Tomart's Price Guide to
GOLDEN BOOK®
COLLECTIBLES

by Rebecca Greason

Edited by Tom Tumbusch

Color Photography by Tom Schwartz

Black & White Photography by Tom Schwartz,
Tom Tumbusch and Rebecca Greason

Wallace-Homestead Book Company
Radnor, Pennsylvania

DEDICATION

**To every Golden Alumni
who shares the happy memory,
"This was my favorite book
when I was little!"**

Prices listed are based on the author's experience and are presented as a guide for information purposes only. No one is obligated in any way to buy, sell or trade according to these prices. Condition, rarity, demand and the reader's desire to own determine the actual price paid. No offer to buy or sell at the prices listed is intended or made. Buying and selling is conducted at the consumer's risk. Neither the author nor the publisher assumes any liability for any losses suffered for use of, or any typographic errors contained in, this book. The numeric code system used in this book is not consistent with previous collectible guides published by Tomart Publications. All value estimates are presented in U.S. dollars. The dollar sign is omitted to avoid needless repetition.

Notice of Copyright Ownership

Golden®, Golden Book®, A Little Golden Book® and associated trademarks, trademark designs and designations are the property of Western Publishing Company, Inc., Racine, Wisconsin 53404 and are used with permission.

The distinctive simulated foil strip and trade dress designs displayed on the covers of this book are registered trademarks of Western Publishing Company, Inc., Racine, Wisconsin and are used under license.

ACKNOWLEDGEMENTS

In Memoriam: To my **Grandmother Greason**, who always kept a well-worn copy of *The Poky Little Puppy*™ on the bottom bookshelf!

... To all the **Golden Book® collectors** who have asked, "Are you going to include ...?" Your questions and comments have helped to make this book as thorough a coverage as possible.

... To **Brian Schulman**, who got me hooked on Little Golden Books®. And for the use of some books from his private collection for pictures. ... To **Kathi Diehl**, for letting *Dumbo* (in dust jacket) out of the house for pictures, along with a whole pile of other special Golden Books! ... To **Barbara and Bill Yoffee**, of the Children's Book Adoption Agency, for "placing" some great Little Golden Books in my collection (where they will be well cared for). Special thanks, also, for reviewing the manuscript. ... To **Nancy Best**, "The Best In Dolls", for the use of the character dolls in the color sections. ... To **Sheva Golkow**, for information on foreign edition LGBs — and for not getting mayonnaise on *Doctor Dan*. ... To **Drusilla Jones**, self-appointed (and much appreciated) one-person cheering squad, fountain of ideas, and "information central" for Golden Book contacts. ... To **Janie Wentz** and her fearless X-acto knife, for trimming many, many, many little pictures in return for an unending supply of Mickey Mouse Band-Aids. ... To **Bob Welbaum** for last minute assistance.

Special thanks to **Tom Tumbusch**, for his editorial expertise, for getting excited about Golden Books, and most of all, for the opportunity to see this long planned-for book published. ... To **Rebecca Trissel**, who deserves a Purple Heart and a Golden Keyboard for making a readable book out of a "Swiss cheese" manuscript.

To **Mary Janaky** and the staff of Western Publishing Company for assistance in providing the information requested and arranging the rights for this publication.

The color photography is the work of **Tom Schwartz**, **Terry Cavanaugh**, and **Robert Hock**. Page imaging was done by Type One Graphic and color separations by Printing Preparations.

Last, but far from least ... to **John**, for scrounging through countless grubby book boxes, toy stores and book shows in search of "gold." And for never doubting that "the book" would some-day happen, even when I was ready to give up. Yes, you are whole bunches more important to me than Little Golden Books!

TABLE OF CONTENTS

The Sunday Book Supplement *for May 19, 1946 of the* Chicago Tribune *ran this full page color picture of Elizabeth Orton Jones' cover art for* Little Red Riding Hood *(LE0420).*

COLOR PLATES

ABOUT THE AUTHOR

Rebecca Greason, of Hershey, PA, owns and operates "Rebecca of SunnyBook Farm", specializing in out-of-print and collectible children's books, and related collectibles. She exhibits at major antique, collectible and toy shows as well as book shows on the East Coast.

Before becoming immersed in the book field, she was art director for a large publishing firm and later a free-lance artist. She has received both national and regional awards for excellence in graphic design. In addition, she has also pursued fine art and photography and has had articles published in several national newsletters.

She began collecting and researching LGBs in the early '80s and has expanded the collection over the years to include Big, Tiny and in-between Golden Books. Prize possessions among the over 1400 books in her collection are several Golden Books from the personal library of Lucille Ogle, who was responsible for developing the original "Golden Dozen" LGBs.

Toy and book tie-ins are a favorite collector combination. Here a Japanese tin plate toy truck teams up with The Good Humor Man *(LE5500). Truck courtesy of Al Marwick.*

Life ad offering LE2030

Announcing

LITTLE GOLDEN BOOKS

A new series of 25¢ books for children

To be published October 1st by Simon and Schuster

In the September 19, 1942 issue of Publisher's Weekly, *the Poky Little Puppy crawled out from under his first fence to help announce Little Golden Books. The four-page spread (first page shown above) included a full-page color picture from Mother Goose, a complete listing of the first 12 books and a statement of the "hows, whys and wherefores" of Little Golden Books. Forty years later, Poky was on hand again to help celebrate the 40th anniversary of Golden Books, gracing the cover of the 1982 book catalog from Western.*

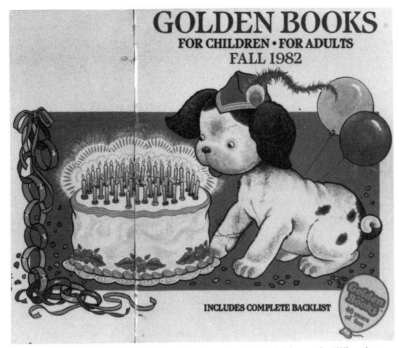

GOLDEN BOOKS
FOR CHILDREN · FOR ADULTS
FALL 1982

INCLUDES COMPLETE BACKLIST

Jerald Kellman, commenting in Publisher's Weekly, *April 9, 1982, said:* "What began as a modest attempt to put inexpensive children's books into supermarkets and chain stores - at a time when the country was at war, toys were scarce, book stores were limited to big cities and libraries were less accessible - has grown into a publishing colossus". *Eight hundred million copies were in print by 1982, the billion mark was passed 5 years later. With their "Golden Anniversary" not far off, and Golden Books continuing to grow and thrive, The Poky Little Puppy is undoubtedly grooming himself for the biggest celebration yet.*

FOREWORD

Golden Books are the most successful mass-market children's books ever produced, with Little Golden Books leading the parade. It was inevitable that these colorful books with their familiar gold spines and nostalgic tug would evidently find their way from the toy chests of America to collector's shelves.

As the demand for older Golden Books has grown, increased interest in more recent titles and related collectibles has also grown, and the need for an authoritative and comprehensive guide to the field has become increasingly evident. This book has been prepared in response to that need, and covers not only the Golden series which have already proven themselves in the collectibles market (such as Giant and Little Golden Books), but also the broader spectrum of Golden publications and related collectibles which are becoming of more interest to collectors.

This book contains the majority of books and related items produced under the Golden imprint, but it was not possible to include every item produced. The main emphasis is on the hardcover series produced for younger readers. Several soft cover series are also included in addition to records, promotional items, puzzles and other spin-offs. Golden comic books are not included.

This book is intended to serve three functions: 1) To be an informative guide to the many Golden publications and related collectibles. 2) To list, as completely as possible, the various books and other items produced, in a format which enables easy identification. 3) To provide an estimate of values. Regarding the last, it should be noted that price guides are out-of-date the day they roll off the press. Prices go up and down and may vary from one area to another. The price ranges shown in this book are, however, relative to each other at the time of publication. In that context, and with condition taken into account, prices can be adjusted for local demand factors and changes in market trends.

STRIKING GOLD

The advent of Golden Books in 1942 and the overwhelming success of the original 12 titles, was the result of an unique combination of circumstances and preparation.

The publishing of story books designed especially to entertain children—or at least provide instruction in an enjoyable manner—began to blossom in the late 1800s. Although a variety of inexpensive books had been produced since the early 1900's, they were not usually available in great quantity. Generally lacking in both originality of text and illustration, they were also poorly constructed.

Western Printing and Lithographing Co., later to become Western Publishing Company, had experimented with the marketing of low-priced children's books several times previous to the advent of Little Golden Books. They had also pioneered the concept of year-round sales of children's books, which in the early part of the century were generally available only for the holidays. Distributing the books through variety store outlets as well as book dealers was also a Western innovation. Given this background and Western's already established reputation for diversity and expansion, it seems only natural, in retrospect, Western should be the company who made the first serious effort to produce an ongoing line of low-priced, yet high quality illustrated books for children.

In the early 1940s, Georges Duplaix and Lucille Ogle of the Artists and Writers Guide (the creative book design division of Western Printing) were considering the possibility of producing an inexpensive line of uniform size, colorful children's books. Meanwhile, Simon and Schuster, a well-established New York publishing firm under the direction of then-president Leon Shimkin, was looking for a novel product with which to introduce its newly organized children's department to the public.

While involved with S&S on another book project, Duplaix discussed with Albert Leventhal, sales manager for S&S, the possibility of a low-priced series of children's books. Both Leventhal and Shimkin were receptive to the idea, and 12 pilot titles were prepared by Lucille Ogle. Western Printing, which had acquired the nation's first sheet-fed 4-color offset presses in the '30s, had the technical capability needed to produce these colorful books. Printed in a large enough volume, the books could be retailed at 25¢, a price attractive enough to outdistance competing 50¢ books and appeal to limited budgets. With publisher, production staff and printer all in agreement, Little Golden Books went to press.

War time shortages were the hot topic of the day and toys were among the early victims of rationing. It was a rather austere children's market when the first 12 Little Golden Books arrived in October of 1942. Colorful, durable, inexpensive—almost a toy in themselves—they were designed to be handled by children, stashed in toy chests, played with and loved. Within 5 months, one and a half million copies had been sold and the books were into their third printing. Simon and Schuster had clearly "struck gold" and the rush was on.

The enthusiastic reception of Little Golden Books prompted the creation of other Golden series. Giant, Big and Tiny Golden Books quickly followed. By 1951, records, puzzles and even Little Golden writing paper were among the many products advertised.

Initially, the Artists and Writers Guild provided the editorial and design work for the products, with S&S and Western as joint owners. In 1944, S&S set up a new graphics division, Sandpiper Press, with Duplaix in charge. The combination of these different entities provided a rather cumbersome copyright statement, but each did their part to insure a quality product. Little Golden Books were firmly established as a series and have had a profound influence on the children's book market, not only in America, but worldwide.

In 1958, Western Printing and Affiliated Publishers, Inc. (later to be Pocket Books, Inc.) bought out Simon and Schuster's interest in Golden Books and the Golden Press was formed. In 1960, Western Printing and Lithographing Co. became Western Publishing Co., Inc. They acquired Pocket Book's part in the Golden line in 1964 and became sole owner of the series and its many products.

The multiplicity of Golden Book series introduced over the years has been augmented with many other innovations … books in Braille, merchandise promotions, cassette tapes and videos, to name a few. The recent "Little Golden Book Land" series incorporates a whole line of related products, including plush toys, ceramic figures and party paper goods in addition to books, puzzles and other ephemera.

Brief histories of the many Golden publications and products will be included in the introduction preceding each category.

WHY COLLECT GOLDEN BOOKS?

Collecting anything—stamps, old bottles, primitive tools or books—has many self satisfying rewards. Finding a sought after title in some junk shop is like discovering gold. Every antique shop or flea market provides the thrill of the hunt and the chance to meet others who share a collecting interest.

Each item in a collection becomes a trophy which the collector has found, bought, won in an auction or otherwise traded to obtain. To collect is to succeed at your own pace under whatever terms and goals you set for yourself. Collecting provides a comfortable niche in a highly competitive world— one that the collector controls—as opposed, for example, to job or other pressures they cannot. And collectors "know" that if they lose interest, they can "get more" than they paid for the collection when it is sold.

Everything is collected by somebody. The infinite variety of

what many might consider to be the "odd-ball" collector's items can be confirmed in any collecting journal. Golden Books, with their diverse appeal, have become a well recognized entity in the collectibles market.

WHAT MAKES GOLDEN BOOKS SO COLLECTIBLE?

Golden Books offer something for everyone … from childhood memories to specialized collector categories.

From the inception of the original Little Golden Book line in 1942, the idea of collecting (or assembling) a complete library of Golden Books was actively promoted by the publishers. Many of the series are uniform in size and easily identifiable, an attribute of mass-market publishing which lends itself to collectibility. The policy of numbering each book—which prevailed throughout the early series—provided ready-made parameters for defining a collection.

Under the auspices of the Artists and Writers Guild, as well as the influence of the Disney Studios, many of the best know children's authors and illustrators have been involved with Golden publications. Collectors avidly seek work done by their favorites.

The licensing of Disney characters and many other TV and comic personalities has provided many items of interest to collectors of movie, TV and comic memorabilia. In addition, there are books which feature toys, dolls, Band-Aids™, and a variety of activities. Paper dolls and other cut-out & assemble projects also enjoy specific collector appeal.

Giant Golden Books and their miniscule counterparts, Tiny Golden Books, were found on book dealer's shelves long before Little Golden Books were considered collectible. In the mid-1980s, as Little Golden Book collecting began to take off, a heightened interest was also taken in other Golden Books. Today almost any Golden Book—and there is a diverse variety of Golden series—is looked upon with interest by collectors.

WHO IS COLLECTING GOLDEN BOOKS?

The people who collect Golden publications fall into five categories:

1. Consumers who purchase the book to entertain or educate a child, to be used and discarded as the child grows older.

2. People who are interested in children's literature and especially the effect of mass market children's books on young people in this century.

3. People who may have owned or wanted to own a particular book or item as a child.

4. Collectors who purchase memorabilia to add to their collection. These people may confine their interest to one or more specialities or collect everything from a given time period.

5. Dealers and investors who buy Golden Book collectibles with the intent of realizing a profit from their knowledge and interest.

The last three groups often interact with each other, and are interdependent for the purposes of buying, selling and trading.

HOW TO FIND GOLDEN BOOKS

Western Publishing produced the billionth Little Golden Book in 1986 so plenty survive for collectors. The appeal of collecting is heightened by the number of books that can still be found at low prices. A considerable collection can be amassed in a short time even on a limited budget by visiting flea markets, thrift shops, library sales and yard sales. But "the fun is in the search", and as the books are assembled and the collection begins to take shape, there are books in any of the Golden series that are a challenge to locate. This is where dealers and speciality shows come into play.

Shows: Golden Books have not yet attained the status where they are specially featured items at prestigious book shows and gallery auctions. However, more dealers are starting to cater to Golden Book collectors and stacks of these books are beginning to show up more frequently at antique toy and advertising shows as well as book and paper shows. The larger the event, the better your chances of striking "gold", although smaller shows can also yield some great finds.

In addition to the events listed below, there are many more shows held periodically throughout the United States where Golden collectibles can be found. Ads for these shows can be found in collector publications. An annual *Directory of Antiquarian Book Fairs and Paper Shows* is also available through Isaiah Thomas Books, 980 Main St., Worchester, MA 01603.

Big-D Super Collectibles Show (July)
Sheraton Park Central
Dallas, TX

Brimfield Associate's
"Atlantique City" Show (March)
Atlantic City, NJ

Glendale Antiquarian Book Fair (April & October)
Glendale/Santa Monica, CA

Great Eastern U.S.
Antique Book, Paper, Advertising
and Collectables show (April & October)
Fairgrounds
Allentown, PA

New York is Book Country (September)
47th to 58th Streets & Fifth Avenue
New York, NY

Printer's Row Book Fair (June)
Dearborn Street
Chicago, IL

AB Bookman's Weekly Magazine publishes an annual issue dedicated to children's books as well as a yearbook which lists many children's book dealers. Both publications are good sources for finding dealers who specialize in children's books. Many listed dealers offer sales catalogs or provide search services for specific titles. (AB Bookman, P.O. Box AB, Clifton, NJ 07015)

Collector newspapers and magazines carry classified ad sections where dealers and collectors advertise for books wanted and/or books for sale. In addition, one will find ads for specialty dealers (dolls, toys, Disneyana, characters, etc) which may also prove to be good sources for Golden Books

Local dealers and shops: The classified section of the telephone book is a good place to locate local book dealers. A telephone call is all it takes to find out if a particular dealer handles Golden Books. When contacting a dealer, it is best to have some idea of the specific books you are looking for ... perhaps even a list to give to the dealer.

PRICE GUIDES

Values for Golden Books listed in general antique price guides should be viewed with considerable skepticism. Rarely is the edition cited, or adequate information given as to the condition of the book. Descriptions given may apply to several different versions of the same book.

One general price guide that does contain a separate section on Little Golden Books and has made an effort to correctly list the books and their current values is *Warman's Guide to Americana and Collectibles*, edited by Harry Rinker (Wallace-Homestead Book Company, Radnor, PA 19089).

A specialized guide dealing primarily with the Little Golden Book series, *Collecting Little Golden Books* by Steve Santi is also available (Books Americana, Inc., Florence, AL 35630).

REFERENCE BOOKS

Aside from articles and ads appearing in *Publisher's Weekly*, very little information has appeared in print concerning Golden Books. Barbara Bader's *American Picturebooks from Noah's Ark to The Beast Within* (Macmillan, 1976) devotes an entire chapter to Golden Books, and provides an excellent commentary on the subject. There is also a wealth of information contained throughout the book on many of the authors and illustrators who have been involved with Golden Books.

Another reference source dealing exclusively with the Little Golden series, is Dee Jones' *Bibliography of the Little Golden Books* (Greenwood Press, 1987). This is a technical compilation, listing Little Golden Books issued from 1942 through 1985. While the book lacks pictures, it is a thorough examination of the LGB line in all its various aspects with complete bibliographic descriptions.

HOW TO USE THIS BOOK

Tomart's Price Guide to Golden Book Collectibles was designed to be an authoritative and easy to use collector's guide. It utilizes an identification system designed to create a standard identification number for each individual book and associated item.

No one has yet cataloged all the books and related items produced under the Golden imprint. However, this system contains the framework in which they may be listed.

The format is a classification system—similar to the yellow pages of a telephone book. If you want to locate a Giant Golden Book, flip through the pages until you find classification numbers beginning with *G* and read the alphabetical category headings until you find "Giant Golden Books." Classification headings have been established according to the Golden series name printed on each book (Little Golden Book, Tiny Golden Book, etc). Series are categorized without the "Golden" prefix. There is one general category entitled "Golden Books" which lists publications which are not part of any specific series. Cross-references and special notes are used throughout to help direct the reader.

Almost all Golden Books were imprinted with numbers by the publisher. Where these numbers already serve as an established reference for collectors, they have been incorporated into the Tomart identity code. Items in these categories are listed numerically. For classifications where there were no numbers or it was impractical to use the Golden code number, books are listed alphabetically by cover title.

The classification system is standardized for the most part. However, if there was a more effective way to communicate more information in less space, a different approach was used.

Each item has been assigned a Tomart identity code number consisting of 2 letters and 4 numbers. Use of these numbers in dealer and distributor ads and collector's correspondence is encouraged. Permission for such use to conduct buying, selling, and trading of Golden Books and collectibles is hereby granted. Some items in this volume have been previously listed in Tomart's Disneyana series and *Space Adventure* book. This book utilizes a different system and the code numbers are NOT consistent with previous publications.

The identity codes also serve to match the correct listing to a nearby photo. There are photographs for as many listings as possible, but unfortunately, not all items can be depicted. In some large classifications, such as "Records", a cross section of available material is used for illustration.

BOOK LISTING FORMAT

At each classification there is a brief introductory comment on the material covered, followed by item listings. Every effort has been made to provide the best information currently available. Data is most reliable for the closed series, to which no new titles will be added. Previously uncataloged items are constantly being discovered. This is especially true in series where no numerical format could be relied upon to compile a complete list.

Where information may be limited or incomplete, it has still been provided in order to alert collectors to rare or obscure items that may have been previously overlooked. Comments or suggestions are welcome from collectors having additional information to supplement or help clarify material in this guide.

Books are listed by cover title. Instances where the cover title and inside title page differ will be noted with the listings. For alphabetizing purposes, *A* and *The* have been disregarded at the beginning of titles. Books popularly know by a portion of their full title have been cross-referenced as fully as possible in the Index.

Value range reflects a low price for items in "good" condition to a high for items in "as new" condition. Values given are for 1st editions unless stated otherwise. See section below for a complete discussion of values.

The copyright date is shown as "©1948." For books with more than one copyright date, the most recent is listed. For most books, the copyright and publication date are the same. However, copyrights are good for 100 years beyond death of author, and the actual publication date of reissued titles will not be the same as the stated copyright date. Books previously

copyrighted in another form or by another publisher will also have differing copyright and publication dates.

The publication date is shown as "/p1955" and will be indicated when the actual publication date differs from the copyright. For example, a book listed as "©1948/p1955(D)" would have been originally copyrighted in 1948 and published in its present form in 1955 as a "D"—or 4th—printing. Copyright holders other than Western Publishing Company are shown following the date.

Books are listed as first editions, unless another edition/printing is noted.

Many books published between 1942 and 1947 were issued with dust jackets. In the case of Little Golden Books, a blue spine denotes a book issued with dust jacket. Big and Giant Books had no such identifying feature, and information concerning which books in these series were issued with dust jackets is incomplete. Books known to have had a dust jacket will be noted.

Remarks following listings contain information on awards, variations and cover styles.

IDENTIFICATION OF FIRST EDITIONS

The determination of a first edition or specific printing of a given book is always of importance to book collectors. While it is unusual for children's books to carry much printing information beyond the original copyright date, Golden Books more often than not include imprint information or printing codes which make it possible to determine the printing.

In many instances the precise printing is fully spelled out, as in "2nd printing, July 1945." When letter codes are used to identify printings, an "A" copy of a book is, in most instances, a first edition. A "B" copy is generally a second printing rather than a second edition. To be a true second edition, the book would have to have been changed substantially, whereas most subsequent printings of Golden Books are the same as the original printing. "C" indicates a third printing, etc.

Some of the older Golden Books which have been reprinted and are currently available on the retail market are imprinted with "A" codes. The copyright may state the original copyright date, or a recent date which would be a copyright renewal. Familiarity with the series and cross-referencing of titles with information available in this guide should provide adequate information to determine which of these books are actually new to the series or merely reprints of previously published books.

A variety of formats have been used to signify printings, most of which employ a letter or number code. The particular method used for each series will be noted at the series introductory statement.

Golden Book collectors seem to thrive on the minute differences between printings, as well as the broad changes associated with a new edition. Many of these variations will be noted at the individual title listing.

THE VALUES IN THIS PRICE GUIDE

This book is a collector's and dealer's guide to average prices, in a range of conditions. The real value of any collectible is what a buyer is willing to pay. No more. No less. Prices are constantly changing—up and down.

Many factors have a bearing on each transaction. Not the least of which are perceived value, emotional appeal or competitive drive for ownership. Few people actually need Golden Books and collectibles, but many buy them to fulfill an emotional desire. Dealers usually want the highest return they can get and continually test collectors with higher prices. Values rise and fall at the whim of collector's willingness to pay the asking price.

Supply and demand—always factors in measuring value—are a bit more predictable for those knowledgeable in a given area of collectibles. These people have a feel for how often they see a given item become available for sale. Since everyone has different experiences, however, there are many different ideas concerning which items are rarer and more valuable.

The availability of items listed in this book is definitely limited. No one can say how limited, but it is certain no more originals will be manufactured. The quantities of collectible Golden Books range anywhere from thousands up into millions. Generally, the titles which generate the most interest originally were the titles produced in the largest quantities. By 1953, over half of the 200 titles in the LGB series had sold over 1 million copies each. And since there were so many of them produced back then, early printings still turn up on a regular basis on book shelves, in attics and even warehouses.

New books are being published under the Golden imprint daily and first editions disappear quickly from retail shelves. Many titles published within the last 10 years are out-of-print and have become collectible. New editions fulfill the demand of many new collectors coming into the hobby. Of course, many of these new collectors have an interest in the older material also. Often they keep up with the new material while specializing in selected categories of older items. A high demand exists for rare items, as well as some common ones ... and the value of these items outperforms the market as a whole ... at least until the supply catches up with the demand.

There is no ready retail market for a large collection of Golden Books. There have been numerous examples in recent years where collections of nostalgia collectibles were sold at auctions or estate sales at a fraction of the estimated value. Except for a limited number of high demand items, the process of turning a good sized collection back into cash can be long and expensive.

Collecting should be pursued for the interest and satisfaction involved. There are much better investments at most financial institutions. *Fortune, Business Week* and other business publi-

cations have done extensive articles on the pitfalls of speculating in what these magazines categorize as "exotic investments."

This book reports market prices based on items sold or traded by dealers and collectors nationwide. It reflects sales on the whole, with the understanding an auction price is the one all other bidders refused to pay.

Collectors who buy at yard sales and flea markets generally purchase for less. Often they have first choice of items offered for sale; sometimes at exceptional bargain prices. But they also incur substantial time and travel expenses.

Book dealer catalogs, mail and gallery auctions are preferred by collectors who don't have the time or ability to visit major shows. Money spent and current resale value also tend to be of less concern to the catalog or auction buyer. Catalog buyers must respond with alacrity to obtain choice items, while the winning auction bidder must outlast the others who have an emotional fix on ownership or perhaps need the specific piece to "complete" a collection.

It's difficult to say who actually spends more money in pursuit of their collecting interest ... the aggressive hunter at low cost outlets or the catalog or auction buyer. This much is sure, there are substantial costs involved beyond the money spent for collectibles by the original buyer not normally considered in the "price." And higher overhead costs are included in auction sales where the "price" includes everything.

What it all boils down to is the two ways in which Golden collectibles are sold: pre-priced or by auction to the highest bidder.

Every attempt has been made to have this price guide reflect the market in its broadest sense. The research effort covers extensive travel each year to leading book, paper, toy and antique shows. Auction prices are monitored and many leading dealer catalogs and lists are reviewed. The values in this edition are a compilation of information received through November 1990.

The very existence of a price guide will affect the market— increasing prices, introducing the hobby to many new collectors, as well as opening new areas of interest to established collectors. This is to be expected. However, the advantages of a published record of accepted values outweigh the disadvantages. Among these advantages are the protection of financial investment, easier insurability (and collection) in the event of loss, a better basis for collector trading, item identification, a forum for new discoveries, preservation of more items and photos helpful in spotting unmarked or unfamiliar items. Price guides often inspire more dealer interest.

There are two more factors affecting value that we can measure more precisely: rarity and condition.

RARITY

Some Golden Books were available for years after they were first published. While first editions or early printings of some of these books may be difficult to obtain, later editions are quite common. For example, *The Country Mouse and The City Mouse*, first published in 1961, is still in print and a very common title … except in its first edition. On the other hand, some books produced in the '70s and '80s went out-of-print quickly and are very difficult to find. *Hiram's Red Shirt*, published in 1981, is an example. Rarity, however, doesn't always equate to value. In book collecting, the strongest demand is often generated by people wishing to obtain items of special interest. Thus, rarity is only a part of value. Character popularity, cross-overs to other collecting fields (such as Disneyana, puzzles, paper dolls, etc) and subject matter (aviation, ice cream, Christmas, etc) as well as author/illustrator popularity are also strong factors influencing value.

Be wary of international editions billed as "rare." More often than not, such items are rare in the United States, but are easily found in their countries of origin. While some foreign Golden Book titles were never printed in the United States, many others are identical to their American printings. As such, they are considered to be equivalent for the purposes of identification and worth. The values in this price guide are based on research within the United States.

CONDITION

Condition, like beauty, is in the eye of the beholder. When money becomes involved, the eye seems to take on an added dimension of X-ray vision or rose-colored glasses—depending on whether you are buying or selling.

However, let there be no mistake about the price spreads set down on the following pages. The top price refers to books in "as new" condition—activity portions unused, no tears, never repaired, free of any defects whatsoever, selling in a top market. These books were probably never read and especially never kept in a toy chest.

The low end price describes items in "good" condition. That means, first and foremost, the book is complete, with both covers intact and no pages missing. Edges that show wear, bumped corners, rubbed covers and similar shortcomings are factors that depreciate value and relegate such items to the complete, but "good" classification. Of course, some complete items with excessive wear, page and cover tears, heavy scribble marks, tape and other mistreatment are less than good; either poor or only a filler until a better book is found. The value of poor condition items would obviously be less than the lowest price shown.

The range between "good" and "as new" is the condition in which most items will be found. "Very good" and "fine" are the most common grades used. In general, a "fine" condition item will be one with only minor wear, marks, scratches, blemishes, etc. The item has been in circulation—used, but given care. The value would be somewhat less than the average in the price range as true "as new" items command a premium.

It is not possible to evaluate every contingency affecting the condition of books, especially children's books, and assign them to a particular grade. Any attempt to do so would prove cumbersome and would, at best, still be woefully inadequate.

The general guidelines established here, together with the careful noting of any defects when describing a book should prove sufficient for most evaluations.

Location also has some influence on price. In Los Angeles and New York, prices are often substantially higher. Selling prices are lowest in the Midwest—especially around Chicago and in Indiana, Ohio and Pennsylvania. Items still become available on a regular basis in these areas and thereby fulfill demand. Realizing that these regional price situations exist, and that isolated individuals will always let emotions rule in auction bidding, the values represented in this guide are average estimates taking into account what a given item has sold for over a period of time.

Rarity, condition and the amount of material available in the market place all have a direct effect on value. The overriding factor, however, is the number of individuals who wish to acquire any given title and have the money to satisfy their desire.

All prices shown in this book are U.S. dollar values with the dollar signs removed to avoid repetition.

ABBREVIATIONS

adp	Adapted by
arr	Arranger, arranged by
BCE	Book Club Edition
BGB	Big Golden Book
BLGB	Big Little Golden Book
©	Copyright (date or by)
CTW	Children's Television Workshop
dj	Dust jacket
dwg	Drawings
ed	Editor, edited by
FLGB	First Little Golden Book
GB	Golden Book
GGB	Giant Golden Book
GLGB	Giant Little Golden Book
GP	Golden Press
GPI	Golden Press, Inc.
illus	Illustrator, illustrated by
LG	Little Golden
LGB	Little Golden Book
LGBL	Little Golden Book Land
LLGB	Little Little Golden Book
MMC	Mickey Mouse Club
pp	Pages
p	Publication (date)
sel	Selected (by)
S&S	Simon & Schuster
trans	Translated by
w/	With
w/o	Without
WD	Walt Disney
WDCo	Walt Disney Company
WDL	Walt Disney Library
WDLL	Walt Disney Little Library
WDP	Walt Disney Prod.
WDS	Walt Disney Studios
WL	Walter Lantz
WPC	Western Publishing Co.
WRC	Weekly Reader Club

AB1101   AB1102

AB1103   AB1104

AB1105   AB1106

AB1107   AB1108

AB1111   AB1112

ACTIVITY BOOKS

Activity books appear throughout the various Golden series. Categories include Little, Big, Giant and Golden Books; Funtime; Fun-To-Learn; Stamp Books and Toy Books.

In 1961, an ad on the back of Little Golden Books listed several New Golden Activity Books. These books do not form a distinct activity series, but were simply grouped together for advertising purposes. Books listed in the ad can be located through the alphabetical index.

AD BACKS

"Ad backs" appeared on the back covers of Little Golden Books from 1956 through 1964. They contain a wealth of information about the various LGB series, as well as other Golden Book series. They are also useful in determining the probable publication year of books whose copyright date and year of publication differ. Ads are listed in chronological sequence, with reference by book number to the earliest LGB on which the ad appeared. Since these ads were later used on other books and some ran for several years, the listing also includes the year(s) in which a particular ad was used. Ads were run at random within their time periods. Therefore, several different ad backs can appear on the same LGB within one printing.

Information on the items advertised can be found at the categories noted.

AB1101 **Big Golden Books for Growing Minds**
(1956-57, LGB 254) (Giant Golden Books)

AB1102 **Walt Disney's Library of Big Golden Books**
(1956-57, LGB D57) (Big Golden Books–
Disney, Giant Golden Books)

AB1103 **Golden Nature Guides**
(1957, LGB 284) (Guides)

AB1104 **Giant Little Golden Books**
(1958, LGB 323) (Giant Little Golden Books)

AB1105 **Golden Stamp Books**
(1958-59, LGB 334) (Stamp Books)

AB1106 **Golden Library of Knowledge**
(1958-59, LGB 339) (Library of Knowledge)

AB1107 **Craft and Hobby Books**
(1960, LGB 361) (Craft and Hobby Books)

AB1109   AB1110

AB1113   AB1114

AB1108 **Giant Golden Books for Growing Minds**
(1959-60, LGB 374) (Giant Golden Books)

AB1109 **Golden Guides**
(1959-60, LGB 382) (Guides)

AB1110 **Golden Capitol Adventure Kits**
(1960, LGB 380) (Collectibles–Toys & Games)

AB1111 **Golden Guides to Nature and Science**
(1960-63, LGB 414) (Guides)

AB1112 **De Luxe Golden Books**
(1961, LGB 409) (De Luxe Golden Books)

AB1113 **New Golden Activity Books**
(1961, LGB 410) (Big Golden Books, Golden
Activity Books, Giant Golden Books, Giant Golden
Punch-out Books)

AB1114 **Walt Disney Big Golden Books**
(1961, LGB 423) (Big Golden Books–Disney,
Giant Golden Books)

AB1115 **De Luxe Golden Books**
(1961, LGB 427) (De Luxe Golden Books)

AB1116 **Golden Books for the Very Young**
(1961, LGB 428) (Big Golden Books)

AB1117 **Fun-to-Learn Golden Books**
(1961, LGB 429) (Fun-to-Learn)

AB1118 **Golden Library of Knowledge**
(1961-62, LGB 425) (Library of Knowledge)

AB1119 **Golden Beginning Readers**
(1961-63, LGB 432) (Read-It-Yourself)

AB1120 **De Luxe Golden Books**
(1962-63, LGB 465) (De Luxe Golden Books)

AB1121 **Craft and Hobby Books**
(1962-63, LGB 467) (Craft & Hobby Books)

AB1122 **Giant Golden Books for Growing Minds**
(1962-63, LGB 471) (Giant Golden Books)

AB1123 **De Luxe Golden Books**
(1962-63, LGB 478) (De Luxe Golden Books)

AB1124 **Panorama Books**
(1963, LGB 534) (Panorama Books)

AB1125 **Golden Question and Answer Books**
(1963-64, LGB 533) (Adventure Books)

AB1126 **Golden Workbooks**
(1963-64, LGB 537) (Key to Learning Program)

AB1115   AB1116

AB1117   AB1118

AB1119   AB1120

AB1121   AB1122

AB1123   AB1124

AB1125   AB1126

AB1127   AB1128

AB1127 **Golden Quiz–Me Books**
(1963-64, LGB 539) (Junior Golden Guides)
AB1128 **Golden Funtime Books**
(1963-64, LGB 541) (Funtime Books)
AB1129 **Fiction for Boys and Girls**
(1964, LGB 527) (Junior Fiction Series)
AB1130 **Golden Happy Books**
(1964, LGB 542) (Happy Books)
AB1131 **Golden Play and Learn Books**
(1964, LGB 543) (Play and Learn Books)
AB1132 **Golden Read-It-Yourself Books**
(1964, LGB 546) (Read-It-Yourself Books)

AB1129   AB1130

ADVENTURE BOOKS (Question & Answer)

A library of science-hobby books, soft cover, 7" x 10", 96 pages illustrated in black and white with directions for activities and experiments. The text was preceeded by a Question–Answer page, which the young learner would be able to answer after having worked through the book. Photos and drawings for the books were prepared by specialists in their respective fields. The books were advertised on LGBs in 1963 and 1964, and are included here more as an explanatory reference than as established collectibles.

AB1131   AB1132

AD1101	**Birds** by William Jerr	1 - 3
AD1104	**Chemistry** by Lazer Goldberg	1 - 2
AD1106	**Coins** by Eva Knox Evans	1 - 3
AD1111	**Growing Plants** by Frances M. Miner	1 - 2
AD1114	**Human Biology** by Otto B. Burgdorf	1 - 2
AD1116	**Human Mind, The** by Dr. James G. Miller	1 - 2
AD1120	**Insects** by Alice Gray	1 - 3
AD1127	**Magnetism** by Dr. Frances L. Behnke	1 - 2
AD1132	**Nature Craft** by Richard A. Dempewolff	1 - 2
AD1140	**Rocks** by Eva Knox Evans	1 - 2
AD1145	**Shells** by Eva Knox Evans	1 - 3
AD1150	**Stars** by Thomas D. Nicholson	1 - 3
AD1165	**Underwater Life** by Dr. Charleton Ray	1 - 2
AD1170	**Weather** by Harry Milgrom	1 - 3

AD1140   AD1170

ALMANACS

Golden Almanacs are year-round books with stories, poems and projects keyed to the seasons, months and holidays. When first published in 1944, *The Golden Almanac* was simply part of "The Golden Library." Later listings assign it to the "Big Golden" series, although the series identification does not always appear on the book especially in the earlier printings. The *New Golden Almanac* is identified as a BGB. Both are listed with Big Golden Books.

BEGINNING READERS

Golden has always had a pronounced interest in producing quality products to help children develop learning skills.

Beginning Readers was one of several series aimed at developing reading skills. The series was merged with Read-It-Yourself Books and are listed under that heading. The current production "Easy Reader" series also helps children perfect reading abilities. Easy Reader's strong reliance on licensed characters increases their potential entry into the collectible field.

BIG & LITTLE BOOKS

Advertised as "a big book with a complete little book inside", 2 titles are recorded. The "little book" was in an envelope inside the big book. These books were advertised in the late '40s.

| BA1010 | **Big Elephant and The Little Mouse, The** Title noted, but copy unavailable verification. | ? |
| BA1015 | **Big Farmer Big & Little Farmer Little** by Kathryn & Byron Jackson illus by Feodor Rojankovsky Title noted, but copy unavailable for verification. | ? |

BB1110

BB1267

BB1040

BB1265

BB1160

BB1215

BB1255

BIG GOLDEN BOOKS

When large size books were first published in 1944, they were simply listed as "The Golden Library", with the "Big" and "Giant" designations appearing around 1947. These designations were used on the cover of most large format books through the late '60s, when the series names fell into disuse as the larger books began to be offered to retailers in assorted lots, grouped by price, rather than in specified series. Although "Big" and "Giant" designations have appeared sporadically on books in the past 20 years, it has only been within the past year that "Big Golden Books" have once more been established as a defined series. Books from the intervening years which carried no "Big Golden" identification, but were definitely qualified as such by style and format, are included in this listing. A complete list of Big Golden Books has not yet been compiled, but a majority of the titles are covered here. We invite reader comments to help assemble a full list for future updates of this guide.

Big Golden Books have been published in a variety of sizes and binding styles. Within the series there are four identifiable styles:

(1) Hard cover books with spine showing book number, title and publisher. Approximately 9-1/2" x 12-3/4", this size and format is the most common style found in the Big Golden series. Number of pages and style of end papers varies with individual books. Edition information is shown with the copy-

right notice or on the inside front cover in the lower left or top right corner as a letter code followed by a double price code.

(2) Same as above, except books are 9" x 11-1/2".

(3) Hard cover book with gold and black triangle pattern foil spine. Books were side-stitched in the same manner as Little Golden Books. This binding style was used in the late '50s. Books were 9-1/4" x 12-1/2" with end papers in an overall "snowflake" pattern. Edition information was usually located on the last page in the lower right corner as a letter code, when provided. Additional titles published in the same format were listed on the back cover. All books were numbered in the "10000" series, although that numbering is not unique to this binding style.

(4) Hard cover books with the familiar gold foil spine used in the LGB series as well as the same side-staple binding. These 8" x 11" Big Golden Books all had "8000" series numbers and were published in the late '50s and early '60s. End papers had an overall flower pattern and the number of pages varied. A list of additional titles in this format was carried on the back cover. Printing is noted on last page in lower right corner.

Various titles throughout the series have been published in all four styles. There are also many older Big Golden Books which do not fit these standard formats. The reference pictures are in scale with one another and show the proportional differences. Current production Big Golden Books vary in size from 9-1/2" x 11-3/4" to 8" x 10-1/2". Many classic Big Golden titles are

THE BIG GOLDEN

ANIMAL

A B C

BB1305

THE BIG GOLDEN BOOK OF

BIBLE STORIES

BB1315

BIRDS

Child's First Book About Our Most Familiar Birds

BB1365

BUGS BUNNY in

Escape From Noddington Castle

BB1400

now being reprinted under the Merrigold imprint.

Because many Big Golden Books were reprinted from previously published titles with no indication of actual publication date, a chronological listing is not possible. Also, although book numbers were assigned to all titles, a great many books on the secondary market have lost their spines, making collector identification by book number difficult. In addition, the numbering system has been altered several times, with numbers changed and/or reassigned to other titles. Listing is arranged alphabetically by title; Tomart codes are not related to original book numbers.

BB1000	**Animal Stories** by Georges Duplaix, illus by Feodor Rojankovsky ©1944. 62pp. An abridged version of GB1070, 32 stories.	5 - 15
BB1030	**Animals of Farmer Jones** by Leah Gale, illus by Richard Scarry ©1953, 28pp (See also: LE2110, LE2820)	3 - 10
BB1040	**Animals' Merry Christmas, The** by Kathryn Jackson, illus by Richard Scarry ©1950, 32pp. Six stories from GB1090. Style 3 binding.	5 - 15
BB1080	**Baby Animals** written & illus by Garth Williams ©1952, 28pp (See also: LE2740, LE5170)	3 - 8
BB1110	**Baby Farm Animals** written & illus by Garth Williams ©1953, 28pp. 1959 printing shown. Style 1 binding. (See also: LE3330, LE4640)	3 - 8
BB1130	**Baby's House** by Gelolo McHugh, illus by Mary Blair ©1950, 28pp. (See also: LE0800)	5 - 10
BB1160	**Baby's Mother Goose** (Nursery Rhymes), illus by Eloise Wilkin ©1958, 24pp. 1976 printing shown. (See also: GE1050)	10 - 30
BB1180	**Bedtime Tales** by Hazel Packard, illus by Corinne Malvern ©1951, 192pp. A treasury of 36 favorite stories.	8 - 20
BB1200	**Benji: Fastest Dog in the West, Joe Camp's** by Gina Ingoglia (adp), illus by Werner Willis ©1978, 28pp (See also: LF1650)	3 - 8
BB1215	**Betsy's Adventure** written & illus by Gwyneth Mamlock	3 - 8

	©1964, 28pp	
BB1235	**Bible Picture Stories from the Old Testament** Stories retold by Carol Mullen ©1973, 20pp	3 - 8
BB1255	**Big and Little** written & illus by Joe Kaufman ©1966, 28pp	2 - 7
BB1265	**Big Brown Bear, The** by Georges Duplaix, illus by Gustaf Tenggren ©1947, 28pp. Unstated 1st.	5 - 14
BB1267	Same as BB1265 New cover illustration. No printing stated. (See also: LE0890, LE3350)	8 - 18
BB1285	**Big Elephant, The** by Kathryn & Byron Jackson, illus by Feodor Rojankovsky ©1949, 28pp (See also LG1470)	8 - 25
BB1305	**Big Golden Animal ABC, The** (ABC), illus by Garth Williams ©1957, 28pp (See also: LG0970)	4 - 10
BB1315	**Big Golden Book of Bible Stories** (Old & New Testaments), illus by Schnorr Von Carolsfeld, colored by Fritz Kredel ©1958 by Christliche Verlagsanstalt, Konstanz (illus), 70pp. Style 2 binding.	8 - 20
BB1365	**Birds** by Jane Werner Watson, illus by Eloise Wilkin ©1958, 28pp. Shown in Goldencraft Library binding. (See also: LF1840, GD5110)	5 - 15
BB1400	**Bugs Bunny: Escape from Noddington Castle** by Kennon Graham, illus by Darrell Baker ©1980 by Warner Bros., Inc., 24pp	3 - 8
BB1420	**Bugs Bunny's Book** by Annie North Bedford, illus by Warner Bros, adp by Jack Bradbury & Campbell Grant ©1951 by Warner Bros. Cartoons, Inc., 56pp. Games on front & back end papers.	8 - 20
BB1440	**Caroline at the Ranch** written & illus by Pierre Probst, trans by Debra Dabrowska ©1961 by Librairie Hachette, 28pp No edition noted.	10 - 40

17

BB1420

BB1440
BB1500
BB1480

BB1520

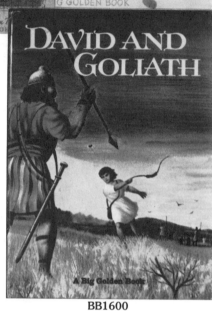

BB1540

BB1600

BB1442	**Caroline in Europe**	10 - 40
	written & illus by Pierre Probst,	
	trans by Susan Witty	
	©1961 by Librairie Hachette 28 pp	
BB1480	**Child's Garden of Verses, A**	8 - 20
	by Robert Louis Stevenson,	
	illus by Alice & Martin Provensen	
	©1951, 68pp	
BB1500	**Color Kittens, The**	8 - 20
	by Margaret Wise Brown,	
	illus by Alice & Martin Provensen	
	©1958, 28pp. 1st thus. Previously published	
	as LE0860 in 1949. (See also: LE4360)	
BB1520	**Cookie Monster and the Cookie Tree**	2 - 8
	by David Koor, illus by Joe Mathieu	
	©1977 by CTW & Muppets, Inc., 24pp	
	(See also: LF1590)	
BB1540	**Counting Rhymes**	3 - 10
	(Nursery Rhyme), illus by Corinne Malvern	
	©1947, 24pp (See also: LE0120, LE2570)	

Dale Evans' Prayer Book (See BB3350)

BB1600	**David and Goliath**	4 - 8
	by Barbara Shook Hazen, illus by Robert J. Lee	
	©1968, 28pp (See also: LF1100)	
BB1630	**Dennis the Menace and Ruff**	4 - 10
	by Carl Memling,	

illus by Hawley Pratt & Lee Holly
©1959 by Hall Syndicate, Inc., 28pp. Cover
art is different from LGB, content is the same.
(See also: LE3860)

BB1680	**Dressed Up Rabbit, The**	5 - 12
	written & illus by Gerda Muller	
	©1972 by WPC and Editions de Deux	
	Coqs d'Or, 32pp	
BB1720	**Eloise Wilkin's Book of Poems**	5 - 15
	by Deborah Wilkin Springett,	
	illus by Eloise Wilkin	
	©1988 by Deborah Wilkin Springett (text),	
	Eloise Wilkin (illus), 28pp. The pictures were	
	inspired by the poems, which were written	
	by Eloise's daughter. Eloise's last book.	
BB1740	**Favorite Fairy Tales**	10 - 35
	(Fairy Tales), illus by Feodor Rojankovsky	
	©1949, 281pp	
BB1750	**Favorite Mother Goose Rhymes**	3 - 9
	(Nursery Rhymes), illus by Richard Scarry	
	©1978, 24pp (See also: BB2980)	
BB1760	**First Noel, The**	12 - 30
	(Gospel of St. Luke),	
	illus by Alice & Martin Provensen	
	©1959, 28pp. Award: 1959 NY Times	
	Best Illustrated.	

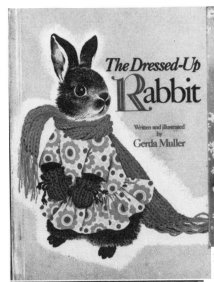

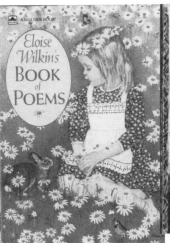

BB1680   BB1720

BB1770

BB1810

BB1880

BB1850

BB1870

BB1770   **Five Bedtime Stories**   5 - 12
          (Fairy Tales), illus by Gustaf Tenggren
          ©1957, 48pp. Stories compiled from
          LE0020, LE1790 & LE2000. Style 4
          binding. (See also: GD5020)

BB1790   **Five Fairy Tales**   ?
          Title noted, but copy unavailable for verification.

BB1810   **Flintstones, The**   5 - 20
          by Carl Memling,
          illus by Hawley Pratt & Al White
          ©1962 by Hanna-Barbera Productions Inc.,
          36pp

BB1850   **Frosty The Snowman**   3 - 10
          by Annie North Bedford,
          illus by Corinne Malvern
          ©1951 by Hill and Range Songs, Inc., 24pp
          1979 printing shown. (See also: LE1420)

BB1870   **Funny Bunny**   9 - 30
          by Rachel Learnard,
          illus by Alice & Martin Provensen
          ©1950, 28pp. Pop-up inside front
          cover. See color plate. (See also: LG1020)

BB1880   **Fuzzy Duckling, The**   3 - 8
          by Jane Werner,
          illus by Alice & Martin Provensen
          ©1949, 24pp. 1977 printing shown.
          (See also: LE0780, LE5570)

BB1900

BB1900   **Gay Purr-ee**   8 - 18
          by Carl Memling , illus by Al White
          ©1962 by UPA Pictures, 24pp.
          Based on the same film as LE4880,
          but contents are different.

BB1930   **Gergely's Golden Circus**   10 - 25
          by Peter Archer, illus by Tibor Gergely
          ©1954, 28pp

BB1970   BB1975   BB1995   BB2090

BB2030

BB2070

BB2098

BB1950 **Gingerbread Man, The**   2 - 8
(Nursery Tale), illus by Bonnie & Bill Rutherford
©1963, 28pp

BB1970 **Golden Almanac, The**   5 - 15
by Dorothy Bennett, illus by Masha
©1944, 96pp. No Golden identification.
S&S only. Almanac starts with January.

BB1975 Same as BB1970, in dj, different design   10 - 30
than cover.

BB1995 **Golden Bedtime Book, The**   5 - 15
by Kathryn Jackson, illus by Richard Scarry
©1955, 236pp. Story-a-day book, 366 stories.

BB2030 **Golden Birthday Book, The**   3 - 6
by Margaret Wise Brown,
illus by Leonard Weisgard
©1989 by Roberta B. Rauch (text),
Leonard Weisgard (illus), 28pp. A previously
unpublished story by this well-known author.

BB2050 **Golden Book of Favorite Tales**   ?
(Fairy Tales), illus by Feodor Rojankovsky
Title noted, but copy unavailable for verification.
(See BB1740)

BB2070 **Golden Book of Little Verses, The**   5 - 15
by Miriam Clark Potter, illus by Mary Blair
©1953, 28pp. Some later printings show
cover title as *Little Verses*.

BB2090 **Golden Book of Nursery Tales, The**   5 - 20

by Jane Werner, illus by Tibor Gergely
©1948, 128pp. 1st edition is spiral bound;
later printings are case bound.
(See also: ST1030)

BB2098 **Golden Book of Poems for the Very Young** 9 - 20
by Louis Untermeyer (ed),
illus by Joan Walsh Anglund
©1971, 34pp. Selections from DL1240.

BB2100 **Golden Book of Poetry, The**   8 - 20
by Jane Werner (ed), illus by Gertrude Elliott
©1949, 68pp

BB2120 **Golden Book of Storytime Tales**   8 - 20
sel by the Golden Press Editors,
illus by Sharon Kane
©1962, 164pp. Later issued as a
Golden Pleasure Book in 1964.

BB2140 **Golden Book of 365 Bedtime Stories, The** 5 - 10
by Kathryn Jackson, illus by Richard Scarry
©1955, 236pp. Same as BB1995, but
365 stories.

BB2160 **Golden Book of Words**   3 - 10
by Jane Werner Watson,
illus by Cornelius DeWitt
©1949, 78pp (See also: LE0450)

BB2165 **Golden Book of Words, The**   3 - 6
by Selma Lola Chambers, illus by Louis Cary
©1974, 24pp (See also: LG0120)

BB2180 **Golden Bunny & Seventeen Other Stories** 10 - 25

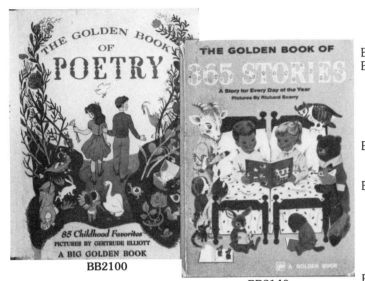

BB2100

BB2140

by Margaret Wise Brown,
illus by Leonard Weisgard
©1953, 28pp. 1981 reissue shown.

BB2184	Same as BB2180, reissued in 1989	3 - 8
BB2210	**Golden Christmas Book, The**	10 - 30

by Gertrude Crampton,
illus by Corinne Malvern
©1947, 96pp. Unstated 1st. Honeycomb
Christmas tree inside front cover. See color
plate.

BB2215	Same as BB2210, later edition w/o honey-comb tree inside front cover. Same cover and contents.	6 - 20
BB2220	**Golden Christmas Book, The**	5 - 18

by Gertrude Crampton,
illus by Corinne Malvern
©1955, 32pp. An abridged version of
the 1947 book. "A" editions noted for
both style 1 & 3 bindings. New cover design.

Golden Christmas Manger, The (See Toy Books)

BB2260	**Golden Christmas Tree, The**	3 - 8

by Jan Wahl, illus by Leonard Weisgard
©1988 by Jan Wahl (text), Leonard
Weisgard (illus), 28pp. This book, together
with BB2184, BB2310 and BB2030 form
a quartet of especially delightful, elegantly
illustrated and designed Big Golden Books.

Golden Circus, The (See Fuzzy Books)

BB2310	**Golden Egg Book, The**	8 - 25

by Margaret Wise Brown,
illus by Leonard Weisgard
©1947, 28pp. Gilt decorations on cover.
(See also: LE4560)

BB2340	**Golden Funny Book, The**	5 - 10

by Gertrude Crampton, illus by J.P. Miller
©1950, 76pp

BB2360	**Golden Grab Bag, The**	5 - 20

by Jerome Wycoff (ed), illus by Tibor Gergely
©1951, 76pp

BB2450	**Golden Song Book**	15 - 25

by Katherine Tyler Wessels,
illus by Gertrude Elliott
©1945, 76pp. 1st edition specially bound
in brown cloth, issued in dj w/light
green background.

BB2452	Same as BB2450, w/pictorial cover. Same design as 1st edition dj except light yellow background.	5 - 18

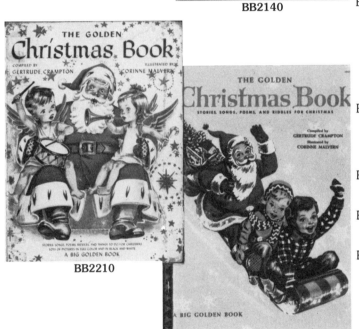

BB2210

BB2220

BB2260

BB2310

BB2184

BB2340　　　　　BB2360　　　　　BB2470　　　　　BB2520

BB2455　**Golden Song Book, The (New)**　　3 - 8
by Katherine Tyler Wessels,
illus by Kathy Allert
©1981, 48pp. An abridged version of
the original book (BB2450), reissued
w/all new illustrations.

BB2470　**Golden Story Treasury, The**　　5 - 20
(Anthology), illus by Tibor Gergely
©1951, 48pp

BB2520　**Golden Treasure Book, The**　　5 - 20
by Kathryn & Byron Jackson, et al;
illus by Cornelius DeWitt, et al
©1951, 192pp

BB2540　**Golden Treasury of Caroline &
Her Friends**　　30 - 85
written & illus by Pierre Probst,
©1953 by Librairie Hachette
Printed in France by Brodart/Topan.
Unpaged thick quarto.

BB2560　**Good Morning, Farm**　　5 - 10
by Betty Ren Wright, illus by Fred Weinan
©1964, 32pp. Published by Whitman
in 1964 as a Giant Tell-a-Tale.

BB2580　**Great Big Animal Book, The**　　5 - 18
written & illus by Feodor Rojankovsky
©1950, 28pp. Shown in Goldencraft
binding.

BB2560　　　　　BB2450

BB2590　**Great Big Car & Truck Book**　　4 - 8
illus by Richard Scarry
©1951, 20pp

BB2600　**Great Big Fire Engine Book, The**　　4 - 10
illus by Tibor Gergely
©1950, 24pp. 1980 printing shown.

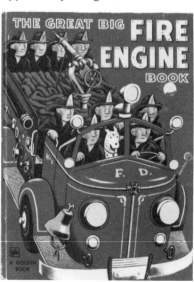

BB2580　　　　　BB2590　　　　　BB2600

BB2630

BB2650

BB2670

BB2730

BB2760 – Front	BB2760 – Back

BB2610	**Great Big Wild Animal Book, The**	4 - 8
	written & illus by Feodor Rojankovsky ©1951, 28pp	
BB2630	**Happy Rabbit, The**	4 - 8
	written & illus by Patricia Barton ©1963 by Golden Pleasure Books, Ltd, 28pp	
BB2650	**Hey There – It's Yogi Bear**	8 - 20
	by Carl Memling, illus by Hawley Pratt ©1956 by Hanna-Barbera Productions, Inc., 28pp. Not the same book as LE5420 of the same title.	
BB2670	**Home for a Bunny**	5 - 15
	by Margaret Wise Brown, illus by Garth Williams ©1956, 32pp (See also: LE5420)	
BB2690	**Howdy Doody in the Wild West**	?
	Title noted, but copy unavailable for verification.	
BB2710	**Huckleberry Hound & Yogi Bear**	?
	Title noted, but copy unavailable for verification.	
BB2730	**I Can Count**	3 - 6
	by Carl Memling, illus by Feodor Rojankovsky ©1963, 28pp	
BB2740	**I Want to Read**	3 - 6
	by Betty Ren Wright, illus by Aliki	

©1965, 20pp

BB2760	**I'm My Mommy/I'm My Daddy**	4 - 8
	by Daniel Wilcox, illus by Mel Crawford ©1976 by CTW & Muppets, Inc., 24pp A turn-about book.	
BB2780	**Jetson's, The**	?
	Title noted, but copy unavailable for verification.	
Judy & Jim (See Toy Books)		
BB2800	**Kittens**	7 - 20
	by Cathleen Schurr & Patricia Scarry, illus by Masha, Gustaf Tenggren & Eloise Wilkin ©1958, 28pp. Compiled from 3 LGBs: LE0010, LE0230, LE1630. (See also: GD5130)	
BB2820	**Lassie and the Secret Friend**	?
	Title noted, but copy unavailable for verification.	
BB2835	**Lassie Finds a Way**	5 - 15
	by Irwin Shapiro, illus by Hamilton Greene ©1957 by Lassie Programs, Inc., 28pp.	
BB2850	**Litterbugs Come in Every Size**	3 - 6
	by Norah Smaridge, illus by Charles Bracke ©1972, 32pp	
BB2865	**Little Black Sambo**	10 - 35
	by Helen Bannerman,	

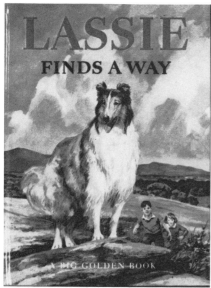

BB2835

BB2865

BB2890

BB2930

BB2960

BB2970

BB3060

BB3064

illus by Bonnie & Bill Rutherford
©1961/p1976(1st), 20pp. First
Golden Press printing. Previously
published as a Top-Top Book.

BB2890 **Little Red Caboose, The**   5 - 12
by Marian Potter, illus by Tibor Gergely
©1953, 28pp. (See also: LE1620, LE3190)

BB2930 **Miss Jaster's Garden**   5 - 18
written & illus by N.M. Bodecker
©1972, 28pp. A Big Golden Mystery Story.

BB2950 **Molly and Mike**   ?
Title noted, but copy unavailable for verification.
Advertised on LGB ad back in 1961.

BB2960 **Monster at the End of This Book, The**   5 - 12
by Jon Stone, illus by Mike Smollin
©1977 by CTW & Muppets, Inc., 24pp
(See also: LF3160)

BB2970 **Mother Goose**   5 - 18
(Nursery Rhymes), illus by Corinne Malvern
©1953, 64pp

BB2980 **Mother Goose, Richard Scarry's**   3 - 7
(Nursery Rhymes), illus by Richard Scarry
©1983, 24pp. Reissued w/new title.
See BB1750.

    Mouse's House (See Fuzzy Books)

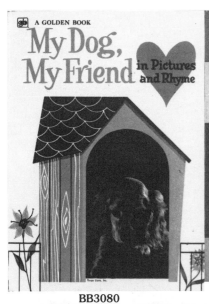

BB3080

BB3090

BB3120

BB3160

BB3210

BB3230

BB3250

BB3010 **My Big Book of the Outdoors**   5 - 12
by Jane Werner Watson, illus by Eloise Wilkin
©1958/p1983, 28pp. Formerly titled:
Wonders of Nature (BB4060).
(See also: LE2930)

BB3020 **My Big Book of the Seasons**   5 - 12
by Bertha Morris Parker, illus by Eloise Wilkin
©1966/p1983, 28pp. Formerly titled:
Wonders of the Seasons (BB4070).

BB3040 **My Big Golden Counting Book**   5 - 15
by Lilian Moore, illus by Garth Williams
©1956, 24pp (See also: LE4340)

BB3060 **My Christmas Treasury**   8 - 20
(Anthology), illus by Lowell Hess
©1957, 32pp (See also: GD5030)

BB3064 Same as BB3060, ©1957/p1968(B),   3 - 12
28pp. New cover design.

BB3080 **My Dog, My Friend**   3 - 9
illus by Sidney Rafilson (& photos)
©1966/p1972, 28pp. Real photos of
dogs combined with illustrations and
rhymes. Previously published as a
Giant Tell-a-Tale (Whitman).

BB3090 **My First Golden Dictionary**   4 - 9
by Mary Reed & Edith Osswald,

illus by Richard Scarry
©1957, 20pp. (See also: LE0900)

BB3095 Same as BB3090, new cover deisgn,   3 - 6
contents the same.

BB3120 **Never Talk to Strangers**   3 - 6
by Irma Joyce, illus by George Buckett
©1967, 20pp. 1989 printing shown.

BB3140 **New Baby, The**   7 - 18
by Harold & Ruth Shane, illus by Eloise Wilkin
©1975, 24pp (See also: LE2910)

BB3160 **New Golden Almanac, The**   5 - 14
by Kathryn Jackson, illus by Richard Scarry
©1952, 128pp. Almanac begins w/March.

BB3180 **New Testament Bible Stories**   3 - 6
(New Testament), retold by Carol Mullen
©1973, 20pp

BB3210 **Nicky Goes to the Doctor**   6 - 10
written & illus by Richard Scarry
©1972 by Richard Scarry, 32pp.
Also published as a Look-Look Book.

BB3220 **Night Before Christmas, Tenggren's**   12 - 35
by Clement C. Moore, illus by Gustaf Tenggren
©1951, 28pp

BB3230 **Night Before Christmas, The**   5 - 18
by Clement C. Moore, illus by Corinne Malvern

The Pink Elephant with Golden Spots

BB3290

PIGGY WIGLET and the Great Adventure

BB3280

Tenggren's Pirates, Ships, and Sailors

26 stories and poems by Kathryn and Byron Jackson

BB3300

The POKY LITTLE PUPPY'S First Christmas

BB3330

The POKY LITTLE PUPPY

A BIG GOLDEN BOOK

BB3320

Raggedy Ann
A Thank You, Please, and I Love You Book

BB3410

©1950/p1958(A), 28pp. Contents same as
LE0200.

BB3250	**Noah's Ark**	3 - 6
	by Barbara Shook Hazen, illus by Tibor Gergely ©1969, 24pp (See also: LF1090)	
BB3270	**Pebbles (Flintstone)**	?
	Title noted, but copy unavailable for verification.	
BB3280	**Piggy Wiglet and the Great Adventure**	4 - 9
	by David L. Harrison, illus by Les Gray ©1973, 20pp	
BB3290	**Pink Elephant with Golden Spots, The**	4 - 9
	written & illus by Philippe & Réjane Fix ©1971, 28pp. First Golden Press printing. Previously published by Editions des Deux Coqs d'Or, Paris, 1970.	
BB3300	**Pirates, Ships & Sailors**	8 - 20
	by Kathryn & Byron Jackson, illus by Gustaf Tenggren ©1950, 62pp. Contents selected from GB2360. 1971 printing shown.	
BB3310	**Poky Little Puppy, The**	3 - 10
	by Janette Sebring Lowry, illus by Gustaf Tenggren ©1942, 24pp (See also: LE0080)	
BB3320	**Poky Little Puppy & Patchwork Blanket**	5 - 12
	written & illus by Jean Chandler ©1983, 24pp	

BB3330	**Poky Little Puppy's First Christmas, The**	5 - 12
	by Adelaide Holl, illus by Florence Sarah Winship ©1973, 20pp	
BB3350	**Prayer Book for Children**	5 - 18
	by Dale Evans Rogers, illus by Eleanor Dart ©1956 by Dale Evans Enterprises, 28pp	
BB3360	**Prayers for Children**	4 - 12
	(Anthology), illus by Eloise Wilkin ©1952, 28pp (See also: LE2050)	
BB3380	**Pussy Willow**	6 - 20
	by Margaret Wise Brown, illus by Leonard Weisgard ©1951, 26pp (See also: LE3140)	
BB3400	**Raggedy Andy: The I Can Do It, You Can Do It Book**	4 - 10
	by Norah Smaridge, illus by June Goldsborough ©1969 by Bobbs-Merrill Co. Inc., 24pp	
BB3410	**Raggedy Ann: A Thank You/Please and I Love You Book**	4 - 10
	by Norah Smaridge, illus by June Goldsborough ©1969 by Bobbs-Merrill Co., Inc., 24pp. 1981 printing shown.	
BB3430	**Rin Tin Tin and the Hidden Treasure**	8 - 20
	by Charles Spain Verral, illus by Mel Crawford ©1958 by Screen Gems, Inc., 28pp	

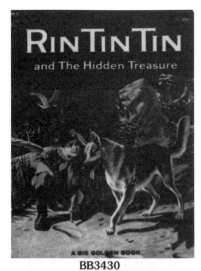

BB3430

BB3480

BB3540

BB3510 BB3530

as issued in 1981. 1988 reprints were issued w/o dj.

BB3530 **Santa Claus Book, The** 15 - 30
by Kathryn Jackson (ed),
illus by Retta Worcester
©1952, 128pp

BB3540 **Scuffy the Tugboat** 3 - 8
by Gertrude Crampton, illus by Tibor Gergely
©1955, 24pp. 1974 printing shown.
(See also: LE0300, LE3630)

BB3560 **Snowy, The Little White Horse** 5 - 12
by Suzanne Reynolds,
illus by Studio Brambilla
©1962/p1965 by Imperial Cancer
Research Fund (text) ,©1964 by
Mondadori-Western Printing (illus), 28pp

BB3580 **Spotty Finds a Playmate** 3 - 10
by Mary Brooks & Bruce Carrick,
illus by Mary Brooks
©1963, 28pp

BB3590 **Stories from Mary Poppins** 8 - 20
by P.L. Travers, illus by Gertrude Elliott
©1952, 36pp. Selected and abridged from
the original stories. Does not include any of
the stories done for the Little Golden series.

BB3440 **Road Runner: A Very Scary Lesson** 2 - 7
by Russell K. Shroeder,
illus by Phil DeLara & Bob Totten
©1974 by Warner Bros., Inc., 24pp
(See also: LF1220)

BB3450 **Rojankovsky's ABC: Alphabet of Many
Things** 8 - 20
(ABC), illus by Feodor Rojankovsky
©1970, 28pp

BB3470 **Roy Rogers, King of the Cowboys** 10 - 35
by John McLeod
©1955 by Roy Rogers Enterprises, 94pp.
Printed in Great Britain by Purnell & Sons
Ltd. Cover photo of Roy on Trigger. Inside
stories do not include any of the stories in the
Little Golden series.

BB3480 **Rudolph the Red-Nosed Reindeer** 3 - 10
by Robert L. May, adp by Janette
Sebring Lowrey, illus by Richard Scarry
©1958 by Robert L. May, 24pp.
(See also: LE3310)

BB3490 **Saggy Baggy Elephant's Great Big
Counting Book** 3 - 9
illus by Manny Campana
©1983, 24pp

BB3510 **Sailor Dog, The** 7 - 15
by Margaret Wise Brown, illus by Garth Williams
©1952, 32pp. 1981 printing shown.
(See also: LE1560)

BB3511 Same as BB3510, in dj of same design, 10 - 20

BB3560 BB3580

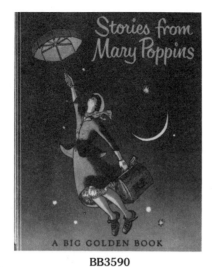

BB3590

BB3600

BB3660

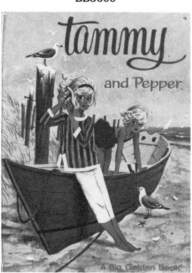

BB3620

BB3640

BB3680

BB3600	**Storytime Tales** (Anthology), illus by Corinne Malvern ©1950, 208pp. Unstated 1st. 8-1/4" x 10-3/4".	8 - 20	BB3740	**Top Cat** by Carl Memling, illus by Hawley Pratt & Al White ©1963 by Hanna-Barbera Productions, Inc., 28pp	10 - 20
BB3620	**Tale of Peter Rabbit, The** by Beatrix Potter, illus by Rod Ruth ©1963, 24pp	2 - 4	BB3760	**True Story of Smokey the Bear, The** by Jane Werner Watson, illus by Feodor Rojankovsky ©1955, 28pp	3 - 15
BB3640	**Tammy & Pepper** by Kathryn Hitte, illus by Mel Crawford ©1964 by Ideal Toy Corp., 28pp	4 - 10	BB3765	Same as BB3760, but smaller format ©1955/p1958, 28pp	2 - 10
BB3660	**Tenggren's Story Book** (Anthology), illus by Gustaf Tenggren ©1948, 68pp. An abridged version of GB2600. Nine stories selected from the original collection.	8 - 20	BB3780	**Weekly Reader Parade, The** by the editors of *Weekly Reader*, illus by Alice & Martin Provensen, Feodor Rojankovsky, et al. ©1947, 116pp. Unstated 1st. No Golden identification on book.	7 - 12
BB3680	**Three Bears, The** (Nursery Tale), illus by Feodor Rojankovsky ©1948, 28pp. 1966 printing shown. (See also: LE0470)	3 - 10	BB3781	Same as BB3780, in dj of same design as cover. "A Big Golden Book Special" is noted on the inside flap of the dj.	10 - 18
BB3690	**Three Bedtime Stories** (Fairy Tales), illus by Garth Williams ©1958, 24pp (See also: LE3090)	3 - 10	BB3790	**Whales** by Jane Werner Watson, illus by Rod Ruth ©1978, 24pp (See also: LF1710)	3 - 9
BB3700	**Three Little Kittens** (Nursery Rhyme), illus by Masha ©1942 (See also: LE0010, LE2250, LE2880, LE3810)	8 - 20	BB3810	**Whatever Happens to Kittens?** by Bill Hall, illus by Virginia Parsons ©1967, 28pp. This title, like many other Big Golden Books, is now in print under the Merrigold Press.	3 - 8
BB3730	**Tootle** by Gertrude Crampton, illus by Tibor Gergely ©1945, 28pp (See also: LE0210)	3 - 8	BB3820	**Whatever Happens to Puppies?**	3 - 8

28

BB3690

BB3760

BB3740

BB3810

BB3820

BB3900

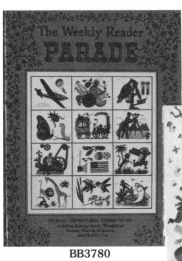

BB3780

BB4040

by Bill Hall, illus by Virginia Parsons
©1965, 24pp

BB4060

BB4070

BB4090

BB5020   BD1010   BD1020   BD1045

BB4070 **Wonders of the Seasons, The**   5 - 20
  by Bertha Morris Parker, illus by Eloise Wilkin
  ©1966, 28pp

BB4090 **Woody Woodpecker: Pirate Treasure**   3 - 7
  ©1979 by Walter Lantz Productions,
  Inc., 24pp

BB5020 **Yogi Bear**   5 - 15
  by Carl Memling,
  illus by Norm McGary & Hawley Pratt
  ©1961 by Hanna-Barbera Productions,
  Inc., 28pp

BB5030 **Yogi Bear/A Christmas Visit**   5 - 12
  by S. Quentin Hyatt,
  illus by Sylvia & Burnett Mattinson
  ©1961 by Hanna-Barbera Productions,
  Inc., 24pp (See also: LE4330)

BIG GOLDEN BOOKS—DISNEY

 Although the Disney titles were not separated from the regular titles in the Big series as they were in the LG series, we have grouped them together in view of collector interest. The same general series notes apply. Many of the older books were published in several different binding styles, and as both Big Golden Books and Walt Disney's Library. The values apply to all styles, unless otherwise noted. Later reprints with less pages, plain end papers, etc., are obviously worth less.

 To avoid needless repetition, the prefix "Walt Disney's" is not listed at the beginning of each title, unless it is an integral part

of the title (as in *Walt Disney's Circus*). All characters, devices and illustrations are copyrighted by Walt Disney Productions.

BD1010 **Adventures of Mr. Toad, The**   10 - 45
  illus by Walt Disney Studios,
  adp by John Hench
  ©1949 by WDP, 28pp. Adapted from
  the WD film *Ichabod and Mr. Toad*,
  based on Kenneth Graham's *The*
  Wind in the Willows.

BD1020 **Adventures of Robin Hood**   9 - 20
  ©1955 by WDP, 46pp. Adapted from
  the WD film starring Richard Greene.
  Illustrated w/photo stills from the movie.

BD1030 **Alice in Wonderland**   9 - 30
  by Lewis Carroll, illus by WDS,
  adp by Al Dempster
  ©1951 by WDP, 28pp. 1st edition
  has gilt decorations on cover and a
  special border on the pages.

BD1035 Same as BD1030, later edition,   3 - 12
  w/o gilt on cover & page border design.

BD1045 **Andy Burnett**   4 - 15
  by Charles Spain Verral,
  illus by E. Joseph Dreany
  ©1958 by WDP, 44pp. Adapted from
  the WD TV series, based on the book
  by Stewart Edward White.

BD1055 **Babes in Toyland**   3 - 12

BD1030

BD1035

BD1070

BD1055

BD1065

BD1080

BD1100

by George Sherman & Mary Carey,
illus by WDS, adp by Lowell Hess
©1961 by WDP, 28pp. Based on
the WD film *Babes in Toyland.*

BD1065 **Bambi**   18 - 35
illus by WDS
©1941 by WDP, 56pp w/4 fold-out
pictures inserted in front of text.
Published by S&S, no Golden Book
identification. First book in what was
to become the "Walt Disney's Library"
series of the large format books.

BD1066 Same as BD1065, in dj of same design   25 - 45

BD1068 Same as BD1065, but later edition   10 - 30
published without fold-out pictures.

BD1070 **Bambi**   4 - 12
illus by WDS, adp by Melvin Shaw
©1949 by WDP, 28pp. Adapted from
the WD film, based on the story by
Felix Salten. (See also: FZ1010)

BD1080 **Bambi**   3 - 8
©1984/p1986 by WD Co., 20pp
(See also: LI2150)

BD1100 **Bedknobs and Broomsticks**   2 - 8
©1971 by WDP, 28pp. Adapted from
the WD film. Unstated 1st.

BD1130 **Bongo**   8 - 30

BD1130

BD1160

BD1200

BD1240

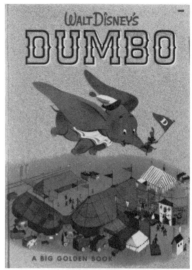

BD1340

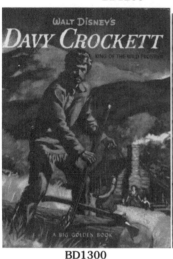

BD1300

BD1310

BD1250

BD1350

illus by Edgar Starr
©1947 by WDP, 28pp. Adapted from
the WD film *Fun and Fancy Free*,
based on the story by Sinclair Lewis.

BD1160 **Bunny Book** 6 - 25
by Jane Werner, illus by WDS,
adp by Dick Kelsey & Bill Justice
©1951 by WDP, 28pp. No edition
stated. (See also: LI0210, LI1110)

BD1200 **Chicken Little** 2 - 7
©1965/p1983 by WDP, 24pp.
Formerly appeared in BD1720.

BD1240 **Cinderella** 10 - 35
by Jane Werner (adp), illus by WDS,
adp by Retta Worcester
©1950(A) by WDP, 28pp. 1st edition
has gilt decoration throughout, honeycomb pumpkin inside front cover.

BD1241 Same as BD1240, later printing 4 - 12
without gilt decorations and pumpkin.

BD1250 **Cinderella** 3 - 8
©1986 by WD Co., 20pp (See also: LI2160)

BD1300 **Davy Crockett King of the Wild Frontier** 8 - 25
by Elizabeth Beecher, illus by WDS,
adp by Al Schmidt
©1955 by WDP, 48pp

BD1310 **Davy Crockett and Mike Fink** 8 - 25
by Irwin Shapiro (adp), illus by WDS (photos)

©1955 by WDP, 46pp. Based on the TV
series.

BD1320 **Donald Duck It's Playtime!** 3 - 8
illus by WDS
©1981 by WDP, 24pp

BD1340 **Dumbo** 7 - 20
by Annie North Bedford, illus by WDS,
adp by Dick Kelsey
©1955 by WDP, 28pp

BD1350 **Dumbo** 3 - 8
by Teddy Slater (adp),
illus by Ron Dias & Annie Guenther
©1988 by WD Co., 20pp

BD1380 **Favorite Stories, WD** 6 - 20
illus by Bob Moore, Milt Banta,
Al Dempster & Bob Grant
©1957 by WDP, 36pp. A compilation
of 3 LG books (LI0030, LI0060 & LI0100)
(See also: GD5040)

BD1400 **Great Locomotive Chase, The** 4 - 15
by Charles Spain Verral,
illus by Graham Kaye (adp)
©1956 by WDP, 44pp. Adapted from
the WD film.

BD1450 **Jungle Book, The** 3 - 9
by Jean Lewis, illus by WDS
©1967 by WDP, 28pp. Adapted from
the WD film, based on the Mowgli
stories by Rudyard Kipling.

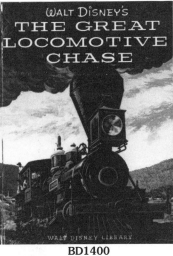

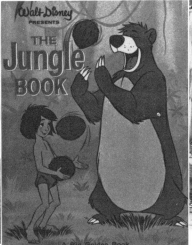

BD1380

BD1400

BD1450

BD1460

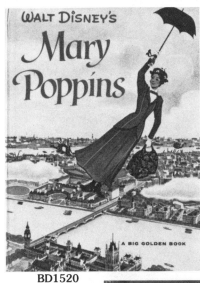

BD1480

BD1520

BD1610

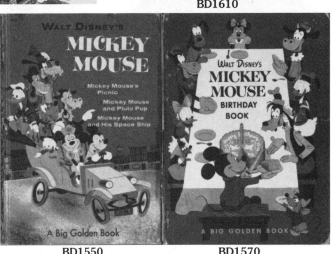

BD1550

BD1570

BD1460	**Jungle Book, The**	2 - 6

BD1460 **Jungle Book, The**   2 - 6
by Annie North Bedford,
illus by WDS, adp by Mel Crawford
©1990 by WD Co., 20pp. Contents
same as LI1200, published in 1967.

BD1480 **Lady & the Tramp**   6 - 20
illus by WDP, adp by Claude Coats
©1955 by WDP, 32pp. Adapted from
the WD film, based on the story by
Ward Greene.

BD1490 Same as BD1480, WDL edition, different   6 - 20
binding style. Number of pages shortened by
eliminating free end papers. 28pp.

BD1520 **Mary Poppins**   5 - 10
by Annie North Bedford (adp),
illus by Grace Clarke
©1964 by WDP, 1963 by P.L. Travers,
28pp. Adapted from the WD film,
based on the original stories by P.L. Travers.

BD1550 **Mickey Mouse**   4 - 15
illus by WDS
©1953 by WDP, 36pp. A compilation
of 3 Disney LGBs: LI0150, LI0200 &
LI0250. Cover art same as LI0250.

BD1570 **Mickey Mouse Birthday Book**   8 - 20
by Annie North Bedford (sel),
illus by WDS, adp by Campbell Grant
©1953 by WDP, 64pp

BD1610 **Mickey Mouse in Hideaway Island**   2 - 6
©1980 by WDP, 24pp

BD1625 **Mickey Mouse The Kitten Sitters**   2 - 6
©1976 by WDP, 24pp

BD1660 **Mickey's Christmas Carol**   2 - 6
illus by Ron Dias
©1990 by WD Co., 20pp. New cover
art, contents same as LI2070.

BD1680 **Mother Goose**   8 - 25
illus by WDS, adp by Al Dempster

BD1660

BD1680

BD1690

BD1720

BD1740

BD1760

BD1780

©1949 by WDP, 28pp. A classic Disney title, available in many formats from a variety of publishers. (See also: LI0510, LI0790)

BD1690 Same as BD1680, with new cover. 2 - 7
Inside text & illustrations remained the same. ©1970 by WDP

BD1720 **Nursery Tales** 8 - 20
by Kathleen Daly (adp), illus by WDS, adp by Norm McGary
©1965 by WDP, 62pp (See also: LI1250)

BD1740 **Old Yeller** 7 - 18
by Willis Lindquist, illus by WDS, adp by Robert Doremus
©1958 by WDP, 32pp. Adapted from the WD film, based on the novel by Fred Gipson. (See also: LI0650)

BD1760 **101 Dalmatians** (10540) 5 - 18
by Carl Buettner (adp), illus by WDS, adp by Norm McGary & Sylvia Mattison
©1961 by WDP, 32pp. Adapted from the WD film, based on the original story by Dodie Smith. Published in varying BG formats. Number of pages varies w/format, content essentially the same.

BD1780 **Perri** 4 - 12
by Emily Broun (adp), illus by Dick Kelsey
©1957 by WDP, 28pp. Based on the

original story by Felix Salten.

BD1800 **Peter Pan** 4 - 15
illus by WDS, adp by John Hench & Al Dempster
©1952 by WDP, 32pp. Adapted from the WD film, based on the story by James Barrie.

BD1820 **Peter Pan** 2 - 6
©1987 by WD Co., 20pp. New cover art and contents adapted from BD1800.

BD1840 **Pinocchio** 8 - 20
by Steffi Fletcher (adp), illus WDS, adp by Al Dempster
©1953 by WDP, 28pp. Adapted from the WD film, based on the story by Collodi.

BD1850 Same as BD1840, later edition w/plain 5 - 12
background cover.

BD1860 **Pinocchio** 2 - 6
©1984/p1986 by WD Co., 20pp. New cover art, contents adapted from BD1840.

Robin Hood (See BD1020)

BD1900 **Savage Sam** 4 - 15
by Carl Memling, illus by Mel Crawford
©1963 by WDP, 28pp. Adapted from the WD film, based on the story by Fred Gipson.

BD1920 **Sleeping Beauty** 8 - 20
by Jane Werner Watson, illus by WDS, adp by Earl Eyvind & Julius Svendsen

WALT DISNEY'S
Peter Pan

BD1800

Walt Disney's
Peter Pan

BD1820

WALT DISNEY'S
Pinocchio

BD1840

Walt Disney's
PINOCCHIO

BD1860

Savage Sam

A BIG GOLDEN BOOK

BD1900

WALT DISNEY'S
Sleeping Beauty

A BIG GOLDEN BOOK

BD1920

Walt Disney's
Snow White
and the Seven Dwarfs

A GOLDEN BOOK

BD1960

WALT DISNEY'S
Sleeping Beauty

BD1940

©1957 by WDP. A much abridged version of GD2460

BD1930	Same as BD1920, smaller format.	5 - 12
BD1940	**Sleeping Beauty**	3 - 12
	©1986 by WD Co., 20pp (See also: LI2180)	
BD1960	**Snow White and the Seven Dwarfs**	4 - 15
	by Jane Werner (adp), illus by WDS, adp by Campbell Grant © 1952 by WDP, 28pp	
BD1970	Same as BD1960, later edition, 24 pp, with plain end papers.	3 - 10
BD1980	**Snow White and the Seven Dwarfs**	3 - 12
	©1984/p1986 by WD Co., 20pp (See also: LI2080)	
BD2010	**Storybook of Peter Pan**	8 - 20
	by Annie North Bedford (adp), illus by Campbell Grant ©1969 by WDP. Adapted from the WD film, based on the story by James Barrie	
BD2030	**Sword in the Stone, The**	9 - 20
	by Carl Memling, illus by WDS, adp by Al White ©1963 by WDP, 28pp. Adapted from the WD film, based on the story by T.H. White.	
BD2060	**Treasure Chest, WD**	8 - 30
	illus by WDS ©1948 by WDP. 14 favorite WD stories, no repeats from LGBs.	

Walt Disney's
SNOW WHITE
And The Seven Dwarfs

A GOLDEN BOOK

BD1980

Walt Disney PRESENTS THE STORYBOOK OF
Peter Pan

A BIG GOLDEN BOOK

BD2010

BD2080 **20,000 Leagues Under the Sea**   4 - 12
by Elizabeth Beecher, illus by WDS,
adp by Grant Campbell
©1954 by WDP, 64pp. Adapted from the
WD film, based on the story by Jules Verne.

BD2100 **Ugly Dachshund, The**   8 - 20
by Carl Memling (adp), illus by Mel Crawford
©1965 by WDP, 28pp. Adapted from
the WD film.

BD2150 **Walt Disney's Circus**   10 - 30
illus by WDS
©1944 by WDP, 32pp. A slightly different
binding than FZ1040. Issued w/o dj, but
still w/fuzzy cover & pages.

BD2200 **Winnie-the-Pooh A Tight Squeeze**   2 - 8
by A.A. Milne, illus by WDS, adp by Al White
©1965 by WDS (illus), ©1954 by A.A.
Milne (text), 28pp

BD2210 **Winnie-the-Pooh and Eeyore's Birthday**   2 - 8
by A.A. Milne, illus by WDS,
adp by Norm McGary & Bill Lorencz
©1965 by WDS (illus), ©1954 by A.A.
Milne (text), 20pp.

BD2220 **Winnie-the-Pooh Meets Tigger**   2 - 8
by A.A. Milne, illus by WDS
©1968 by WDP (illus), ©1956 by A.A.
Milne (text), 20pp.

BD2230 **Winnie-the-Pooh The Unbouncing of Tigger**   2 - 8
by A.A. Milne, illus by WDS
©1974 by WDP (illus), ©1956 by A.A.
Milne (text), 24pp.

BD2260 **Zorro**   4 - 15
by Irving Werstin (adp), illus by John Steel
©1958 by WDP, 32pp. Adapted from the
WD TV series, based on the Johnston McCulley
character. Cover same as LE0680, but
contents are different. Soft cover editions of
several large format Golden Books have been
noted. How many books were published in
this format has not been determined.

BIG LITTLE GOLDEN BOOKS

A spin-off from the LGB series, Big LGBs are designed with
slightly older readers in mind, although they do include some
titles available in the Little Golden series. Books are 8" x 8-
1/4", 24 pages, with the same spine as LGBs. They have been

BD2030

BD2080

BD2150

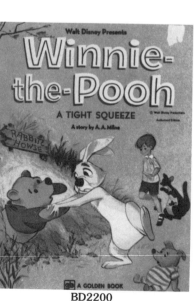

BD2060

BD2100

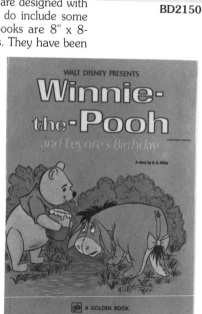

BD2210

BD2200

BD2220	BD2230	BD2260

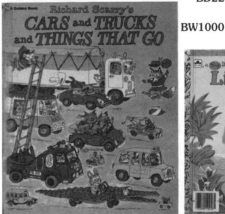

BW1000

published both in hard cover and soft cover. Most books are numbered in a 10xxx series, with the last 3 digits derived form the ISBN number. Edition information is carried with the copyright data. The series began in 1986, and most titles are still in print. Copies can be found readily at flea markets and yard sales for 25¢ - $1.

BOOK CLUB EDITIONS (and Weekly Reader Books)

Children's books are a regular part of Book Club fare, and many Golden Books have been published in this form. Some of the books have a notice with the copyright date that states "Book Club Edition" (BCE) and date; however, most BCEs are unmarked. "Weekly Reader" (WRC) books are a juvenile "book club" in effect, and several Golden titles have been included in that series. Often, the stories are combined, as in the two books shown. Most Book Club and Weekly Reader books sell for $4 and under.

BW1000 **Cars and Trucks and Things That Go** (BCE)   1 - 3
written & illus by Richard Scarry
©1974 by Richard Scarry, 70pp. Noted "First Book Club Edition, 1975." An overall smaller book than the original Golden Book printing.

BW1020 **Little Peewee/Sylvester** (WR)   1 - 3
©1967 (WRC), 63pp. A combination of LE0525 and a Read-It-Yourself book.

BW1040 **Whispering Rabbit and Other Stories** (WR)   1 - 3
by Margaret Wise Brown, illus by Garth Williams ©1965, 63pp. A combination of several LGBs with a selection from LE0460, LE1990, LE4560

BW1040	BW1020

Big Little Golden Books, part of the growing Little Golden Book family, were introduced in 1986. Over 60 titles were published by 1990.

CL2803

Golden Classic™
Library
for ages 8-10

Golden
Junior Classic™
Library
for ages 4-7

CL2808

CHILDREN'S TELEVISION WORKSHOP: CTW/GOLDEN

Children's Television Workshop, producers of "Sesame Street", has published many educational books featuring Sesame Street characters, which are marked "CTW/Golden" and/or "Sesame Street/Golden Press." The books are designed to be used independently of the television program, so they are accessible to all children. CTW books are produced by several publishers, not only Golden Press, and do not constitute a specialized series for the purposes of this book. Sesame Street Books have been included in many Golden Book series since the early '70s. A category listing is included in the Appendix.

CLASSIC LIBRARY (Golden Classic and Golden Junior Classic)

Introduced in 1986, as a collection of the best loved children's literature of all time, "Golden Junior Classics" are geared to ages 4-7; "Golden Classics" to ages 8-10. Books are 7-1/4" x 9-1/4" with the "Golden Classic" design in the upper right corner of the front cover. Personalized Golden Classic bookplates and a book embosser were offered as "library accessories" to help promote the new series. Sets of the original 8 Golden Junior Classics were also offered as prizes in the "Billion Golden Memories" celebration. Most Golden Classics, which are unabridged versions of the original stories, retail for $8.95; Junior Classics for $4.95.

Junior Classics

CL2800 **Three Little Pigs and Other Nursery Tales** 1 - 3
(Nursery Tales), illus by Christopher Santoro
©1986 by Christopher Santoro (illus), 48pp

CL2801 **Golden Goose and Other Tales of Good Fortune** 1 - 3
(Nursery Tales), illus by S. D. Schindler
©1986 by S.D. Schindler (illus), 48pp

CL2802 **Jack and the Beanstalk and Other Favorite Folk Tales** 1 - 3
(Folk Tales), illus by Richard Walz
©1986 by Richard Walz (illus), 48pp

CL2803 **Cinderella and Other Favorite Fairy Tales** 1 - 3
by Eric Suben (ed), illus by Darcy May
©1986 by Darcy May (illus), 48pp

CL2804 **Emperor's New Clothes and Other Nonsense Stories** 1 - 3
(Fairy Tales), illus by Kathy Milone
©1986 by Kathy Milone (illus), 48pp

CL2805 **Jabberwocky and Other Nonsense Verses** 1 - 3
by H.E. Casterline (ed), illus by Jean Chandler
©1986 by Jean Chandler (illus), 48pp

CL2806 **Mother Goose and Other Nursery Rhymes** 1 - 3
(Nursery Rhymes), illus by Ann Schweninger
©1986 by Ann Schweninger (illus), 48pp

CL2807 **Beauty and the Beast and Other Tales of Enchantment** 1 - 3
(Fairy Tales), illus by Jean Chambless-Rigie
©1986 by Jean Chambless-Rigie (illus), 48pp

CL2808 **Alladin and the Wonderful Lamp and Other Tales of Adventure** 1 - 3
by Linda C. Falken (ed), illus by Anthony Accado
©1987 by Anthony Accado (illus), 48pp

CL2809 **Wynken, Blyken, and Nod and Other Bedtime Poems** 1 - 3
by Linda C. Falken (sel), illus by Karen Milone
©1987 by Kathy Milone (illus), 48pp

Classics

CL7110 **Adventures of Tom Sawyer, The** 2 - 5
by Mark Twain, illus by Luis Dominguez
©1986 by Luis Dominguez (illus), 304pp

CL7111 **Alice in Wonderland & Through the Looking Glass** 2 - 5
by Lewis Carroll, illus by Kathy Mitchell
©1986 by Kathy Mitchell (illus), 256pp

CL7112 **Black Beauty** 2 - 5
by Anna Sewell, illus by Tony Chen
©1986 by Tony Chen (illus), 256 pp

CL7113 **Grimm's Fairy Tales** 2 - 5
by Jacob & Wilhelm Grimm,
illus by Richard Walz
©1986 by Richard Walz (illus), 384pp

CL7114 **Heidi** 2 - 5
by Johanna Spyri, illus by Judith Cheng
©1986 by Judith Cheng (illus), 352pp

CL7115 **Wizard of Oz, The** 2 - 5
by L. Frank Baum, illus by Kathy Mitchell
©1986 by Kathy Mitchell (illus), 176pp

CL7116 **Little Women** 2 - 7
by Louisa May Alcott, illus by Michael Adams
©1987 by Michael Adams (illus), 640pp

CL7117 **Wind in the Willows, The** 2 - 5
by Kenneth Grahame, illus by Peter Barrett
©1987 by Peter Barrett (illus), 224pp

CR1050   CR1070

CRAFT AND HOBBY BOOKS

Craft and Hobby Books were advertised on LGB backs in 1960, 1962 and 1963. Well illustrated in full color, they continue to be of special interest to camp directors, teachers, scout masters and others. The books were published in Goldencraft library editions as well as regular trade editions.

While the covers do not state, "Golden Craft & Hobby Books", they are, however, easily recognized by their titles as craft and hobby books, and have been grouped together as such rather than being included under the general "Golden Book" heading.

Books are hard cover, generally 8-1/2" x 11" or larger. Printing information is usually found in the lower left corner of the front inside cover or a front end paper as a letter code followed by a double price code.

CR1010	**Camping and Camp Crafts** by Gordon Lynn, illus by Ernest Kurt Barth ©1959, 212pp	3 - 10
CR1020	**Chemistry Experiments** by R. Brent, illus by Harry Lazarus ©1961, 112pp	2 - 6
CR1022	Same as CR1020, later edition, cover variation.	2 - 6
CR1030	**Crafts and Hobbies** by W. Ben Hunt ©1957, 104pp. Advertised w/2 different covers.	3 - 10
CR1032	Same as CR1030, later edition, cover variation.	2 - 8
CR1040	**Gardening** by F. Gianonni & Seymour Reit, illus by William Sayles & Tom Tierney ©1961, 68pp	4 - 10
CR1050	**Indian Crafts and Lore** written & illus by W. Ben Hunt ©1954, 104pp	5 - 12
CR1054	Same as CR1050, later edition, new cover design.	3 - 9
CR1060	**Nature Crafts** by John R. Saunders ©1958, 104pp	2 - 6
CR1070	**Wild Animal Pets** written & illus by Roy Pinney (photos) ©1959 by GP, 68pp. Goldencraft binding shown.	2 - 6

DE LUXE GOLDEN BOOKS

Although the "deluxe" connotation is also used on books in other Golden categories, this special series was set apart by its educational content, designed to widen the young readers' horizons, adding to their knowledge of themselves and the world. Some books were written especially for the De Luxe series; others were adapted from books already published and made into special editions for young people. De Luxe Golden Books were featured in several different ads on LGBs between 1961 and 1963. Books with dust jackets are valued at 25- 50% over the values listed. Not all volumes were published in dust jackets; verified copies are stated with listings. Several of the titles were also issued in soft cover.

DL1030	**Courtis-Watters Illustrated Golden Dictionary, The** by Stuart A. Courtis & Garnette Watters 1951/p1961. First issued by Golden in 1951, this revised one-volume edition was especially edited for the De Luxe series. (See also: ID1010)	5 - 10
DL1050	**Epic of Man, The** by the editors of *LIFE* and Lincoln Barnett, adp by Eugene Rachlis ©1962, 176pp. A special edition for young readers.	5 - 10
DL1070	**Golden Anniversary Book of Scouting** by R.D. Bezucha, illus by Norman Rockwell, et al ©1959 by Boy Scouts of America & GPI 166pp. Issued in dj of same design	10 - 20

DL1050   DL1070

DL1080   DL1120

DL1080   **Golden Book of America**   5 - 10
by Irwin Shapiro (adp)
©1957 by American Heritage Pub. Co.,
216pp. Adapted from *American Heritage
Magazine*. Issued in dj of same design.

DL1085   Same as DL1080, soft cover   2 - 6

DL1120   **Golden Book of the American Revolution**   5 - 10
by Fred Cook (adp)
©1959 by American Heritage Pub. Co.,

194pp. Adapted from *American Heritage
Magazine*.

DL1140   **Golden Book of the Civil War**   5 - 15
by Charles Flato
©1961 by American Heritage Pub. Co.,
216pp. Adapted for young readers from the
*American Heritage Picture History of the
Civil War*. Edition not stated.

DL1160   **Golden Picture Book of Knowledge**   3 - 8
written & illus by Herbert Pothorn
©1961 by Droemersche Verlagsanstalt Th.
Knaur Nachf, 165pp. 1st American edition.

DL1200   **Golden Treasury of Myths & Legends**   10 - 35
by Anne Terry White,
illus by Alice & Martin Provensen
©1959, 166pp. Adapted from the world's
greatest classics. Although marked a "Giant
Golden Book", this book is properly classified
with this series.

DL1220   **Golden Treasury of Natural History, The**   5 - 10
by Bertha Morris Parker
©1952, 216pp. Unstated 1st. Illustrated
w/paintings from the Golden Nature Guides
and *The Golden Book of Animal Stamps*,
as well as other sources. (See also: DL1370)

DL1221   Same as DL1220, in dj, different design   7 - 15

DL1224   Same as DL1220, pictorial cover   5 - 10
Later printing, pictorial cover same
as original dust jacket.

DL1240   **Golden Treasury of Poetry, The**   12 - 40
by Louis Untermeyer (sel),
illus by Joan Walsh Anglund
©1959 by GPI, 324pp. 1962 printing shown.
Excerpts from this book have been published
in many different Golden series. (See GG3160,
GG3340, TR1000)

DL1280   **Human Body, The/What It Is and
How It Works**   5 - 10
by Mitchell Wilson, illus by Cornelius DeWitt
©1959, 140pp. Shown in Goldencraft
binding.

DL1330   **Living Desert, Walt Disney's**   5 - 10
by Jane Werner Watson & Staff, WDS
©1954 by WDP, 124pp. A True-Life
Adventure Series.

DL1370   **New Golden Treasury of Natural History**   3 - 9
by Bertha Morris Parker
©1968, 384pp. A revised edition of DL1220.

DL1390   **Our Friend the Atom, Walt Disney's**   5 - 10
by Heinz Haber, illus by WDS

DL1140   DL1160

DL1200   DL1220

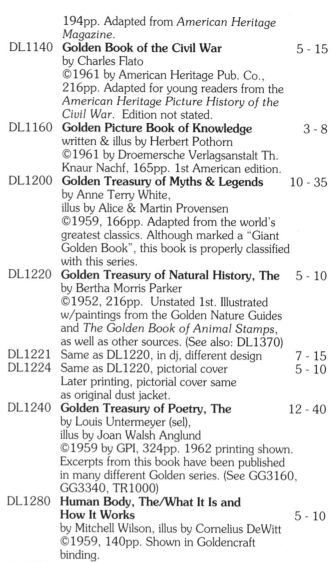

DL1221   DL1280   DL1240   DL1370

| DL1410 | DL1540 | DL1600 | DR3302 |

©1956 by WDP, 166pp. Bound in red cover, title on spine only. Issued in pictorial dj of different design.

DL1410 **People and Places, Walt Disney's**   5 - 10
by Jane Werner Watson & Staff, WDS
©1959 by WDP, 176pp. Adapted from the True-Life Adventure Series. Issued in dj of same design.

DL1450 **Sea Around Us, The**   5 - 10
by Rachel Carson
©1959, 166pp. A special edition for young people.

DL1470 **Story of Geology, The**   3 - 8
by Jerome Wycoff
©1960, 178pp

DL1490 **Vanishing Prairie, The–Walt Disney's**   5 - 10
by Jane Werner Watson & Staff, WDS
©1955 by WDP, 124pp. A True-Life Adventure.

DL1510 **Wonders of Life on Earth, The**   3 - 8
by editors of *Life*, adp by Sarel Einer
©1961 by Time, Inc., 216pp

DL1530 **World of Science, The**   3 - 8
by Jane Werner Watson, color photos by Wilson & MacPherson Hole, et al
©1958, 216pp. Issued in dj designed by William Dugan

DL1540 **World We Live In, The**   3 - 8
by editors of *Life* and Lincoln Barnett, adp by Jane Werner Watson
©1956 by Time, Inc., 216pp. A special edition for young readers. Issued in dj of same design.

DL1580 **World's Greatest Religions, The**   5 - 10
by editors of *Life* & Henry R. Luce
©1958 by Time, Inc., 118pp

DL1600 **Worlds of Nature, Walt Disney's**   5 - 10
by Rutherford Platt & Staff, WDS
© by WDP, 176pp. A Treasury of True-Life Adventures. Issued in dj of same design.

DISNEY RHYMING STORYBOOK
A short series of 4 books, each 7-1/4" X 10" in glossy pictorial covers. A pre-school series with short, rhymed stories featuring favorite Disney characters.

DR3300 **Winnie-the-Pooh Gets Shipwrecked**   3 - 5

by Vince Jefferds, illus by WDS
©1985 by WDP, 32pp

DR3301 **Wooly Bird Meets Winnie-the-Pooh**   3 - 5
by Vince Jefferds, illus by WDS
©1985 by WDP, 32pp

DR3302 **Peter Pan & the Troll**   3 - 5
by Vince Jefferds, illus by WDS
©1985 by WDP, 32pp

DR3303 **Mickey & Donald in the Tickle Grass**   3 - 5
by Vince Jefferds, illus by WDS
©1985 by WDP, 32pp

ENCYCLOPEDIA, GOLDEN
The *Golden Book Encyclopedia*, compiled by a voluminous staff of editors and artists, was another product of Golden's determination to provide interesting, factual and effective learning books. First published in 1959, the set was the only encyclopedia at the time that was geared to young grade-school children. Each 96-page, 8-1/2" x 11" volume has full color illustrations on every page, with articles "entertainingly written" to make learning an adventure, without sacrificing either accuracy or authority.

EG1010 **Golden Book Encyclopedia, The**   16 - 48
by Bertha Morris Parker (ed)
© 1959, 16 vols, 96pp each. Pages numbered consecutively throughout the set, index in last volume. Cover illustration differs with each volume.

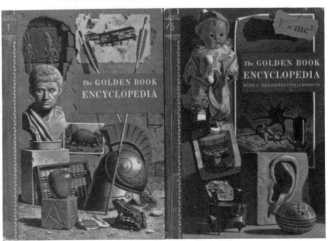

EG1010 - Vols 1 and 5

| EG1040 | EG1060 |

EG1015   Individual volumes of EG1010, each   1 - 3
EG1040   Same as EG1015, each   1 - 3
              Shown in Goldencraft binding, 1970 edition.
EG1060   **Golden Book Encyclopedia, The (revised)** 20 - 60
              by Patricia A. Reynolds, (ed), WPC;
              and Lawrence T. Lorimer, Macmillan
              Educational Co.
              ©1987, 20 vols, 96pp each. A thoroughly
              revised and expanded version, issued in 1987
              under a new editorial staff. Pages numbered
              individually per volume, index in Vol. 20.
EG1065   Individual volumes of EG1060, each   1 - 3

ENCYCLOPEDIA OF NATURAL SCIENCE

Edited by Herbert Zim, this 16-volume set enhances and amplifies much of the information in the Nature Guide series and other Golden series dealing with natural science. The volumes are illustrated with drawings and photos, and the contents are advertised as "a world survey" of all fields of natural history. As is usual with most golden reference sets, the matieral is presented in such a manner that it is not only stimulating to young learners, but also provides much useful information even on an adult level. The volumes are uniform in size with other Golden reference works.

EN1010   **Encyclopedia of Natural Science**   16 - 48
              edited by Herbert S. Zim
              ©1962, 16 volumes
EN1015   Individual volumes of EN1010, each   1 - 3

| EN1010 - *Vol 3* | EN1010 - *Vol 6* |

First Little Golden Books

FIRST LITTLE GOLDEN BOOKS

These small format books were designed to appeal to toddlers and serve as a "stepping stone" to LGBs. Some books repeat previously published LGB titles (*Happy Man and His Dump Truck*, for example) in exactly the same format as the LGB. Others have adapted previous books with new illustrations (*I Can Fly* and *Busy Timmy*). The bulk of the series, however, is entirely new stories. Disney titles are included. No listing of additional titles is provided in the books as with LGBs, and a current list of all titles in the FLGB series has not yet been assembled.

The series began in 1981, with books retailing for 69¢ each. New titles are added to the series each year. All books are 5-1/2" x 5-7/8" with the familiar LG spine and 24pp text. Similar in size to "Tell-a-Tale" books (FLGBs are slightly shorter), the side stapled format provides a more durable book. Printing information is shown as a letter code following the copyright date.

Collectibility at present is limited, but, like most small format books, the series show promise of increased collector interest. Most of the books are still available on the retail market and many are currently into multiple reprints. With books this new, however, collectibility is generally limited to first editions.

One particular title that has already generated interest is *I Can Fly* (previously published as LGB 1-92). The FLGB version is illustrated by Jan Brett, and 1st edition copies sell for $1-3. Most secondary copies in this series, however, are generally found at flea markets and yard sales and go for 10¢-25¢.

FORTY-NINERS

Advertised as a new series of big picture books designed for children who had outgrown LGBs, the "49er" series stressed books with more factual texts, as opposed to the mostly "story" content or pre-school learning emphasized in LGBs.

Books were 7-1/4" x 10", with illustrated end papers. The "Golden Forty-Niner" name included a logo depicting a Conestoga wagon. Their saddle stitch construction did not have the durability of LGBs, and spines are often missing. Printing information is shown on the lower left corner of the inside cover, as a letter followed by a double price code. Information is limited for this series, and more titles may have been published.

FR1020   FR1030

FN4910	**Animals from All Over the World** (4901) by Willia Lindquist, illus by James Gordon Irving & Sy Barlowe ©1956, 30pp	3 - 6
FN4920	**Presidents of the United States** (4902) by Irwin Shapiro, illus by Mel Crawford & Edwin Schmidt ©1956, 30pp	3 - 6
FN4930	**Wonders of the World** (4903) by Herbert J. Bernhard, illus by George Solonwitsch, Ted Chaiko & Robert Moynihan ©1956, 30pp	3 - 6
FN4940	**Cowboys** (4904) by Francis Sayers, illus by Hans Helwig & Frank Bolle ©1956, 30pp	4 - 10
FN4950	**Bible Stories** (4905) by Jonathan Braddock, illus by Steele Savage ©1956, 28pp	3 - 6
FN4960	**Night Before Christmas, The** (4906) by Clement C. Moore, illus by Eloise Wilkin ©1956 by Simon & Schuster, 28pp. With the exception of a new title page spread, this book uses the same illustrations as LE2410. The LGB is in full color, while the 49er alternates full-color pages with black and white. Picture shows both front and back.	8 - 12

FN4960 - Back   **FN4960 - Front**

FRAGRANCE BOOKS (see Scratch & Sniff)

FUN-TO-LEARN

A special series of educational books that stressed enjoyment in learning. Stories were combined with games, skits, activities, nature walks and handicrafts.

Books in the Fun-to-Learn series originally had a small slate design on the cover, enclosing the words "Fun-To-Learn" and numbers beginning with "FL". Later printings drop the slate design and the "FL". Book titles begin with "The Golden Picture Book of ...". They were advertised on LGBs in 1961, although the series was initiated in the mid-50s. Colorful, well illustrated volumes, they were published in both pictorial cover format and Golden craft library editions. Printing information is

found on the lower left corner of the front end paper as a letter code followed by a double price code.

FR1010	**Words/How They Look and What They Tell** (FL-1) by Jane Werner Watson, illus by Cornelius DeWitt ©1954, 64pp	2 - 6
FR1020	**Numbers/What They Look Like & What They Do** (FL-2) by Edith Osswald & Mary Reed, illus by Corinne Malvern ©1954 by GP, 48pp. LE2430 adapted some of the text from this book into the smaller LGB format, with new illustrations. Shown in Goldencraft binding.	2 - 6
FR1030	**School Days** (FL-3) by Kathryn Jackson, illus by Violet LaMont ©1954 by S&S, 48pp	2 - 8
FR1040	**Golden Picture Dictionary, The** (FL-4) by Lilian Moore, illus by Beth & Joe Krush, cover by Violet LaMont ©1954, 80pp	2 - 8
FR1050	**Stories to Read and Hear** (FL-5) by Lilian Moore, illus by Corinne Malvern ©1955, 48pp	4 - 10
FR1060	**Poems/To Read and Learn** (FL-6) by Ilse Hayes Govoni & Dorothy Hall Smith, illus by Grace Dalles Clarke ©1955 by S&S, 48pp. Shown in Goldencraft binding.	2 - 6

FR1060   FR1070

FR1090

FR1110

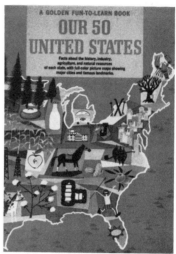

FR1120

FR1070	**Questions and Answers** (FL-7)	2 - 6
	by Horace Elmo, illus by Tibor Gergely ©1957 by Simon & Schuster, 56pp	
FR1080	**Science** (FL-8)	2 - 6
	by Jene Lyon, illus by George Solonewitsch ©1957, 58pp	
FR1090	**Our Sun/And the Worlds Around It** (FL-9)	3 - 8
	by Jene Lyon, illus by George Solonewitsch ©1957, 58pp	
FR1100	**Birds** (FL-10)	4 - 10
	by Clara Hussong, illus by Marjorie Hartwell ©1959, 58pp	
FR1110	**Sea and Shore, The** (FL-11)	3 - 8
	by Marion B. Carr, illus by Sy Barlowe ©1959, 58pp	
FR1120	**Our Fifty States** (FL-12)	3 - 8
	by Eugene & Katherine Sharp Rachlis, illus by Harry McNaught, cover by Don Sibley ©1960/p1961, 58pp	
FR1130	**Nature Walks** (FL-13)	3 - 8
	by Clara Hussong, illus by Marjorie Hartwell ©1961, 58pp	

FT2080

FT3040

FUNTIME BOOKS

A soft cover activity series featuring coloring books, paper dolls, punch-outs, stick-um books and trading card books. Books were varied in size and page length according to activity. Included in the line were Disney characters as well as many other popular TV characters. The series originated as a Pocket Books, Inc. publication, and was introduced as a Golden series during their association with Western as Golden Book publishers. The series was advertised on LGBs in 1963 and 1964.

All books were identified as "Golden Funtime Books" on the cover. They originally sold for 29¢ each. Because of their self-destructive nature, not many examples have survived.

Coloring Books

FT1020	Birds	2 - 5
FT1040	Cars and Trucks	2 - 5
FT1080	Elroy & Astro Jetson	5 - 15
FT1120	Hokey Wolf	5 - 10
FT1160	Lassie	5 - 10
FT1180	Merlin the Magician, WD	5 - 10
FT1200	Mister Magoo	10 - 20
FT1220	My First Coloring Book	1 - 4

Cut-out Coloring Books with cut-outs on inside of covers

FT2060	Mother Goose Cut-out Coloring Book	4 - 8

FT2080	Nursery Tales Cut-out Coloring Book (GF137, 1959)	3 - 10
FT2100	Three Bears Cut-out Coloring Book	3 - 10
FT2130	Walt Disney's Cut-out Coloring Book	8 - 20

Paper Dolls

FT3030	Career Girls	5 - 10
FT3040	Charmin' Chatty (GF237, 1964)	8 - 20
FT3050	Dress Your Doll	5 - 10
FT3080	Mary Poppins (GF238, 1964)	5 - 15
FT3100	Paper Dolls	5 - 10
FT3130	Pollyanna, Walt Disney's (GF163, 1960)	10 - 25
FT3150	Saddle Your Pony	5 - 10
FT3170	Tammy Doll	8 - 20

Punch-Out Books, 12 pages, heavy board

FT4110	Airplanes Old and New	8 - 20
FT4120	Alamo, The	10 - 30
FT4140	Birds (GF157, 1960)	8 - 20
FT4150	Cars Old and New	8 - 20
FT4160	Cinderella (GF211, 1962)	8 - 20
FT4165	Circus (GF158, 1960)	8 - 20
FT4170	Civil War, The	10 - 30
FT4190	Dennis the Menace	8 - 20
FT4200	Dinosaurs	8 - 20
FT4210	Disneyland, Walt Disney's (GF230, 1963)	10 - 40
FT4220	Doll House	10 - 30
FT4240	Dr. Kildare	9 - 24
FT4260	Flintstones, The	10 - 35

FT3080   FT3130

FT4160   FT4380

FT4140   FT4390

FT4165   FT4210

FT4280	Horses	8 - 20
FT4300	Indians (GF110, 1956)	8 - 20
FT4380	Pinocchio, Walt Disney's (GF195, 1961)	10 - 25
FT4390	Popeye (GF177, 1961)	15 - 45
FT4430	Sleeping Beauty, Walt Disney's (GF195, 1959)	15 - 50
FT4450	Toymaker, Walt Disney's (GF196, 1961)	10 - 25
FT4470	Wild West Wagon Train (1957)	8 - 20
FT4490	Zorro, Walt Disney's	10 - 35

Stick-um Books, 12-page book & 2 stick-um pages

FT5160	Goldilocks and the Three Bears (GF191, 1961)	6 - 12
FT5200	Little Red Riding Hood	2 - 6
FT5220	Ludwig Von Drake (GF197, 1961)	10 - 25
FT5240	Mother Goose	6 - 12
FT5260	Numbers	6 - 12
FT5270	Nurse Nancy	10 - 30
FT5330	Three Little Pigs, The	6 - 12
FT5360	Wild Animals (GF162, 1960)	6 - 12

Trading Card Books

FT6120	Animals (1960)	8 - 15
FT6150	Dinosaurs (1961)	8 - 15

FT4430   FT4450

FT5220   FT5160

FZ1040   FZ1050

FZ1010   FZ1020

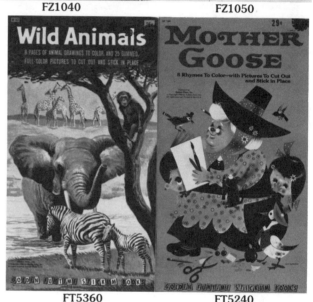

FT5360   FT5240

©1945 by S&S, 32pp (See also: LE3050)

FUZZY BOOKS (Touch-Me Books)

There were 5 Golden Fuzzy Books, all issued with dust jackets, containing 32 full-color pages, with 12 "touch-me" fuzzy pages. They were sometimes listed as part of the Big Golden Book series and sometimes grouped as a separate series. Early titles stated neither "Fuzzy" nor "Golden" on the cover. (*Walt Disney's Circus*, for example, notes only Simon & Schuster as publishers.) Some of the books were later incorporated in other Golden series.

FZ1010 **Bambi, Walt Disney's**   10 - 35
        illus by WDS
        ©1949 by WDP, 32pp. Adapted from the
        WD film, based on the story by Felix Salten.
        (See also: BD1068)
FZ1020 **Golden Circus, The**   7 - 20
        by Kathryn Jackson,
        illus by Alice & Martin Provensen
        ©1950 by Simon & Schuster, 32pp
FZ1030 **Mouse's House**   10 - 20
        by Kathryn Jackson, illus by Richard Scarry
        ©1949 by S&S, 32pp
FZ1040 **Walt Disney's Circus**   10 - 35
        ©1944 by WDP, 32pp (See also: BD2150)
FZ1050 **White Bunny and His Magic Nose, The**   7 - 18
        by Lily Duplaix, illus by Masha

GIANT GOLDEN BOOKS, GIANT DELUXE, GIANT—ACTIVITY & GIANT—DISNEY

Following the phenomenal success of LGBs, large Golden books were introduced in 1944. (Nineteen LGB titles were in print at the time.) S&S had formed a new graphics department, later to be known as Sandpiper Press, with Georges Duplaix in charge and Dorothy Bennett as general editor. Under their direction, the Giant Golden line produced not only story books, but also outstanding educational books. These books were the beginning of a whole new concept in learning books that permeated the entire Golden line: factual, authoritative and easy to understand educational books for younger children designed to make learning fun and exciting. Outstanding authors and editors, experts in their respective fields, were employed to insure the authority of these books.

There is no general book format common to the series. Giant books were originally advertised as being "about 10-1/4" x 13." Although most older Giant Books conform to this general size, there are some distinct variations, especially in newer books designated as "Giant." Exactly what qualified a book as a "Deluxe Edition" is not clear. Books examined that are labeled as "Deluxe Editions" appear comparable to other GGBs. A "Deluxe" connotation has no effect on the relative value of the book in question. Some books issued between 1944 and 1947

GB1010

GB1011

GB1055

GB1030

GB1035

GB1090

had dust jackets. Known jackets are listed.

Title lists appeared on the back of some Big and Giant Books, but no all-inclusive list has been compiled. On rare occasions a newly published book is issued with the "Giant" designation. Edition information is generally listed with the copyright block or shown on the inside front cover in the lower left corner as a letter code followed by a double price code.

GB1010 **Aesop's Fables**   10 - 25
by Louis Untermeyer (sel),
illus by Alice & Martin Provensen
©1965, 92pp. Original cover art shown.

GB1011 Same as GB1010, in dj of same design   20 - 35

GB1015 Same as GB1010, later printing. Cover   8 - 15
art changed to same design as GB1011.

GB1030 **Animal Book, The**   10 - 15
written & illus by Alice & Martin Provensen
©1952, 56pp. Abridged. First published under
the title *The Animal Fair* (See GB1050)

GB1035 **Animal Book, The (Die Neue Arche
Noah)**   10 - 15
German edition of GB1030, but w/complete
text as issued under the title *The Animal Fair*,
GB1050. No copyright or publication date
given.

GB1050 **Animal Fair, The**   10 - 25
written & illus by Alice & Martin Provensen
©1952, 76pp. Also published as *The
Animal Book* (See GB1030). Award: *The
New York Times* Best Illustrated 1952.

GB1055 **Animal Fair, The**   8 - 14
©1952/p1972, 60pp. Reissue of GB1050,
abridged.

GB1070 **Animal Stories**   10 - 25
by Georges Duplaix,
illus by Feodor Rojankovsky
©1944, 92pp. Original cover art shown,
1st edition only.

GB1071 Same as GB1070, as issued in dj of   15 - 35
different design.

GB1075 Same as GB1070, 2nd printing w/cover   10 - 20
art changed to same design as GB1071.

GB1090 **Animals' Merry Christmas, The**   15 - 50
by Kathryn Jackson, illus by Richard Scarry
©1950, 96pp. Pop-up Santa in 1st ed.
(See color plate)

GB1095 **Animal's Merry Christmas, The**   4 - 10
by Kathryn Jackson, illus by Richard Scarry
©1970, 68pp. A soft cover abridged version
of GB1090, with new cover art. Other

GB1070

GB1071

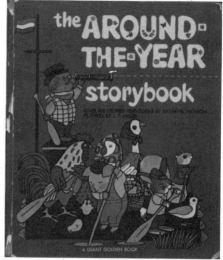

GB1110

GB1095

GB1150

GB1170

abridged versions include Big Golden, Little
Golden and Big Little Golden Books.

GB1110 **Around the Year Storybook**   7 - 12
by Kathryn Jackson, illus by J.P. Miller
©1971/p1974(A), 98pp. Original 1952
edition may differ from this version. Edition
shown at bottom of inside back cover.

GB1140 **Best Mother Goose Ever**   6 - 12
(Nursery Rhymes), illus by Richard Scarry
©1964, 94pp. 50 traditional nursery rhymes.

GB1150 **Best Word Book Ever**   3 - 9
written & illus by Richard Scarry
©1963, 94pp

GB1152 Revised version of GB1150, issued in 1981.   2 - 8
Covers are marked revised version.

GB1170 **Busy, Busy World**   5 - 15
written & illus by Richard Scarry
©1965, 92pp

GB1200 **Cowboys and Indians**   15 - 65
by Kathryn & Byron Jackson,
illus by Gustaf Tenggren
©1948, 96pp. Unstated 1st.

GB1210 Same as GB1200, as reissued in 1968   10 - 35
with new cover art.

GB1250 **Dinosaurs & Other Prehistoric**
Reptiles   5 - 15
by Jane Werner Watson,

GB1200

GB1210

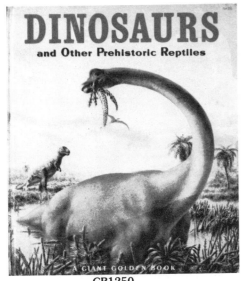

GB1250

GB1270

GB1320

GB1340

GB1345

GB1460

illus by Rudolph F. Zallinger
©1960, 60pp

GB1270 **Dog Stories**   8 - 20
by Elizabeth Coatsworth,
illus by Feodor Rojankovsky
©1953, 66pp. Inside title: *Giant Golden Book of …*

GB1320 **Fairy Tale Book, The**   12 - 45
trans by Marie Ponsot, illus by Adrienne Segur
©1958, 156pp. Illustrated throughout in soft pastels, w/full color pages interspersed.

GB1340 **Farm Stories**   15 - 50
by Kathryn & Byron Jackson,
illus by Gustaf Tenggren
©1946, 92pp. Award:1946 Spring Book Festival (younger). Original cover art shown.

GB1341 Same as GB1340, as issued in dj of same design   15 - 50

GB1345 Same as GB1340, later edition, as issued in dj with new design. Cover art same as GB1340.   15 - 40

GB1400 **Giant Golden Book of Animals**   5 - 12
illus by Wolfgang Suschitzky (photos)
©1958, 96pp

GB1420 **Giant Golden Book of Birds**   10 - 30
by Robert Porter Allen, Oliver L. Austin, Jr., consultant; illus by Arthur Singer
Offered as a bonus book in 1963 with 2-year *Golden Magazine* subscriptions.

GB1460 **Giant Golden Book of Cat Stories**   10 - 35
by Elizabeth Coatsworth,
illus by Feodor Rojankovsky
©1953, 66pp.

GB1480 **Giant Golden Book of Dogs, Cats & Horses**   10 - 30
by Elizabeth Coatsworth & K. Barnes,
illus by Feodor Rojankovsky
©1957, 124pp. Contents compiled from GB1270, GB1460, & GB1520

GB1500 **Giant Golden Book of Elves and Fairies**   35 - 75
by Jane Werner (sel), illus by Garth Williams
©1951, 76pp "… with assorted pixies, mermaids, brownies, witches and leprechauns." A favorite book with collectors and extremely hard to find with spine intact.

GB1520 **Giant Golden Book of Horse Stories, The**   10 - 20
by K. Barnes, illus by Feodor Rojankovsky
©1954, 66pp

GB1480

GB1500

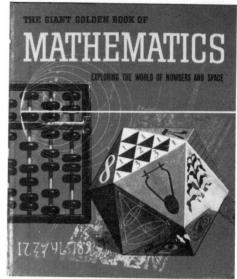

GB1540

GB1600

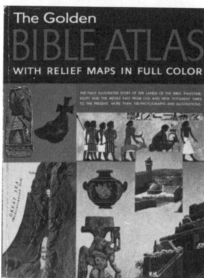

GB1700

GB1710

GB1540   **Giant Golden Book of Mathematics, The**   5 - 10
by Irving Adler, PhD; illus by Lowell Hess
©1960, 92pp

GB1560   **Giant Golden Book of Zoo Animals**   8 - 15
by William Bridges, illus by Scott Johnson
©1962, 60pp

GB1600   **Giant Golden Mother Goose**   15 - 30
by Jane Werner (sel),
illus by Alice & Martin Provensen
©1948, 96pp. Selections from this
book appear in LG1300.

GB1640   **Giant Golden Stamp Book**   ?
Contents compiled from several books in the
Golden Stamp Book series. Shown on LG
ad back, but copy unavailable for verification.

GB1700   **Golden Bible Atlas, The**   5 - 12
by Samuel Terrien, illus by William Bolin
©1957, 98pp. 1966 printing shown.
Previously published as *Lands of the Bible*.

GB1710   **Golden Bible: The New Testament**   8 - 20
by Elsa Jane Werner (sel),
illus by Alice & Martin Provensen
©1953, 96pp. Award: 1953 *The New
York Times* Best Illustrated

GB1720   **Golden Bible: The Old Testament**   8 - 15
by Jane Werner (sel),
illus by Feodor Rojankovsky
©1946 by S&S, 124pp. A deluxe edition.
Unstated 1st. Original cover art shown.

GB1721   Same as GB1720, as issued in dj of   15 - 30
different design.

GB1725   Same as GB1720, later printing w/cover   8 - 15
art same design as GB1721.

GB1790   **Golden Book of Astronomy**   5 - 10
by Rose Wyler & Gerald Ames,
illus by John Polgreen
©1955, 98pp

GB1795   **Golden Book of Aviation, The**   5 - 10
by John Lewellen & Irvin Shapiro,
illus by Harry McNaught
©1959/p1961, 98pp. Previously published
as *The Story of Flight*. (See GB2520)

GB1820   **Golden Book of Biology**   5 - 10
by Gerald Ames & Rose Wyler,
illus by Charles Harper
©1961, 98pp

GB1860   **Golden Book of Fun and Nonsense**   10 - 18
by Louis Untermeyer (sel),
illus by Alice & Martin Provensen

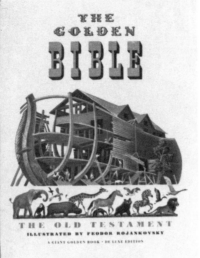

GB1720

GB1721

GB1860

GB1790

GB1920

©1970, 92pp

GB1920 **Golden Book of Science...for Boys & Girls** 5 - 10
by Bertha Morris Parker,
illus by Harry McNaught
©1956, 98pp

GB1950 **Golden Dictionary** 5 - 15
by Ellen Wales Walpole, illus by Gertrude Elliott
©1944, 94pp. Unstated 1st. Original cover
art shown.

GB1951 Same as GB1950, as issued in dj of 8 - 20
different design

GB1955 Same as GB1950, later printing w/cover 5 - 15
art same as GB1951

GB1970 **Golden Encyclopedia** 5 - 20
by Dorothy A. Bennett,
illus by Cornelius DeWitt
©1946, 126pp. A deluxe edition.

GB2010 **Golden Geography** 5 - 10
by Elsa Jane Werner, illus by Cornelius DeWitt
©1952, 96pp. Deluxe edition.
Award: 1954 Boy's Club.

GB2030 **Golden History of the World** 5 - 10
by Jane Werner Watson,
illus by Cornelius DeWitt
©1955, 156pp. Goldencraft edition shown.

GB2050 **Golden Tales from the Arabian Nights** 15 - 40
by Margaret Soifer & Irwin Shapiro,

GB1950

GB1951

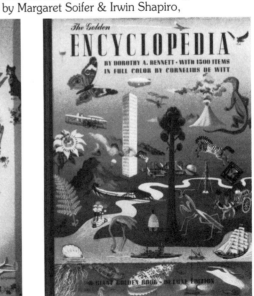

GB1970

GB2010

GB2030

GB2050

GB2070

THE ILIAD AND THE ODYSSEY

GB2150

Japanese Fairy Tales

GB2170

illus by Gustaf Tenggren
©1957, 96pp

GB2070 **Golden Treasury of Wonderful Fairy Tales**   10 - 30
by Wilhelm Hauff (adp), illus by Cremonini ©1961 by Golden Press; ©1958 by Fratelli Fabbri, 156pp. No edition stated. Stories adapted from Marchenalmanach. Copies were given as bonus books w/2-year *Golden Magazine* subscriptions.

GB2150 **Iliad and the Odyssey, The**   10 - 35
by Jane Werner Watson (adp), illus by Alice & Martin Provensen ©1956, 96pp. Adapted from the Greek classics of Homer. The Provensen's favorite book. They spent 3 months in Greece researching the pictures.

GB2170 **Japanese Fairy Tales**   10 - 30
by Mildred Marmur, illus by Benvenuti ©1960 by Fabbri, Milan, 66pp

GB2250 **Magic Butterfly and Other Fairy Tales of Central Europe**   15 - 35
trans by George Obligado,

illus by Ugo Fontana
©1963 by Fabbri Milan, 62pp

GB2270 **McCall's Giant Golden Make-It Book**   5 - 20
by John Peter,
illus by Corinne Malvern & Bob Riley
©1953, 256pp

GB2300 **New Golden Songbook, The**   10 - 25
by Norman Lloyd, illus by Mary Blair ©1955, 96pp. Songs and singing games arranged by Norman Lloyd of the Juilliard School.

GB2340 **New Walt Disney Treasury, The**   5 - 15
©1971 by WDP, 94pp. Stories adapted from 10 favorite WD films. Some stories from the original *Walt Disney Treasury* (GB2690) were revised and included in this book.

GB2345 **New Walt Disney Treasure, The**   2 - 10
Same as GB2340, cover art changed. Reissued thus in 1989.

GB2360 **Pirates, Ships and Sailors, Tenggren's**   15 - 60
by Kathryn Jackson, illus by Gustaf Tenggren ©1950, 96pp (See also: BB3300)

GB2270

GB2340

GB2345

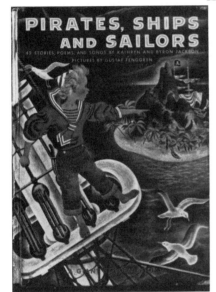

GB2360

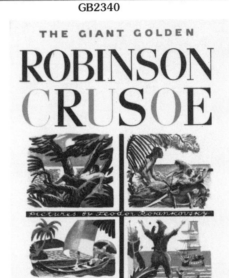

GB2400

GB2460

GB2410

GB2400	**Robinson Crusoe** By Anne Terry White (adp), illus by Feodor Rojankovsky ©1960, 98pp. Based on the novel by Daniel Defoe.	10 - 30
GB2410	Same as GB2400, but soft cover book in much smaller format. Reissued thus in 1977, 96pp.	4 - 8
GB2460	**Sleeping Beauty, Walt Disney** by Jane Werner Watson, illus by WDS, adp by Eyvind Earl & Julius Svendsen ©1957 by WDP, 58pp (See also: BD1920)	8 - 20
GB2480	**Snow Queen, The** retold by Andre Bay, illus by Andrienne Segur ©1961, 136pp. A selection of 11 Russian fairy tales, including *Story of a Nutcracker* by Alexandre Dumas, trans by Marie Ponsot. Offered as a bonus book with 2-year subscrip- tions to *Golden Magazine* in 1963.	10 - 30
GB2520	**Story of Flight, The** by John Lewellen & Irvin Shapiro, illus by Harry McNaught ©1959, 98pp. Republished in 1961 as *The Golden Book of Aviation* (See GB1795).	5 - 10
GB2540	**Storybook Dictionary**	5 - 10

written & illus by Richard Scarry
©1966, 126pp. "A new kind of word book",
w/a complete little story for each word, and a
wealth of Scarry's unique animal characters.

| GB2560 | **Surprise Package, Walt Disney**
by Marion Palmer (adp), illus by WDS
©1944 by WDP, 92pp. One of the first
Disney books produced as part of the Golden
line. Not an uncommon book, but difficult to | 10 - 25 |

53

GB2520

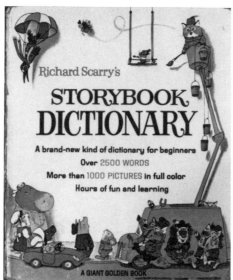

GB2540

GB2560

GB2600

GB2601

GB2650

find with spine intact and in dust jacket.
Original cover art shown.

GB2561 Same as GB2560, as issued in dj of same   15 - 45
design

GB2600 **Tenggren's Story Book**   15 - 30
sel & illus by Gustaf Tenggren
©1944, 89pp. Original cover art shown.
An abridged version was issued at BB3660.

GB2601 Same as GB2600, as issued in dj of   25 - 50
different design.

GB2650 **Uncle Remus Stories, Walt Disney**   15 - 35
by Marion Palmer (retold),
illus by Al Dempster & Bill Justice
©1947 by WDP, 92pp. Adapted from the
WD film, *The Song of the South* and other
Disney adaptions of Joel Chandler Harris'
Uncle Remus stories. Original cover art shown.
Presence of dj of same or different design has
not been verified.

GB2660 Same as GB2650, as issued in 1982 with   10 - 20
new cover art

GB2670 Same as GB2650, cover redesigned.   6 - 12
©1986, 92pp. A phenomenal best seller,
shown in its 42nd printing, 1989, w/contents
still the same as when first published in 1947.

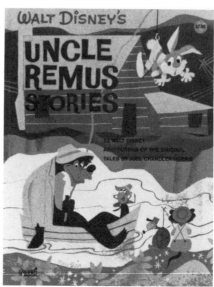

GB2660

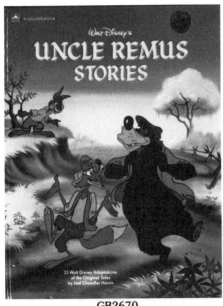

GB2670

GB2690

GC1010

GB2690 **Walt Disney's Treasury**   10 - 35
by Steffi Fletcher & Jane Werner, illus by
WDS, adp by Dick Kelsey & Dick Moores
©1953 by WDP, 140pp. 21 stories adapted
from WD films.

GIANT GOLDEN PUNCH-OUT BOOKS

Giant Punch-out Books were designed with story text close to
the spine, so that when the punch-outs were removed, a tall,
narrow (2-3/4") book remained.

GC1010 **Babes in Toyland, Walt Disney**   5 - 20
by George Sherman, illus by Chester Collum
©1961 by WDP

GC1020 **Giant Golden Punch Out Book**   5 - 20
©1961, 4 stories - train, cowboy, fire engine
and Indian stories.

GC1030 **Giant Golden Punch-Out Book of Animals** 5 - 20
by Kenwood Giles
©1961, 20 wild animal scenes

GC1040 **Pinocchio, Walt Disney's**   8 - 25
illus by Carl Buettner & Norm McGary
©1961 by WDP

GIANT LITTLE GOLDEN BOOKS

Produced between 1957 and 1959, the series is made up of
27 titles. Proportional size is the same as Little Golden Books,
but books vary from 56 to 72 pages in length. Some were done
in full color, others were done in color and duo-tone. Several of
the books were "3 in 1" volumes, made up of books from the
first LG series. End paper design featured stars and toys on a
blue background. The same design framed a list of additional
GLGBs on the back cover. Spine was blue foil in a star pattern.
Printing noted on back page, lower right corner.

GD5010 **My Little Golden Dictionary** (5001)   5 - 10
by Mary Reed & Edith Osswald,
illus by Richard Scarry
©1957, 56pp (See also: LE0900, BB3080)

GD5020 **Five Bedtime Stories** (5002)   5 - 12
(Folk Tales), illus by Gustaf Tenggren
©1957, 56pp. Compiled from LE0020,
LE1790, LE2000 (See also: BB1770)

GD5030 **My Christmas Treasury** (5003)   5 - 12
(Anthology), illus by Lowell Hess
©1957, 72pp (See also: BB3060)

GD5040 **Favorite Stories, Walt Disney** (5004)   5 - 15
illus by WDS, adp by Bob Moore,
Al Dempster & Bob Grant
©1957 by WDP, 72pp. Compiled from
LE0030, LI0060, LI0100 (See also: BB1830)

GD5050 **Donald Duck Treasury** (5005)   7 - 20
by Annie North Bedford & Jane Werner,
illus by WDS, adp by Campbell Grant,
Dick Kelsey & Bill Justice
©1957 by WDP, 56pp. Compiled from
LI0140, LI0180, LI0340

GD5060 **Animal Stories** (5006)   5 - 15
by Miryam, Beth Greiner Hoffman &
George Duplaix, illus by Tibor Gergely
©1957, 56pp. Compiled from LE0770,
LE1700, LE2490

GD5070 **Mother Goose** (5007)   5 - 10
(Nursery Rhymes), illus by Violet LaMont
©1957, 56pp

GD5080 **Dogs** (5008)   5 - 12
by Kathleen N. Daly, illus by Tibor Gergely
©1957, 72pp

GD5090 **Nursery Tales** (5009)   5 - 10
(Folk Tales), illus by Richard Scarry
©1958, 72pp

GD5100 **Wild Animals** (5010)   5 - 10
written & illus by W. Suschitzky (photos)
©1958, 72pp

GD5110 **Birds** (5011)   5 - 15

GD5010   GD5020

by Jane Werner Watson, illus by Eloise Wilkin
©1958, 56pp (See also: LF1840, BB1365)

GD5120 **Adventures of Lassie** (5012)   7 - 20
by Charles Spain Verral & Monica Hill,
illus by E. Joseph Dreany, Mel Crawford
& Lee Ames
©1958 by Lassie Programs, Inc., 56pp.
Compiled from LE2770, LE3070, LE4150

GD5130 **Kittens** (5013)   7 - 20
by Cathleen Schurr & Patricia Scarry,
illus by Masha, Gustaf Tenggren & Eloise Wilkin
©1958, 56pp. Compiled from LE0010,
LE0230, LE1630

GD5140 **Storytime Book, Walt Disney** (5014)   5 - 15
illus by WDS, adp by Bob Grant &
Campbell Grant
©1958 by WDP, 56pp. Compiled from
LI0070, LI0080, LI0090

GD5150 **Off to School** (5015)   5 - 10
by Kathleen Jackson, et al,
illus by Corinne Malvern & Violet LaMont
©1958, 56pp

GD5160 **Mother Goose Rhymes** (5016)   5 - 10
(Nursery Rhymes), illus by Feodor Rojankovsky
©1958, 56pp. Compiled from LE2830,
LE3170 and additional material.

GD5170 **Plants and Animals** (5017)   5 - 10
by Jane Werner Watson, illus by Ted Chaiko
©1958, 56pp

GB5171 **Animaux et Plantes** (7)   5 - 10
Same as GB5170, French edition

GD5180 **Train Stories** (5018)   5 - 10
by Marian Potter, Gertrude Crampton
& Margaret Wise Brown, illus by Tibor Gergely
©1958, 56pp. Compiled from LE0210,
LE1180, LE1620

GD5190 **Cowboys and Indians** (5019)   5 - 15
by Willis Lindquist, illus by Richard Scarry
©1958, 72pp

GD5200 **Fairy Tales** (5020)   5 - 10
by Anne Terry White (adp), illus by Lowell Hess

GD5080   GD5090

GD5100   GD5110

GD5130   GD5140

GD5030   GD5040

GD5160   GD5170

GD5060   GD5070

GD5171   GD5190

GD5200   GD5210

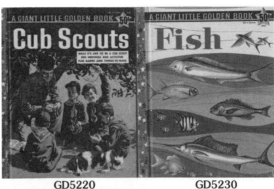

GD5220   GD5230

GD5240   GD5250

GD5260   GD5270

©1958, 72pp. Adapted from the original stories by Hans Christian Andersen.

GD5210 **Captain Kangaroo** (5021)   5 - 15
by Kathleen N. Daly & Barbara Lindsay, illus by Art Seiden & Edwin Schmidt ©1959 by Robert Keeshan Associates, Inc., 56pp. Compiled from LE2610, LE2780, LE3410

GD5220 **Cub Scouts** (5022)   5 - 15
by Bruce Brian, illus by Mel Crawford ©1959, 56pp. With a forward by Ben Statzman, Commissioner of Cubbing.

GD5230 **Fish** (5023)   5 - 10
by Herbert Zim, illus by Jean Zallinger ©1959, 56pp. Zim also edited the Golden Nature Guides.

GD5240 **Quiz Fun** (5024)   5 - 10
by Horace Elmo & Nancy Fielding Hulick, illus by Tibor Gergely ©1959, 56pp

GD5250 **My Magic Slate Book** (5025)   9 - 20
by Carl Memling, illus by William Dugan ©1959, 24pp. Magic slate inside back cover, pencil in front cover.

GD5251 Same as GD5250, book only   5 - 10

GD5260 **This World of Ours** (5026)   5 - 20
by Jane Werner Watson, illus by Eloise Wilkin ©1959, 56pp

GD5270 **My Pets** (5027)   5 - 20
by Patsy Scarry, illus by Eloise Wilkin ©1959, 56pp. Compiled from LE1630, LE2330, LE2500

GIANT STURDY BOOKS

In spite of the "Giant" prefix, Giant Sturdy Books are actually the same proportional size as LGBs (6-3/4" x 8"), but issued with 22 heavy board pages, cased in a regular book binding. The books were brought out in 1958 and some titles were still available through the late '60s. Although some of these books were only designated as "Golden Books", all had the same "sturdy" format and are therefore grouped as a series. Printings are noted inside the front cover, bottom left.

GE1010 **Animal ABC**   ?
Title noted, but copy unavailable for verification.

GE1020 **Baby Animals**   5 - 10
written & illus by Garth Williams ©1952, 22pp (See also: LE2740)

GE1030 **Baby Farm Animals**   5 - 10
written & illus by Garth Williams ©1958 (See also: LE3330)

GE1040 **Baby's First Book**   5 - 10
written & illus by Garth Williams ©1955 (See also: LE3580)

GE1050 **Baby's Mother Goose**   5 - 15
(Nursery Rhymes), illus by Eloise Wilkin ©1958, 22pp. 1969 printing shown. (See also: BB1160)

GE1080 **My First Book about God**   ?
Title noted, but copy unavailable for verification.

GE1090 **My First Counting Book**   5 - 10
by Lilian Moore, illus by Garth Williams ©1956, 22pp (See also: LE4340)

GOLDEN BOOKS

Although the bulk of Golden Book titles are "series" oriented,

GE1020   GE1050

57

GE1090

GE1060

GG2500

GG1120

GG1180

GG1220

GG1300

there are also many books which are not series related. This is especially true of books published since the early '70s, when the Giant and Big series gave way to price range categories for large format books. This general category, therefore, is made up of a selection of books identified only as "A Golden Book".

As there is no reference available that lists all of the books produced by Golden Books, we have attempted to assemble a representative selection, including as many titles as possible that reflect current collector interests. We have even strayed ever so slightly out of the bounds of Golden Books to include a few Golden Press imprints that directly relate to Golden Book collector interests. (Golden Press, which operates under the Consumer Products Division of Western Publishing Co., produces many other books outside the Golden Book line, including cookbooks, craft and hobby books, and books on the arts, history and science.)

As an aid in locating specific titles, an alphabetical index to all books listed in this guide is included at the back of the book.

GG1760

GG1700

GG1360

GG1740

GG1780

GG1800

written & illus by Richard Scarry, et al.
©1968, 288pp

GG1500 **Big Golden Book of Fairy Tales**   4 - 12
retold by Lornie Lette-Hodge,
illus by Beverlie Manson
©1982, 160pp. 11 classic fairy tales.

GG1600 **Birds of the World**   15 - 35
by Oliver Luther Austin, illus by Arthur Singer
©1961, 316pp. A survey of 27 orders and
150 families of birds, edited by Herbert Zim
and illustrated with over 300 specially commissioned full color illustrations, this book was
hailed as a "solid contribution" to birding
literature by Roger Tory Peterson when first
released in 1961.

GG1610 Same as GB1600, reissued in 1983, 320pp   8 - 20

GG1660 **Brontosaurus: The Thunder Lizard**   3 - 6
by Beverly Halstead, illus by Jenny Halstead
©1983, 32pp

GG1700 **Butterflies**   8 - 20
by J.F. Gates Clarke, PhD;
illus by Andre Durenceau
©1963, 68pp. 187 Species illustrated
in full color.

GG1720 **Canterbury Tales of Geoffrey Chaucer**   12 - 25
by A. Kent Hieatt (sel & adp),
illus by Gustaf Tenggren
©1962, 140pp. Adapted from Geoffrey
Chaucer's classic work, with an introduction
by Mark Van Doren.

GG1740 **Cars & Trucks & Things That Go**   5 - 12

written & illus by Richard Scarry
©1974 by Richard Scarry, 70pp

GG1760 **Charge of the Light Brigade, The**   8 - 20
by Alfred, Lord Tennyson;
illus by Alice & Martin Provensen
©1964, 32pp. *The NY Times* Best
Illustrated, 1964.

GG1780 **Children's Bible, The**   3 - 8
Ed. advisors: Rev. Joseph A. Grispino, S.M.,
S.S.L.; Dr. Samuel Terrien, ThD; Rabbi David
H. Wice
©1965 by WPC; ©1962 by Fratelli Fabbri,
Milan, 512 pp. 1979 printing shown.

GG1785 Deluxe edition of GG1780 in slipcase,   5 - 10
with simulated leather cover.

GG1800 **Child's First Book of Nursery Tales, A**   6 - 12
by Selma G. Lanes (sel & adp),
illus by Cyndy Szekeres
©1983 by WPC (text) Cyndy Szekeres (illus),
48pp. Full color Goldencraft binding,
"A" edition shown.

GG1820 **Child's First Book of Poems, A**   5 - 10
(Anthology), illus by Cyndy Szekeres
©1981, 48pp

GG1840 **Chinese Fairy Tales**   15 - 40
trans by Marie Ponsot, illus by Serge Rizzato
©1960(A) by Fabbri, Milan, 156pp.

GG1860 **Christmas Cat, The**   3 - 8
by Isabelle Holland, illus by Kathy Mitchell
©1987 by Isabelle Holland (text),

GG1840

GG1880

GG2120

GG1860

GG1980

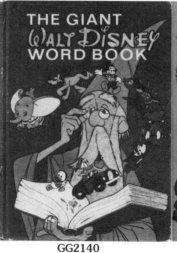

GG2100

GG2060

Kathy Mitchell (illus), 44pp

GG1880 **Christopher for President**   3 - 10
by Addie, illus by Mel Crawford
©1973, 46pp

GG1980 **Ding Dong School, Miss Frances'**   3 - 10
by Frances R. Horwich & Reinald Werrenrath,
Jr., illus by Katherine Evans
©1960, 56pp. The only large format Ding
Dong School book published by Golden. An
earlier copyright date (1953) suggests this
book may have been previously printed by
Rand McNally. (See LH4000.)

GG2040 **Favorite Christmas Carols**   6- 14
by Margaret Boni Bradford (sel & ed),
illus by Peter Spier
©1957, 128pp. Arranged by Norman Lloyd.

GG2060 **Fluppy Dogs: Home for a Fanci Flup,
Disney's**   2 - 6
©1986 by WDCo., 32pp

GG2100 **Four Little Kittens Storybook, The**   3 - 8
by Kathleen N. Daly, illus by Lilian Obligado
©1986(A), 44pp. *The Four Little Kittens*
(LE3220) is reprinted here, followed by their
later adventures. A nice sequel to a favorite LGB.

GG2120 **Funny Fingers**   2 - 9
by Kent Salisbury, illus by Joan Allen
©1971, 16pp. A hole book. Heavy board

GG2140

GG2240

construction, this tall narrow book is 15-1/2"
x 6". Spiral bound.

GG2140 **Giant Walt Disney Word Book**   4 - 12
©1971 by WDP, 142pp

GG2200 **Golden Book of Christmas Tales/
Legends from Many Lands**   8 - 20

GG2200

GG2280

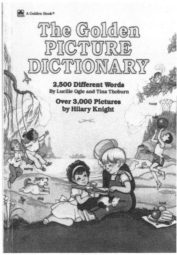

GG2460

GG2250

GG2520

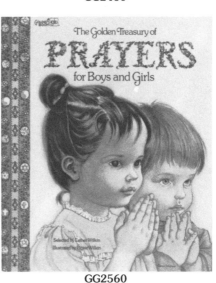

GG2560

by Lillian Lewicki, illus by James Lewicki
©1956 by James & Lillian Lewicki, 28pp

GG2240 **Golden Book of Grimm's Fairy Tales, The** 9 - 18
by Jane Gerruth, illus by Benvenuti
©1973 by Editions des Deux Coqs d'Or,
Paris, 140pp. Retold from the original stories
of Jacob and Wilhelm Grimm. 1st U.S. edition.

GG2280 **Golden Book of Magic/Amazing
Tricks for Young Magicians** 5 - 18
by Clayton Rawson ("The Great Merlini"),
illus by William Dugan
©1964, 104pp. One of the founders of "The
Mystery Writers of America", Rawson performed
under the stage name of "The Great Merlini."
A great compendium of slight-of-hand magic
for young readers.

GG2420 **Golden Christmas Treasury** 3 - 10
by Rick Bunsen (ed), illus by Christopher
Santoro, Kahty Wilburn, et al
©1986, 80pp. New in 1986.

GG2450 **Golden Picture Dictionary** 5 - 15
by Lucille Ogle & Tina Thoburn,
illus by Hilary Knight
©1976 by WPC (text), Hilary Knight (illus),
160pp

GG2460 Same as GG2450, revised edition 3 - 9
©1989 by WPC (text), Hilary Knight (illus),

160pp. Cover art changed.

GG2480 **Golden Puppet Playhouse** 10 - 35
©1961. A "Talent Kit" consisting of 3 hand
puppets, costumes, a complete stage and an
illustrated handbook of play & stage ideas.
Kit included admission tickets!

GG2580 **Golden Storybook of River Bend** 10 - 24
by Patsy Scarry, illus by Tibor Gergely
©1969, 94pp. Republished in 1987 as
Animal Friends All Year Long, GG1160.

GG2520 **Golden Treasury of Animal Stories
& Poems** 3 - 9
by Louis Untermeyer (ed), illus by various artists
©1971/p1979, 324pp

GG2540 **Golden Treasury of Fairy Tales** 5 - 10
by Jacob & Wilhelm Grimm, et al;
illus by Elizabeth Orton Jones, et al
©1985, 46pp. Contents selected from 7
LGB fairy tales.

GG2560 **Golden Treasury of Prayers for
Boys and Girls** 12 - 22
by Esther Wilkin (sel), illus by Eloise Wilkin
©1975, 46pp

GG2620 **Great Alphabet Race, The** 4 - 12
by Janet & Roger Campbell,
illus by Tom O'Sullivan
©1972, 52pp

GG2620

GG2760

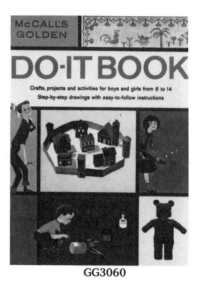
GG3060

GG2660 **Hans Christian Andersen Fairy Tale Book** 15 - 30
by Hans Christian Andersen, trans by Anne Scott, illus by Benvenuti ©1959 by Fratelli Fabbri, Milan, 154pp

GG2700 **Hilary Knight's ABC** 8 - 20
written & illus by Hilary Knight ©1961, 56pp

GG2760 **Hop Aboard! Here We Go!** 5 - 12
written & illus by Richard Scarry ©1972 by Richard Scarry, 48pp

GG2840 **Jungle Book, Walt Disney's** 10 - 20
©1968 by WDP
"A Merry-Go-Round Book". Heavy board construction, spiral bound w/fold-out page inserts designed to form a carousel. Could be hung as a mobile when assembled.

GG2860 **Karen's Curiosity** 9 - 18
written & illus by Alice & Martin Provensen ©1963 Unpaged, small format (5" x 6")
Awards: 1963 *The New York Times* Best Illustrated

GG2862 **Karen's Opposites** 9 - 18
written & illus by Alice & Martin Provensen ©1963 Unpaged, small format (5" x 6")
Awards: 1963 *New York Herald Tribune*, Spring Book Festival, Picture Book Honor.

GG2920 **Legends of America, Walt Disney's** 10 - 18
by Annie North Bedford, illus by WDS, adp by Mel Crawford ©1969 by WDP, 48pp. Stories of 6 legendary American heroes.

GG3000 **Little Monster's Word Book** 4 - 10
written & illus by Mercer Mayer ©1977 by Mercer Mayer, 46pp

GG3020 **Little Willie and Spike** 5 - 10
by Patricia Scarry, illus by Lucinda McQueen ©1986 by Patricia Scarry (text), Lucinda McQueen (illus), 64pp

GG3060 **McCall's Golden Do-It Book** 9 - 14
by Joan Wyckoff (adp) & Nan Comstock (ed), illus by William Dugan ©1960 by McCall Corp & GPI, 156pp. Craft projects and activities.

GG3100 **Mickey Mouse Cookbook, Walt Disney's** 5 - 15
©1975 by WDP, 94pp

GG3101 Same as GG3100, in dj of same design 10 - 25

GG3110 Same as GG3100, revised 3 - 9

GG2840

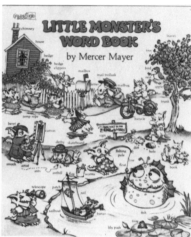
GG3000

GG3020

GG2920

GG3100

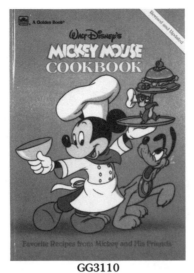

GG3110

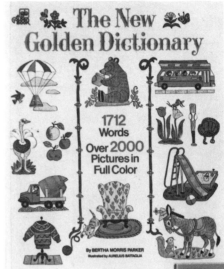

GG3240

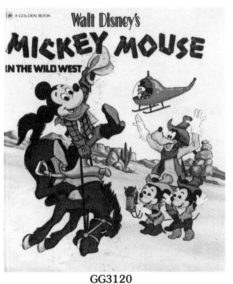

GG3120

GG3130

GG3260

GG3340   GG3160

©1990 @ WDP, 94pp. New cover design.

GG3120 **Mickey Mouse in the Wild West**   9 - 18
©1973 by WDP, 46pp

GG3130 **Minniken, Midgie and Moppet**   4 - 12
by Adelaide Holl, illus by Priscilla Hillman
©1977, 46pp

GG3160 **More Poems**   3 - 9
by Louis Untermeyer (ed),
illus by Joan Walsh Anglund
©1959/p1968, 80pp. A hard bound pocket-
book size edition, distributed by Crown Pub.
in 1968. This edition was also published as a
Golden paperback. Contents selected from
The Golden Treasury of Poetry. (See DL1240)

GG3240 **New Golden Dictionary, The**   3 - 9
by Bertha Morris Parker,
illus by Aurelius Battaglia
©1972, 118pp

GG3260 **Night Before Christmas**   6 - 12
by Clement C. Moore, illus by Cyndy Szekeres
©1983, 28pp. A tiny book, 4-1/4" x 4-3/4",
with Czekeres delightful illustrations presenting
a mouse-size interpretation of this favorite poem.

GG3262 **Night Before Christmas**   3 - 8
by Clement C. Moore, illus by Cyndy Szekeres
©1986, 32pp. Revised and enlarged edition of
GG3260.

GG3280 **One & Only Wacky Word Book**   3 - 8
written & illus by Peter Lippman
©1979, 44pp

GG3290 **101 Animal Stories**   5 - 10
by Anne-Marie Dalmais, trans by Glynis E.
Holland & Brenda Uttley, illus by Benvenuti
©1972 by Editions de Deux Coqs d'Or
& Mondadori, 140pp

GG3300 **One Monster After Another**   6 - 12
written & illus by Mercer Mayer
©1974 by Mercer Mayer, 46pp

GG3320 **Pinocchio**   15 - 35
by Carlo Collodi, illus by Sergio Rizzato
©1963 by Fratelli Fabbri Editori (illus), 118pp
Complete and unabridged, beautifully illustrated
throughout. Large quarto (10-1/2" x 13-1/2")
A deluxe book.

GG3340 **Poems**   3 - 9
by Louis Untermeyer (ed),
illus by Joan Walsh Anglund
©1959/p1968, 80pp. A hard bound pocket-
book size edition, distributed by Crown Pub.
in 1968. This edition was also published as a
Golden paperback. Contents selected from *The
Golden Treasury of Poetry*. (See DL1240)

GG3400 **Read-It-Yourself Storybook, The**   5 - 10
by Leland B. Jacobs (ed),

GG3290

GG3300

GG3320

GG3280

GG3400

GG3420

GG3460

illus by Susan Perl, et al
©1971, 216pp. Seven stories for beginning
readers. A spin off of the "Read-It-Yourself"
Book series.

GG3420 **Rojankovsky's Wonderful Picture Book**   10 - 25
(Anthology), ed by Nina Rojankovsky,
illus by Feodor Rojankovsky
©1972, 118pp. A tribute to an outstanding
illustrator. Contents compiled from many
different works done by the artist between
1933 and 1960.

GG3460 **Russian Fairy Tales**   15 - 30
trans by Marie Ponset, illus by Benvenuti
©1960 by Fabbri Milan, 66pp. 1973
printing shown.

GG3480 **Sails, Rails and Wings**   8 - 14
by Seymour Reit, illus by Roberto Innocenti
©1978, 72pp

GG3500 **Sesame Street Story Land**   3 - 9
(Anthology), illus by Tom Cooke, et al
©1986 by CTW and Muppets, Inc., 192pp

GG3520 **Sesame Street Word Book**   3 - 9
illus by Tom Leigh
©1983 by CTW & Muppets, Inc., 70pp

GG3560 **Sleeping Beauty**   2 - 8
by Charles Perrault, adp by Barbara Shook
Hazen, illus by Shiba Productions (photos)
©1968 by Shiba Productions (photos), 30pp.
A "sturdy page" book, with photo illus of
puppets. Cover has 3-D pictures set in.

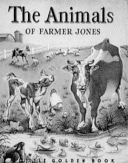

THE GOLDEN
Christmas Book
STORIES, SONGS, POEMS, AND RIDDLES FOR CHRISTMAS

Compiled by
GERTRUDE CRAMPTON
Illustrated by
CORINNE MALVERN

A BIG GOLDEN BOOK

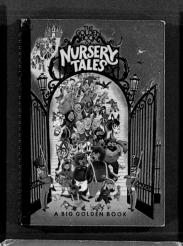

THE
GOLDEN BOOK OF
NURSERY TALES

A BIG GOLDEN BOOK

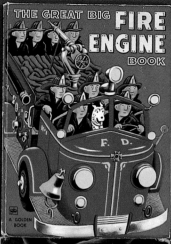

THE GREAT BIG
FIRE ENGINE BOOK

F. D.

A GOLDEN BOOK

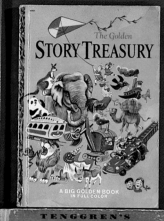

The Golden
STORY TREASURY

A BIG GOLDEN BOOK
IN FULL COLOR

FARM STORIES
100 pictures in full color by
GUSTAF TENGGREN
50 original stories by
K. and B. JACKSON

A GIANT GOLDEN BOOK

FARM STORIES
100 pictures in full color by
GUSTAF TENGGREN
50 original stories by
K. and B. JACKSON

A GIANT GOLDEN BOOK

PIRATES, SHIPS AND SAILORS
42 STORIES, POEMS, AND SONGS BY KATHRYN AND BYRON JACKSON
PICTURES BY GUSTAF TENGGREN

A GIANT GOLDEN BOOK

TENGGREN'S
COWBOYS AND INDIANS
32 STORIES AND RHYMES BY K. AND L. JACKSON
OVER 100 PICTURES IN FULL COLOR BY GUSTAF TENGGREN

A GIANT GOLDEN BOOK

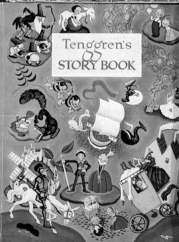

Tenggren's STORY BOOK

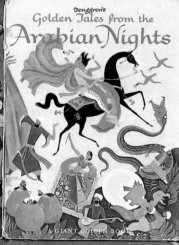

Tenggren's
Golden Tales from the Arabian Nights

A GIANT GOLDEN BOOK

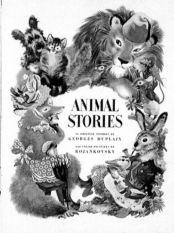

ANIMAL STORIES
50 ORIGINAL STORIES BY
GEORGES DUPLAIX
200 COLOR PICTURES BY
ROJANKOVSKY

ALL CHILDREN LOVE GOLDEN BOOKS

SIMON AND SCHUSTER, PUBLISHERS • ROCKEFELLER CENTER • NEW YORK 20, NEW YORK

THE GIANT GOLDEN BOOK OF
Cat Stories

THE GIANT GOLDEN BOOK OF
ELVES AND FAIRIES

The GIANT GOLDEN
MOTHER GOOSE
367 Childhood Favorites Illustrated in Full Color
By ALICE AND MARTIN PROVENSEN

THE
PROVENSEN
ANIMAL BOOK

A GIANT GOLDEN BOOK

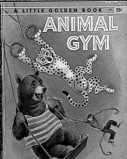

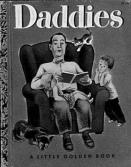

GG3560

GG3620

GG3690

GG3800

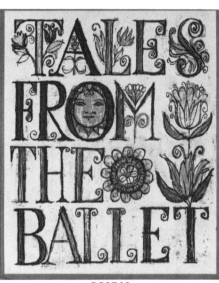

GG3740

GG3741

GG3835

GG3850

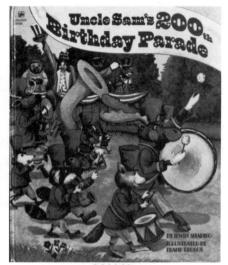

GG3940

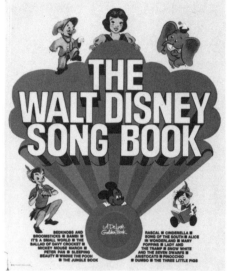

GG3970

GG3970

GH1100

GG3970 **Walt Disney's Story Land**   12 - 20
by Frances Saldinger (sel), illus by WDS
©1962 by WDP, 320pp. 55 favorite
stories adapted from Walt Disney films.

GG3975 Same as GG3970, reissued in 1987   3 - 9
2 million copies of the original book were in
print when it was reissued in 1987 with this
new cover. Contents unchanged.

GG4020 **What Makes It Go?**   4 - 10
written & illus by Joe Kaufman
©1971, 94pp

GG4060 **Wings, Paws, Hoofs and Flippers**   4 - 10
written & illus by Joe Kaufman
©1981, 48pp

GOLDEN HOURS LIBRARY

This library of 12 books was housed in a "grandfather clock" box, and each tiny book (4" x 5-1/4") had a clock in the lower left corner of the cover, with the book number and "The Golden Hours Library identification." Books were 24 pages, with plain color spines and end papers with pastel pictures of children reading. The "library" was copyrighted in 1967, but none of the books show this date. (All books have their original copyright, and no other edition information is given.) All of the stories were originally part of the LGB series. The books from this library also make up the first 12 titles in the Golden Tiny Book series, which was probably a spin-off from this set. See Tiny Books.

GH1000 Golden Hours Library   25 - 55
Set of 12 books in "Grandfather Clock" box

Individual titles in set:

GH1010 **How to Tell Time** (1)   1 - 4
by Jane Werner Watson, illus by Eleanor Dart
©1957, 214pp (See also: LE2850)

GH1020 **Hop, Little Kangaroo!** (2)   1 - 4
by Patricia Scarry, illus by Feodor Rojankovsky
©1965, 24pp (See also: LE5580)

GH1030 **Heidi** (3)   1 - 4
by Johanna Spyri, illus by Corinne Malvern
©1954, 24pp (See also: LE1920)

GH1040 **Four Puppies** (4)   1 - 4
by Anne Heathers, illus by Lilian Obligado
©1960, 24pp (See also: LE4050)

GH1050 **Big Little Book** (5)   1 - 4
by Dorothy Hall Smith, illus by Moritz Kennel
©1962, 24pp (See also: LE4820)

GH1060 **Littlest Racoon, The** (6)   1 - 4
by Peggy Parish, illus by Claude Humbert
©1961, 24pp (See also: LE4570)

GH1070 **Old MacDonald Had a Farm** (7)   1 - 4
(Nursery Song), illus by Moritz Kennel
©1960, 24pp (See also: LE4000)

GH1080 **Tommy's Camping Adventure** (8)   1 - 4
by Gladys Saxon, illus by Mel Crawford
©1962, 24pp (See also: LE4710)

GH1090 **Four Little Kittens** (9)   1 - 4
by Kathleen N. Daly,
illus by Adriana Mazza Saviozzi
©1957, 24pp (See also: LE5300)

GH1100 **Colors Are Nice** (10)   1 - 4
by Adelaide Holl, illus by Leonard Shortall
©1962, 24pp (See also: LE4960)

GH1110 **Rumpelstiltskin and The Princess
and the Pea** (11)   1 - 4
by Hans Christian Andersen,
illus by William J. Dugan
©1962, 24pp (See also: LE4960)

GH1120 **Little Cottontail** (12)   1 - 4
by Carl Memling, illus by Lilian Obligado
©1960, 24pp (See also: LE4140)

GOLDENCRAFT LIBRARY BINDINGS

Whatever they may lack in pictorial appeal, Goldencraft bindings make up in sturdiness. These cloth bindings – found throughout the series – were designed to enable the books to stand up to rugged school and library use.

Goldencraft Library Bindings

Cover illustrations tend to be 2 or 3 colors on a bright cloth binding, although some books in the Little Golden series have been found with full color cover illustrations. Goldencraft identification is usually found on the back cover in a circle design, and the original Golden series may or may not be noted on the book. Goldencraft LGBs have been found with both plain end papers and end papers that have the word "Goldencraft" intertwined with the standard LG design. Larger series books usually have plain end papers, with the illustrated end papers from the regular edition bound in. Printing identification follows the same pattern as the regular editions, and both binding styles are probably made up from the same run.

Most books in Goldencraft bindings have the same value as listed for regular editions. Their appeal, however, is limited. Collectors assembling a series may include Goldencraft copies as a variation, but not in place of a regular pictorial cover edition.

Other examples of Goldencraft bindings are noted throughout the listings.

Golden Guides

GUIDES (Nature, Science, Field, Regional & Handbooks)

This listing is included only as an explanation reference for Golden publications advertised in the LG series. They were advertised on LGB backs in 1957, 1959, 1962 and 1963. (See LG Ad Backs) A complete listing of these books does not fall within the intended purpose of this price guide.

Golden Guides were published in paperback, pocket-size editions as well as deluxe cloth editions. The series was originally edited by Dr. Herbert S. Zim. Most of the titles advertised are still in print, in revised editions. Many new titles have been added, and there are over 50 books among the different divisions. (See: Junior Golden Guides.)

HAPPY BOOKS

With utmost simplicity of text and especially commissioned illustrations, these tall (12-1/4" x 6-3/4") books were 24 pages long and designed to present basic educational concepts to the very young. Some of the books were also published as "Sturdy Happy Books", with heavier pages. The series was introduced

in 1963, and eventually gave way to the current Golden Sturdy Book series. Edition information is carried at the copyright notice or on the last page in the lower right corner. Series still in publication.

As with most simplified text books, the author's name is not always stated. Values are the same for regular and sturdy page editions. The series evolved into the smaller format Sturdy Book series.

HB1010	**ABC** illus by Helen Federico ©1963, 24pp	1 - 4
HB1030	**I Am a Bunny** by Ole Risom, illus by Richard Scarry ©1963, 24pp	1 - 6
HB1040	**I Am a Mouse** by Ole Risom, illus by J.P. Miller ©1963, 24pp	1 - 6
HB1050	**I Am a Puppy** by Ole Risom, illus by Jan Pfloog ©1970, 24pp	1 - 6
HB1080	**Numbers** illus by Helen Federico ©1963, 24pp	1 - 4
HB1140	**Rooster Struts, The**	1 - 6

HB1010   HB1040

HB1050   HB1170

illus by Richard Scarry
©1963, 24pp (See also: SU1300)

HB1160 **Who Says Hoo?**   1 - 4
illus by Murray Tinkelman
©1963, 24pp

HB1170 **Words**   1 - 4
illus by Joe Kaufman
©1963, 24pp

HISTORY OF THE UNITED STATES

The Golden Book *History of the United States* is a 10-volume set, uniform in size with Golden's other "encyclopedic" references. Each volume covers a distinctive period in American History and opens with a folding picture which can be removed for framing, followed by an "important dates" chronology preceding the text. The volumes vary in page length, and cover art for each volume depicts an event from the time period covered.

HI2010 **History of the United States**   15 - 35
by Earl Schenck Miers,
dwgs by Richard P. Kluga
©1963. 10-volume set

HI2015 Individual volumes of HI2010, each   1 - 3

HI2020 **History of the United States, Golden Book** 8 - 18
by Earl Schenck Miers,
dwgs by Richard P. Kluga
©1970, 320pp. Selected from the 10-volume
set (HI2010).

HOME AND HIGH SCHOOL ENCYCLOPEDIA

A 20-volume reference set designed primarily for use by high school students, intended to complement the study curriculum, guide the student in the use of other reference tools and provide stimulus for continued education planning and career choices. The set is well-illustrated throughout with photos and drawings. Each volume has its own unique cover design and the set is uniform in size with other Golden reference works.

HO2010 **Home and High School Encyclopedia** 20 - 45
by Virginia S. Thatcher (ed),
(Robert D. Bezucha, Project Director;
Bertha M. Parker, Project Consultant)
©1961, 20-volume set

HO2015 Individual volumes of HO2010, each   1 - 2

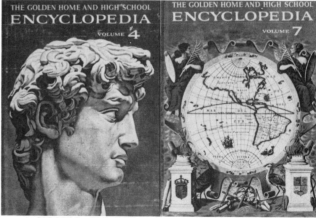

HI2010 - *Vol 2*   HI2010 - *Vol 3*

HO2010 - *Vol 4*   HO2010 - *Vol 7*

ILLUSTRATED CLASSICS, large format

Lengthy, though somewhat abridged, versions of classic literature for older juveniles. Books were hard bound, 7-3/4" x 10-1/4", with pictorial covers and many color illustrations throughout the text. The series gave way to the juvenile book size series of Illustrated Classics which follows this listing. (See also Picture Classics, Classic Library.)

IC1010 **Around the World in 80 Days**   5 - 15
by Jules Verne, George M. Towle (trans),

IC1010

IC2100-IC2280

illus by Libico Maraja
©1962 by Fratelli Fabbri, Editori (illus), 220pp

IC1040 **Gulliver's Travels** 5 - 15
by Jonathan Swift, adp by Sarel Eimerl,
illus by Libico Maraja
©1962, 156pp

IC1060 **King Arthur and the Knights of the
Round Table** 8 - 20
by Sir Thomas Malory, adp by Emma Gelders
Sterne & Barbara Lindsay, illus by Gustaf
Tenggren
©1963, 140pp

IC1080 **Merry Adventures of Robin Hood** 8 - 20
by Howard Pyle, illus by Benvenuti
©1962, 284pp

ILLUSTRATED CLASSICS, small format

5-3/4" x 8-1/2" hard cover books, Golden Illustrated Classics
were largely reprints of the earlier series done under the
Whitman imprint. The books had full color illustrations. Page
length varied, some stories were abridged.

IC2100 **Huckleberry Finn** (12210) 3 - 9
by Mark Twain, illus by Betty Fraser
©1965, 252pp

IC2110 **Heidi** (12211) 4 - 10
by Johanna Spyri, trans by M. Rosenbaum,
illus by June Goldsborough
©1965, 252pp

IC2120 **Rebecca of Sunnybrook Farm** (12212) 4 - 10
by Kate Douglas Wiggin,
illus by June Goldsborough
©1965, 252pp

IC2130 **Little Women** (12213) 3 - 9
by Louisa May Alcott, illus by David K. Stone
©1965, 254pp

IC2140 **Tom Sawyer** (12214) 3 - 9
by Mark Twain, illus by Patty Bolian
©1965, 254pp

IC2150 **Sherlock Holmes** (12215) 3 - 9
by Arthur Conan Doyle, illus by Jo Polseno
©1965, 254pp

IC2160 **Bible Stories** (12216) 3 - 9
by Thea Heineman (ed), illus by Huntley Brown
©1965, 254pp

IC2170 **Black Beauty** (12217) 3 - 9
by Anna Sewell, illus by William Steinel
©1965, 256pp

IC2180 **Wind in the Willows, The** (12218) 3 - 9
by Kenneth Grahame, illus by David K. Stone
©1968, 254pp

IC2190 **Treasure Island** (12219) 3 - 9
by Robert Louis Stevensen,
illus by Don Bolognese
©1965, 254pp

IC2200 **Little Men** (12220) 4 - 10
by Louisa May Alcott, illus by David K. Stone
©1965, 250pp

IC2210 **Heidi's Children** (12221) 4 - 10
by Johanna Spyri, trans by Charles Tritten,
illus by June Goldsborough
©1967, 254pp

IC2220 **Fifty Famous Fairy Tales** (12222) 4 - 10
(Fairy Tales), illus by Robert J. Lee
©1965, 254pp

IC2230 **Freckles** (12223) 3 - 9
by Gene Stratton Porter,
illus by Michael Lowenbein
©1965, 254pp

IC2240 **Eight Cousins** (12224) 3 - 9
by Louisa May Alcott, illus by Reisie Lonette
©1965, 254pp

IC2250 **Beautiful Joe** (12225) 3 - 9
by Marshall Saunders,
illus by Robert MacLean
©1965, 254pp

IC2260 **Red Badge of Courage, The** (12226) 3 - 9
by Stephen Crane, illus by Harvey Kidder
©1968, 254pp

IC2270 **Tales of Edgar Allen Poe** (12227) 3 - 9
by Edgar Allen Poe, illus by Ati Forberg
©1965, 254pp

IC2280 **Heidi Grows Up** (12228) 4 - 10
by Charles Tritten, illus by Jean Coquillet
©1966, 210pp

ID1040 - *Vol 1*   ID1040 - *Vol 2*

ID1040 - *Vol 5*   ID1040 - *Vol 6*

ILLUSTRATED DICTIONARY (Courtis–Watters Dictionary)

The Courtis-Watters Dictionary has a long history. The concept is based on *The Picture Dictionary for Children*, created by the same editors, published by E.M. Hale in 1939. This early version, while illustrated, had very limited color. The first Golden appearance of the *Courtis-Watters Dictionary* was a one-volume edition in 1951, followed by several revisions and the publication of a six-volume set. Other dictionaries which were variations of this same work appeared under the titles: *Giant All-Color Dictionary*, *Learn at Home Illustrated Dictionary* and *Illustrated Junior Dictionary*. See also: DL1030.

ID1010	**Illustrated Golden Dictionary for Young Readers**	8 - 12
	by Stuart A. Courtis & Garnette Watters, illus by Beth and Joe Krush ©1951, 554pp, 7554 words w/2120 pictures. Revised versions of this basic work were still in print into the early '80s.	
ID1040	**Golden Book Illustrated Dictionary, The**	12 - 36
	by Stuart A. Courtis & Garnette Watters ©1951/p1961(revised), 6-volume set, over 10,000 words w/3000 pictures in color. An expanded version of the *Courtis-Watters Dictionary*, this was the first multi-volume publication of the book. Released in 1961 it was edited for use by older grade school children and intended as a "step up" from the *Golden Dictionary* (see GB1950). The set is uniform in size with other Golden reference books.	
ID1042	Individual volumes of ID1040, each	1 - 3

JUNIOR CLASSICS – see Classic Library

JUNIOR FICTION SERIES

A juvenile fiction series, offering mystery, suspense and adventure stories for boys and girls. Published in both hard cover and paperback form, with color covers and a frontispiece in black and white, 5-5/8" x 7-3/4".

The series noted here were advertised on LGB ad backs in 1964. Other juvenile mystery and adventure series were produced by both Whitman and Golden.

Junior Fiction - Girls Series:
Kathy Martin Stories

First book had blue & green diamond design on the spine, the rest had blue & white. Josephine Jones was a pseudonym for Barbara Lindsay & E.G. Sterne.

JF1010	**Cap for Kathy, A** (1)	3 - 8
	by Josephine James, illus by John Firnic ©1960	
JF1020	**Junior Nurse** (2)	3 - 8
	by Josephine James, illus by William Plummer ©1960	
JF1030	**Senior Nurse** (3)	3 - 8
	by Josephine James, illus by Kenneth Rossi ©1961	
JF1040	**Patient in 202, The** (4)	2 - 6
	by Josephine James, illus by William Plummer ©1961	
JF1050	**Assignment in Alaska** (5)	2 - 6
	by Josephine James, illus by William Plummer ©1961	
JF1060	**Private Nurse** (6)	2 - 6
	by Josephine James, illus by William Plummer ©1962	
JF1070	**Search for an Island** (7)	2 - 6
	by Josephine James, illus by William Plummer ©1963	
JF1080	**Sierra Adventure** (8)	2 - 6
	by Josephine James, illus by William Plummer ©1964	
JF1090	**Courage in Crisis** (9)	2 - 6
	by Josephine James, illus by William Plummer ©1964	
JF1100	**Off-Duty Nurse** (10)	2 - 6
	by Josephine James, illus by Stan Klimley ©1964	
JF1110	**An Affair of the Heart** (11)	2 - 6
	by Josephine James, illus by Stan Klimley ©1965	
JF1120	**Peace Corps Nurse** (12)	2 - 6
	by Josephine James, illus by Stan Klimley ©1965	
JF1130	**African Adventure** (13)	2 - 6
	by Josephine James, illus by Stan Klimley ©1965	

Vicky Loring Stories (pink & green diamonds on spine)

JF2010	**Career for Vicky, A** (1)	3 - 7
	by Wynn Kincade, illus by Mel Crawford ©1962	
JF2020	**Golden Buttons** (2)	3 - 7
	by Wynn Kincade, illus by Mel Crawford ©1963	
JF2030	**Double Deception** (3)	?
	by Wynn Kincade, illus by Mel Crawford Title noted, but copy unavailable for verification.	

JF2020   JF8010

Penny of Paintrock Stories (Penny Linstrom)
Green & yellow diamonds on spine

JF3010	**Phantom Stallion, The** (1)	2 - 6
	by Jane & Paul Annixter, illus by Robert Schultz	
	©1961	
JF3020	**Penny of Paintrock** (2)	2 - 6
	by Jane & Paul Annixter, illus by Albert Micale	
	©1962	

Junior Fiction - Boys Series
Brains Benton Mystery Series
George Wyatt was apparently a pseudonym. Real author(s) name unknown.

JF6010	**Case of the Missing Message, The** (1)	2 - 5
	by Charles Spain Verral, illus by Hamilton Green	
	©1959	
JF6020	**Case of the Counterfeit Coin, The** (2)	2 - 5
	by George Wyatt, illus by Hamilton Green	
	©1960	
JF6030	**Case of the Stolen Dummy, The** (3)	2 - 5
	by George Wyatt, illus by Walter Dey	
	©1961	
JF6040	**Case of the Roving Rolls, The** (4)	2 - 5
	by George Wyatt, illus by Al Schmidt	
	©1961	
JF6050	**Case of the Waltzing Mouse, The** (5)	2 - 5
	by George Wyatt, illus by Al Schmidt	
	©1961	
JF6060	**Case of the Painted Dragon, The** (6)	2 - 5
	by George Wyatt, illus by Hamilton Green	
	©1961	

Dig Allen Science Fiction Series

JF7010	**Forgotten Star**	2 - 6
	by Joseph Greene, illus by Myron Strauss	
	©1959	
JF7020	**Captains in Space**	2 - 6
	by Joseph Greene, illus by Myron Strauss	
	©1959	
JF7030	**Journey to Jupiter**	2 - 6
	by Joseph Greene, illus by Walter Dey	
	©1961	
JF7040	**Trappers of Venus**	2 - 6
	by Joseph Greene, illus by Charles Beck	
	©1961	
JF7050	**Lost City of Uranus**	2 - 6
	by Joseph Greene, illus by Phil Maron	
	©1962	
JF7060	**Robots**	2 - 6
	by Joseph Greene, illus by Myron Strauss	
	©1962	

Ellery Queen, Jr., Mystery Series
Eight previous EQ, Jr. mystery stories had been written under

the same name (a pseudonym for Frederick Dannay & Manfred Lee), but these 2 titles published by Golden are not generally considered a part of that series.

JF8010	**Mystery of the Merry Magician, The**	3 - 7
	by Ellery Queen, Jr., illus by Robert Magnusen	
	©1961, 188pp	
JF8020	**Mystery of the Vanished Victim, The**	3 - 7
	by Ellery Queen, Jr., illus by Robert Magnusen	
	©1962, 188pp	

JG1010-JG1070

JUNIOR GOLDEN GUIDES (Quiz-Me Books)

As the name implies, these books were a spin-off from the regular Golden Nature Guides, designed especially for younger readers. The text was followed by a series of questions, hence the "Quiz-Me" connotation. (Shown on the cover in the upper left corner.) These 4" x 5" books were presented in full color, and sold for 25¢. The books were advertised on LGBs in 1963 and 1964.

JG1010	**Birds**	1 - 4
	by George B. Stevenson	
JG1020	**Cats**	1 - 3
	by Brenda Biram	
JG1030	**Dogs**	1 - 3
	by Mary B. Irving	
JG1040	**Dinosaurs**	1 - 3
	by Brenda Biram	
JG1050	**Planes and Pilots**	1 - 3
	by James A. Hathway	
JG1060	**Snakes**	1 - 4
	by George S. Fichter	
JG1070	**Wonders of the World**	1 - 3
	by James A. Hathway	

KEY TO LEARNING PROGRAM (Golden Workbooks)

Seven workbooks on math and science, keyed to Grades 1 through 4, were produced as part of the "Key to Learning" program. These books were advertised on the backs of LGBs in 1963 and 1964. A contemporary equivalent of these books would be the "Golden Step Ahead" workbooks which are currently in publication.

LIBRARY OF KNOWLEDGE

Books in this series were originally issued in the same proportional size as LGBs, but with 56 pages. Illustrated with drawings, art and photos, the series was supervised by Dr. Herbert S. Zim, editor of the Golden Nature Guides, and a leading authority on science education.

The "Library of Knowledge" logo incorporated an oak tree, which was used on the back cover and repeated in a pattern on the end papers. About mid-series, the back cover was changed to advertise additional books in the series. A list of titles (not always complete, as stated in the books) was also noted on the inside back cover. Paper spines had a leather-texture design and were various colors. Printing identification is in the lower right corner of the back page. The series began in 1958, and ads ran on LGB backs in 1958 and '59. The original series books have 4-digit numbers beginning with "77xx."

Library of Knowledge, 7700 Series: (6-3/4" x 8")

LB7010   **White Wilderness, Walt Disney** (7701)   3 - 10
      by Robert Louvain & staff of WDS
      ©1958 by WDP, 56pp. A True-Life Adventure.

LB7020   **Indians of the Old West** (7702)   2 - 8
      by Anne Terry White
      ©1958 by American Heritage Pub. Co., 56pp

LB7030   **Famous American Ships** (7703)   2 - 8
      by Walter Franklin
      ©1958 by American Heritage Pub. Co., 56pp

LB7040   **Birds of the World** (7704)   1 - 6
      by Eunice Holsaert, illus by Arthur Singer,
      James Irving & Arnold Ryan
      ©1957, 56pp

LB7050   **Wildlife of the West** (7705)   3 - 10
      by Robert Louvain & staff of WDS
      ©1958 by WDP, 56pp. A True-Life Adventure.

LB7060   **Butterflies and Moths** (7706)   1 - 6
      by Richard A. Martin, illus by Rudolf Freund,
      James Irving & Eloise Wilkin
      ©1958, 56pp

LB7070   **Sea, The** (7707)   1 - 5
      by the editors of *Life* and Lincoln Barnett,
      text adp by Emma Sterne & Barbara Lindsay
      ©1958 by Time, Inc., 56pp. Adapted
      from the pages of *Life* magazine.

LB7080   **Prehistoric Animals** (7708)   1 - 8
      by the editors of *Life* and Lincoln Barnett,
      text adp by Jane Werner Watson
      ©1958 by Time, Inc., 56pp. Adapted
      from the pages of *Life* magazine.

LB7090   **Mathematics** (7709)   1 - 6
      by Irving Adler, illus by Lowell Hess
      ©1958, 56pp

LB7100   **Space Flight** (7710)   2 - 10
      by Lester Del Rey, illus by John Polgreen
      ©1959 by WPC; ©1958 by General
      Mills, Inc., 56pp

LB7110   **Engines** (7711)   1 - 6
      by L. Sprague de Camp, illus by Jack Coggins
      ©1959, 56pp

LB7120   **Animals and Their Travels** (7712)   1 - 6
      by Richard A. Martin, illus w/photos,
      maps by Ray Pioch
      ©1959, 56pp

LB7130   **Moon, The** (7713)   1 - 6
      by Otto Binder, illus by George Solonevich
      ©1959, 56pp

LB7010   LB7020

LB7030   LB7040

LB7050   LB7060

LB7070   LB7080

LB7090   LB7100

LB7110   **LB7120**

LB7150   **LB7160**

LB7140   **Insect World** (7714)   1 - 6
by Norman M. Lobsenz
©1959, 56pp

LB7150   **Submarines** (7715)   2 - 8
by Edward C. Stephens, illus by Jack Coggins,
cover by Lowell Hess
©1959, 56pp

LB7160   **Atoms** (7716)   1 - 6
by Jerry Korn, illus by Norbert Van Houten
©1959, 56pp

LB7170   **World of Ants, The** (7717)   1 - 6
by G. Collins Wheat, illus by Eric Mose
©1959, 56pp

In 1961, the books were changed to 7" x 9-1/2", with the numbers changed to a "78xx" series. All of the original books were reissued in this larger format, and many new titles were added to the series. The books contained 54 pages, covers and end papers remained the same, and the back covers carried ads for additional books in the series. Edition information, if noted, is generally carried with the copyright notice. Ads for the revised series appeared on LGBs 1961 and 1962.

Library of Knowledge, 7800 Series: (7" x 9-1/2")

LB8010   **White Wilderness, Walt Disney** (7801)   2 - 10
by Robert Louvain & staff of WDS
©1958 by WDP, 54pp. A True-Life Adventure.

LB8020   **Indians of the Old West** (7802)   1 - 8
by Anne Terry White
©1958/p1961 by American Heritage Pub.
Co, 54pp

LB8030   **Famous American Ships** (7803)   1 - 6
by Walter Franklin
©1958/p1961, 54pp. Adapted from
American Heritage magazine.

LB8040   **Birds of the World** (7804)   1 - 6
by Eunice Holsaert, illus by Arthur Singer,
James Irving & Arnold Ryan
©1957/p1961, 54pp

LB8050   **Wildlife of the West** (7805)   2 - 10
by Robert Louvain & staff of WDS
©1961 by WDP, 54pp. A True-Life Adventure.

LB8060   **Butterflies and Moths** (7806)   1 - 5
by Richard A. Martin, illus by Rudolf Freund,
James Gordon Irving & Eloise Wilkin
©1958/p1961, 54pp

LB8070   **Sea, The** (7807)   1 - 5
by the editors of *Life* and Lincoln Barnett,
text adp by Emma Sterne & Barbara Lindsay
©1958/p1961 by Time, Inc., 54pp. Adapted
from the pages of *Life* magazine.

LB8080   **Prehistoric Animals** (7808)   1 - 8
by the editors of *Life* and Lincoln Barnett,
text adp by Jame Werner Watson
©1958/p1961 by Time Inc., 54pp. Adapted
from the pages of *Life* magazine.

LB8090   **Mathematics** (7809)   1 - 6
by Irving Adler, illus by Lowell Hess
©1958/p1961, 54pp

LB8110   **Engines** (7811)   1 - 6
by L. Sprague de Camp, illus by Jack Coggins
©1961, 54pp

LB8120   **Animals and Their Travels** (7812)   1 - 5
by Richard A. Martin, illus w/photos,
maps by Ray Pioch
©1959/p1961, 54pp

LB8130   **Moon, The** (7813)   1 - 6
by Otto Binder, illus by George Solonevich
©1961, 54pp

LB8140   **Insect World, The** (7814)   2 - 8
by Norman M. Lobenz
©1959/p1961, 54pp. Revised edition

LB8150   **Submarines** (7815)   2 - 8
by Edward C. Stephens, illus by Jack Coggins,
cover by Lowell Hess
©1959/p1961, 54pp

LB8160   **Atoms** (7816)   1 - 6
by Jerry Korn, illus by Norbert Van Houten
©1961, 54pp

LB8170   **World of Ants, The** (7817)   1 - 6
by G. Collins Wheat, illus by Eric Mose
©1959/p1961, 54pp

LB8180   **Planets** (7818)   1 - 6
by Otto Oscar Binder,
illus by George Solonevitch
©1959/p1961, 54pp

LB8190   **Fishes and How They Live** (7819)   2 - 8
by George S. Fichter, illus by Rene Martin &
James Gordon Irving
©1960/p1961, 54pp

LB8200   **Reptiles and Their Way of Life** (7820)   2 - 8
by George S. Fichter; illus by Sy Barlowe,
James Gordon Irving & Arnold W. Ryan
©1960/p1961, 54pp

LB8210   **Rocks and How They Were Formed** (7821)   2 - 8
by Herbert S. Zim; illus by Harry McNaught,

LB8190   **LB8210**

Raymond Perlman, Arch & Miriam Hurford
©1961, 54pp

LB8220 **Story of Maps and Map Making** (7822)   1 - 6
by James A Hathway, illus by Harry McNaught
©1960/p1961, 54pp

LB8230 **Early Automobiles** (7823)   3 - 12
by Eugene Rachlis, illus by Jack Coggins,
cover by Leslie Saalburg
©1961, 54pp

LB8240 **Flying Animals** (7824)   2 - 8
by George S. Fichter, illus by Jean Zallinger
©1961, 54pp

LB8250 **Energy and Power** (7825)   1 - 6
by L. Sprague De Camp,
illus by Weimer Pursell & Fred Eng
©1962, 54pp

LB8260 **Polar Regions** (7826)   1 - 5
by Walter Sullivan, illus by Ray Pioch & photos
©1962, 54pp

LB8270 **Body in Action, The** (7827)   1 - 5
text adp by Ann Reit from *The Human Body*
by Mitchell Wilson, illus by Cornelius DeWitt
©1962, 54pp

LB8280 **Vision** (7828)   1 - 5
by Janette Rainwater, illus by Weimer Pursell
©1962, 54pp

LB8320 **Whales and Dolphins** (7832)   2 - 8
by G. Collins Wheat
©1963

LB8330 **Wonders of Animal Life** (7833)   1 - 6
by editors of *Life* & Lincoln Barnett,
adp by Sarel Eimerl
©1963 by Time, Inc., 54pp

LB8340 **Marvels of the Earth** (7834)   1 - 5
by Jerome Wyckoff (adp),
illus by William Sayles & Harry McNaught
©1964, 54pp

LIFT AND LOOK BOOKS

Books are 6-3/4" x 8", 22 pages long, with "life and look" flaps incorporated in the illustrations. A recent series, the stories incorporate many familiar LGB characters.

LC3000 **Bialosky's Big Mystery**   2 - 5
by Anne Kostick, illus by Jerry Joyner
©1985, 24pp

LC3010 **Curious Little Kitten Plays Hide-and-Seek**   2 - 5
by Sarah Leslie, illus by Maggie Swanson
©1985, 24pp

LC3020 **Saggy Baggy Elephant and the New Dance**   2 - 5
by Sarah Leslie, illus by Frank Renkiewicz
©1985, 24pp

LC3030 **Poky Little Puppy and the Lost Bone**   2 - 5
by Sarah Leslie, illus by Jean Chandler
©1985, 24pp

LB8230   LB8240

LB8250   LB8260

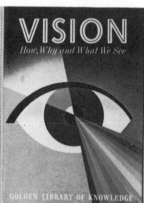
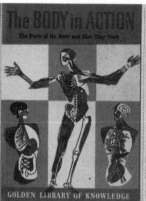

LB8270   LB8280

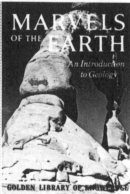

LB8340

LC3030   LC3010   LC3020   LC3000

LD3700   LD3710

LD3720   LD3730

LD3740   LD3770

LITTLE GOLDEN BOOK LAND

A major promotion by Western launched in 1989, "Little Golden Book Land" features the characters who have come to be instantly identified with LGBs: Poky Little Puppy, Shy Little Kitten, Tawny Scrawny Lion, Tootle and Scuffy, in new adventures in "A Magical Place." Items for the promotion are included in every aspect of the Golden line: storybooks, activity books, puzzles, games, audio cassettes, videos and more. LGB Land characters have also been licensed by Golden, with plush toys by Hasbro/Playskool and gift items by Enesco among the many products being offered. Some of the items available are listed in the Collectibles section.

LGBL stories are also found in Big, Little, First Little and Look-Look Books, with more titles in the planning stages. The LGB versions are the same size and configuration as regular LGBs, but these books have their own numbering system, with special end paper and back cover designs, as well as a special "LGB Land" logo on the cover. All of the Little Golden titles have been repeated in the Big Golden format, with identical covers and contents only slightly varied.

LD3700   **Welcome to Little Golden Book Land** (370)   1 - 3
            by Cindy West, illus by Mateu
            ©1989, 24pp
LD3710   **Poky Little Puppy's Special Day** (371)   1 - 3
            by Cindy West, illus by Keenan Jones
            ©1989, 24pp
LD3720   **Shy Little Kitten's Secret Place** (372)   1 - 3
            by Jim Lawrence, illus by Keenan Jones
            ©1989, 24pp
LD3730   **Saggy Baggy Elephant/No Place for Me** (373)   1 - 3
            by Gina Ingoglia, illus by Richard Walz
            ©1989, 24pp
LD3740   **Tootle and Katy Caboose/A Special Treasure** (374)   1 - 3
            by Gina Ingoglia, illus by Isidre Mones
            ©1989, 24pp
LD3750   **Scuffy's Underground Adventure** (375)   1 - 3
            by Mary Carey, illus by Darrel Baker
            ©1989, 24pp
LD3760   **Baby Brown Bear's Big Bellyache** (376)   1 - 3
            by Eugene Bradley Coco, illus by John Nez
            ©1989, 24pp
LD3770   **Tawny Scrawny Lion Saves the Day** (377)   1 - 3
            by Michael Teitelbaum, illus by Art & Kim Ellis
            ©1989, 24pp

LITTLE GOLDEN BOOKS

Over 1,000 LGBs have been published since 1942. A complete collection of LGBs occupies about 33 running feet of shelf space, depending on how many "variation" copies you include! Many of the original books issued in the '40s and '50s are still in print, and new titles are added to the series on a regular basis. In *American Picture Books from Noah's Ark to the Beast Within*, Barbara Bader makes the following observation concerning the initial success of LGBs in the late '40s: "In those years, they commanded the kind of serious attention ordinarily reserved for trade books, a recognition of the general interest in them – of the fact that they were being purchased not only in lieu of expensive books or of no books at all, but in addition to other books, for themselves. It is not just that Golden Books flooded the market with cheap books, as was often said. The books had caught the public fancy." A phenomenal success story in the field of mass media children's books, they came into their own as a collectible in the mid '80s.

All LGBs are 6-3/4" x 8", with a variety of distinct design formats, most of which incorporate the famous "Golden Spine." Changes and variations in format are noted at each series.

Dating Books Actual publication dates for most of the reissued LGBs and cover variations are included in this guide and stated with the listings. However, the guidelines noted below, as well as the format changes given in the listings, can be used to determine approximate publication time for any books not covered:

(1) **Numerical listing** (reissued books only): Compare the copyright date of books numerically preceding or following the book in question. For example, *Poky Little Puppy* was reissued as #271, with books published in 1957.

(2) **Book lists:** Compare copyright dates for the last book in both the regular and Disney series listed at the back of the book in question. This method works best with books published through the late '60s, and loses effectiveness in later years, when lists ran for 2 and 3 years without changes.

(3) **Back cover advertisements:** See "Ad Backs" for years in which these different ads were used.

(4) **Book price**
        25¢ (1942-1962)
        29¢ (1962-1968)
        39¢ (1968-1974)
        49¢ (1974-1977)
        59¢ (1977-1979)

69¢ (1979-1980) In 1980, price codes appear on the back of the books, but prices are still stated.

89¢ (1981-1986) Price remained stated until sometime in 1985, when price code is moved to the front cover.

99¢ (1988 -) Price in code only.

Price changes generally take place within a given year. For example, books from 1962 can be found with both 25¢ and 29¢ prices. Some books have prices over stamped, reflecting a change from the time they were printed to the time when they were released. Books today retail for 99¢ to $1.26.

Most of the LGBs are collected by series and book number, and are listed here in that manner. However, in order to provide a composite reference to all Little Golden Books, regardless of series or book number, a special alphabetical index has been provided in the Appendix. (See Little Golden Book Index)

Edition information is shown in several ways:

(1) Notation on title page or back of title page, usually with copyright information.

(2) Letter code on the last page of the book, generally in the lower right corner of the page. It may be necessary to "lift" the spine slightly to see it. In a few instances, the letter will appear at bottom center or top right.

(3) No printing notation at all, which indicates a 1st. This is common for books printed between 1969 and 1973, and some of the books done in the late '40s. Only the first editions are unmarked, later printings are indicated.

Guidelines for determining condition and establishing book values are stated in the Foreword. Most listings are given for books in their first editions, but we have also included many later printings and variant copies that are of interest to collectors. While it is not possible to cover every variation for every book, the examples listed may serve as guidelines for similar variations. Obvious factors which affect value, such as 24-page and 28-page editions of books originally published with 42 pages, partial activities and modern reprints (the 46th printing of *The Night Before Christmas*, for instance) should be gauged in relationship to stated values for original books and no attempt has been made to evaluate them here.

All original LGB book numbers are given in parentheses following the title. The Tomart code adapts this number as follows: the first 3 digits correspond to the original LGB book number; i.e., LE0010 = LGB 1. The last digit indicates a variation of the same book. "0" indicates the book as first printed, higher numbers for later variations. LE0420, for example, is *Little Red Riding Hood*. LE0425 is the same book in puzzle edition.

All books are pictured as first editions, unless stated otherwise. When a variation is listed, or when a title is repeated later in the list, the first printing in which the book was issued in that form is noted. In cases where the exact printing may not be known, the printing code of the book shown is given, followed by a question mark.

Comments on text changes in later printings which do not call for a separate listing are preceded by the letter of the printing in which they occur. For example, "F: Song added, last page."

Little Golden Books - 1st Series (1942-1970)

All books are listed as originally assigned in numerical order. Numbers later assigned to a new title will be found in the 2nd Series. With a few aberrations, the list is also fairly chronological. Some books repeat within the series, but in every instance it is the first time a book was assigned to that particular number and the book also "belongs" in a chronological sense. (For comparison purposes, redesigns of these original titles, *when issued at the same number*, are included, even though the new design may have been implemented after 1970.) Although first editions of the earliest books (1 to 20) are difficult to locate (and dust jackets even more so), the hardest books to find are generally from the '60s. Special collector interest is aroused by books with complete activities ... puzzles, Band-Aids™, decals, etc.

Because there are so many format changes, they are included in the listings as they occur.

LE0010   **Three Little Kittens** (1)   8 - 20
(Nursery Tale), illus by Masha
©1942, 42pp, Q: Song added to last page
One of the most popular LGBs, it was into its 3rd printing (150,000 copies total) 6 weeks after publication. (See also: GD5130, BB3700, LE2250, LE2880, LE3810)

LE0011   Same as LE0010, in dj of same design   15 - 35

1942 General Format   42 pages, color and black and white illustrations. Illustrated end papers and stained book edges, printed in a variety of colors. Full color cover with "A Little Golden Book" in black letters at bottom. Books with blue spines issued in dust jacket (#1-28, 30 & 34). Dust jacket was a duplicate of the cover. Back cover design included a list of other LGB titles. This format common to the series through book #28. (NOTE: 24-page "war editions" were issued from 1943 to 1945, and are usually marked "first printing, this edition" on back of title page.)

LE0020   **Bedtime Stories** (2)   8 - 20
by Leah Gale, illus by Gustaf Tenggren
©1942, 42pp. Originally published w/5 stories, shortened to 3 in later versions. (See also: GD5020, LE2390, LE3640, LE5380)

1942 Back Cover   LE0010

LE0020   LE0030

LE0040   LE0050

LE0060   LE0065

LE0070   LE0075

Front End Paper   LE0080

LE0090   LE0095

LE0100   LE0104

LE0021	Same as LE0020, in dj of same design	15 - 35
LE0030	**Alphabet from A to Z, The** (3)	8 - 15
	by Leah Gale, illus by Vivienne Blake ©1942, 42pp, R: Song added to last page.	
LE0031	Same as LE0030, in dj of same design	15 - 25
LE0040	**Mother Goose** (4)	5 - 18
	by Phyllis Fraser, illus by Gertrude Elliott ©1942, 42pp (See also: LE2400)	
LE0041	Same as LE0040, in dj of same design	15 - 25
LE0050	**Prayers for Children** (5)	5 - 15
	illus by Rachel Taft Dixon ©1942, 42pp, S: Song added to last page. Prayer changed on pgs 36-37. Many slight illustration variations in early printings.	
LE0051	Same as LE0050, in dj of same design	15 - 25
LE0060	**Little Red Hen** (6)	5 - 18
	(Nursery Tale), illus by Rudolf Freund ©1942, 42pp (See also: LE2960, LE5190)	
LE0061	Same as LE0060, in dj of same design	15 - 30
LE0065	Same as LE0060, ©1942/p1952(M), 28pp. New cover art.	4 - 10
LE0070	**Nursery Songs** (7)	8 - 20
	by Leah Gale, illus by Corinne Malvern, cover art by Louise Altson ©1952, 42pp (See also: LE5290)	
LE0071	Same as LE0070, in dj of same design	15 - 30
LE0075	Same as LE0070, ©1942/p1948(L?), 42pp. New cover art by Corinne Malvern. Exact printing when the cover art was changed has not been determined. (See also: LE5290)	5 - 15
LE0080	**Poky Little Puppy, The** (8)	8 - 20
	by Janette Sebring Lowrey, illus by Gustaf Tenggren ©1942, 42pp. In 1986, when the billionth LGB rolled off the press, it was a copy of *Poky*. The most popular original title in the LGB series, sales of this book alone accounted for over 13 million of those books. (See also: BB3330, LE2710, LE5060)	
LE0081	Same as LE0080, in dj of same design	15 - 35

Front end paper for the original format depicted animals reading books. The book plate, a device which is found in all of the LG series, reinforced the idea that these books were designed to "belong" to the child.

LE0090	**Golden Book of Fairy Tales** (9)	8 - 18
	by Leah Gale, illus by Winfield Hoskins ©1942, 42pp	
LE0091	Same as LE0090, in dj of same design	15 - 30
LE0095	**First Little Golden Book of Fairy Tales** (9)	5 - 15
	by Leah Gale, illus by Gertrude Elliott ©1946(A), 42pp. Inside title: *Golden Book of Fairy Tales*. All new illustrations. Text same as previous book.	
LE0096	Same as LE0095, in dj of same design	15 - 25
LE0100	**Baby's Book** (10)	9 - 18
	by Janette Sebring Lowrey, illus by Bob Smith, cover by Louise Altson ©1942, 42pp. Three versions of this book were printed. Inside text and illustrations are the same for all 3.	
LE0101	Same as LE0100, in dj of same design	20 - 30
LE0104	**My First Book** (10)	9 - 18
	by Janette Sebring Lowrey, illus by Bob Smith ©1942/p1948(F), 42pp. Previously titled: *Baby's Book*	
LE0105	Same as LE0104, in dj of same design	20 - 30
LE0107	Same as LE0104, ©1942/p1949(G), 42pp. New cover art only.	8 - 15

| LE0108 | Same as LE0107, in dj of same design | 15 - 25 |
| LE0110 | **Animals of Farmer Jones** (11) | 8 - 18 |

by Leah Gale, illus by Rudolf Freund
©1942, 42pp. Later books with this
title use the same text, but have all new
illustrations. (See also: LE2110)

LE0111	Same as LE0110, in dj of same design	18 - 30
LE0120	**This Little Piggy and Other Counting**	
	Rhymes (12)	8 - 20

by Phyllis Fraser, illus by Roberta Paflin
©1942, 42pp. Limited to 7 printings
between 1942 & 1947. All printings
were issued with dust jackets.

| LE0121 | Same as LE0120, in dj of same design | 20 - 35 |
| LE0125 | **Counting Rhymes** (12) | 9 - 15 |

(Nursery Rhymes), illus by Corinne Malvern
©1942/p1946(A), 42pp. A new book,
repeating only a few rhymes from LE0120.
All new illustrations. (See also: BB1540,
LE2570, LE3610)

| LE0126 | Same as LE0125, in dj of same design | 15 - 25 |
| LE0130 | **Golden Book of Birds, The** (13) | 5 - 12 |

by Hazel Lockwood,
illus by Feodor Rojankovsky
©1943, 42pp

| LE0131 | Same as LE0130, in dj of same design | 15 - 20 |
| LE0140 | **Nursery Tales** (14) | 8 - 20 |

(Nursery Tales), illus by Masha
©1943, 42pp. I: Song added, last page.

| LE0141 | Same as LE0140, in dj of same design | 18 - 30 |
| LE0150 | **Lively Little Rabbit** (15) | 5 - 20 |

by Ariane, illus by Gustaf Tenggren
©1943, 42pp. N: Song added, last page.
(See also: LE5510)

| LE0151 | Same as LE0150, in dj of same design | 15 - 25 |
| LE0155 | Same as LE0150, ©1943/p1953(O), | 3 - 8 |

24pp. New cover, artist not noted.

| LE0160 | **Golden Book of Flowers, The** (16) | 5 - 12 |

by Mabel Witman, illus by Mac Harshberger
©1943, 42pp.

| LE0161 | Same as LE0160, in dj of same design | 15 - 20 |

Back end paper: same design as front, without bookplate.
Design contained within page, as opposed to later design which
bleeds off the edge.

| LE0170 | **Hansel and Gretel** (17) | 8 - 15 |

by Jacob & Wilhelm Grimm,
illus by Erika Weihs
©1945, 42pp. Copyright shown as 1943
and 1945 in different books. Actual date
of publication, June 1945.

| LE0175 | Same as LE0170, ©1945/p1953(H), | 5 - 12 |

28pp. New cover art by Eloise Wilkin.
Both "H" and "I" printings were originally
done in the same format as LE0170. This
book, which was issued later, may have been
made up from old press sheets, which

LE0107   LE0110

LE0120   LE0125

LE0130   LE0140

LE0150   LE0155

LE0160   *Back End Paper*

LE0170   LE0175

LE0180   LE0190

LE0200   LE0204

LE0205   LE0207

LE0210   LE0220

1946 Back Cover   LE0230

would account for the odd cover/contents combination. (See also: LE2170: cover)

LE0180	**Day in the Jungle, A** (18) by Janette Sebring Lowrey, illus by Tibor Gergely ©1943, 28pp. First LGB w/Tibor Gergely illustrations.	7 - 15
LE0181	Same as LE0180, in dj of same design	15 - 25
LE0190	**My First Book of Bible Stories** (19) by Mary Ann Walton, illus by Emmy Ferand ©1943, 42pp	8 - 15
LE0191	Same as LE0190, in dj of same design	15 - 25
LE0200	**Night Before Christmas, The** (20) by Clement C. Moore, illus by Cornelius DeWitt ©1946, 42pp. Unstated 1st. C: 2 songs added, end of book.	8 - 25
LE0201	Same as LE0200, in dj of same design	15 - 35
LE0204	**Night Before Christmas, The** (20) by Clement C. Moore, illus by Corinne Malvern ©1949, 28pp. Printings "A" through "D" have this cover design. All new illustrations. Gilt decorations throughout. No songs. Cover artist not noted.	8 - 15
LE0205	Same as LE0204, ©1949/p1951(E), E: 1st printing, new cover, contents unchanged. By 1952, 4 million copies had been sold. Gilt decorations through "J", which comes in both gilt and plain pages.	3 - 10
LE0207	Same as LE0204, ©1949, 24pp. 31st printing, 1975 shown, w/type style for title changed. Other minor variations took place over the 30 years this best selling book was in print. All have about the same value. Different LGB versions appear at LE2410 & LG1170. See Index for copies in other Golden series.	1 - 4
LE0210	**Tootle** (21) by Gertrude Crampton, illus by Tibor Gergely ©1945, 42pp. Until the 1970s, all *Tootle* books were issued at this number. Value remains high for 42-page books, but drops for later 28-page and 24-page editions. (See also: BB3730, GD5180)	3 - 20
LE0211	Same as LE0210, in dj of same design	15 - 30
LE0220	**Toys** (22) by Edith Osswald, illus by Masha ©1946, 42 pp	8 - 15
LE0221	Same as LE0220, in dj of same design	15 - 25
LE0230	**Shy Little Kitten** (23) by Cathleen Schurr, illus by Gustaf Tenggren ©1946, 42pp. Unstated 1st. (See also: GD5130, LE2480, LE4940)	8 - 20
LE0231	Same as LE0230, in dj of same design	18 - 30

Back cover: Book lists were carried in several different styles. Authors and/or artists were listed with the titles up to Book #27. Number of columns changed to 2 and 3 as books were added to the series.

LE0240	**New House in the Forest** (24) by Lucy Sprague Mitchell, illus by Eloise Wilkin ©1946, 42pp. Unstated 1st. Bank Street Book	10 - 18
LE0241	Same as LE0240, in dj of same design	20 - 35
LE0250	**Taxi That Hurried, The** (25) by Lucy Sprague Mitchell, Irma Simonton Black & Jessie Stanton, illus by Tibor Gergely ©1946, 42pp. Unstated 1st. Bank Street Book	5 - 15

| LE0240 | | LE0250 |

LE0260   LE0265

LE0270   LE0280

LE0290   LE0300

1947 End papers

LE0310   LE0320

LE0251   Same as LE0250, in dj of same design   20 - 30
LE0260   **Christmas Carols** (26)   4 - 10
    by Marjorie Wyckoff, illus by Corinne Malvern
    ©1946, 42pp (See also: LE5950)
LE0261   Same as LE0260, in dj of same design   2 - 7
LE0265   Same as LE0260, ©1946/p1953(G), 28pp.   2 - 7
    New cover art, 28pp. 7 songs dropped.
    (See also: LE5950)
LE0267   Same as LE0265, w/green background cover. 1 - 5
    ©1946/p1968, 24pp. Same carols as
    LE0265, some illustrations move for 24-page
    format.
LE0270   **Story of Jesus** (27)   6 - 12
    by Beatrice Alexander, illus by Steffie Lerch
    ©1946, 42pp. Unstated 1st.
LE0271   Same as LE0270, in dj of same design   15 - 20
LE0280   **Chip Chip** (28)   7 - 12
    by Norman Wright, illus by Nino Carbe
    ©1947, 42pp. Unstated 1st.
LE0281   Same as LE0280, in dj of same design   15 - 25
LE0290   **Noises and Mr. Flibberty-Jib** (29)   8 - 18
    by Gertrude Crampton, illus by Eloise Wilkin
    ©1947, 42pp
LE0300   **Scuffy the Tugboat and His**   9 - 18
    Adventures Down the River (30)
    by Gertrude Crampton, illus by Tibor Gergely
    ©1946, 42pp
    (See also: BB3540, LE2440, LE3630)
LE0301   Same as LE0300, in dj of same design   20 - 35

1947 Format Change: LGBs #30 and #34 were the last two books issued with dust jackets. LGBs #29, #31, #32 and all books from #35 on were issued without dust jackets. Covers on these books have a glossy finish. Various designs of gold paper spines (sometimes now aged to brown) were used, until a spine with the same design as the back cover became standard in 1948. (Transitional period, books #29–#52.) End paper design, printed in gold only, now incorporated the words "Little Golden Books" and was enlarged to bleed off the page. Book price began to appear on some back covers in 1947.

LE0310   **Circus Time** (31)   6 - 12
    by Marion Conger, illus by Tibor Gergely
    ©1948, 42pp
LE0320   **Fix It, Please!** (32)   8 - 14
    by Lucy Sprague Mitchell, illus by Eloise Wilkin
    ©1947, 42pp. Bank Street Book
LE0330   **Let's Go Shopping w/Peter & Penny** (33)   5 - 10
    written & illus by Lenora Combes
    ©1948, 42pp. F: Song added, last page.
LE0340   **Little Golden Book of Hymns, The** (34)   5 - 10
    by Elsa Jane Werner, illus by Corinne Malvern
    ©1947, 42pp. Unstated 1st. D(1949): 28pp,
    11 songs dropped (1949) (See also: LE3920)
LE0350   **Happy Family, The** (35)   7 - 15
    by Nicole, illus by Gertrude Elliott
    ©1947, 42pp. Unstated 1st (See also: LE2160)

LE0330   LE0340

LE0350   LE0360

LE0370   LE0380

LE0390   LE0400

LE0410   LE0415

LE0420   LE0425

LE0351   Same as LE0350, in dj of same design   20 - 30

LE0360   **Saggy Baggy Elephant, The** (36)   6 - 14
         by Kathryn & Byron Jackson
         illus by Gustaf Tenggren
         ©1947, 42pp (See also: LE3850)

LE0370   **Year on the Farm, A** (37)   6 - 12
         by Lucy Sprague Mitchell,
         illus by Richard Floethe
         ©1948, 42pp. Bank Street Book

LE0380   **Little Golden Book of Poetry, The** (38)   5 - 10
         (Anthology), illus by Corinne Malvern
         ©1947, 42pp

LE0390   **Animal Babies** (39)   6 - 10
         by Kathryn & Byron Jackson,
         illus by Adele Werber
         ©1947, 42pp

LE0400   **Singing Games** (40)   5 - 10
         by Katherine Tyler Wessells,
         illus by Corinne Malvern
         ©1947, 42pp

LE0410   **New Baby, The** (41)   5 - 18
         by Ruth & Harold Shane, illus by Eloise Wilkin
         ©1948, 42pp. Title color changed from pink
         to blue for 2nd (B) printing.
         (See also: LE2910, LE5410)

LE0415   Same as LE0410, ©1948/p1954(G), 28pp.   5 - 12
         New cover.

LE0420   **Little Red Riding Hood** (42)   5 - 14
         written & illus by Elizabeth Orton Jones
         ©1948, 42pp. Cottage drawings are of the
         artist's home in Mason, NH, which now
         houses an herb and gift shop called
         "Pickity Place."

LE0425   Same as LE0420, puzzle edition   15 - 30
         ©1948/p1951(G), 28pp

LE0426   Same as LE0425, lacking puzzle   2 - 5

  Puzzle Books: Puzzles were set in a frame in the back
cover. The front cover carried a color headline, "A Little
Golden Book with a Real Jig Saw Puzzle." A listing of all books
with puzzles is carried in the category section of the appendix.

LE0430   **Little Pond in the Woods** (43)   5 - 12
         by Muriel Ward, illus by Tibor Gergely
         ©1948, 42pp

LE0440   **Come Play House** (44)   8 - 20
         by Edith Osswald, illus by Eloise Wilkin
         ©1948, 42pp. Also said to be issued as
         Come Play With Me, but no copies have
         been verified.

LE0450   **Little Golden Book of Words, The** (45)   4 - 9
         by Selma Lola Chambers, illus by Gertrude Elliott
         ©1948, 42pp.

LE0455   Same as LE0450, ©1948/p1954(J), 28pp   2 - 5
         Cover background changed to red. Illustration
         changes for 28-page layout. Later printings
         show cover title of *Words* only.

LE0430   LE0440

LE0472   LE0470

LE0460   LE0455

LE0480   LE0490

LE0500   LE0510

LE0460	**Golden Sleepy Book, The** (46)	5 - 12
	by Margaret Wise Brown,	
	illus by Garth Williams	
	©1948, 42pp (See also: LG0140)	
LE0470	**Three Bears, The** (47)	8 - 16
	(Fairy Tale), illus by Feodor Rojankovsky	
	©1948, 42pp. Cover art shown used	
	for 1st edition only.	
LE0472	Same as LE0470, ©1948(B), 42pp.	3 - 10
	New cover art. Contents unchanged. (See	
	also: BB3680)	
LE0480	**Year in the City, A** (48)	6 - 12
	by Lucy Sprague Mitchell, illus by Tibor Gergely	
	©1948, 42pp. Bank Street Book	
LE0490	**Mr. Noah and His Family** (49)	5 - 10
	by Jane Werner	
	illus by Alice & Martin Provensen	
	©1948, 28pp	

28-Page Books: Beginning with *Mr. Noah*, the transition from 42 to 28 pages took place between 1948 and 1950. By shortening the number of pages, the books could have color pictures throughout, without a change in price. The shorter books were actually better suited to the short attention span of young readers. Later editions of 42-page books start to use duo-tone process on black and white pages.

LE0500	**Busy Timmy** (50)	6 - 12
	by Kathryn & Byron Jackson	
	illus by Eloise Wilkin	
	©1948, 28pp (See also: LE4520)	
LE0510	**Seven Sneezes, The** (51)	9 - 15
	by Olga Cabral, illus by Tibor Gergely	
	©1948, 42pp	
LE0520	**Little Peewee, or Now Open the Box** (52)	7 - 12
	by Dorothy Kunhardt, illus by J.P. Miller	
	©1948, 42pp. This title used for printings	
	"A" through "F."	
LE0525	**Little Peewee, the Circus Dog, or Now Open the Box** (52)	7 - 15
	by Dorothy Kunhardt, illus by J.P. Miller	
	©1948/p1949(G), 42pp. This title variation	
	used for "G" and later printings. Contents	
	unchanged.	

LE0520   LE0525

LE0530   LE0540

LE0560   LE0550

LE0570   LE0580

LE0590   LE0600

LE0610   LE0620

LE0630   LE0640

LE0530	**Up in the Attic/A Story ABC** (53) by Hilda K. Williams, illus by Corinne Malvern ©1948, 42pp	6 - 12
LE0540	**Pat-a-Cake/Baby's Mother Goose** (54) (Nursery Rhyme), illus by Aurelius Battaglia ©1948, 28pp (See also: LE3030, LE4220)	5 - 10
LE0550	**Name for Kitty, A** (55) by Phyllis McGinley, illus by Feodor Rojankovsky ©1948, 28pp (See also: LG1380)	5 - 10
LE0560	**Our Puppy** (56) by Elsa Ruth Nast, illus by Feodor Rojankovsky ©1948, 28pp (See also: LE2920)	6 - 12

Book Numbers begin to appear on the front cover. Sometimes in the upper right corner in bold type, sometimes in the lower left in very small type.

LE0570	**Little Black Sambo** (57) by Helen Bannerman, illus by Gustaf Tenggren ©1948, 42pp	20 - 55
LE0580	**What Am I?** (58) by Ruth Leon, illus by Cornelius DeWitt ©1949, 28pp (See also: LE5090)	5 - 10
LE0585	Same as LE0580, puzzle edition ©1949/p1950(E), 28pp	15 - 30
LE0586	Same as LE0585, lacking puzzle	2 - 5
LE0590	**Nursery Rhymes** (59) (Nursery Rhyme), illus by Gertrude Elliott ©1948, 28pp	5 - 12
LE0600	**Guess Who Lives Here?** (60) by Louise Woodcock, illus by Eloise Wilkin ©1949, 42pp. Bank Street Book	6 - 10
LE0610	**Good Morning, Good Night** (61) by Jane Werner, illus by Eloise Wilkin ©1948, 42pp	9 - 16
LE0620	**We Like to do Things** (62) by Walter M. Mason, illus by Steffie Lerch ©1949, 42pp	6 - 12

1949: The Golden Library of Books ... Big, Giant, Tiny, Toy and Fuzzy Books, as well as Little Golden Records and Golden Story Books are noted with some of the book lists.

LE0630	**Tommy's Wonderful Rides** (63) by Helen Palmer, illus by J.P. Miller ©1948, 42pp	5 - 10
LE0640	**Five Little Firemen** (64) by Margaret Wise Brown & Edith Thacher Hurd, illus by Tibor Gergely ©1948, 42pp. H: Music score added, last page. (See also: LE3010)	7 - 14
LE0650	**Gaston and Josephine** (65) by Georges Duplaix, illus by Feodor Rojankovsky ©1948, 42pp. An abridged version of the book Oxford had published for Duplaix in 1933.	8 - 16
LE0660	**Two Little Miners** (66) by Margaret Wise Brown & Edith Thacher Hurd, illus by Richard Scarry ©1949, 42pp. Earliest title illustrated by Richard Scarry.	6 - 14

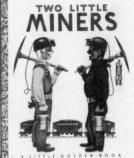

LE0650   LE0660

LE0670	**Jolly Barnyard, The** (67)	5 - 12	

LE0670 **Jolly Barnyard, The** (67) 5 - 12
by Annie North Bedford, illus by Tibor Gergely
©1950, 28pp (See also: LG0700)

LE0672 Same as LE0670, puzzle edition 15 - 35
©1950/p1950(B), 28pp

LE0673 Same as LE0672, lacking puzzle 2 - 5

LE0680 **Little Galoshes** (68) 8 - 14
by Kathryn & Byron Jackson, illus by J.P. Miller
©1949, 42pp

LE0690 **Bobby and His Airplanes** (69) 5 - 12
by Helen Palmer, illus by Tibor Gergely
©1949, 42pp

LE0700 **When You Were a Baby** (70) 5 - 10
by Rita Eng, illus by Corinne Malvern
©1949, 42pp (See also: LE4350)

LE0710 **Johnny's Machines** (71) 5 - 10
by Helen Palmer, illus by Cornelius DeWitt
©1949 by WDP, 42pp. Adapted from
Walt Disney's *Melody Time*.

LE0720 **Bugs Bunny** (72) 5 - 12
by Warner Bros. Cartoons, illus by Warner
Bros. Cartoons, adp by Tom McKimson, Al
Dempster
©1949 by Warner Bros. Cartoons, Inc., 42pp
(See also: LE3120, LE4750)

Bugs Bunny was the first licensed character to appear in the regular LGB series. Soon to be followed by Howdy Doody and others. Character books are listed by subject in the Appendix.

LE0730 **Little Yip-Yip and His Bark** (73) 5 - 12
by Kathryn & Byron Jackson,
illus by Tibor Gergely
©1950, 42pp

First book with Character back: #73, #76, #82, #87 and #88 use this format, which becomes standard with book #91. Overall format change is described following #90.

LE0740 **Little Golden Funny Book, The** (74) 5 - 10
by Gertrude Crampton, illus by J.P. Miller
©1950, 42pp

LE0750 **Katie the Kitten** (75) 6 - 12
by Kathryn & Byron Jackson,
illus by Alice & Martin Provensen
©1949, 42pp (See also: LP1205)

LE0755 Same as LE0750, puzzle edition 15 - 35
©1949/p1950(E), 42pp

LE0757 Same as LE0755, lacking puzzle 2 - 5

LE0760 **Wonderful House, The** (76) 8 - 12
by Margaret Wise Brown, illus by J.P. Miller
©1950, 42pp

LE0770 **Happy Man and His Dump Truck, The** (77) 6 - 14
by Miryam, illus by Tibor Gergely
©1950, 28pp (See also: GD5060, LE5200)

LE0772 Same as LE0770, puzzle edition 15 - 35
©1950/p1950(B), 28pp

LE0773 Same as LE0772, lacking puzzle 3 - 9

LE0780 **Fuzzy Duckling, The** (78) 4 - 9
by Jane Werner,

LE0670   LE0680

LE0690   LE0700

LE0710   LE0720

LE0730   LE0740

LE0750   LE0760

LE0770   LE0780

LE0790   LE0800

illus by Alice & Martin Provensen
©1949, 28pp (See also: LE5570)

LE0790	**Little Trapper, The** (79)	5 - 10

by Kathryn & Byron Jackson,
illus by Gustaf Tenggren
©1950, 28pp

LE0800	**Baby's House** (80)	5 - 10

by Gelolo McHugh, illus by Mary Blair
©1950, 28pp (See also: BB1130)

LE0805	Same as LE0800, puzzle edition	15 - 35

©1950/p1950(B), 28pp

LE0806	Same as LE0805, lacking puzzle	2 - 6
LE0810	**Duck and His Friends** (81)	4 - 10

by Kathryn & Byron Jackson
illus by Richard Scarry
©1949, 28pp

LE0820	**Pets for Peter** (82) (puzzle edition)	20 - 35

by Jane Werner, illus by Aurelius Battaglia
©1950(A), 28pp

LE0821	Same as LE0820, lacking puzzle	5 - 10
LE0822	Same as LE0820, not puzzle edition	5 - 10

©1950/p1952(B), 28pp

LE0830	**How Big** (83)	5 - 10

written & illus by Corinne Malvern
©1949, 28pp

LE0835	Same as LE0830, ©1949/p1971, 24pp.	2 - 6

New cover.

LE0840	**Surprise for Sally** (84)	9 - 14

by Helen Crowninshield,
illus by Corinne Malvern
©1950, 42pp. Published with both LG back
and Character frame back. Neither book has
printing stated. LG back published first.

LE0850	**Susie's New Stove, The Little Chef's Cookbook** (85)	12 - 22

by Annie North Bedford,
illus by Corinne Malvern
©1950, 42pp. A cookbook/storybook,
featuring the "Little Chef" toy stove produced
by Tacoma Metal Products. (See color plate)

LE0860	**Color Kittens, The** (86)	8 - 20

by Margaret Wise Brown,
illus by Alice & Martin Provensen
©1949, 28pp. Both unstated 1sts and
copies marked "A" were printed. (See
also: BB1500, LE4360)

LE0865	Same as LE0860, puzzle edition	15 - 40

©1949/p1950, 28pp. Printing not
stated. Song added, last page.

LE0866	Same as LE0865, lacking puzzle	3 - 8
LE0870	**Marvelous Merry-Go-Round, The** (87)	7 - 12

by Jane Werner, illus by J.P. Miller
©1950, 42pp

LE0880	**Day at the Zoo, A** (88)	5 - 12

by Marion Conger, illus by Tibor Gergely
©1950, 42pp. Unstated 1st. (See also: LE3240)

LE0810   LE0820

LE0830   LE0835

LE0840   LE0850

LE0860   LE0870

LE0880   LE0890

| LE0890 | **Big Brown Bear, The** (89) | 5 - 10 |

LE0890 **Big Brown Bear, The** (89)   5 - 10
by Georges Duplaix, illus by Gustaf Tenggren
©1947/p1949(A), 42pp

LE0900 **My Little Golden Dictionary** (90)   4 - 10
by Mary Reed & Edith Osswald,
illus by Richard Scarry
©1949, 56pp. Both unmarked & "A" printings exist. The last book to have an LG back,
it was published in a 56-page numbered
format. (See also: BB3090, GD5010)

1950 Format Change: Back cover design changed to an
LGB character frame surrounding book list. (Young readers
were encouraged to identify all these famous LG characters!)
End papers were redesigned to include LGB characters in full
color. Book plate now states "This LGB belongs to." Spine
retained the same design, but was changed to gold foil. Those
that have a "silver" look are actually gold spines with the gilt
worn off. (NOTE: Some of the transitional books between #73
and #91 have original end papers, with new back and spine
only.) Book numbers are included on the front cover in upper
right corner.

LE0910 **Little Fat Policeman, The** (91)   5 - 12
by Margaret Wise Brown & Edith Thacher
Hurd, illus by Alice & Martin Provensen
©1950, 42pp

LE0920 **I Can Fly** (92)   5 - 12
by Ruth Krauss, illus by Mary Blair
©1950, 42pp. Bank Street Book. 1951
The New York Tribune Spring Book
Festival Award (Picture Honor Book)

LE0930 **Brave Cowboy Bill** (93) (puzzle edition)   20 - 35
by Kathryn & Byron Jackson,
illus by Richard Scarry
©1950, 42pp. Both "A" and "B"
printings have puzzle.

LE0931 Same as LE0930, lacking puzzle   6 - 10

LE0940 **Jerry at School** (94) (puzzle edition)   12 - 20
by Kathryn & Byron Jackson,
illus by Corinne Malvern
©1950(A), 28pp

LE0941 Same as LE0940, lacking puzzle   6 - 10

LE0942 Same as LE0940, "B" printing, not a
puzzle edition   6 - 10

LE0950 **Christmas in the Country** (95)   5 - 12
by Barbara Collyer & John R. Foley,
illus by Retta Worcester
©1950, 28pp

LE0960 **When I Grow Up** (96) (puzzle edition)   15 - 35
by Kay Mace, illus by Corinne Malvern
©1950(A), 42pp

LE0961 Same as LE0960, lacking puzzle   6 - 10

LE0970 **Little Benny Wanted a Pony** (97)   12 - 20
by Oliver Barrett, illus by Richard Scarry
©1950, 42pp. Unstated 1st. Fold-out
mask in back of book.

LE0971 Same as LE0970, lacking mask   4 - 9

LE0980 **Bugs Bunny's Birthday** (98)   5 - 12
by Elizabeth Beecher, illus by Warner Bros.
Cartoons, adp by Ralph Heimdahl & Al
Dempster
©1950 by Warner Bros. Cartoons, Inc., 28pp

LE0990 **Howdy Doody's Circus** (99)   9 - 16
by Edward Kean,
illus by Liz Dauber & Dan Gormley
©1950 by Robert E. (Bob) Smith, 28pp.
Theme song, last page.

LE1000 **Little Boy with a Big Horn** (100)   5 - 10
by Jack Bechdolt, illus by Aurelius Battaglia
©1950, 42pp

LE0900   *1950: Back Cover*

1950: End Papers   LE0910

LE0920   LE0930

LE0940   LE0950

LE0960   LE0970

LE0980   LE0990

LE0120   LE1030

LE1070   LE1080

LE1090   LE1100

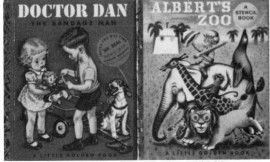

LE1110   LE1120

LE1000   LE1010

LE1010	**Little Golden ABC, The** (101) (puzzle ed) (Alphabet), illus by Cornelius DeWitt ©1951(A), 28pp	15 - 30
LE1011	Same as LE1010, lacking puzzle	2 - 7
LE1015	Same as LE1010, not puzzle edition ©1951/p1953(B), 28pp	2 - 7

28-page format now fully established for books from #101 through #245.

LE1020	**Ukelele and Her New Doll** (102) (puzzle ed) by Clara Louise Grant, illus by Campbell Grant ©1951, 28pp	20 - 35
LE1021	Same as LE1020, lacking puzzle	6 - 10
LE1030	**Christopher and the Columbus** (103) by Kathryn & Byron Jackson, illus by Tibor Gergely ©1951, 28pp	5 - 10

No book published in 1951 (104, 105, 106)

LE1070	**Kitten's Surprise, The** (107) by Nina, illus by Feodor Rojankovsky ©1951, 28pp (See also: LG1390)	5 - 10
LE1080	**Two Little Gardeners** (108) by Margaret Wise Brown & Edith Thacher Hurd, illus by Gertrude Elliott ©1951, 28pp	5 - 10
LE1090	**Little Golden Holiday Book, The** (109) by Marion Conger, illus by Eloise Wilkin ©1951, 28pp	8 - 14
LE1100	**Day at the Beach, A** (110) by Kathryn & Byron Jackson, illus by Corinne Malvern ©1951, 28pp	5 - 10
LE1110	**Doctor Dan, The Bandage Man** (111) by Helen Gaspard, illus by Corinne Malvern ©1950, 28pp. Produced in cooperation with Johnson & Johnson, the book included 6 Band-Aids™. Released with an extensive ad campaign, including TV ads by J&J, the book had an unprecedented 1st printing of 1,600,000 copies. (See also: LE2950)	15 - 25
LE1111	Same as LE1110, lacking Band-Aids	6 - 10
LE1120	**Albert's Zoo** (112) by Jane Werner, illus by Richard Scarry ©1951, 28pp. A stencil book.	10 - 16
LE1121	Same as LE1120, w/punched stencils on pages	5 - 10
LE1120	Same as LE1120, without stencils	2 - 6
LE1130	**Little Golden Paper Dolls, The** (113) written & illus by Hilda Miloche & Wilma Kane ©1951, 28pp. Dolls on heavy board. Last page has 2 beds to keep the dolls in & a closet for the clothes. (See also: LE2800, LH1030, LH1470)	15 - 30
LE1131	Same as LE1130, w/all dolls & clothes, cut	12 - 25
LE1132	Same as LE1130, no dolls or clothes	1 - 6
LE1135	Same as LE1130, ©1951/p1952(B), 28pp	15 - 30

New cover. Dolls on heavy board, no closet/
bed at back. (See also: LE2800, LH1030,
LH1470)

LE1136   Same as LE1135, w/all dolls & clothes, cut 12 - 25

LE1137   Same as LE1135, no dolls or clothes   1 - 6

LE1140   **Pantaloon** (114)   4 - 9
           by Kathryn Jackson, illus by Leonard Weisgard
           ©1951(A), 28pp. 1st editions of this book
           have both plain & die-cut covers.

LE1141   Same as LE1140, w/die-cut door in cover.   4 - 9
           Area of die-cut is slightly grayed in picture
           for identification.

  No book published in 1951 (115)

LE1160   **Laddie and the Little Rabbit** (116)   5 - 10
           written & illus by William P. Gottlieb (photos)
           ©1952 by S&S (text), Curriculum Films, Inc.
           (photos), 28pp

LE1170   **Tom and Jerry** (117)   4 - 10
           by MGM Cartoons, illus by MGM Cartoons,
           adp by Don Mac Laughlin & Harvey Eisenberg
           ©1951 by Loew's Inc., 28pp
           (See also: LE5610)

LE1180   **Train to Timbuctoo, The** (118)   5 - 10
           by Margaret Wise Brown, illus by Art Seiden
           ©1951, 28pp (See also: GD5180)

LE1190   **Day at the Playground, A** (119)   8 - 20
           by Miriam Schlein, illus by Eloise Wilkin
           ©1951, 28pp

LE1200   **Bugs Bunny and the Indians** (120)   5 - 12
           by Annie North Bedford, illus by Warner Bros.
           Cartoons, adp by Dick Kelsey & Tom McKimson
           ©1951 by Warner Bros. Cartoons, Inc., 28pp
           (See also: LE4300)

LE1210   **Howdy Doody and Clarabell** (121)   8 - 15
           by Edward Kean, illus by Art Seiden
           ©1951 by Kagran Corp., 28pp

LE1220   **Lucky Mrs. Ticklefeather** (122)   6 - 12
           by Dorothy Kunhardt, illus by J.P. Miller
           ©1951, 28pp

LE1230   **Happy Birthday** (123)   10 - 20
           by Elsa Ruth Nast, illus by Retta Worcester
           ©1952, 40pp. Party cut-outs. Original

LE1160   LE1170

LE1180   LE1190

LE1200   LE1210

LE1130   LE1135

LE1220   LE1230

LE1140   LE1141

LE1240   LE1250

LE1260   LE1280

LE1290   LE1300

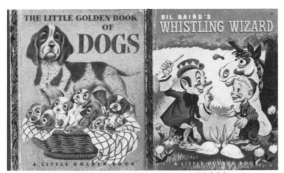

LE1310   LE1320

LE1330   LE1340

LE1350   LE1360

price: 35¢ for this special 40pp book.
(See also: LE3840)

LE1231	Same as LE1230, lacking cut-outs	1 - 5
LE1240	**Robert and His New Friends** (124)	4 - 9
	by Nina Schneider, illus by Corinne Malvern ©1951, 28pp	
LE1250	**Boats** (125)	5 - 10
	by Ruth Mabee Lachman, illus by Lenora & Herbert Combes ©1951, 28pp (See also: LE3390, LE5010)	
LE1260	**Gingerbread Shop, The** (126)	5 - 12
	by P.L. Travers, illus by Gertrude Elliott ©1952, 28pp. A Mary Poppins book.	

No book published in 1952 (127)

LE1280	**Mister Dog/The Dog Who Belonged to Himself** (128)	10 - 18
	by Margaret Wise Brown, illus by Garth Williams ©1952, 28pp	
L1290	**Tex and His Toys** (129)	10 - 16
	by Elsa Ruth Nast, illus by Corinne Malvern ©1952, 28pp. Cut-outs. Came w/roll of Texel Tape®.	
LE1291	Same as LE1290, lacking tape, but uncut	3 - 8
LE1292	Same as LE1290, lacking tape, toys cut out. Most copies found are in this condition.	1 - 3
LE1300	**What If?** (130)	5 - 10
	by Helen & Henry Tanous, illus by J.P. Miller ©1951, 28pp	
LE1310	**Little Golden Book of Dogs, The** (131)	5 - 12
	by Nita Jonas, illus by Tibor Gergely ©1952, 28pp (See also: LE2600, LE3910, LE5320)	
LE1320	**Whistling Wizard, Bil Baird's** (132)	6 - 14
	by Alan Stern & Rupert Pray, illus by Mel Crawford ©1952 by Bil and Cora Baird, 28pp. Based on the TV puppet show.	
LE1330	**Rainy Day Play Book** (133)	3 - 9
	by Marion Conger & Natalie Young, illus by Corinne Malvern ©1951, 28pp (See also: LG0210)	
LE1340	**Seven Little Postmen** (134)	5 - 10
	by Margaret Wise Brown & Edith Thacher Hurd, illus by Tibor Gergely ©1952, 28pp (See also: LE5040)	
LE1350	**Howdy Doody and the Princess** (135)	8 - 15
	by Edward Kean, illus by Art Seiden ©1952 by Kagran Corp., 28pp. Copies of this book also found as LGB 133. LGB 135 is correct number.	
LE1360	**Bugs Bunny Gets a Job** (136)	5 - 12
	by Annie North Bedford, illus by Warner Bros. Cartoons, adp by Tony Strobl & Don MacLaughlin ©1952 by Warner Bros. Cartoons, Inc., 28pp	
LE1370	**Puss in Boots** (137)	5 - 9

LE1370   LE1380

by Kathryn Jackson, illus by J.P. Miller
©1952, 28pp. Based on the Charles Perrault
story. (See also: LE3590)

LE1380 **Tawny Scrawny Lion** (138)   5 - 10
by Kathryn Jackson, illus by Gustaf Tenggren
©1952, 28pp

LE1385 Same as LE1380, ©1952/p1978(J), 24pp   1 - 3
New cover art.

LE1390 **Fun with Decals** (139)   12 - 20
by Elsa Ruth Nast, illus by Corinne Malvern
©1952, 28pp. W/page of Meyercord decals.

LE1400 **Mr. Wigg's Birthday Party** (140)   5 - 12
by P.L. Travers, illus by Gertrude Elliott
©1952, 28pp. A Mary Poppins book.

LE1410 **Wheels** (141)   5 - 10
by Kathryn Jackson, illus by Leonard Weisgard
©1952, 28pp

LE1420 **Frosty the Snowman** (142)   3 - 10
by Annie North Bedford,
illus by Corinne Malvern
©1951 by Hill and Range Songs, Inc., 28pp
Adapted from the song. N: (1964) has
Christmas spine. (See also: LG1350)

LE1423 Same as LE1420, ©1951/P1971(U), 24pp   2 - 5
Cover background changed to green.

LE1426 Same as LE1420, ©1951/p1976(Z) by   1 - 3
Hill and Range Songs, Inc., 24pp
New cover art.

LE1430 **Here Comes the Parade** (143)   5 - 10
by Kathryn Jackson, illus by Richard Scarry
©1951, 28pp. A Christmas parade of LGB
characters.

LE1440 **Road to Oz, The** (144)   9 - 18
by Peter Archer (adp), illus by Harry McNaught
©1951 by Maud Gage Baum, 28pp. Based
on the story by L. Frank Baum.

LE1450 **Woody Woodpecker (Joins the Circus)** (145) 4 - 9
by Annie North Bedford, illus by Walter Lantz
Studios, adp by Riley Thomson
©1951 by Walter Lantz Productions, Inc.,
28pp (See also: LE3300)

LE1460 **Magic Compass, The** (146)   6 - 14
by P.L. Travers, illus by Gertrude Elliott
©1953, 28pp. A Mary Poppins book

LE1470 **Hopalong Cassidy and the Bar-20
Cowboy** (147)   9 - 18
by Elizabeth Beecher, illus by Sahula-Dycke
©1952 by Doubleday and Co., 28pp.
Starring William Boyd; based on the
characters created by Clarence Mulford.

LE1480 **Little Golden Book of Uncle Wiggily** (148) 5 - 12
by Howard R. Garis, illus by Mel Crawford
©1953 by Howard R. Garis, 28pp. Based
on the story "Uncle Wiggily and the Alligator"

LE1490 **Indian, Indian** (149)   3 - 8
by Charlotte Zolotow, illus by Leonard Weisgard

LE1385   LE1390

LE1400   LE1410

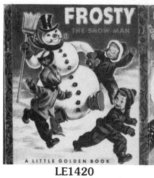

LE1420   LE1426

LE1430   LE1440

LE1450   LE1460   LE1470   LE1480

LE1490　　　　　　LE1500

LE1510　　　　　　LE1520

LE1530　　　　　　LE1540

LE1550　　　　　　LE1560

LE1570　　　　　　LE1580

©1952, 28pp

LE1500　**Rootie Kazootie, Detective** (150)　　10 - 18
by Steve Carlin, illus by Mel Crawford
©1953 by Rootie Kazootie, Inc., 24pp

LE1510　**Emerald City of Oz** (151)　　9 - 22
by Peter Archer (adp), illus by Harry McNaught
©1952 by Maud Gage Baum, 28pp. Based
on the story by L. Frank Baum.

LE1520　**All Aboard!** (152)　　4 - 9
by Marion Conger, illus by Corinne Malvern
©1952, 28pp

LE1530　**Thumbelina** (153)　　4 - 9
by Hans Christian Andersen,
illus by Gustaf Tenggren
©1953, 28pp (See also: LE5140)

LE1540　**Nurse Nancy** (154)　　15 - 25
by Kathryn Jackson, illus by Corinne Malvern
©1952, 28pp. Came w/an assortment
of Johnson & Johnson Band-Aids™.
(See also: LE3460, LE4730)

LE1541　Same as LE1540, lacking Band-Aids　　6 - 10

LE1550　**Little Eskimo, The** (155)　　3 - 8
by Kathryn Jackson, illus by Leonard Weisgard
©1952, 28pp

LE1560　**Sailor Dog, The** (156)　　8 - 14
by Margaret Wise Brown, illus by Garth Williams
©1953, 28pp (See also: BB3510)

LE1570　**Doctor Squash/The Doll Doctor** (157)　　4 - 9
by Margaret Wise Brown, illus by J.P. Miller
©1952, 28pp

LE1580　**Christmas Story, The** (158)　　5 - 10
by Jane Werner, illus by Eloise Wilkin
©1952, 28pp (See also: LG0240)

LE1590　**Tin Woodman of Oz, The** (159)　　9 - 18
by Peter Archer (adp), illus by Harry McNaught
©1952 by Maud Gage Baum, 28pp. Based
on the story by L. Frank Baum.

LE1600　**Danny Beaver's Secret** (160)　　5 - 10
by Patricia Scarry, illus by Richard Scarry
©1953, 28pp

LE1610　**Topsy Turvy Circus** (161)　　5 - 10
by Georges Duplaix, illus by Gustaf Tenggren

LE1590　　　　　　LE1600

LE1610　　　　　　LE1620

©1953, 28pp. Adapted from the story published by Duplaix in 1940.

LE1620 **Little Red Caboose, The** (162)   4 - 9
by Marian Potter, illus by Tibor Gergely
©1953, 28pp (See also: BB2890, GD5180, LE3190)

LE1630 **My Kitten** (163)   7 - 12
by Patricia Scarry, illus by Eloise Wilkin
©1953, 28pp (See also: GD5130, GD5270, LE3000, LE5280)

LE1640 **Bugs Bunny at the County Fair** (164)   5 - 10
by Elizabeth Beecher, illus by Warner Bros. Cartoons, adp by Fred Abranz & Don MacLaughlin
©1953 by Warner Bros. Cartoons, Inc., 28pp

LE1650 **Gingerbread Man, The** (165)   5 - 12
by Nancy Nolte, illus by Richard Scarry
©1953, 28pp (See also: LE4370)

LE1660 **Wiggles** (166)   7 - 14
by Louise Woodcock, illus by Eloise Wilkin
©1953, 28pp

LE1670 **Animal Friends** (167)   5 - 10
by Jane Werner, illus by Garth Williams
©1953, 28pp (See also: LG0220)

LE1680 **My Teddy Bear** (168)   8 - 14
by Richard Scarry, illus by Eloise Wilkin
©1953, 28pp (See also: LE4480)

LE1690 **Rabbit and His Friends** (169)   4 - 9
written & illus by Richard Scarry
©1953, 28pp

LE1700 **Merry Shipwreck, The** (170)   6 - 12
by Georges Duplaix, illus by Tibor Gergely
©1953, 28pp (See also: GD5070)

LE1710 **Howdy Doody's Lucky Trip** (171)   9 - 18
by Edward Kean, illus by Harry McNaught
©1953 by Kagran Corp., 28pp

1953 Format change: Back cover copy changed, book list moved to inside back cover. Front end paper remained the same, but back end paper with book list was printed in sepia with different LGB characters surrounding the list. Book number on front cover was followed by price.

Outlets for LGBs had grown to 120,000 with supermarkets in the lead. Over 300,000,000 Golden Books were in print, and LGBs were not without competitors. Bonnie, Elf, Treasure and Wonder Books were among the many rivals. Few of these series survived the inevitable market shake-down that followed.

LE1720 **Howdy Doody in Funland** (172)   9 - 18
by Edward Kean, illus by Art Seiden
©1953 by Kagran Corp., 28pp

LE1730 **Three Billy Goats Gruff and the Wolf and the Kids** (173)   5 - 10
(Fairy Tale), illus by Richard Scarry
©1953, 28pp

LE1740 **Bible Stories of Boys and Girls** (174)   4 - 8
by Jane Werner, illus by Rachel Taft Dixon & Marjorie Hartwell

1953 Format change: End papers

LE1630   LE1640

LE1650   LE1660

LE1670   LE1680

LE1690   LE1700

LE1710   *1953 Back Cover*

LE1720   LE1730

LE1740   LE1750

LE1760   LE1770

LE1780   LE1790

LE1800   LE1810

©1953, 28pp

LE1750 Uncle Mistletoe (175)   8 - 22
by Jane Werner, illus by Corinne Malvern
©1953, characters property of Marshall Field
& Co., 28pp. Uncle Mistletoe and Aunt Holly
were used as Christmas promotions by Marshall
Field & Co. in the early '50s. Marshall Field
was one of the original companies to place
advance orders for LGBs when they were first
released in 1942.

**LE1760 Little Golden Cut-Out Christmas
Manger** (176)   6 - 12
by Jane Werner, illus by Steffie Lerch
©1953, 28pp. Value is for complete, uncut
book. No price given for cut book, as once
scenes are cut, there is nothing left.

LE1770 Roy Rogers and the New Cowboy (177)   9 - 18
by Annie North Bedford,
illus by Hans Helweg & Mel Crawford
©1953 by Roy Rogers Enterprises, 28pp

LE1780 Brave Little Tailor, The (178)   3 - 8
(Fairy Tale), illus by J.P. Miller
©1953, 28pp

LE1790 Jack and the Beanstalk (179)   5 - 10
(Folk Tale), illus by Gustaf Tenggren
©1953, 28pp (See also: GD5020, LE2810,
LE4200)

LE1800 Airplanes (180)   5 - 10
by Ruth Mabee Lachman,
illus by Lenora & Herbert Combes
©1953, 28pp (See also: LE3730)

LE1810 Tom and Jerry Meet Little Quack (181) 5 - 10
written & illus by MGM Cartoons, adp
by Don MacLaughlin & Harvey Eisenberg
©1953 by Loew's Inc., 28pp. Reprinted as
LE3110 in 1958, then later reprinted in the
'70s at this number ... which is why #181
copies are found which are newer than some
issued at #311.

   Laddie and the Little Rabbit (182) not published at this
number. (See LE1160)

LE1830 Bugs Bunny at the Easter Party (183)   5 - 10
by Kathryn Hitte, illus by Warner Bros.
Cartoons, adp by Tony Strobl & Ben Kudo
©1953 by Warner Bros. Cartoons, Inc., 28pp

LE1840 Howdy Doody and His Magic Hat (184)   9 - 18
by Edward Kean, illus by Art Seiden
©1954 by Kagran Corp., 28pp. Based
on the UPA cartoon.

   1954 "A Little Golden Book" is moved to the top of the
front cover, between two rule lines. With few exceptions (#187,
#188, #205 and #211, as well as some older titles released at
a new number), this format is standard until 1963.

LE1850 Laddie the Superdog (185)   5 - 10
written & illus by William P. Gottlieb (photos)
©1954 by Curriculum Films, Inc. (photos), 28pp

LE1830   LE1840

| LE1860 | **Madeline** (186) | 8 - 14 |

written & illus by Ludwig Bemelmans
©1954 by Ludwig Bemelmans, 28pp.
Madeline was a Caldecott honor book when
it was first published by S&S in 1940.

| LE1870 | **Daddies** (187) | 5 - 15 |

by Janet Frank, illus by Tibor Gergely
©1953, 28pp

| LE1880 | **Hi Ho! Three in a Row** (188) | 9 - 18 |

by Louise Woodcock, illus by Eloise Wilkin
©1954, 28pp. A Bank Street Book

| LE1890 | **Musicians of Bremen, The** (189) | 4 - 9 |

by Jacob & Wilhelm Grimm, illus by J.P. Miller
©1954, 28pp

| LE1900 | **Rootie Kazootie, Baseball Star** (190) | 9 - 14 |

by Steve Carlin, illus by Mel Crawford
©1954 by Steven R. Carlin, 28pp

| LE1910 | **Party Pig, The** (191) | 8 - 15 |

by Kathryn & Byron Jackson,
illus by Richard Scarry
©1954, 28pp

| LE1920 | **Heidi** (192) | 5 - 10 |

illus by Corinne Malvern
©1954, 28pp. Adapted from story by
Johanna Spyri. (See also: LE2580, LE4700)

| LE1930 | **Paper Doll Wedding, The** (193) | 15 - 30 |

written & illus by Hilda Miloche & Wilma Kane
©1954, 28pp. Dolls on heavy board, clothes
closet on back page. (See also: LH1220)

LE1931	Same as LE1930, all dolls & clothes cut	20 - 30
LE1932	Same as LE1930, no dolls or clothes	2 - 6
LE1940	**Twelve Dancing Princesses, The** (194)	6 - 14

by Jacob & Wilhelm Grimm,
Jane Werner (adp), illus by Sheilah Beckett
©1954, 28pp

| LE1950 | **Roy Rogers and Cowboy Toby** (195) | 8 - 16 |

by Elizabeth Beecher, illus by Mel Crawford
©1954 by Roy Rogers Enterprises, 28pp

| LE1960 | **Georgie Finds a Grandpa** (196) | 6 - 14 |

by Miriam Young, illus by Eloise Wilkin
©1954, 28pp

| LE1970 | **Tom and Jerry's Merry Christmas** (197) | 4 - 9 |

LE1890   LE1900

LE1910   LE1920

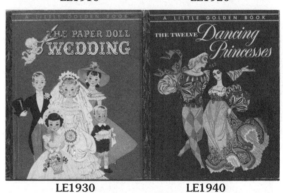

LE1930   LE1940

LE1950   LE1960

LE1850   LE1860

LE1970   LE1980

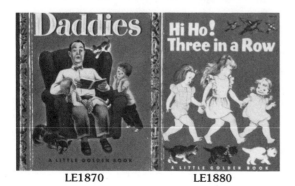

LE1870   LE1880

LE1990   LE2000

LE2010   LE2020

LE2030   LE2040

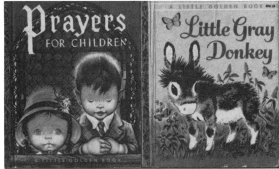

LE2050   LE2060

by Peter Archer, illus by MGM Cartoons,
adp by Harvey Eisenberg & Samuel Armstrong
©1954 by Loew's Inc., 28pp

LE1980 **First Bible Stories** (198)   6 - 14
by Jane Werner, illus by Eloise Wilkin
©1954, 28pp

LE1990 **Friendly Book, The** (199)   5 - 10
by Margaret Wise Brown, illus by Garth Williams
©1954, 18pp (See also: LE5920, LG1160)

LE2000 **Golden Goose, The** (200)   6 - 12
by Jacob & Wilhelm Grimm,
illus by Gustaf Tenggren
©1954, 28pp (See also: GD5020, LE4870)

LE2010 **From Then to Now** (201)   4 - 9
by J.P. Leventhal, illus by Tibor Gergely
©1954, 28pp

LE2020 **Little Indian** (202)   3 - 8
by Margaret Wise Brown, illus by Richard Scarry
©1954, 28pp

LE2030 **Little Lulu and Her Magic Tricks** (203)   14 - 22
written & illus by Marge Henderson Buell
©1954 by Marjorie Henderson Buell, 28pp
Came w/a pack of Kleenex™ in the cover &
instructions for 3 tricks. A first printing of
2,250,000 copies was released in May, 1954,
with full page ads for the book in *Life*, *Look*,
Woman's Day and *Family Circle*. An animated
figure of Little Lulu holding the book was
made for retail displays.

LE2031 Same as LE2030, without Kleenex, but table 6 - 12
cover in place. (Books without table cover
are considered uncollectible.)

LE2040 **Howdy Doody and Mr. Bluster** (204)   9 - 20
by Edward Kean, illus by Elias Marge
©1954 by Kagran Corp., 28pp

LE2050 **Prayers for Children** (205)   3 - 8
(Anthology), illus by Eloise Wilkin
©1952, 28pp. Not the same content as
LE0050.

LE2060 **Little Gray Donkey** (206)   4 - 10
by Alice Lunt, illus by Tibor Gergely
©1954, 28pp

LE2070 **Open Up My Suitcase** (207)   5 - 12
by Alice Low, illus by Corinne Malvern
©1954, 28pp

LE2080 **Tiger's Adventure** (208)   5 - 10
written & illus by William P. Gottlieb (photos)
©1954, photos ©1951 by Curriculum Films,
Inc., 28pp (See also: LE3510)

LE2090 **Little Red Hen, The** (209)   3 - 9
(Folk Tale), illus by J.P. Miller
©1954, 28pp. All new illustrations. Not the
same as LE0060 (See also: LE2960, LE5190)

LE2100 **Kitten Who Thought He Was a
Mouse, The** (210)   9 - 18
by Miriam Norton, illus by Garth Williams

LE2070   LE2080

LE2090   LE2100

©1954, 28pp
LE2110 **Animals of Farmer Jones, The** (211)   3 - 8
by Leah Gale, illus by Richard Scarry
©1953, 28pp. All new illustrations. Same
text as LE0110 (See also: LE2820)
LE2120 **Pierre Bear** (212)   6 - 14
by Patricia Scarry, illus by Richard Scarry
©1954, 28pp
LE2130 **Dale Evans and the Lost Gold Mine** (213)   6 - 14
by Monica Hill, illus by Mel Crawford
©1954 by Dale Evans Enterprises, Inc., 28pp
LE2140 **Linda and Her Little Sister** (214)   8 - 20
by Esther Wilkin, illus by Eloise Wilkin
©1954, 28pp
LE2150 **Bunny Book, The** (215)   5 - 9
by Patricia Scarry, illus by Richard Scarry
©1955, 28pp
LE2160 **Happy Family, The** (216)   9 - 18
by Nicole, illus by Corinne Malvern
©1955, 28pp. All new illustrations and
major text revisions from LE0350.
LE2170 **Hansel and Gretel** (217)   3 - 10
by Jacob & Wilhelm Grimm,
illus by Eloise Wilkin
©1955(A), 24pp. A unique situation, with
"A" copies actually issued after "B" copies.
All books checked have the same markings.
Cover was previously used for some printings
of LE0170, inside illustrations are all new.
(See also: LE4910)
LE2171 Same as LE2170, ©1954(B), 28pp   3 - 10
Published before books marked "A". Note
copyright date and number of pages.
LE2180 **House That Jack Built, The** (218)   5 - 10
(Nursery Rhyme), illus by J.P. Miller
©1954, 28pp
LE2190 **Giant with the Three Golden Hairs** (219)   5 - 10
by Jacob & Wilhelm Grimm,
illus by Gustaf Tenggren
©1955, 28pp
LE2200 **Pony for Tony, A** (220)   6 - 12
written & illus by William P. Gottlieb (photos)
©1955, 28pp
LE2210 **Annie Oakley and the Rustlers** (221)   7 - 14
by Ann McGovern, illus by Mel Crawford
©1955 by Annie Oakley Enterprises, Inc.,
28pp
LE2220 **Circus ABC, The** (222)   7 - 14
by Kathryn Jackson, illus by J.P. Miller
©1955, 28pp

1955: Book list returned to the back cover, and the previous end paper format was used. The price appears in a color block between the rule lines on the front cover, with the book number first appearing under the block, later to the left of it.

Over 200 LGB titles were in print and the LGB Activity series had begun. Before the end of the year, the number of

LE2110   LE2120

LE2130   LE2140

LE2150   LE2160

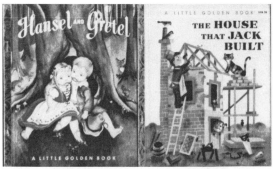

LE2170   LE2180

LE2190   LE2200

LE2210   LE2220

1955: Back Cover   LE2230

LE2240   LE2250

LE2260   LE2270

LE2280   LE2290

LE2300   LE2310

LGBs in print had gone up to more than 300.

LE2230	**It's Howdy Doody Time** (223)	12 - 24
	by Edward Kean, illus by Art Seiden ©1955 by Kagran Corp., 28pp	
LE2240	**Smokey the Bear** (224)	5 - 10
	by Jane Werner, illus by Richard Scarry ©1955, 28pp (See also: LE4810)	
LE2250	**Three Little Kittens, The** (225)	5 - 12
	(Nursery Rhymes), illus by Masha ©1942/p1955(A), 28pp (See also: BB3700, LE0010, LE2880, LE3810)	
LE2260	**Rootie Kazootie Joins the Circus** (226)	10 - 18
	by Steve Carlin, illus by Mel Crawford ©1955 by Steven R. Carlin, 28pp	
LE2270	**Twins, The** (227)	10 - 20
	by Ruth & Harold Shane, illus by Eloise Wilkin ©1955, 28pp	
LE2280	**Snow White and Rose Red** (228)	5 - 10
	(Fairy Tale), illus by Gustaf Tenggren ©1955, 28pp	
LE2290	**Houses** (229)	5 - 10
	by Elsa Jane Werner, illus by Tibor Gergely ©1955, 28pp. With a place to draw a house picture on the last page.	
LE2300	**Gene Autry** (230)	8 - 14
	by Steffi Fletcher, illus by Mel Crawford ©1955 by Gene Autry, 28pp	
LE2310	**Roy Rogers and the Mountain Lion** (231)	9 - 20
	by Ann McGovern, illus by Mel Crawford ©1955 by Frontiers, Inc., 28pp	

Skyscrapers (232) (Not Published) This book is listed in several LGB book lists, but no copies have ever been found and it is generally assumed that it was never published.

LE2330	**My Puppy** (233)	7 - 12
	by Patricia Scarry, illus by Eloise Wilkin ©1955, 28pp (See also: GD5270, LE4690)	
LE2340	**J. Fred Muggs** (234)	5 - 10
	by Irwin Shapiro, illus by Edwin Schmidt ©1955 by J. Fred Muggs Enterprises, 28pp. Based on the NBC TV program.	
LE2350	**Tom and Jerry's Party** (235)	3 - 8
	by Steffi Fletcher, illus by MGM Cartoons,	

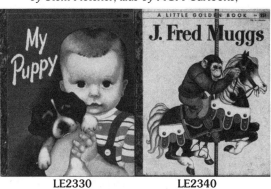

LE2330   LE2340

LE2350   LE2360

adp by Harvey Eisenberg & Samuel Armstrong
©1955 by Loew's, Inc., 28pp

LE2360 **Heroes of the Bible** (236) 3 - 8
by Jane Werner Watson, illus by Rachel
Taft Dixon & Marjorie Hartwell
©1955, 28pp

LE2370 **Howdy Doody and Santa Claus** (237) 9 - 18
by Edward Kean, illus by Art Seiden
©1955 by Kagran Corp., 28pp

LE2380 **Five Pennies to Spend** (238) 5 - 10
by Miriam Young, illus by Corinne Malvern
©1955, 28pp

LE2390 **Bedtime Stories** (239) 5 - 7
(Fairy Tale), illus by Gustaf Tenggren
©1942/p1955(A), 28pp. New cover art.
Shortened to 3 stories. (See also: LE0020,
LE3640, LE5380)

LE2400 **Mother Goose** (240) 5 - 10
by Phyllis Fraser, illus by Gertrude Elliott
©1942/p1955(A), 28pp. New cover.
Edited version of LE0040.

LE2410 **Night Before Christmas, The** (241) 10 - 20
by Clement C. Moore, illus by Eloise Wilkin
©1955, 28pp. Different illustrations than
LE0200. Both books were in print at the
same time. (See also: FN4960)

LE2420 **Our World/A Beginner's Introduction
to Geography** (242) 3 - 8
by Jane Werner Watson, illus by William Sayles
©1955, 28pp (See also: LE5340)

LE2430 **Numbers** (243) 2 - 6
by Mary Reed & Edith Osswald,
illus by Violet LaMont
©1955, 28pp. Adapted from a "Fun-to-
Learn" book. (See also: LE3370)

LE2440 **Scuffy the Tugboat** (244) 4 - 10
by Gertrude Crampton, illus by Tibor Gergely
©1955(A), 28pp. New cover art. (See also:
BB3540, LE0300, LE3630)

LE2450 **Out of My Window** (245) 6 - 14
by Alice Low, illus by Polly Jackson
©1955, 24pp

24-page format: #245 was the first 24-page book. #246
was the last 28-page book. From #247 to the present, all
books are 24 pages.

LE2460 **Rin Tin Tin and Rusty** (246) 5 - 12
by Monica Hill, illus by Mel Crawford
©1955 by Screen Gems, Inc., 28pp

LE2470 **Happy Days** (247) 3 - 8
by Janet Frank, illus by Eleanor Dart
©1955, 24pp

LE2480 **Shy Little Kitten** (248) 4 - 10
by Cathleen Schurr, illus by Gustaf Tenggren
©1946/p1956(A), 24pp. New cover art,
artist not noted. Minor inside illustration
moves to accommodate 24-page book.

LE2370   LE2380

LE2390   LE2400

LE2410   LE2420

LE2430   LE2440

LE2450   LE2460

LE2470   LE2480

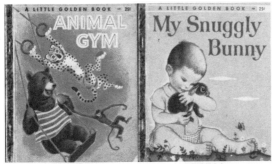

LE2490

LE2500

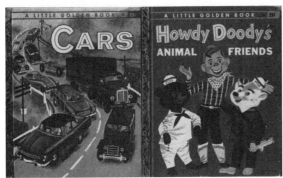

LE2510

LE2520

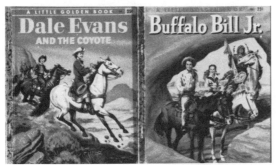

LE2530

LE2540

1956 Format Change

LE2550

LE2560

(See also: LE0230, LE4940)

LE2490 **Animal Gym** (249)   6 - 12
by Beth Greiner Hoffman, illus by Tibor Gergely
©1956, 24pp

LE2500 **My Snuggly Bunny** (250)   8 - 12
by Patricia Scarry, illus by Eloise Wilkin
©1956, 24pp (See also: GD5270)

LE2510 **Cars** (251)   6 - 12
by Kathryn Jackson, illus by William J. Dugan
©1956, 24pp

LE2520 **Howdy Doody's Animal Friends** (252)   9 - 18
by Kathleen N. Daly, illus by Art Seiden
©1956 by Kagran Corp., 24pp

LE2530 **Dale Evans and the Coyote** (253)   6 - 14
by Gladys Wyatt, illus by E. Joseph Dreany
©1956 by Dale Evans Enterprises, Inc., 24pp

LE2540 **Buffalo Bill, Jr.** (254)   5 - 10
by Gladys Wyatt, illus by Hamilton Greene
©1956 by Flying A Productions, 24pp.
Based on the TV program.

1956 Format change: Ads for other Golden series begin to appear on LGB back covers. A number of different ads were run between 1955 and 1964. For a full description, see "Ad Backs" (AB1000). The first few books with ad backs have no book list, but by #257 the list is carried again on the inside back cover. The character frame is used with the list, but it is reversed from the way it was printed on the back cover.

LE2550 **Lassie Shows the Way** (255)   5 - 10
by Monica Hill, illus by Lee Ames
©1956, 24pp (See also: LE4150)

LE2560 **Daniel Boone** (256)   4 - 9
by Irwin Shapiro, illus by Miriam Story Hurford
©1956, 24pp

LE2570 **Counting Rhymes** (257)   3 - 7
(Nursery Rhymes), illus by Corinne Malvern
©1947/p1956(A), 24pp. New cover art.
Edited version of LE0125. (See also: BB1540, LE0125)

LE2580 **Heidi** (258)   3 - 7
illus by Corinne Malvern
©1954/p1956(A), 24pp. Adapted from the story by Johanna Spyri. (See also: LE1930, LE4700)

LE2590 **Roy Rogers and the Indian Sign** (259)   9 - 20
by Gladys Wyatt, illus by Mel Crawford
©1956 by Frontiers, Inc., 24pp

LE2600 **Dogs (The Little Golden Book of)** (260)   5 - 12
by Nita Jonas, illus by Tibor Gergely
©1952/p1956(A), 24pp. New cover art.
Cover title change from LE1310. (See also: LE1310, LE3910, LE5320)

LE2610 **Captain Kangaroo** (261)   5 - 9
by Kathleen N. Daly, illus by Art Seiden
©1956 by Keeshan-Miller Enterprises
Corp., 24pp. Based on the CBS TV
program. (See also: GD5210)

LE2570

LE2580

No book published in 1956 (262)

LE2630 **Lone Ranger, The** (263) 9 - 18
by Steffi Fletcher, illus by E. Joseph Dreany
©1956 by The Lone Ranger, Inc., 24pp

No book published in 1956 (264)

LE2650 **Pal and Peter** (265) 3 - 9
written & illus by William P. Gottlieb (photos)
©1956, 24pp

LE2660 **Winky Dink** (266) 6 - 12
by Ann McGovern, illus by Richard Scarry
©1956 by Marvel Screen Enterprises, Inc.,
24pp. Based on the CBS TV program,
"Winky Dink and You."

LE2670 **Gene Autry and Champion** (267) 8 - 14
by Monica Hill, illus by Frank Bolle
©1956 by Gene Autry, 24pp

LE2680 **My Little Golden Book About God** (268) 3 - 9
by Jane Werner Watson, illus by Eloise Wilkin
©1956, 24pp

LE2690 **My Little Golden Book About Travel** (269) 3 - 9
by Kathleen N. Daly, illus by Tibor Gergely
©1956, 24pp

LE2700 **My Little Golden Book About the Sky** (270) 3 - 9
by Rose Wyler, illus by Tibor Gergely
©1956, 24pp

LE2710 **Poky Little Puppy, The** (271) 3 - 9
by Janette Sebring Lowrey,
illus by Gustaf Tenggren
©1942/p1956(A), 24pp (See also: BB3330,
LE0080, LE5060)

LE2720 **Farmyard Friends** (272) 3 - 9
written & illus by William P. Gottlieb (photos)
©1956, 24pp (See also: LE4290)

LE2730 **Romper Room Do Bees/A Book of
Manners** (273) 3 - 8
by Nancy Claster, illus by Eleanor Dart
©1956, 24pp

LE2740 **Baby Animals** (274) 3 - 8
written & illus by Garth Williams
©1957, 24pp (See also: BB1080, LE5170)

LE2750 **Annie Oakley Sharpshooter** (275) 7 - 14

LE2650   LE2660

LE2670   LE2680

LE2690   LE2700

LE2590   LE2600

LE2710   LE2720

LE2610   LE2630

LE2730   LE2740

LE2750   LE2760

LE2770   LE2780

LE2790   LE2800

LE2810   LE2820

LE2830   LE2840

by Charles Spain Verral,
illus by E. Joseph Dreany
©1956 by Annie Oakley Enterprises, Inc.,
24pp

LE2760	**Rin Tin Tin and the Lost Indian** (276)	5 - 12

by Monica Hill, illus by Hamilton Greene
©1956 by Screen Gems, Inc., 24pp

LE2770	**Lassie and the Daring Rescue** (277)	6 - 12

by Charles Spain Verral,
illus by E. Joseph Dreany
©1956 by Lassie Programs, Inc., 24pp
(See also: GD5120)

LE2780	**Captain Kangaroo and the Panda** (278)	5 - 10

by Kathleen N. Daly, illus by Edwin Schmidt
©1957 by Keeshan-Miller Enterprises Corp.,
24pp (See also: GD5210, LE4210)

LE2790	**My Baby Brother** (279)	10 - 20

by Patricia Scarry, illus by Eloise Wilkin
©1956, 24pp

LE2800	**Little Golden Paper Dolls, The** (280)	15 - 30

written & illus by Hilda Miloche & Wilma Kane
©1951/p1956(A), 24pp. Reissued with
original cover art, light blue background.
(See also: LE1130, LH0030, LH1470)

LE2801	Same as LE2800, w/all dolls & clothes, cut	12 - 25
LE2802	Same as LE2800, no dolls or clothes	1 - 6
LE2810	**Jack and the Beanstalk** (281)	5 - 10

(Folk Tale), illus by Gustaf Tenggren
©1953/p1956(A), 24pp. New cover art
(See also: LE1790, LE4200)

LE2820	**Animals of Farmer Jones, The** (282)	3 - 8

by Leah Gale, illus by Richard Scarry
©1953/p1956(A), 24pp (See also: LE2110)

LE2830	**Little Golden Mother Goose, The** (283)	4 - 9

(Nursery Rhymes), illus by Feodor Rojankovsky
©1957, 24pp (See also: GD5160, LE3900,
LE4720)

LE2840	**About the Seashore** (284)	4 - 9

by Kathleen N. Daly, illus by Tibor Gergely
©1957, 24pp. Inside title: *A Little Golden
Book About the Seashore.*

LE2850	**How to Tell Time** (285)	6 - 12

by Jane Werner Watson, illus by Eleanor Dart
©1957, 24pp w/cover die-cut to show clock.
Clock face w/movable hands, marked "Gruen",
printed on fold-out page. Only book in this LG
series identified as "A Little Golden Activity
Book".

LE2851	Same as LE2850, ©1957/p1961(F), 24pp	4 - 10

Clock face on single page, no longer marked
"Gruen".

LE2858	Same as LE2850, ©1957/p1967(H), 20pp	2 - 6

Soft cover book, w/clock face and hands
inside front cover.

LE2860	**Fury** (286)	5 - 12

by Kathleen Irwin, illus by Mel Crawford

LE2850   LE2860

©1957 by Vision Productions, Inc., 24pp

LE2870 **Cleo** (287)   5 - 10
by Irwin Shapiro,
illus by Durward B. Graybill (photos)
©1957 by Norden Productions, 24pp.
Cleo was featured on the TV program
"The People's Choice."

LE2880 **Three Little Kittens** (288)   4 - 9
(Nursery Rhymes), illus by Masha
©1942/p1957(Y?), 24pp. Earliest printing
at this number not determined. (See also:
BB3700, LE0010, LE2250, LE3810)

LE2890 **Child's Garden of Verses, A** (289)   6 - 12
by Robert Louis Stevenson, illus by Eloise Wilkin
©1957, 24pp (See also: LE4930)

LE2900 **Circus Boy** (290)   6 - 15
by Irwin Shapiro, illus by Joan Walsh Anglund
©1957 by Norbert Productions, Inc., 24pp.
Based on the TV program.

LE2910 **New Baby, The** (291)   5 - 10
by Ruth & Harold Shane, illus by Eloise Wilkin
©1948/p1957(J), 24pp (See also: LE0410,
LE5410)

LE2915 Same as LE2910, ©1975(A), 24pp.   2 - 6
All new illustrations and revised text.
(See also: LE0410, LE5410)

LE2920 **Our Puppy** (292)   5 - 10
by Elsa Ruth Nast, illus by Feodor Rojankovsky
©1957(E), 24pp. E: earliest printing at this
number. (See also: LE0560)

LE2930 **Wonders of Nature** (293)   4 - 10
by Jane Werner Watson, illus by Eloise Wilkin
©1957, 24pp (See also: BB4060)

LE2940 **Brave Eagle** (294)   5 - 10
by Charles Spain Verral, illus by Si Vanderlaan
©1957 by Frontiers, Inc., 24pp.
Based on the TV program.

LE2950 **Doctor Dan, The Bandage Man** (295)   15 - 25
by Helen Gaspard, illus by Corinne Malvern
©1957(C), 24pp. C: earliest printing at this
number. New cover art. Came w/Band-Aids.
(See also: LE1110)

LE2951 Same as LE2950, lacking Band-Aids   6 - 10

LE2960 **Little Red Hen, The** (296)   2 - 7
(Folk Tale), illus by J.P. Miller, cover by
Rudolf Freund
©1954/p1957(C), 24pp. C: earliest printing
at this number (See also: LE2090, LE5190)

LE2970 **Lone Ranger and Tonto, The** (297)   9 - 18
by Charles Spain Verral, illus by Edwin Schmidt
©1957 by The Lone Ranger, Inc., 24pp
Based on the TV program.

LE2980 **My Christmas Book** (298)   5 - 10
(Anthology), illus by Sheilah Beckett,
cover by Richard Scarry
©1957, 24pp. Inside title: *My Little*

LE2870   LE2880

LE2890   LE2900

LE2910   LE2915

LE2920   LE2930

LE2940   LE2950

LE2960   LE2970

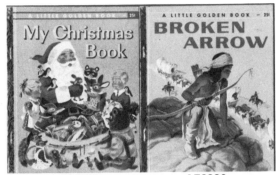

LE2980   LE2990

LE3000   LE3010

LE3020   LE3030

LE3040   LE3050

LE3060   LE3070

Golden Christmas Book.

LE2990	**Broken Arrow** (299)	5 - 10

by Charles Spain Verral, illus by Mel Crawford
©1957 by TCF - Television Productions,
Inc., 24pp. Based on the TV program.

LE3000	**My Kitten** (300)	6 - 10

by Patricia Scarry, illus by Eloise Wilkin
©1953/p1957(B), 24pp. B: earliest printing
at this number (See also: LE1630, LE5280)

LE3010	**Five Little Firemen** (301)	3 - 9

by Margaret Wise Brown & Edith Thacher
Hurd, illus by Tibor Gergely
©1949/p1957(N), 24pp. N: earliest known
printing at this number. (See also: LE0640)

LE3020	**New Kittens, The** (302)	6 - 10

written & illus by William P. Gottlieb (photos)
©1957, 24pp

LE3030	**Baby's Mother Goose/Pat-a-Cake** (303)	5 - 12

(Nursery Rhymes), illus by Aurelius Battaglia
©1948/p1957(A), 24pp. Formerly titled:
Pat-a-Cake, LE0540 (See also: LE4220)

LE3040	**Rin-Tin-Tin and the Outlaw** (304)	5 - 12

by Charles Spain Verral, illus by Mel Crawford
©1957 by Screen Gems, Inc., 24pp

LE3050	**White Bunny and His Magic Nose** (305)	5 - 10

by Lily Duplaix, illus by Feodor Rojankovsky
©1957, 24pp. Illustrations are different than
the "Fuzzy" book. Cover shown, 1st ed. only.

LE3051	Same as LE3050, ©1957/p1965(B), 24pp	2 - 5

Cover has plain background in light yellow.

LE3052	Same as LE3050, ©1957/p1965(C), 24pp	1 - 3

Cover has plain background in bright red.

LE3060	**Red Little Golden Book of Fairy Tales** (306)	3 - 9

by Jacob & Wilhelm Grimm & Hans Christian
Andersen, illus by William J. Dugan
©1958, 24pp. Later reprinted as LE4980.

LE3070	**Lassie and Her Day in the Sun** (307)	5 - 10

by Charles Spain Verral, illus by Mel Crawford
©1958 by Lassie Programs, Inc., 24pp
(See also: GD5120, LE5180)

LE3080	**Jack's Adventure** (308)	3 - 9

by Edith Thacher Hurd, illus by J.P. Miller
©1958, 24pp

LE3090	**Three Bedtime Stories** (309)	3 - 9

(Fairy Tale), illus by Garth Williams
©1958, 24pp (See also: BB3690)

LE3100	**Lone Ranger and the Talking Pony** (310)	10 - 20

by Emily Broun, illus by Frank Bolle
©1958 by The Lone Ranger, Inc., 24pp

LE3110	**Tom and Jerry Meet Little Quack** (311)	3 - 7

written & illus by MGM Cartoons, adp by
Don MacLaughlin & Harvey Eisenberg
©1953/p1958(B), by Loew's Inc., 24pp.
"B" is probably the earliest printing at this
number. (See also: LE1810)

LE3120	**Bugs Bunny** (312)	5 - 10

LE3080   LE3090

written & illus by Warner Bros. Cartoons, adp by Tom McKimson & Al Dempster ©1949/p1958(I) by Warner Bros. Cartoons, Inc., 24pp. May also be "H" printing at this number. LE0720 runs through "G" at least. (See also: LE0720, LE4750)

LE3130   **Peter Rabbit** (313)   5 - 10
by Beatrix Potter,
illus by Adriana Mazza Saviozzi
©1958, 24pp. Inside title: *The Tale of Peter Rabbit* (See also: LE5050, LG0830)

LE3140   **Pussy Willow** (314)   5 - 10
by Margaret Wise Brown,
illus by Leonard Weisgard
©1951/p1958(A), 24pp. Cover w/autumn
gold background 1st edition only. Previously
published as BB3380 (See also: LG0070)

LE3142   Same as LE3140, ©1951/p1965(B), 24pp   3 - 8
Cover design changed to plain white background.

LE3150   **Life and Legend of Wyatt Earp®, The** (315) 6 - 12
by Monica Hill, illus by Mel Crawford
©1958 by Wyatt Earp Enterprizes, Inc., 24pp

Barker the Puppy (316) Not published

LE3170   **More Mother Goose Rhymes** (317)   5 - 10
(Nursery Rhymes), illus by Feodor Rojankovsky
©1958, 24pp (See also: GD5160)

LE3180   **Cheyenne** (318)   5 - 10
by Charles Spain Verral, illus by Al Schmidt
©1958 by Warner Bros. Productions, Inc.,
24pp

LE3190   **Little Red Caboose, The** (319)   2 - 6
by Marian Potter, illus by Tibor Gergely
©1953/p1958(C), 24pp. C: earliest printing
at this number(See also: BB2890, LE1620)

LE3200   **Gunsmoke** (320)   9 - 14
by Seymour Reit, illus by E. Joseph Dreany
©1958 by CBS, Inc., 24pp

Day at the Zoo, A (321) See LE3240

LE3220   **Four Little Kittens** (322)   4 - 9
by Kathleen N. Daly,
illus by Adriana Mazza Saviozzi
©1957, 24pp. A continuation of this story
was published as BB2800. (See also: LE5300)

LE3230   **Ali Baba and the Forty Thieves** (323)   5 - 10
illus by Lowell Hess
©1958, 24pp. A story from *1001 Arabian
Nights*.

LE3240   **Day at the Zoo, A** (324)   3 - 8
by Marion Conger, illus by Tibor Gergely
©1950/p1958(D), 24pp. D: earliest printing
at this number. (See also: LE0880)

LE3250   **Play Ball!** (325)   6 - 12
by Charles Spain Verral, illus by Gerald McCann
©1958, 24pp. "A First Book About Baseball"

LE3260   **Wagon Train** (326)   6 - 12

LE3120   LE3130

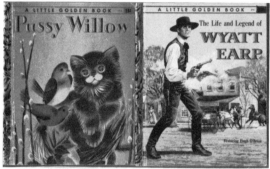

LE3140   LE3150

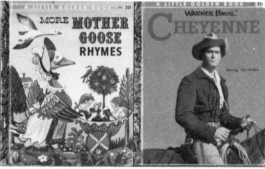

LE3170   LE3180

LE3190   LE3200

LE3100   LE3110

LE3220   LE3230

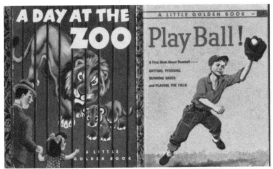

LE3240   LE3250

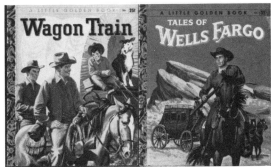

LE3260   LE3280

LE3290   LE3300

LE3310   LE3320

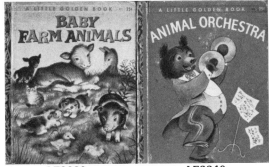

LE3330   LE3340

by Emily Broun, illus by Frank Bolle
©1958 by Revue Productions, Inc., 24pp
No book published in 1958 (327)

LE3280	**Tales of Wells Fargo: Danger at Mesa Flats** (328)	7 - 14
	by Leon Lazarus, illus by John Leone ©1958 by Overland Productions, Inc., 24pp	
LE3290	**Animals' Merry Christmas, The** (329)	5 - 12
	by Kathryn Jackson, illus by Richard Scarry ©1958, 24pp. Contents selected from GB1090.	
LE3300	**Woody Woodpecker (Joins the Circus)** (330)	2 - 7
	by Annie North Bedford, illus by Walter Lantz Studios, adp by Riley Thompson ©1952/P1958(C) by Walter Lantz Productions, Inc., 24pp. C: earliest printing at this number. (See also: LE1450)	
LE3310	**Rudolph the Red-Nosed Reindeer** (331)	3 - 9
	by Barbara Shook Hazen, illus by Richard Scarry ©1958 by Robert L. May, 24pp. Adapted from the story by Robert L. May. Published by arrangement with Maxton Pub., Inc. (See also: BB3480)	
LE3320	**Wild Animal Babies** (332)	3 - 8
	by Kathleen N. Daly, illus by Feodor Rojankovsky ©1958, 24pp	
LE3330	**Baby Farm Animals** (333)	3 - 8
	written & illus by Garth Williams ©1958, 24pp (See also: BB1110, LE4640)	
LE3340	**Animal Orchestra** (334)	6 - 12
	by Ilo Orleans, illus by Tibor Gergely ©1958, 24pp	
LE3350	**Big Brown Bear, The** (335)	3 - 7
	by Georges Duplaix, illus by Gustaf Tenggren ©1947/p1958(D), 24pp. D: earliest printing at this number. (See also: BB1267, LE0890)	
LE3355	Same as LE3350, ©1947/p1973(6th), 24pp Cover has blue background, type style for title changed.	1 - 4
LE3360	**Fury Takes the Jump** (336)	5 - 12
	by Seymour Reit, illus by Mel Crawford ©1958 by Television Programs of America, Inc., 24pp	
LE3370	**Numbers** (337)	2 - 6
	by Mary Reed & Edith Osswald, illus by Violet LaMont ©1955/p1958(B), 24pp. B: earliest printing at this number. (See also: LE2430)	
LE3375	Same as LE3370, ©1955/p1968(L), 24pp Cover background changed to yellow.	1 - 4
LE3380	**Deep Blue Sea, The** (338)	4 - 9
	by Bertha Morris Parker & Kathleen N. Daly, illus by Tibor Gergely ©1958, 24pp	
LE3390	**Boats** (339)	3 - 8
	by Ruth Mabee Lachman,	

LE3350   LE3360

illus by Lenora & Herbert Combes
©1951/p1958(C), 24pp. Earliest printing at this number is "C". Cover variation: color of ocean liner hull changed from previous edition. (See also: LE1250, LE5010).

1958: Golden Press, NY. Western & Affiliated Publishers Co. bought out S&S's share in Golden Books in 1958, and "Golden Press" begins to appear on the title page and the book list. By #354 this is standard. The new name was accompanied by the Golden "Lion" logo.

LE3400   **My Baby Sister** (340)   9 - 14
       by Patricia Scarry, illus by Sharon Koester
       ©1958, 24pp

LE3410   **Captain Kangaroo's Surprise Party** (341)   5 - 10
       by Barbara Lindsay, illus by Edwin Schmidt
       ©1958 by Robert Keeshan Assoc., Inc.,
       24pp (See also: GD5210)

LE3420   **Exploring Space** (342)   4 - 9
       by Rose Wyler, illus by Tibor Gergely,
       cover by George Solonewitsch
       ©1958, 24pp

LE3430   **Lassie and the Lost Explorer** (343)   6 - 12
       by Leon Lazarus, illus by Frank Bolle
       ©1958 by Lassie Programs, Inc., 24pp
No book published in 1958 (344, 345)

LE3460   **Nurse Nancy** (346)   12 - 25
       by Kathryn Jackson, illus by Corinne Malvern
       ©1958(C), 24pp. Cover background changed
       to red. C: earliest printing at this number.
       Came w/Band-Aids. (See also: LE1540,
       LE4730)

LE3461   Same as LE3460, lacking Band-Aids   4 - 10

LE3470   **Leave It to Beaver** (347)   9 - 20
       by Lawrence Alson, illus by Mel Crawford
       ©1959 by Galmaco Productions, Inc., 24pp

LE3480   **Nursery Songs** (348)   3 - 9
       by Leah Gale, illus by Adriana Mazza Saviozzi
       ©1959, 24pp. An edited version of LE0070,
       with all new illustrations.

LE3490   **Animal Alphabet from A to Z** (349)   8 - 12
       by Barbara Shook Hazen, illus by Adele Werber
       ©1958, 24pp
No book published in 1959 (350)

LE3510   **Tiger's Adventure** (351)   3 - 7
       written & illus by William P. Gottlieb (photos)
       ©1954/p1958(B), 24pp. B: earliest printing
       at this number. (See also: LE2080)

LE3520   **We Help Mommy** (352)   4 - 12
       by Jean Cushman, illus by Eloise Wilkin
       ©1959, 24pp

LE3530   **Tom Thumb** (353)   3 - 7
       by Carl Memling, illus by William J. Dugan
       ©1958 by Loew's Inc., 24pp. Based on
       the MGM film.

LE3540   **Maverick** (354)   6 - 12
       by Carl Memling, illus by John Leone

LE3390   LE3400

LE3410   LE3420

LE3430   LE3460

LE3470   LE3480

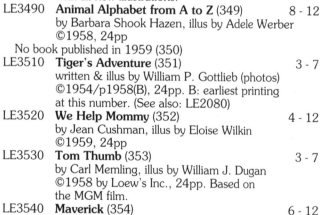

LE3370   LE3380

LE3490   LE3510

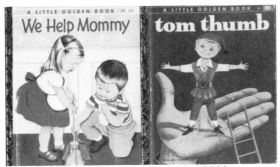

LE3520   LE3530

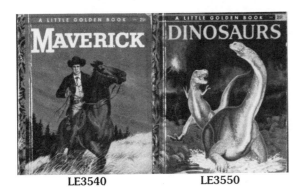

LE3540   LE3550

LE3560   LE3570

LE3580   LE3590

LE3630   LE3640

     ©1959 by Warner Bros. Productions, Inc., 24pp

LE3550   **Dinosaurs** (355)   4 - 9
     by Jane Werner Watson,
     illus by William de J. Rutherfoord
     ©1959, 24pp

LE3560   **Steve Canyon** (356)   6 - 12
     written & illus by Milton Caniff
     ©1959 by Field Enterprises, Inc., 24pp

LE3570   **Helicopters** (357)   8 - 12
     by Carl Memling, illus by Mel Crawford
     ©1959, 24pp. Inside title: *The Little
     Golden Book of Helicopters*.

LE3580   **Baby's First Book** (358)   6 - 10
     written & illus by Garth Williams
     ©1959, 24pp (See also: LE4890)

LE3590   **Puss in Boots** (359)   3 - 8
     by Kathryn Jackson, illus by J.P. Miller
     ©1959, 24pp. Based on the Charles
     Perrault story. (See also: LE1370)

LE3600   **Party in Shariland** (360)   6 - 14
     by Ann McGovern,
     illus by Doris & Marion Henderson
     ©1959 by California National Productions, Inc.,
     24pp. Featuring Shari Lewis & her puppets.

LE3610   **Counting Rhymes** (361)   4 - 9
     (Nursery Rhymes), illus by Sharon Kane
     ©1960, 24pp. All new text and illustrations.
     Not a reprint of LE0120, LE2570.

  Tarzan (362) Not published. See LE5490

LE3630   **Scuffy, the Tugboat** (363)   2 - 7
     by Gertrude Crampton, illus by Tibor Gergely
     ©1955/p1958(C), 24pp. C: earliest printing
     at this number. (See also: BB3540, LE0300,
     LE2440)

LE3640   **Bedtime Stories** (364)   3 - 7
     (Fairy Tale), illus by Gustaf Tenggren
     ©1942/p1958(D), 24pp. D: earliest printing
     at this number. Inside text & illustrations the
     same as LE2390, just rearranged for 24-page
     book. (See also: LE0020, LE2390, LE5380)

No book published in 1959 (365)

LE3600   LE3610

LE3660   LE3670

LE3660	**Cars and Trucks** (366)	3 - 7
	illus by Richard Scarry	
	©1959, 24pp (See also: BB2590)	
LE3670	**Lion's Paw, The** (367)	3 - 9
	by Jane Werner Watson, illus by Gustaf Tenggren	
	©1959, 24pp. Inside subtitle: *A Tale of African Animals.*	
LE3680	**Baby's First Christmas** (368)	8 - 14
	by Esther Wilkin, illus by Eloise Wilkin	
	©1959, 24pp	
LE3690	**Little Golden Picture Dictionary** (369)	3 - 7
	by Nancy Fielding Hulick, illus by Tibor Gergely	
	©1959, 24pp. Not the same book as LG0180.	
LE3700	**New Puppy, The** (370)	4 - 9
	by Kathleen N. Daly, illus by Lilian Obligado	
	©1959, 24pp (See also: LG1410)	
LE3710	**Aladdin and His Magic Lamp** (371)	5 - 12
	by Kathleen N. Daly, illus by Lowell Hess	
	©1959, 24pp. A story from *1001 Arabian Nights.*	
LE3720	**Woody Woodpecker/Drawing Fun for Beginners** (372)	9 - 16
	by Carl Buettner, illus by Harvey Eisenberg & Norm McGary	
	©1959 by Walter Lantz Productions, Inc., 24pp	
LE3730	**Airplanes** (373)	5 - 10
	by Ruth Mabee Lachman, illus by Steele Savage	
	©1959, 24pp. All new illustrations, text adapted from 1953 version, LE1800.	
LE3740	**Blue Book of Fairy Tales, The** (374)	4 - 10
	(Fairy Tales), illus by Gordon Laite	
	©1959, 24pp	
LE3750	**Chipmunks' Merry Christmas, The** (375)	3 - 7
	by David Corwin, illus by Richard Scarry	
	©1959 by Monarch Music Co., Inc., 24pp. *The Chipmunk Song* in story setting.	
LE3760	**Huckleberry Hound Builds a House** (376)	4 - 10
	by Ann McGovern, illus by Harvey Eisenberg & Al White	
	©1959 by Hanna-Barbera Productions, Inc., 24pp	
LE3770	**Naughty Bunny** (377)	6 - 12
	written & illus by Richard Scarry	
	©1959, 24pp	
LE3780	**Ruff and Reddy** (378)	5 - 10
	by Ann McGovern, illus by Harvey Eisenberg & Al White	
	©1959 by Hanna-Barbera Productions, Inc., 24pp (See also: LE4770)	
LE3790	**Animal Dictionary** (379)	3 - 8
	by Jane Werner Watson, illus by Feodor Rojankovsky	
	©1960, 24pp (See also: LE5330)	
LE3800	**Birds of All Kinds** (380)	4 - 8
	written & illus by Walter Ferguson	
	©1959, 24pp	

LE3680   LE3690

LE3700   LE3710

LE3720   LE3730

LE3740   LE3750

LE3760   LE3770

LE3780   LE3790

LE3800   LE3810

LE3820   LE3830

LE3840   LE3850

LE3860   LE3870

LE3810	**Three Little Kittens** (381)	2 - 7

(Nursery Rhymes), illus by Masha
©1942/p1959(Z), 24pp. Z: earliest printing
at this number. (See also: BB3700, LE0010,
LE2250, LE2880)

LE3820   Fire Engines (382)   4 - 10
illus by Tibor Gergely
©1959, 24pp. Inside title: *The Little Golden
Fire Engine Book*. (See also: BB2600)

LE3830   Baby Listens (383)   8 - 14
by Esther Wilkin, illus by Eloise Wilkin
1960, 24pp

LE3840   Happy Birthday (384)   8 - 12
by Elsa Ruth Nast, illus by Retta Worcester
©1960, 24pp. Cut-Outs. Inside title: *How to
Have a Happy Birthday*. Cut copies have no
collector value. An abridged version of LE2470.

LE3850   Saggy Baggy Elephant, The (385)   3 - 6
by Kathryn & Byron Jackson,
illus by Gustaf Tenggren
©1947/p1959(L), 24pp. L: earliest printing
at this number. (See also: LE0360)

LE3860   Dennis the Menace and Ruff (386)   5 - 10
by Carl Memling,
illus by Hawley Pratt & Lee Holley
©1959 by Hall Syndicate, Inc., 24pp

LE3870   Smokey and His Animal Friends (387)   5 - 12
by Charles Spain Verral, illus by Mel Crawford
©1960, 24pp

LE3880   Our Flag (388)   2 - 7
by Carl Memling, illus by Stephen Cook
©1960, 24pp

LE3890   Cowboy A-B-C (389)   5 - 10
by Gladys R. Saxon, illus by Jerry Smath
©1960, 24pp

LE3900   Little Golden Mother Goose, The (390) 3 - 6
(Nursery Rhymes), illus by Feodor Rojankovsky
©1957/p1960(D), 24pp. D: earliest (and only)
printing at this number. (See also: GD5070,
LE2830, LE4720)

LE3910   Dogs (391)   4 - 9
by Nita Jonas, illus by Tibor Gergely
©1952/p1960(E), 24pp. Earliest printing
at this number. (See also: LE1310, LE2600,
LE5320)

LE3920   Hymns (392)   2 - 5
by Elsa Jane Werner, illus by Corinne Malvern
©1947/p1960(I), 24pp. I: earliest printing
at this number. Inside title: *The Little Golden
Book of Hymns*. (See also: LE0340)

LE3930   Happy Little Whale, The (393)   3 - 10
by Jane Werner Watson, as told by Kenneth
Norris, illus by Tibor Gergely
©1960, 24pp

LE3940   Wild Animals (394)   3 - 7
written & illus by Feodor Rojankovsky

LE3880   LE3890

LE3900   LE3910

©1960, 24pp (See also: LE4990)

LE3950 **Yogi Bear** (395)   5 - 12
by S. Quentin Hyatt,
illus by M. Kawaguchi & Bob Barritt
©1960 by Hanna-Barbera Productions,
Inc., 24pp

LE3960 **Animal Quiz** (396)   3 - 8
by Nancy Fielding Hulick, illus by Mel Crawford
©1960, 24pp

No book published in 1960 (397)

LE3980 **Quick Draw McGraw** (398)   5 - 10
by Carl Memling,
illus by Hawley Pratt & Al White
©1960 by Hanna-Barbera Productions,
Inc., 24pp

LE3990 **Doctor Dan at the Circus** (399) 12 - 25
by Pauline Wilkins, illus by Katherine Sampson
©1960, 24pp. W/2 circus-design Band-Aids.

LE3991 Same as LE3990, lacking Band-Aids 4 - 10

LE4000 **Old MacDonald Had a Farm** (400) 2 - 8
(Nursery Song), illus by Moritz Kennel
©1960, 24pp

No book published in 1960 (401, 402)

LG4030 **Huckleberry Hound and the
Christmas Sleigh** (403)   4 - 10
by Pat Cherr, illus by Charles Satterfield
©1960 by Hanna-Barbera Productions,
Inc., 24pp

LE4035 Same as LE4030, ©1960/p1964(E) 3 - 7
Yellow cover background & Christmas spine

LE4040 **Baby Looks** (404)   8 - 14
by Esther Wilkin, illus by Eloise Wilkin
©1960, 24pp.

LE4050 **Four Puppies** (405)   5 - 10
by Anne Heathers, illus by Lilian Obligado
©1960, 24pp

LE4060 **Huckleberry Hound and His Friends** (406) 4 - 10
by Pat Cherr,
illus by Ben De Nunez & Bob Totten
©1960 by Hanna-Barbera Productions,
Inc., 24pp

LE4070 **Day on the Farm, A** (407)   4 - 9
by Nancy Fielding Hulick, illus by J.P. Miller

LE3960   LE3980

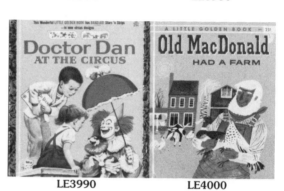

LE3990   LE4000

LE4030   LE4035

LE4040   LE4050

LE3920   LE3930

LE3940   LE3950

LE4060   LE4070

LE4080   LE4082

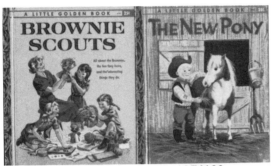

LE4090   LE4100

LE4110   LE4120

LE4130   LE4140

LE4150   LE4170

©1960, 24pp

LE4080 **Rocky and His Friends** (408)   5 - 12
by Ann McGovern,
illus by Ben De Nunez & Al White
©1960 by P.A.T. Ward Productions Inc., 24pp

LE4082 Same as LE4080 ©1973(B)   3 - 7
New cover art, copyright date changed.
Contents unchanged.

LE4090 **Brownie Scouts** (409)   5 - 9
by Lillian Gardner Soskin, illus by Louise Rumely
©1961, 24pp

LE4100 **New Pony, The** (410)   5 - 10
by Blanche Chenery Perrin,
illus by Dagmar Wilson
©1961, 24pp

LE4110 **Sly Little Bear and Other Bears** (411)   4 - 9
by Kathryn Jackson, illus by Scott Johnston
©1960, 24pp

LE4120 **Dennis the Menace/Quiet Afternoon** (412) 5 - 10
by Carl Memling, illus by Lee Holley
©1960 by Hall Syndicate, Inc., 24pp.
Based on the Hank Ketcham character.

LE4130 **Chicken Little** (413)   2 - 6
by Vivienne Benstead, illus by Richard Scarry
©1960, 24pp.

LE4131 Same as LE4130, ©1960/p1963(D), 24pp   1 - 3
Cover design changed to plain green back-
ground

LE4140 **Little Cottontail** (414)   4 - 9
by Carl Memling, illus by Lilian Obligado
©1960, 24pp

LE4150 **Lassie Shows the Way** (415)   4 - 9
by Monica Hill, illus by Lee Ames
©1956/p1960(D), 24pp. D: earliest printing
at this number. (See also: GD5120, LE2550)
No book published in 1960 (416)

LE4170 **Loopy de Loop Goes West** (417)   5 - 10
by Kathryn Hitte, illus by George Santos
©1960 by Hanna-Barbera Productions,
Inc., 24pp

LE4180 **My Dolly and Me** (418)   8 - 12
by Patricia Scarry , illus by Eloise Wilkin
©1960, 24pp

LE4190 **Rupert the Rhinoceros** (419)   4 - 10
by Carl Memling, illus by Tibor Gergely
©1960, 24pp

LE4200 **Jack and the Beanstalk** (420)   3 - 7
(Folk Tale), illus by Gustaf Tenggren
©1956/p1960(A), 24pp (See also: LE1790,
LE2810)

LE4210 **Captain Kangaroo and the Panda** (421)   4 - 8
by Kathleen N. Daly, illus by Edwin Schmidt
©1957/p1960(D?) by Keeshan-Miller
Enterprises Corp., 24pp. Earliest printing at
this number not determined. (See also:
GD5210, LE2780)

LE4180   LE4190

LE4220 **Baby's Mother Goose/Pat-a-Cake** (422)   4 - 8
(Nursery Rhyme), illus by Aurelius Battaglia
©1948/p1960(D), 24pp. D: earliest printing
at this number. (See also: LE0540, LE3030)

LE4230 **Smokey Bear and the Campers** (423)   5 - 12
by S. Quentin Hyatt, illus by Mel Crawford
©1961, 24pp

LE4240 **My Little Golden Book of Jokes** (424)   4 - 9
by George Wolfson, illus by Tibor Gergely
©1961, 24pp. Inside title: *Jokes.*

LE4250 **I'm an Indian Today** (425)   3 - 8
by Kathryn Hitte, illus by William J. Dugan
©1961, 24pp

LE4260 **Country Mouse and the City Mouse** (426)   2 - 9
by Patricia Scarry, illus by Richard Scarry
©1961, 24pp (3 Aesop Fables)

LE4270 **Captain Kangaroo and the Beaver** (427)   5 - 10
by Carl Memling, illus by Marie Nonnast
©1961 by Robert Keeshan Assoc., Inc., 24pp

LE4280 **Home for a Bunny** (428)   4 - 9
by Margaret Wise Brown, illus by Garth Williams
©1961, 24pp (See also: BB2670)

LE4290 **Farmyard Friends** (429)   3 - 9
written & illus by William P. Gottlieb (photos)
©1956/p1961(B), 24pp. B: earliest printing
at this number (See also: LE2720)

LE4300 **Bugs Bunny and the Indians** (430)   3 - 7
by Annie North Bedford, illus by Warner Bros.
Cartoons, adp by Dick Kelsey & Tom McKimson
©1951/p1961(D) by Warner Bros. Cartoons,
Inc., 24pp. D: earliest printing at this number
(See also: LE1200)

LE4310 **National Velvet** (431)   4 - 9
by Kathryn Hitte, illus by Mel Crawford
©1961 by MGM, Inc., 24pp. Based on
the NBC TV program.

LE4320 **Dennis the Menace Waits for Santa
Claus** (432)   5 - 12
by Carl Memling, illus by Al Weisman
©1961 by Hall Syndicate, Inc., 24pp

LE4330 **Yogi Bear/A Christmas Visit** (433)   5 - 10
by S. Quentin Hyatt,

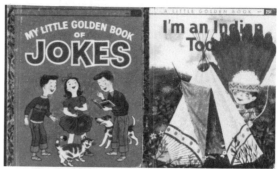

LE4240   LE4250

LE4260   LE4270

LE4280   LE4290

LE4300   LE4310

LE4200   LE4210

LE4320   LE4330

LE4220   LE4230

LE4340   LE4350

LE4360   LE4370

LE4390   LE4400

LE4410   LE4420

illus by Sylvia & Burnett Mattinson
©1961 by Hanna-Barbera Productions,
Inc., 24pp (See also: BB5030)

LE4335 Same as LE4330, ©1961/p1963(E), 24pp   2 - 6
Cover art changed to plain background in blue,
Christmas spine.

LE4340 **My First Counting Book** (434)   3 - 7
by Lilian Moore, illus by Garth Williams
©1957/p1961(A), 24pp (See also: BB3040)

LE4350 **When You Were a Baby** (435)   3 - 9
by Rita Eng, illus by Corinne Malvern
©1949/p1961(E), 24pp (See also: LE0700)

LE4360 **Color Kittens, The** (436)   3 - 8
by Margaret Wise Brown,
illus by Alice & Martin Provensen
©1949/p1961(C), 24pp. C: earliest printing
at this number. New cover design. (See also:
BB1500, LE0860)

LE4370 **Gingerbread Man, The** (437)   4 - 10
by Nancy Nolte, illus by Richard Scarry
©1961(A), 24pp. New cover art. (See also:
LE1650)

No book published in 1961 (438)

LE4390 **Make Way for the Thruway** (439)   5 - 10
by Caroline Emerson, illus by Tibor Gergely
©1961, 24pp (See also: LG0260)

LE4400 **Bobby the Dog** (440)   6 - 12
written & illus by Pierre Probst
©1954 by Librairie Hachette; ©1961
by Golden Press, 24pp

LE4410 **Bunny's Magic Tricks** (441)   6 - 12
by Janet & Alex D'Amato,
illus by Judy & Barry Martin
©1962, 24pp. Fold-over page tricks.

LE4420 **Cindy Bear/featuring Yogi Bear** (442) 8 - 12
by Jean Klinordlinger,
illus by Harvey Eisenberg & Milli Jancar
©1961 by Hanna-Barbera Productions,
Inc., 24pp

LE4430 **Puff the Blue Kitten** (443)   9 - 15
written & illus by Pierre Probst
©1952 by Librairie Hachette, ©1961 by
Golden Press, 24pp

LE4440 **Hokey Wolf and Ding-A-Ling** (444)   8 - 12
by S. Quentin Hyatt,
illus by Frans Van Lamsweerde
©1961 by Hanna-Barbera Productions,
Inc., 24pp

LE4450 **Woody Woodpecker Takes a Trip** (445)   4 - 9
by Ann McGovern,
illus by Al White & Ben De Nunez
©1961 by Walter Lantz Productions,
Inc., 24pp

LE4460 **Bozo the Clown** (446)   5 - 10
by Carl Buettner, illus by Charles Satterfield
©1961 by Capitol Records, Inc., 24pp

LE4430   LE4440

LE4450   LE4460

LE4470	**Good Night, Little Bear** (447)	4 - 9

by Patricia Scarry, illus by Richard Scarry
©1961, 24pp

LE4480	**My Teddy Bear** (448)	8 - 12

by Patricia Scarry, illus by Eloise Wilkin
©1953/p1961(I?), 24pp. Earlier printings
may have been made at this number. LE1680
runs through "E" at least.

LE4490	**Yakky Doodle and Chopper** (449)	8 - 14

by Pat Cherr,
illus by Al White & Hawley Pratt
©1962 by Hanna-Barbera Productions,
Inc., 24pp

LE4500	**Flintstones, The** (450)	6 - 12

written & illus by Mel Crawford
©1961 by Hanna-Barbera Productions, Inc.,
24pp

Night Before Christmas (450) Not issued at this number in
1961/1962. Book number is a transitional stocking code number, appearing on copies of LE0207 printed in 1982.

LE4510	**Ten Little Animals** (451)	3 - 8

by Carl Memling, illus by Feodor Rojankovsky
©1961, 24pp

LE4520	**Busy Timmy** (452)	5 - 10

by Kathryn & Byron Jackson,
illus by Eloise Wilkin
©1948/p1961(G), 24pp. G: earliest known
printing at this number. (See also: LE0500)

LE4530	**Top Cat** (453)	6 - 12

by Carl Memling,
illus by Hawley Pratt & Al White
©1962 by Barbera-Hanna Pictures, 24pp

Sticks (453) Not published

1962: Price change to 29¢. Begins with book #453,
becomes standard with #471. Lots of books in this time period
are over stamped in gold with the new price.

LE4540	**Pixie and Dixie and Mr. Jinks** (454)	8 - 14

written by Carl Buettner, illus by Carl Buettner
and Sylvia & Burnett Mattinson
©1961 by Hanna-Barbera Productions, Inc.,
24pp. Three figures to cut out and assemble.

LE4541	Same as LE4540, lacking cut-out figures	5 - 10
LE4550	**Machines** (455)	4 - 9

written & illus by William J. Dugan
©1961, 24pp

LE4560	**Golden Egg Book, The** (456)	5 - 10

by Margaret Wise Brown,
illus by Lilian Obligado
©1962, 24pp. Cover shown, 1st edition only.
All illustrations different than BB2310.

LE4565	Same as LE4560, ©1962/p1963(B)	2 - 6

Cover art changed to plain red background.

LE4570	**Littlest Raccoon** (457)	4 - 9

by Peggy Parish, illus by Claude Humbert
©1961, 24pp

LE4580	**Huckleberry Hound/Safety Signs** (458)	7 - 12

LE4470   LE4480

LE4490   LE4500

LE4510   LE4520

LE4530   LE4540

LE4550   LE4560

LE4570   LE4580

LE4590   LE4600

LE4610   LE4620

LE4630   LE4640

LE4650   LE4660

LE4670   LE4680

by Ann McGovern, illus by Al White
©1961 by Hanna-Barbera Productions,
Inc., 24pp. Published in cooperation with
the National Safety Council.

LE4590	**Horses** (459)	4 - 9
	by Blanche Chenery Perrin, illus by Hamilton Greene ©1962, 24pp	
LE4600	**My Little Golden Book of Manners** (460)	3 - 7
	by Peggy Parish, illus by Richard Scarry ©1962, 24pp. First editions can be found priced at both 25¢ and 29¢.	
LE4610	**Pick Up Sticks** (461)	6 - 12
	by Pauline Wilkins, illus by Piet Pfloog ©1962, 24pp	
LE4620	**Bullwinkle** (462)	6 - 12
	by David Corwyn, illus by Hawley Pratt & Harry Garo ©1962 by P.A.T. Ward Productions Inc., 24pp	
LE4630	**Wait-for-Me Kitten, The** (463)	5 - 10
	by Patricia Scarry, illus by Lilian Obligado ©1962, 24pp	
LE4640	**Baby Farm Animals** (464)	2 - 6
	written & illus by Garth Williams ©1958/1962(D), 24pp (See also: BB1110, LE0330)	
LE4650	**My Little Golden Animal Book** (465)	5 - 10
	by Elizabeth MacPherson, illus by Moritz Kennel ©1962, 24pp	
LE4660	**Baby Dear™** (466)	8 - 14
	by Esther Wilkin, illus by Eloise Wilkin ©1962, 24pp. "Baby Dear" is a doll designed by Eloise Wilkin and manufactured by Vogue Dolls, Inc. (See color plate)	
LE4670	**Where is the Poky Little Puppy?** (467)	5 - 10
	by Janette Sebring Lowrey, illus by Gustaf Tenggren ©1962, 24pp	
LE4680	**We Help Daddy** (468)	4 - 12
	by Mini Stein, illus by Eloise Wilkin ©1962, 24pp	
LE4690	**My Puppy** (469)	6 - 10
	by Patricia Scarry, illus by Eloise Wilkin ©1955/p1962(D), 24pp. D: earliest printing at this number. (See also: LE2330)	
LE4700	**Heidi** (470)	2 - 6
	illus by Corinne Malvern ©1954/p1962(G), 24pp. G: earliest printing at this number. Adapted from the story by Johanna Spyri. (See also: LE1920, LE2580)	
LE4710	**Tommy's Camping Adventure** (471)	4 - 10
	by Gladys R. Saxon, illus by Mel Crawford ©1962, 24pp	
LE4720	**Little Golden Mother Goose, The** (472)	3 - 6

LE4690   LE4700

(Nursery Rhyme), illus by Feodor Rojankovsky
©1957/p1962(F), 24pp. F: earliest printing
at this number. (See also: LE2830, LE3900)

LE4730 **Nurse Nancy** (473) 12 - 25
by Kathryn Jackson, illus by Corinne Malvern
©1958/p1962(D), 24pp. D: earliest printing
at this number. Came w/Band-Aids.
(See also: LE1540, LE3460)

LE4731 Same as LE4730, lacking Band-Aids 4 - 10

LE4740 **Touché Turtle** (474) 8 - 14
by Carl Memling, illus by Al White, Norm
McGary & Bill Lorencz
©1962 by Hanna-Barbera Productions,
Inc., 24pp

LE4750 **Bugs Bunny** (475) 3 - 7
written & illus by Warner Bros. Cartoons,
adp by Tom McKimson & Al Dempster
©1949/p1962(K), 24pp. K: earliest printing
at this number. (See also: LE0720, LE3120)

LE4760 **Little Lulu, Marge's** (476) 8 - 14
by Gina Ingoglia Weiner,
illus by Woody Kimbrell & Al White
©1962 by Marjorie Henderson Buell, 24pp

LE4770 **Ruff and Reddy** (477) 5 - 10
by Ann McGovern,
illus by Harvey Eisenberg & Al White
©1959/p1962(C) by Hanna-Barbera Productions, Inc., 24pp. Earliest printing at this
number not determined. (See also: LE3780)

LE4780 **Christmas ABC, The** (478) 8 - 14
by Florence Johnson, illus by Eloise Wilkin
©1962, 24pp

LE4790 **Rusty Goes to School** (479) 6 - 12
written & illus by Pierre Probst,
trans by Ann Weingarden
©1955 by Librairie Hachette, ©1962 by
Golden Press, 24pp

LE4800 **Tommy Visits the Doctor** (480) 4 - 9
by Jean H. Seligmann & Milton I.
Levin, M.D.; illus by Richard Scarry
©1969, 24pp

LE4810 **Smokey the Bear** (481) 3 - 9
by Jane Werner, illus by Richard Scarry
©1955/p1962(F), 24pp. F: earliest printing
at this number.

LE4815 Same as LE4810, ©1955/p1963(G) 2 - 6
Cover background changed to yellow.

LE4820 **Big Little Book, The** (482) 4 - 9
by Dorothy Hall Smith, illus by Moritz Kennel
©1962, 24pp

LE4830 **Mister Ed/The Talking Horse** (483) 7 - 14
by Barbara Shook Hazen, illus by Mel Crawford
©1962 by The Mr. Ed Company, 24pp

LE4840 **Play Street** (484) 8 - 14
by Esther Wilkin, illus by Joan Esley
©1962, 24pp

LE4730   LE4740

LE4750   LE4760

LE4770   LE4780

LE4790   LE4800

LE4710   LE4720

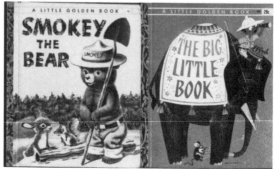

LE4810   LE4820

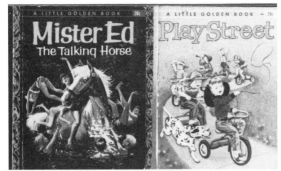

LE4830   LE4840

LE4850   LE4860

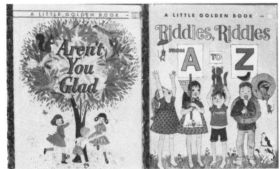

LE4870   LE4880

LE4890   LE4900

LE4930   LE4935

LE4850	**Bozo Finds a Friend** (485) by Tom Golberg, illus by Hawley Pratt & Al White ©1962 by Capitol Records, Inc. & Larry Harmon Pictures, Inc., 24pp	5 - 10
LE4860	**Corky** (486) by Patricia Scarry, illus by Irma Wilde ©1962, 24pp	4 - 10
LE4870	**Golden Goose, The** (487) by Jacob & Wilhelm Grimm, illus by Gustaf Tenggren ©1954/p1962(B), 24pp. B: earliest printing at this number (See also: LE2000)	6 - 10
LE4880	**Gay Purr-ee** (488) by Carl Memling; illus by Hawley Pratt, Harland Young & Herb Fillmore ©1962 by UPA Pictures, Inc., 24pp. Based on the UPA film. (See also: BB1900)	5 - 12
LE4890	**Aren't You Glad?** (489) by Charlotte Zolotow, illus by Elaine Kurtz ©1962, 24pp	3 - 8
LE4900	**Riddles, Riddles/From A to Z** (490) by Carl Memling, illus by Trina Schart ©1962, 24pp	4 - 10
LE4910	**Hansel and Gretel** (491) by Jacob & Wilhelm Grimm, illus by Eloise Wilkin ©1954/p1962(J), 24pp. J: earliest printing at this number. (See also: LE2170)	3 - 8
LE4920	**Supercar** (492) by George Sherman, illus by Mel Crawford ©1962 by Independent Television Corp., 24pp	9 - 18
LE4930	**Child's Garden of Verses, A** (493) by Robert Louis Stevenson, illus by Eloise Wilkin ©1962(B), 24pp. Earliest printing at this number. (See also: LE2890)	6 - 14
LE4935	Same as LE4930, ©1957/p1969(E) Reissued w/original cover art. (See also: LE2890)	1 - 6
LE4940	**Shy Little Kitten, The** (494)	2 - 7

LE4910   LE4920

LE4940   LE4942

by Cathleen Schurr, illus by Gustaf Tenggren
©1946/p1962(C), 24pp. C: earliest printing
at this number. (See also: LE0230, LE2480)

LE4942 Same as LE4940, ©1946/p1965(D), 24pp   1 - 5
First printing thus, w/cover design as shown.
Contents unchanged.

LE4950 **I Have a Secret/First Counting Book** (495) 5 - 12
by Carl Memling, illus by Joseph Giordano
©1962, 24pp

LE4960 **Colors are Nice** (496)   2 - 6
by Adelaide Holl, illus by Leonard Shortall
©1962, 24pp

LE4970 **Dick Tracy** (497)   8 - 16
by Carl Memling,
illus by Hawley Pratt & Al White
©1962 by Chicago Tribune-New York
News Syndicate Inc., 24pp

LE4980 **Rumpelstiltskin and the Princess and
the Pea** (498)   3 - 9
by Jacob & Wilhelm Grimm and Hans Christian
Andersen, illus by William J. Dugan
©1962(A), 24pp. Previously titled: *The Red
Little Golden Book of Fairy Tales* (LE3060).
New cover illustration, contents unchanged.

LE4990 **Wild Animals** (499)   1 - 5
written & illus by Feodor Rojankovsky
©1960/p1962(B), 24pp. B: earliest printing
at this number. (See also: LE3940)

LE5000 **Jetsons, The** (500)   10 - 20
by Carl Memling,
illus by Hawley Pratt & Al White
©1962 by Hanna-Barbera Productions,
Inc., 24pp

LE5010 **Boats** (501)   3 - 8
by Ruth Mabee Lachman,
illus by Lenora & Herbert Combes
©1951/p1962(E), 24pp. E: earliest printing
at this number. (See also: LE1250, LE3390)

LE5020 **Wally Gator** (502)   8 - 14
by Tom Golberg,
illus by Hawley Pratt & Bill Lorencz
©1963 by Hanna-Barbera Productions,
Inc., 24pp

No book published in 1963 (503)

LE5040 **Seven Little Postmen** (504)   3 - 9
by Margaret Wise Brown & Edith Thacher
Hurd, illus by Tibor Gergely
©1952/p1963(C), 24pp. C: earliest printing
at this number. (See also: LE1340)

LE5050 **Peter Rabbit** (505)   3 - 8
by Beatrix Potter, illus by Adriana Mazza Saviozzi
©1958/p1963(C), 24pp. C: earliest printing
at this number. Cover background changed to
yellow. Inside title: *The Tale of Peter Rabbit*.
(See also: LE3130, LG0830)

LE5052 Same as LE5050, ©1958/p1968(E), 24pp 2 - 6

LE4950   LE4960

LE4970   LE4980

LE4990   LE5000

LE5010   LE5020

LE5040   LE5050

LE5052   LE5054

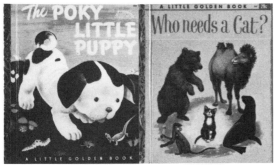

| LE5060 | LE5070 |

| LE5080 | LE5090 |

| LE5110 | LE5115 |

| LE5120 | LE5140 |

| LE5160 | LE5170 |

E: New cover illustration, contents unchanged.

LE5054   Same as LE5050, ©1970(F), 24pp   1 - 5
F: New cover, as shown. New copyright date.

LE5060   **Poky Little Puppy, The** (506)   2 - 6
by Janette Sebring Lowrey,
illus by Gustaf Tenggren
©1942/p1962(C?), 24pp. Earliest printing
at this number not determined. (See also:
BB3330, LE0080, LE2710)

LE5070   **Who Needs a Cat?** (507)   3 - 9
by Clara Cassidy, illus by Audean Johnson
©1963, 24pp

LE5080   **Lippy the Lion and Hardy Har Har** (508)   5 - 12
by Gina Ingoglia Weiner,
illus by Hawley Pratt & Norm McGary
©1963 by Hanna-Barbera Productions,
Inc., 24pp

LE5090   **What Am I?** (509)   3 - 8
by Ruth Leon, illus by Cornelius DeWitt
©1949/p1963(G), 24pp. G: earliest printing
at this number. (See also: LE0580)

No book published in 1963 (510)

LE5110   **Visit to the Children's Zoo, A** (511)   4 - 9
by Barbara Shook Hazen, illus by Mel Crawford
©1963, 24pp. Based on the Children's
Zoo in Central Park, NYC.

LE5115   Same as LE5110, ©1963/p1969(C), 24pp   2 - 6
Cover variation w/yellow background.

LE5120   **Chipmunk's ABC** (512)   3 - 7
by Roberta Miller, illus by Richard Scarry
©1963, 24pp

Baby Sister (513) Title noted, but no copy available for verification. Probably not published at this number (See LE3400)

LE5140   **Thumbelina** (514)   3 - 7
by Hans Christian Andersen,
illus by Gustaf Tenggren
©1953/p1963(B), 24pp. B: earliest printing at
this number. New cover art. (See also: LE1530)

Lisa and the Eleven Swans (515) Not published

LE5160   **Cow Went Over the Mountain, The** (516)   3 - 8
by Jeanette Krinsley, illus by Feodor Rojankovsky
©1963, 24pp

LE5170   **Baby Animals** (517)   2 - 6
written & illus by Garth Williams
©1956/P1963(H), 24pp. H: earliest printing
at this number. (See also: BB1080, LE2740)

LE5180   **Lassie and Her Day in the Sun** (518)   3 - 7
by Charles Spain Verral, illus by Mel Crawford
©1958/p1963(D) by Lassie Programs, Inc.,
24pp. D: earliest printing at this number.
(See also: LE3070)

LE5190   **Little Red Hen, The** (519)   2 - 6
(Folk Tale), illus by J.P. Miller, cover art by
Rudolf Freund
©1954/p1963(H), 24pp. H: earliest printing
at this number. (See also: LE2090, LE2960)

| *Ad Back* | LE5180 |

LE5195   Same as LE5190, ©1954/p1977(Q), 24pp   1 - 4
       Reissued w/ cover by J.P. Miller. (See also:
       LE2090).

LE5200   **Happy Man and His Dump Truck** (520)   5 - 10
       by Miryam, illus by Tibor Gergely
       ©1950/p1963(D), 24pp. Earliest printing at
       this number not determined. (See also:
       LE0770)

LE5210   **Fun for Hunkydory** (521)   5 - 12
       by May Justus, illus by Sue d'Avignon
       ©1963, 24pp

LE5220   **Jamie Looks** (522)   5 - 10
       by Adelaide Holl, illus by Eloise Wilkin
       ©1963, 24pp

LE5230   **Bow Wow! Meow! A First Book of**
       Sounds (523)   3 - 10
       by Melanie Bellah, illus by Trina Schart
       ©1963, 24pp. (See also: LG1560)

LE5231   Same as LE5230, ©1963/p1970(D), 24pp   2 - 4
       Type style of title changed.
   No book printed 1963 (524)

LE5250   **My Word Book** (525)   3 - 7
       by Roberta Miller, illus by Claude Humbert
       ©1963, 24pp

LE5260   **Twelve Days of Christmas, The** (526)   5 - 10
       (Christmas Carol), illus by Tony De Luna
       ©1963, 24pp. 1st edition has Christmas spine.

1963-64 Christmas spine. A red spine with silver bells was
used on Christmas books in 1963 and 1964.

LE5270   **Romper Room Exercise Book** (527)   3 - 8
       by Nancy Claster, illus by Sergio Leone
       ©1964 by Romper Room, Inc., 24pp

LE5280   **My Kitten** (528)   6 - 10
       by Patricia Scarry, illus by Eloise Wilkin
       ©1953/p1963(D?), 24pp. Earliest printing
       at this number not determined. (See also:
       LE1630, LE3000)

LE5290   **Nursery Rhymes** (529)   3 - 9
       (Nursery Rhymes), illus by Corinne Malvern
       ©1947/p1963(A), 24pp. A combination
       of LE0070 (*Nursery Songs*) and LE0400
       (*Singing Games*).

LE5300   **Four Little Kittens** (530)   4 - 9
       by Kathleen N. Daly,
       illus by Adriana Mazza Saviozzi
       ©1957/p1963(D?), 24pp. Earliest printing
       at this number not determined. (See also:
       GG2100, LE3220)

LE5310   **Pebbles Flintstone** (531)   7 - 15
       by Jean Lewis, illus by Mel Crawford
       ©1963 by Hanna-Barbera Productions,
       Inc., 24pp

LE5320   **Dogs** (532)   2 - 7
       by Nita Jonas, illus by Tibor Gergely
       ©1952/p1963(F), 24pp. F: earliest printing
       at this number. Cover background changed

LE5190   LE5195

LE5200   LE5210

LE5220   LE5230

LE5250   LE5260

LE5270   LE5280

LE5290   LE5300

LE5310   LE5320

LE5330   LE5340

LE5370   LE5380

LE5390   LE5400

LE5410   LE5420

to beige. (See also: LE1310, LE2600, LE3910)

1963: "A Little Golden Book" was changed to script wording on front cover. Price and number still carried on cover with number often moved to left side at top.

LE5330 **Animal Dictionary** (533)   2 - 6
by Jane Werner Watson,
illus by Feodor Rojankovsky
©1960/p1963(B), 24pp. B: earliest printing
at this number. (See also: LE3790)

LE5340 **First Golden Geography** (534)   3 - 8
by Jane Werner Watson, illus by William Sayles
©1955/p1963(B), 24pp. B: earliest printing
at this number. New title. Formerly titled:
Our World (LE2420)

Dennis the Menace and Ruff (535) Not Published at this number (See: LE3860)

No book published in 1963 (536)

LE5370 **Beany Goes to Sea** (537)   6 - 14
by Monica Hill,
illus by Hawley Pratt & Bill Lorencz
©1963 by Robert E. (Bob) Clampett,
24pp. A "Beany and Cecil" story.

LE5380 **Bedtime Stories** (538)   3 - 7
(Nursery Rhymes), illus by Gustaf Tenggren
©1942/p1963(H), 24pp. H: earliest printing
at this number. Cover art same as original
edition, LE0020. (See also: LE2390, LE3640)

LE5390 **Cave Kids** (539)   5 - 10
by Bruce R. Carrick, illus by Mel Crawford
©1963 by Hanna-Barbera Productions, Inc.,
24pp. Not a part of the "Flintstones" series,
but often collected as a "go with".

LE5400 **Bamm-Bamm with Pebbles Flintstone** (540) 7 - 15
by Jean Lewis,
illus by Hawley Pratt & Norm McGary
©1963 by Hanna-Barbera Productions,
Inc., 24pp

LE5410 **New Baby, The** (541)   3 - 7
by Ruth & Harold Shane, illus by Eloise Wilkin
©1948/p1964(O), 24pp. O: earliest printing
at this number. (See also: LE0410, LE2910)

LE5420 **Hey There– It's Yogi Bear!** (542)   6 - 12
by Carl Memling,
illus by Hawley Pratt & Al White
©1964 by Hanna-Barbera Productions,
Inc., 24pp

1964: End papers redesigned to include new script "LGB" and printed in one color. Several colors were experimented with until the sepia tone which is still used today became standard. (NOTE: Books #546–549 have end papers same style as used in 1947. A possible explanation is that some old preprintd stock was found and used.)

LE5430 **ABC Rhymes** (543)   2 - 6
by Carl Memling,
illus by Roland Rodegast & Grace Clarke
©1964, 24pp

1964: End papers redesigned

LE5435   Same as LE5430, ©1970, 24pp   1 - 4
          Reissued w/new cover art. Contents un-
          changed. Book shown is 1977 printing.
No book published in 1964 (544, 545)
LE5460   **Fireball XL5** (546)   8 - 20
          by Barbara Shook Hazen,
          illus by Hawley Pratt & Al White
          ©1964 by Independent Television Corp.,
          24pp
LE5470   **Magilla Gorilla** (547)   5 - 10
          by Bruce R. Carrick,
          illus by Hawley Pratt & Al White
          ©1964 by Hanna-Barbera Productions,
          Inc., 24pp
LE5480   **Little Engine That Could, The** (548)   3 - 8
          by Watty Piper (retold),
          illus by George & Doris Hauman
          ©1954/p1964(A) by Platt & Munk Co.,
          24pp. First LGB printing.
LE5490   **Tarzan** (549)   8 - 12
          by Gina Ingoglia Weiner, illus by Mel Crawford
          ©1964 by Edgar Rice Burroughs, Inc., 24pp
LE5500   **Good Humor Man, The** (550)   12 - 40
          by Kathleen N. Daly, illus by Tibor Gergely
          ©1964, 24pp
LE5510   **Lively Little Rabbit, The** (551)   2 - 6
          by Ariane, illus by Gustaf Tenggren
          ©1943/p1964(P), 24pp. P: earliest printing
          at this number. (See also: LE0150)

1965: Character Frame used on back cover once more.
Two Hanna-Barbera characters have replaced Bongo and
Sleepy Bear.

   Over a billion Golden Books had been distributed world-wide,
and Western, which had become the sole owner of Golden
Books in 1964, was well established as the world's leading publisher of books for children.

LE5520   **We Like Kindergarten** (552)   3 - 10
          by Clara Cassidy, illus by Eloise Wilkin
          ©1965, 24pp
LE5530   **Jingle Bells** (553)   3 - 6
          by Kathleen N. Daly, illus by J.P. Miller
          ©1964, 24pp. Based on the carol.
          1st editions have Christmas spine.
LE5534   Same as LE5530, ©1964/p1972(C), 24pp   1 - 4
          New cover art.
LE5540   **Charmin' Chatty™** (554)   5 - 12
          by Barbara Shook Hazen,
          illus by Dagmar Wilson
          ©1964 by Mattel, Inc., 24pp. Story features
          the Mattel doll. (See color plate)
LE5550   **Pepper™ Plays Nurse** (555)   5 - 10
          by Gina Ingoglia Weiner, illus by John Fernie
          ©1964 by Ideal Toy Corp., 24pp. Pepper
          is a doll by Ideal.
LE5560   **Peter Potamus** (556)   6 - 12
          by Carl Memling,

LE5430   LE5435

LE5460   LE5470

LE5480   LE5490

LE5500   LE5510

1965: Back Cover   LE5520

LE5530   LE5534

LE5540   LE5550

LE5560   LE5570

LE5580   LE5590

LE5600   LE5610

LE5620   LE5630

illus by Hawley Pratt & Bill Lorencz
©1964 by Hanna-Barbera Productions,
Inc., 24pp

LE5570   **Fuzzy Duckling, The** (557)   2 - 6
by Jane Werner,
illus by Alice & Martin Provensen
©1949/p1964(F), 24pp. F: earliest printing
at this number. (See also: LE0780)

LE5580   **Hop, Little Kangaroo!** (558)   2 - 6
by Patricia Scarry, illus by Feodor Rojankovsky
©1965, 24pp

LE5590   **Betsy McCall** (559) (Paper Doll)   15 - 25
by Selma Robinson, illus by Ginnie Hofmann
©1965 by McCall Corp., 24pp. Betsy McCall
paper dolls were a regular *McCall's* magazine
feature. Her clothes were available in full-size
pattern for girls. A Betsy McCall doll was also
marketed. (See color plate)

LE5591   Same as LE5590, w/doll & all clothes, cut   15 - 20
LE5592   Same as LE5590, no doll or clothes   2 - 6
LE5600   **Animal Friends** (560)   3 - 9
by Jane Werner, illus by Garth Williams
©1953/p1965(?), 24pp. Printing not stated.
Cover type changed. (See also: LE1670,
LG0220)

LE5610   **Tom and Jerry** (561)   1 - 6
written & illus by MGM Cartoons, adp by
Don MacLaughlin & Harvey Eisenberg
©1951/p1965(E) by Loew's Inc., 24pp.
Cover background changed to red.
(See also: LE1170)

LE5620   **Good Little, Bad Little Girl** (562)   5 - 12
by Esther Wilkin, illus by Eloise Wilkin
©1965, 24pp

1965: Spine changed to the design presently in use, with
chickens, bears, flowers, et al.

LE5630   **Mr. Puffer Bill Train Engineer** (563)   5 - 10
by Leone Arlandson, illus by Tibor Gergely
©1965, 24pp

LE5640   **New Brother, New Sister** (564)   5 - 10
by Joan Fiedler, illus by Joan Esley
©1966, 24pp

LE5650   **Dragon in a Wagon, A** (565)   2 - 8
by Janette Rainwater,
illus by John Martin Gilbert
©1966, 24pp

No book published in 1967 (566)

LE5670   **Play With Me** (567)   5 - 10
by Esther Wilkin, illus by Eloise Wilkin
©1967, 24pp

LE5680   **Where Is the Bear?** (568)   2 - 7
by Betty Hubka, illus by Mel Crawford
©1967, 24pp (See also: LG0110)

LE5690   **Little Mommy** (569)   6 - 12
written & illus by Sharon Kane
©1967, 24pp

LE5640   LE5650

LE5700 **Things in My House** (570) 2 - 7
written & illus by Joe Kaufman
©1968, 24pp. (See also: LG1120)
No book published in 1968 (571, 572)
LE5730 **Animals on the Farm** (573) 2 - 6
written & illus by Jan Pfloog
©1968, 24pp

Colored spine: Some LGBs have been found with colored spines. These may have been bound on by the publisher to finish out a run or else were applied on the secondary market in lieu of a missing gold spine.
LE5740 **So Big** (574) 3 - 9
by Esther Wilkin, illus by Eloise Wilkin
©1968, 24pp
No book published in 1968 (575)
LE5760 **Animal Daddies and My Daddy** (576) 2 - 6
by Barbara Shook Hazen,
illus by Ilse-Margret Vogel
©1968, 24pp
LE5770 **Hush, Hush, It's Sleepytime** (577) 4 - 10
by Peggy Parish, illus by Mel Crawford
©1968, 24pp (See also: LG0510)
LE5780 **When I Grow Up** (578) 3 - 8
written & illus by Ilse-Margret Vogel
©1968, 24pp. Not same book as LE0960.
LE5790 **Ookpik The Arctic Owl** (579) 5 - 12
by Barbara Shook Hazen,
illus by Beverley Edwards
©1968 by H.M. the Queen in Right of
Canada, 24pp. Ookpik books and toys are
licensed by the Fort Chimo Co-operative
Association. (See also: GG1060)

1968: Price change to 39¢. A few 1968 books carry no price notation. By 1969 books are imprinted 39¢.
LE5800 **Sam the Firehouse Cat** (580) 4 - 9
written & illus by Virginia Parsons
©1968, 24pp
LE5810 **Chitty Chitty Bang Bang** (581) 5 - 10
by Jean Lewis (adp), illus by Gordon Laite
©1968 by Glidrose Productions, Ltd and
Warfield Productions, Ltd., 24pp. Unstated
1st. Based on the Ian Fleming story.
LE5820 **Wonderful School, The** (582) 2 - 6
by May Justus, illus by Hilde Hoffman
©1969, 24pp
LE5830 **Little Book, The** (583) 3 - 9
by Sherl Horvarth, illus by Eloise Wilkin
©1969, 24pp
LE5840 **Animal Counting Book** (584) 2 - 6
(Nursery Rhymes), illus by Moritz Kennel
©1969, 24pp. Adapted from the nursery
rhyme, "Over in the Meadow."
LE5850 **Raggedy Ann and Fido** (585) 3 - 8
by Barbara Shook Hazen,
illus by Rochelle Boonshaft

LE5690   LE5700

LE5730   LE5740

LE5760   LE5770

LE5780   LE5790

LE5670   LE5680

LE5800   LE5810

LE5820   LE5830

LE5840   LE5850

LE5860   LE5870

LE5880   LE5890

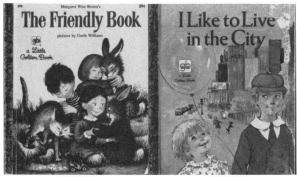

LE5920   LE5930

©1969 by Bobbs-Merrill Co., 24pp.
1st editions are marked "A" and do not have
"GB" logo. 2nd printings are unstated, but
book has "GB" logo on front.

LE5860	**Rags** (586)	2 -7
	by Patricia Scarry, illus by J.P. Miller	
	©1970, 24pp (See also: LG0780)	
LE5870	**Charlie** (587)	2 - 6
	by Diane Fox Downs, illus by Lilian Obligado	
	©1970, 24pp	
LE5880	**Boy With a Drum, The** (588)	4 - 10
	by David L. Harrison, illus by Eloise Wilkin	
	©1969, 24pp	
LE5890	**Mother Goose, Eloise Wilkin's** (589)	3 - 12
	(Nursery Rhymes), illus by Eloise Wilkin	
	©1961/p1970, 24pp. 1st printing stated	
	"1970 edition".	
LE5900	**Tiny Tawny Kitten** (590)	2 - 6
	by Barbara Shook Hazen, illus by Jan Pfloog	
	©1969, 24pp	
LE5910	**Old Mother Hubbard** (591)	2 - 6
	(Nursery Rhymes), illus by Aurelius Battaglia	
	©1970, 24pp	
LE5920	**Friendly Book, The** (592)	2 - 6
	by Margaret Wise Brown, illus by Garth Williams	
	©1954/p1970(A), 24pp. Book shown is	
	1972, 3rd printing thus. (See also: LG1160)	
LE5930	**I Like to Live in the City** (593)	3 - 8
	by Margaret Hillert, illus by Lilian Obligado	
	©1970, 24pp. Unstated 1st.	

1970: Cover change. A new Golden Book logo appeared on the back cover, surrounded by LGB characters. The first design, with a dark blue background, was short-lived. Redesigned, with a chartreuse background and a different arrangement of LGB characters, this back cover was used into 1971. "Children see a lot in Little Golden Books" proclaimed the design ... and the eyes in the logo, when used on the front cover, always "look" towards the LGB identification.

LE5940   **1–2–3 Juggle With Me/Counting Book** (594) 2 - 6
         written & illus by Ilse-Margret Vogel
         ©1970, 24pp

LE5900   LE5910

1970 Back Cover   LE5940

LE5950 **Christmas Carols** (595)   2 - 7
by Marjorie Wyckoff, illus by Corinne Malvern
©1946/p1969(Q), 24pp. Q: earliest printing
at this number. (See also: LE0260)

LE5955 Same as LE5950, ©1972(R), 24pp   1 - 3
R: earliest printing w/new cover art. Cover
artist not noted. New copyright date,
contents unchanged.

LE5960 **Jenny's New Brother** (596)   5 - 15
by Elaine Evans, illus by Joan Esley
©1970, 24pp.

No book published in 1970 (597)

LE5980 **Bozo and the Hide 'n' Seek Elephant** (598) 5 - 10
by William Johnston,
illus by Allan Hubbard & Milli Jancar
©1968/p1970(A) by Larry Harmon
Picture Corp., 24pp. First LGB printing.

LE5990 **Let's Visit the Dentist** (599)   3 - 10
by Patricia Scarry, illus by Dagmar Wilson
©1970, 24pp. Approved by the
American Dental Association.

No book published in 1970 (600)

LE5950   LE5955

LE5960   LE5980

LE5990   *1970: New Logo*

Little Golden Books – 2nd Series (1971-1978)

In 1971, the publishers began to reassign numbers to new titles, and also use numbers that had been "skipped" in the first series. (Some of these numbers had been assigned a title, but were never published. For example, #365 was assigned to *Animal Friends*, which was never printed at that number. The number wasn't used until it was published as *Baby's Birthday* in 1972.)

The listing is numerical and contains only new books published between 1971 and 1978. Many of the books from the first series continued in print, at their original numbers.

The book format is the same as that used in the end of the first series, with a back cover change in 1973. Books in this series with no edition information are first editions, later printings are always stated. All books are 24 pages.

1972: The "Sesame Street Bookmobile" appears on the back of some of the Sesame Street Books.

1973: Back cover design changes to a Little Golden train (pulled by Tootle) on a green background.

1976: Sesame Street characters join the LG Train party. This back cover design remained in effect until 1983.

LF1020 **Daisy Dog's Wake Up Book** (102)   2 - 6
written & illus by Ilse-Margret Vogel
©1974, 24pp

LF1030 **Fritzie Goes Home** (103)   2 - 6
by Kate Emery Pogue, illus by Sally Augustiny
©1974, 24pp

LF1040 **Just Watch Me! Funny Things to Be
and See** (104)   2 - 6
by Eileen Daly, illus by Frank Aloise
©1975, 24pp

LF1050 **Never Pat a Bear/A Book About Signs** (105) 2 - 6
by Mabel Watts, illus by Art Seiden
©1971, 24pp

LF1060 **Magic Next Door, The** (106)   3 - 9
by Evelyn Swetnam, illus by Judy Stang
©1971, 24pp

1972 Back   *1973 Back*

LF1020   LF1030

LF1040　　　　　　　LF1050

LF1060　　　　　　　LF1070

LF1080

LF1070	**Woodsy Owl and the Trail Bikers** (107)	1 - 4

by Kennon Graham, illus by Frank McSavage
©1974, 24pp. Woodsy Owl was the symbol
for the National Environmental Campaign.

LF1080	**ABC is for Christmas** (108)	1 - 5

by Jane Werner Watson, illus by Sally Augustiny
©1974, 24pp

LF1090	**Noah's Ark** (109)	2 - 8

by Barbara Shook Hazen, illus by Tibor Gergely
©1969/p1974, 24pp (See also: BB3250)

LF1100	**David and Goliath** (110)	1 - 4

by Barbara Shook Hazen, illus by Robert J. Lee
©1974, 24pp (See also: BB1600)

LF1110	**I Think About God/Two Stories About**	
	My Day (111)	1 - 5

by Sue Val & Norah Smaridge,
illus by Christiane Cassan & Trina Hyman
©1965/p1972, 24pp

LF1120	**Book of God's Gifts, A** (112)	1 - 4

by Mary Michaels White & Ruth Hannon,
illus by Idellette Bordigoni & Rick Schreter
©1972, 24pp

LF1130	**Little Crow** (113)	2 - 6

by Caroline McDermott, illus by Andy Aldrich
©1974, 24pp

LF1140	**Stories of Jesus** (114)	1 - 4

by Jean H. Richards, illus by Ati Forberg
©1974, 24pp

LF1150	**My Home** (115)	2 - 4

by Renee Bartowski, illus by Rosalind O. Fry
©1971, 24pp

LF1160	**Where Did the Baby Go?** (116)	2 - 8

by Sheila Hayes, illus by Eloise Wilkin
©1974, 24pp

LF1170	**Pano the Train** (117)	2 - 6

by Sharon Holaves, illus by Giannini
©1975, 24pp

LF1180	**Wizard of Oz, The** (119)	2 - 9

by Mary Carey (retold),
illus by Don Turner, Jason Studios
©1975, 24pp. Based on the story by

LF1100　　　　　　　LF1110

LF1120　　　　　　　LF1130

LF1140　　　　　　　LF1150

LF1160　　　　　　　LF1170

L. Frank Baum.

LF1200   **Oscar's Book** (120)   2 - 6
by Jeffrey Moss, illus by Michael Gross
©1975 by CTW & Muppets, Inc., 24pp

LF1210   **Santa's Surprise Book** (121)   1 - 5
by Joan Potter Elwart,
illus by Florence Sarah Winship
©1966/p1973, 24pp. Previously published
as a Whitman Big Tell-a-Tale.

LF1220   **Road Runner/A Very Scary Lesson** (122)   1 - 6
by Russell K. Schroeder,
illus by Phil DeLara & Bob Totten
©1974 by Warner Bros., Inc., 24pp

LF1230   **Remarkably Strong Pippi Longstocking** (123) 2 - 8
by Cecily Hogan (retold),
illus by Don Turner, Jason Studios
©1974 by G.G. Communications, Inc., 24pp
Based on the story by Astrid Lindgren.

LF1240   **Tom and Jerry's Photo Finish** (124)   3 - 10
by Jean Lewis, illus by Al Anderson
©1974 by MGM, Inc., 24pp. Soft cover
book shown. Hard cover printings do exist,
but are difficult to locate. See "LGB - Soft
Cover Books" section for more information
on soft cover printings.

LF1250   **Barbie** (125)   2 - 8
by Betty Biesterveld
©1974 by Mattel, Inc., 24pp. Book
depicts "American Girl" style Barbie.

LF1260   **Scooby-Doo and the Pirate Treasure** (126)   3 - 9
by Jean Lewis,
illus by William Lorencz & Michael Arens
©1974 by Hanna-Barbera Productions,
Inc., 24pp

LF1270   **Bugs Bunny and the Carrot Machine** (127)   2 - 8
by Clark Carlisle,
illus by Anthony Strobl & Bob Totten
©1971 by Warner Bros., Inc., 24pp

LF1280   **Twany Scrawny Lion and the Clever
Monkey, The** (128)   2 - 7
by Mary Carey, illus by Milli Jancar
©1974, 24pp

LF1290   **Bouncy Baby Bunny Finds His Bed** (129)   1 - 5
by Joan Bowden, illus by Christine Westerberg
©1974, 24pp

LF1300   **Poky Little Puppy Follows His Nose
Home, The** (130)   2 - 8
by Adelaide Holl, illus by Alex C. Miclat
©1975, 24pp

LF1310   **New Friends for the Saggy Baggy
Elephant** (131)   1 - 6
by Adelaide Holl,
illus by Jan Neely & Peter Alvarado
©1975, 24pp

LF1330   **Mister Rogers' Neighborhood/**

LF1190   LF1200

LF1210   LF1220

LF1230   LF1240

LF1250   LF1260

LF1270   LF1280

LF1290   LF1300

LF1310   LF1330

<table>
<tr><td></td><td>Henrietta Meets Someone New (133)</td><td>2 - 6</td></tr>
<tr><td></td><td>by Fred M. Rogers, illus by Jason Art Studios
©1974 by Small World Enterprises, Inc., 24pp</td><td></td></tr>
<tr><td>LF1340</td><td>Waltons and the Birthday Present, The (134)
by Jane Godfrey
©1975 by Lorimar Prod., Inc., 24pp</td><td>1 - 6</td></tr>
<tr><td>LF1350</td><td>Underdog and the Disappearing Ice Cream (135)
by Mary Ann Forn, illus by Jason Art Studios
©1975 by T.T.V. & Leonardo Television
Prods, Inc., 24pp</td><td>2 - 7</td></tr>
<tr><td>LF1360</td><td>Land of the Lost/The Surprise Guests (136)
by Kennon Graham, illus by Fred Irvin
©1975 by Sid and Marty Krofft Television
Productions, Inc., 24pp</td><td>2 - 7</td></tr>
<tr><td>LF1370</td><td>Magic Friend-Maker, The (137)
by Gladys Baker Bond, illus by Stina Nagel
©1966/p1975, 24pp</td><td>3 - 10</td></tr>
<tr><td>LF1390</td><td>Raggedy Ann and Andy/The Little Gray Kitten (139)
by Polly Curren, illus by June Goldsborough
©1975 by The Bobbs-Merrill Co., Inc., 24pp</td><td>1 - 5</td></tr>
<tr><td>LF1400</td><td>Pink Panther in the Haunted House (140)
by Kennon Graham,
illus by Darrell Baker, Jason Studios
©1975 by Mirisch-Geoffrey DFE, 24pp</td><td>2 - 6</td></tr>
<tr><td>LF1410</td><td>Tweety Plays Catch the Puddy Tat (141)
by Eileen Daly,
illus by Peter Alvarado & William Lorencz
©1975 by Warner Bros., Inc., 24pp</td><td>2 - 6</td></tr>
<tr><td>LF1430</td><td>Runaway Squash, The (143)
by Gale Wiersum (retold), illus by Bunky
©1976 by Alphaventure, 24pp. Adapted from
"The Big Blue Marble." (The first International
Children's Communication Network.)</td><td>1 - 5</td></tr>
<tr><td>LF1440</td><td>My Christmas Treasury (144)
by Gale Wiersum, illus by Sylvia Emrich
©1976, 24pp</td><td>1 - 5</td></tr>
<tr><td>LF1450</td><td>Bugs Bunny/Too Many Carrots (145)
by Jean Lewis,
illus by Peter Alvarado & Bob Totten
©1976 by Warner Bros., Inc., 24pp</td><td>2 - 6</td></tr>
<tr><td>LF1460</td><td>Porky Pig and Bugs Bunny/Just Like Magic (146)
by Stella Williams Nathan,
illus by Bob Totten & Tom McKimson
©1976 by Warner Bros., Inc., 24pp</td><td>2 - 6</td></tr>
<tr><td>LF1470</td><td>Where Jesus Lived (147)
by Jane Werner Watson, illus by Ronald LeHew
©1977, 24pp</td><td>1 - 4</td></tr>
<tr><td>LF1480</td><td>Ginghams: The Backward Picnic, The (148)
by Joan Chase Bowden,
illus by JoAnne E. Koenig, Creative Studios I, Inc.
©1976, 24pp</td><td>2 - 7</td></tr>
<tr><td>LF1490</td><td>Woody Woodpecker at the Circus (149)
by Stella Williams Nathan,</td><td>1 - 6</td></tr>
</table>

LF1340   LF1350

LF1360   LF1370

LF1390   LF1400

LF1410   LF1430

LF1440   LF1450

illus by Frank McSavage
©1976 by Walter Lantz Prod., Inc., 24pp

LF1500 **Cats** (150)   1 - 4
by Laura French, illus by Mel Crawford
©1976, 24pp

LF1510 **Wild Kingdom, Marlin Perkin's** (151)   2 - 7
by Esta Meier, illus by James Seward,
Creative Studios I, Inc.,
©1976 by Don Meier Prod., 24pp

LF1520 **Big Enough Helper, The** (152)   1 - 6
by Nancy Hall, illus by Tom O'Sullivan
©1976, 24pp

LF1530 **Bible Stories from the Old Testament** (153)   1 - 4
by Sing Lee, illus by Jim Robison
©1977, 24pp

LF1540 **Animal's Christmas Eve, The** (154)   2 - 6
by Gale Wiersum, illus by Jim Robison
©1977, 24pp

LF1550 **Shazam! A Circus Adventure** (155)   2 - 6
by Bob Ottum, illus by Kurt Shafenberger
©1977 by DC Comics, Inc., 24pp

LF1560 **Raggedy Ann and Andy Help Santa
Claus** (156)   1 - 5
by Polly Curren, illus by June Goldsborough
©1977 by The Bobbs-Merrill Co., Inc., 24pp

LF1570 **Big Bird's Red Book** (157)   1 - 5
by Rosanne & Jonathan Cerf,
illus by Michael J. Smollin
©1977 by CTW & Muppets, Inc., 24pp

LF1590 **Cookie Monster and the Cookie Tree** (159)   1 - 5
by David Korr, illus by Joe Mathieu
©1977 by CTW & Muppets, Inc., 24pp

LF1600 **Donny and Marie/The Top Secret
Project** (160)   2 - 6
by Laura French, illus by Jan Neely
©1977 by Osbro Prod., Inc., 24pp

LF1610 **Bugs Bunny, Pioneer** (161)   2 - 6
by Fern G. Brown, illus by Darrell Baker
©1977 by Warner Bros., Inc., 24pp

LF1620 **The Fairy Princess: Superstar Barbie** (162)   2 - 7
by Anne Foster,
illus by Jim Robison & Fred Irvin

LF1500   LF1510

LF1520   LF1530

LF1540   LF1550

LF1560   LF1570

LF1460   LF1470

LF1480   LF1490

LF1590   LF1600

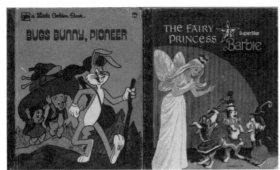

LF1610   LF1620

LF1630   LF1640

LF1650   LF1680

LF1700   LF1710

LF1760   LF1820

©1977 by Mattel, Inc., 24pp
(See color plate)

LF1630	**What Lily Goose Found** (163)	1 - 4
	by Annabelle Sumera,	
	illus by Lorinda Bryan Cauley	
	©1977, 24pp	
LF1640	**Rabbit's Adventure, The** (164)	1 - 4
	by Betty Ren Wright, illus by Maggie Swanson	
	©1977, 24pp	
LF1650	**Benji/Fastest Dog in the West** (165)	1 - 4
	by Gina Ingoglia, illus by Werner Willis	
	©1978 by Mulberry Square Prod., Inc., 24pp	
LF1680	**Circus Is in Town, The** (168)	2 - 6
	by David L. Harrison, illus by Larry Ross	
	©1978, 24pp	
LF1700	**Best of All! A Story About the Farm** (170)	2 - 6
	by Cecily Ruth Hogan,	
	illus by Lorinda Bryan Cauley	
	©1978, 24pp	
LF1710	**Whales** (171)	1 - 4
	by Jane Werner Watson, illus by Rod Ruth	
	©1978, 24pp	
LF1730	**Rabbit is Next, The** (173)	2 - 6
	by Gladys Leithauser & Lois Breitmeyer,	
	illus by Linda Powell	
	©1978, 24pp	
LF1750	**Where Will All the Animals Go?** (175)	1 - 4
	by Sharon Holaves, illus by Leigh Grant	
	©1978, 24pp	
LF1760	**ABC Around the House** (176)	2 - 8
	by Sharon Holaves, illus by Fred Irvin	
	©1978, 24pp. Not the same book as LH1180.	
LF1820	**Gingerbread Man, The** (182)	1 - 4
	(Nursery Tale), illus by Elfrieda	
	©1972, 24pp. Previously published as	
	a Whitman Big Tell-a-Tale.	
LF1840	**Birds** (184)	2 - 8
	by Jane Werner Watson, illus by Eloise Wilkin	
	©1958/p1973, 24pp (See also: BB1365,	
	GD5110)	
LF1850	**Let's Go, Trucks!** (185)	1 - 5
	by David L. Harrison, illus by William Dugan	
	©1973, 24pp	

LF1730   LF1750

LF1840   LF1850

LF1850 **Petey and I** (186)   2 - 8
by Martha Orr Conn, illus by Fred Irvin
©1973, 24pp

LF2040 **Three Bears, The** (204)   1 - 4
by Mabel Watts, illus by June Goldsborough
©1965/p1972, 24pp. Previously published
as a Whitman Big Tell-a-Tale.

LF2320 **Little Red Riding Hood** (232)   1 - 4
by Mabel Watts, illus by Les Gray
©1972, 24pp

LF2620 **Raggedy Ann and the Cookie Snatcher** (262) 1 - 5
by Barbara Shook Hazen,
illus by June Goldsborough
©1972 by the Bobbs-Merrill Co., Inc., 24pp

LF2640 **Just for Fun** (264)   2 - 7
by Patricia Scarry, illus by Richard Scarry
©1960/p1972, 24pp (See also: RE1320)

LF3150 **Together Book, The** (315)   1 - 5
by Revena Dwight, illus by Roger Bradfield
©1971 by CTW & Muppets, Inc., 24pp

LF3160 **Monster at the end of this book, the** (316) 2 - 10
by Jon Stone, illus by Mike Smollin
©1971 by CTW & Muppets, Inc., 24pp

LF3210 **Bert's Hall of Great Inventions** (321) 1 - 5
by Revena Dwight, illus by Roger Bradfield
©1972 by CTW & Muppets, Inc., 24pp

LF3270 **Good-bye, Tonsils** (327)   2 - 6
by Anne Welsh Guy, illus by Frank Vaughn
©1971, 24pp

LF3360 **Mother Goose in the City** (336)   1 - 5
(Nursery Rhymes), illus by Dora Leder
©1974, 24pp

LF3440 **Happy Golden ABC, The** (344)   1 - 5
(ABC), illus by Joan Allen
©1972, 24pp

LF3450 **Smokey Bear Finds a Helper** (345)   2 - 8
by Eileen Daly, illus by Al Anderson
©1972, 24pp

LF3500 **Forest Hotel** (350)   1 - 5
by Barbara Steincrohn Davis, illus by Benvenuti
©1972 by WPC & Editions des Deux
Coqs d'Or, 24pp

LF3620 **Pussycat Tiger, The** (362)   1 - 5
by Joan Chase Bacon, illus by Lilian Obligado
©1972, 24pp

LF3650 **Baby's Birthday** (365)   3 - 10
by Patricia Mowers, illus by Eloise Wilkin
©1972, 24pp

LF3970 **Bear in the Boat, The** (397)   2 - 6
written & illus by Ilse-Margret Vogel
©1972, 24pp

LF4010 **Raggedy Ann and Andy and the
Rainy Day Circus** (401)   2 - 6
by Barbara Shook Hazen,
illus by June Goldsborough
©1973 by The Bobbs-Merrill Co., Inc., 24pp

LF1860   LF2040

LF2320   LF2620

LF2640   LF3150

LF3160   LF3210

LF3270   LF3360

LF3440   LF3450

LF3500   LF3620

LF3650   LF3970

LF4010   LF4020

LF4160   LF4380

LF5150   LF5245

LF4020	**Bravest of All** (402) by Kate Emery Pogue, illus by Al Anderson ©1973, 24pp	2 - 8
LF4160	**Wacky Witch and the Mystery of the King's Gold** (416) by Jean Lewis; illus by Peter Alvarado, A.J. Specter & Bob Totten ©1973, 24pp	2 - 8
LF4380	**Little Red Hen, The** (438) by Evelyn M. Begley, illus by Carl & Mary Hague ©1966/p1973, 24pp. Previously published as a Whitman Big Tell-a-Tale.	1 - 5

My Christmas Treasury (455) Not issued in 1973. Book number is a transitional stocking code number, appearing on copies of LF1440 printed in 1982.

Buck Rogers (500) Not issued in 1973. Book number is a transitional stocking code number. (See LG0020)

Black Hole, The (501) Not issued in 1973. Book number is a transitional stocking code number. (See LI2010)

LF5030	**Corky's Hiccups** (503) by Nicolete Meredith Stack, illus by Tom O'Sullivan ©1968/p1973, 24pp. Previously published as a Whitman Big Tell-a-Tale.	2 - 8
LF5100	**Large and Growly Bear, The** (510) by Gertrude Crampton, illus by J.P. Miller ©1961/p1973, 24pp (See also: RE1380)	2 - 6
LF5150	**Neatos and the Litterbugs in the Mystery of the Missing Ticket, The** (515) by Norah Smaridge, illus by Charles Bracke ©1973, 24pp	1 - 5
LF5240	**Chicken Little** (524) by Stella Williams Nathan, illus by June Goldsborough ©1973, 24pp	1 - 4
LF5360	**Little Boy and the Giant, The** (536) by David L. Harrison, illus by Rosalind O. Fry ©1973, 24pp	1 - 5
LF5440	**Three Little Pigs, The** (544) by Elizabeth Ross, illus by Rosalind O. Fry ©1973, 24pp	1 - 4

LF5030   LF5100

LF5360   LF5440

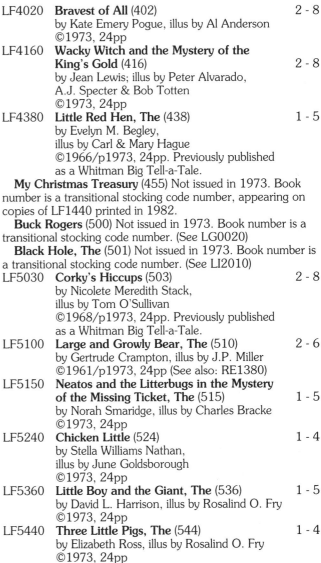

LF5450	**Jack and the Beanstalk** (545) by Stella Williams Nathan, illus by Dora Leder ©1973, 24pp	1 - 5
LF5660	**Cars** (566) by Bob Ottum, illus by William Dugan ©1973, 24pp	1 - 5
LF5710	**My Little Dinosaur** (571) written & illus by Ilse-Margret Vogel ©1971, 24pp	2 - 8
LF5720	**Lassie and the Big Clean-Up Day** (572) by Kennon Graham, illus by Bob Schaar ©1971 by Wrather Corp., 24pp	2 - 9
LF5750	**Who Comes to Your House?** (575) by Margaret Hillert, illus by Tom O'Sullivan ©1973, 24pp	3 - 9
LF5970	**Fly High** (597) written & illus by Virginia Parsons ©1971, 24pp	3 - 10
LF6000	**Susan in the Driver's Seat** (600) by Kathi Gibeault, illus by Jane Ike ©1973, 24pp	3 - 10

1976: **LG Train** added Sesame Street characters. This design used until 1983.

Little Golden Books – 3rd Series (1979 to present)

In 1978, Western adopted a stocking code numbering system for LGBs. Books are grouped in categories: animal stories, fairy tales, Christmas, Disney favorites, etc., and are only available from the publisher in these assortments, and cannot be ordered by title. The first three numbers of the code indicate category. The numbers following the hyphen relate to printing within the category. These numbers do not serve to identify the books for collectors, as they change constantly. Therefore, Tomart codes for this section do not relate to the number shown on the book.

Books are listed chronologically, according to date of publication. It is also increasingly difficult to determine the actual publication date of some of the books. For new titles, a copyright date and an "A" are fairly reliable. However, older books, as well as books published in other series, are reissued as LGB "A" editions, showing only the original copyright and no actual date of publication. In some cases, the only way to approximate the publication date is "knowing" when the book was purchased new. Books copyrighted in 1979 show no edition notation in their first printing. Later printings (2nd, 3rd, etc.) are all noted.

Book Format: All books have 24 pages and use the standard LGB end papers. Back covers have gone through several changes:

1979: Green, with LG Train, no price code, 69¢ on front. Except for a few early 1979 books, numbers are no longer carried with the book list.

1980: Green, with LG Train, price code on back, 69¢ on front.

1981-83: Green, with LG Train, price code on back, 89¢ on front. Golden Sunrise logo begins to appear on books in 1983.

1983-85: Yellow back with LG characters, price code on back, 89¢ on front.

1985-87: Three different back designs were used, all the same basic yellow back with LG characters:

(1) Same design as used since 1983, with price code moved to front cover. No other price noted. Three outside characters are Pink Panther, Color Kitten and Raggedy Ann. This design used in 1985 and 1986, and on a few 1987 books.

(2) Good Night Bear replaces Raggedy Ann. Mostly found on 1986 and a few 1987 books.

(3) Bugs Bunny and Kitten with a ball replace Pink Panther

LF5450   LF5660

LF5710   LF5720

LF5750   LF5970

LF6000   *1976-83: Back Cover*

Back Cover 1983-85   *Back Cover 1987-1990*

LG0010   LG0020

LG0030   LG0040

LG0050   LG0060

LG0070   LG0080

LG0090   LG0100

and Color Kitten. This back cover design has been used exclusively since 1987.

In order to avoid duplication of titles, we are listing only new books published since 1979 and previously published books that have been changed (new title, cover or illustrations) and the approximate date they were issued with this change.

Books this new are generally collectible only in their first editions and in very good or better shape. First editions disappear rapidly from retail outlets.

LG0010 **Amazing Mumford Forgets the Magic Words!, The**   1 - 3
by Patricia Thackray, illus by Normand Chartier
©1979 by CTW & Muppets, Inc., 24pp

LG0020 **Buck Rogers and the Children of Hopetown** 1 - 4
by Ravena Dwight, illus by Kurt Schaffenberger
©1979 by Robert C. Dille, 24pp. LGB number "500" is a transitional stocking code number without the appendix.

LG0030 **Ernie's Work of Art**   1 - 3
by Valjean McLenighan, illus by Joe Mathieu
©1979 by CTW & Muppets, Inc., 24pp

LG0040 **Feelings From A to Z**   1 - 2
by Pat Visser, illus by Rod Ruth
©1979, 24pp

LG0050 **Four Seasons, The**   1 - 3
by Tony Geiss, illus by Tom Cooke
©1979 by CTW & Muppets, Inc., 24pp

LG0060 **Giant Who Wanted Company, The**   1 - 3
by Lee Priestly, illus by Dennis Hockerman
©1979, 24pp

LG0070 **Little Pussycat**   1 - 3
by Margaret Wise Brown,
illus by Leonard Weisgard
©1979, 24pp. Formerly titled: *Pussy Willow*
(LE3140). Book still in print under both titles.
1989 printing shown.

LG0080 **Many Faces of Ernie, The**   1 - 3
by Judy Freudberg, illus by Normand Chartier
©1979 by CTW & Muppets, Inc., 24pp

LG0090 **Raggedy Ann and Andy/Five Birthday in a Row**   2 - 6
by Eileen Daly, illus by Mary S. McClain
©1979 by Bobbs-Merrill Co., Inc., 24pp

LG0100 **What Will I Be?**   1 - 4
by Kathleen Krull Cowles, illus by Eulala Conner
©1979, 24pp

LG0110 **Where is the Bear?**   1 - 2
by Betty Hubka, illus by Mel Crawford
©1978/p1979(D), 24pp. New cover art.
Previously published as LE5680.

LG0120 **Words**   1 - 2
by Selma Lola Chambers, illus by Louis Cary
©1974/p1979, 24pp. All illustrations redone.
Previously published as LE0450. No printing
stated. (See also: LG1200)

LG0110   LG0120

LG0130 **Family Circus/Daddy's Surprise Day** 2 - 5
by Gale Charlotte Wiersum, illus by Bil Keane
©1980 by The Register & Tribune Syndicate,
Inc., 24pp

LG0140 **Sleepy Book, The** 1 - 2
by Margaret Wise Brown, illus by Garth Williams
©1948/p1980, 24pp. Formerly titled: *The
Golden Sleepy Book* (LE0460). New cover art,
yellow background.

LG0150 **Grover's Own Alphabet** 1 - 3
illus by Sal Murdocca
©1978/p1981 by CTW & Muppets, Inc.,
24pp

LG0160 **Hiram's Red Shirt** 2 - 6
by Mabel Watts, illus by Aurelius Battaglia
©1981, 24pp. 1983 D printing shown.

LG0170 **Jenny's Surprise Summer** 1 - 3
written & illus by Eugenie Fernandes
©1981, 24pp

LG0180 **Little Golden Picture Dictionary** 1 - 2
illus by Marie DeJohn
©1981 by WPC, illus by Marie DeJohn,
24pp. 1989 printing shown. Not the same
book as LE3690.

LG0190 **Mr. Bear's Birthday** 1 - 3
by Veva Wilcox, illus by Lyn McClure Butrik
©1981, 24pp

LG0200 **Mr. Bell's Fix-it Shop** 1 - 3
by Ronne Peltzman, illus by Aurelius Battaglia
©1981, 24pp

LG0210 **Rainy Day Play Book** 1 - 2
by Susan Young with Marion Conger &
Natalie Young, illus by Ib Ohlsson
©1981 by WPC, illus by Ib Ohlsson, 24pp.
An adaptation of *The Rainy Day Play Book*
(LE1320). New illustrations.

LG0220 **Very Best Home for Me!, The** 1 - 2
by Jane Werner Watson, illus by Garth Williams
©1953/p1981, 24pp. Formerly titled:
Animal Friends (LE1670, LE5600). New cover
art shown at LG1180.

LG0230 **Chipmunk's ABC** 1 - 2
by Roberta Miller, illus by Richard Scarry
©1963/p1982, 24pp. Cover art changed,
contents same as LE5120. 1985 printing
shown.

LG0240 **Christmas Story, The** 1 - 2
by Jane Werner, illus by Eloise Wilkin
©1952/p1982(A), 24pp. Cover art changed.
Previously published as LE1580.

LG0250 **Color Kittens, The** 1 - 2
by Margaret Wise Brown,
illus by Alice & Martin Provensen
©1977/p1982(Q), 24pp. Cover art changed.
Previously published as LE0560 and LE4860.

LG0130   LG0140

LG0150   LG0160

LG0170   LG0180

LG0190   LG0200

LG0230   LG0240

LG0210   LG0220

LG0250   LG0260

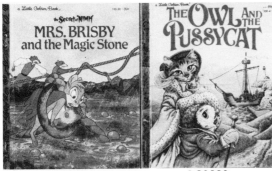

LG0270   LG0280

LG0290   LG0300

LG0310   LG0320

LG0330   LG0340

LG0260	**Make Way for the Highway**	2 - 5
	by Caroline Emerson, illus by Tibor Gergely ©1961/p1982(D), 24pp. Formerly titled: *Make Way for the Thruway* (LE4390)	
LG0270	**Mrs. Brisby and the Magic Stone**	2 - 5
	by Gina Ingoglia, illus by Carol Nicklaus ©1982 by Mrs. Brisby Ltd., 24pp. From the Don Bluth film, *The Secret of Nimh*.	
LG0280	**Owl and the Pussycat, The**	2 - 5
	by Edward Lear, illus by Ruth Sanderson ©1982 by WPC, illus by Ruth Sanderson, 24pp	
LG0290	**Rudolph the Red-Nosed Reindeer Shines Again**	1 - 2
	illus by Darrell Baker ©1982 by Robert L. May, 24pp. Adapted from the story by Robert L. May. Published by arrangement w/Follett Pub. Co.	
LG0300	**When You Were a Baby**	1 - 3
	by Linda Hayward, illus by Ruth Sanderson ©1982 by WPC, illus by Ruth Sanderson, 24pp. New story, not an adaption of LE4350.	
LG0310	**Animal Quiz Book**	1 - 2
	by Edith Kunhardt, illus by Kelly Oechsli ©1983 by WPC, illus by Kelly Oechsli, 24pp	
LG0320	**Best Friends**	2 - 4
	by Catherine Kenworthy, illus by Dyanne Di Salvo-Ryan ©1983 by Catherine Kenworthy (text), Dyanne Di Salvo-Ryan (illus), 24pp	
LG0330	**Cow and the Elephant, The**	1 - 3
	by Claude Clayton Smith, illus by R.Z. Whitlock ©1983 by Claude Clayton Smith (text), R.Z. Whitlock (illus), 24pp	
LG0340	**Dogs**	1 - 3
	by Jean Lewis, illus by Turi MacCombie ©1983 by WPC, illus by Turi MacCombie, 24pp	
LG0350	**Elves and the Shoemaker, The**	1 - 3
	by Eric Suben, illus by Lloyd Bloom ©1983 by WPC, illus by Lloyd Bloom, 24pp 1987 printing shown.	
LG0360	**Fire Fighter's Counting Book, The**	1 - 3
	by Polly Curren, illus by Pat Stewart ©1983 by WPC, illus by Pat Stewart, 24pp 1987 printing shown.	
LG0370	**Good Night, Aunt Lilly**	1 - 3
	by Margaret Madigan, illus by Diane Dawson ©1983 by Margaret Madigan (text), Diane Dawson (illus), 24pp	
LG0380	**Little Golden Book of Jokes and Riddles**	1 - 3
	by E.D. Ebsun (sel), illus by John O'Brien ©1983 by WPC, illus by John O'Brien, 24pp	
LG0390	**Musicians of Breman, The**	1 - 2
	by Ben Cruise (retold), illus by Ann Schweninger ©1983 by WPC, illus by Ann Schweninger, 24pp	

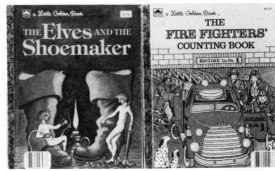

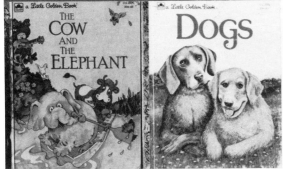

LG0350   LG0360

LG0400 **One of the Family** 1 - 2
by Peggy Archer, illus by Ruth Sanderson
©1983 by WPC, illus by Ruth Sanderson, 24pp

LG0410 **Puppy Love** 1 - 2
by Madeline Sunshine , illus by Carol Nicklaus
©1983 by CTW & Muppets, Inc., 24pp

LG0420 **Right's Animal Farm** 2 - 6
written & illus by Joan Elizabeth Goodman
©1983 by Joan Elizabeth Goodman, 24pp

LG0430 **Store-Bought Doll, The** 1 - 2
by Lois Meyer, illus by Ruth Sanderson
©1983 by WPC (text), Ruth Sanderson (illus),
24pp. Adapted from *Ukelele and Her New Doll* (LE1020).

LG0440 **Theodore Mouse Goes to Sea** 1 - 4
by Michaela Muntean, illus by Lucinda McQueen
©1983 by Michaela Muntean (text),
Lucinda McQueen (illus), 24pp

LG0450 **Twelve Days of Christmas, The** 1 - 3
(Christmas Carol), illus by Mike Eagle
© 1983 by WPC, illus by Mike Eagle, 24pp

LG0460 **Adventures of Goat** 2 - 4
by Lucille Hammond, illus by Eugenie Fernandes
©1984 by Lucille Hammond (text),
Eugenie Fernandes (illus), 24pp. 1986
printing shown.

LG0470 **Biskitts in Double Trouble** 1 - 3
by Gina Ingoglia, illus by John Costanza
©1984 by Hanna-Barbera Productions,
Inc., 24pp

LG0480 **Christmas Donkey, The** 1 - 3
by T. William Taylor, illus by Andrea Brooks
©1984 by T. William Taylor (text),
Andrea Brooks (illus), 24pp

LG0490 **Good-by Day, The** 2 - 5
by Leone Castell Anderson,
illus by Eugenie Fernandes
©1984 by Leone Castell Anderson (text),
Eugenie Fernandes (illus), 24pp. Later printings
retitled: *The Moving Day* (LG1100)

LG0500 **Gull That Lost the Sea, The** 1 - 3
by Claude Clayton Smith,

LG0370   LG0380

LG0390   LG0400

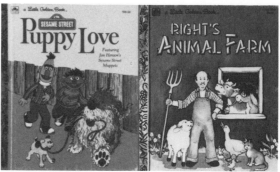

LG0410   LG0420

LG0450   LG0460

LG0430   LG0440

LG0490   LG0500

LG0470   LG0480

146

LG0510

LG0520

LG0530

LG0540

LG0550

LG0560

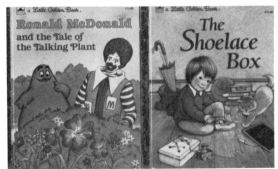

LG0570

LG0580

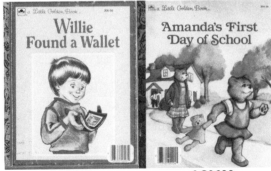

LG0590

LG0600

illus by Lucinda McQueen
©1984 by Claude Clayton Smith (text),
Lucinda McQueen (illus), 24pp

LG0510 **Hush, Hush, It's Sleepytime**   1 - 3
by Peggy Parish, illus by Leonid Pinchevsky
©1984, 24pp. All new illustrations.
Previously published as LE5770.

LG0520 **I Think That It Is Wonderful**   1 - 3
by David Korr, illus by A. Delaney
©1984 by CTW & Muppets, Inc., 24pp

LG0530 **If I Had a Dog**   2 - 5
written & illus by Lilian Obligado
©1984 by Lilian Obligado, 24pp

LG0540 **Inspector Gadget in Africa**   1 - 3
by Sandra Beris, illus by David Gantz
©1984 by DIC Enterprises, 24pp

LG0550 **Polly's Pet**   1 - 3
by Lucille Hammond, illus by Amye Rosenberg
©1984 by Lucille Hammond (text),
Amye Rosenberg (illus), 24pp

LG0560 **Rainbow Brite and the Brook Meadow Deer** 1 - 3
by Sarah Leslie, illus by Roy Wilson
©1984 by Hallmark Cards, Inc., 24pp

LG0570 **Ronald McDonald and the Tale of
the Talking Plant**   2 - 6
by John Albano, illus by John Costanza
©1984 by McDonald's Corp., 24pp

LG0580 **Shoelace Box, The**   1 - 2
by Elizabeth Winthrop, illus by Kathy Wilburn
©1984 by Elizabeth Winthrop Mahony (text),
Kathy Wilburn (illus), 24pp

LG0590 **Willie Found a Wallet**   2 - 5
by Mary Beth Markhamm illus by Lilian Obligado
©1984 by WPC, illus by Lilian Obligado, 24pp
1985 printing shown.

LG0600 **Amanda's First Day of School**   1 - 2
written & illus by Joan Elizabeth Goodman
©1985 by Joan Elizabeth Goodman, 24pp

LG0610 **Bialosky's Special Picnic**   1 - 3
by Leslie McGuire, illus by Jerry Joyner
©1985 by Workman Pub. and Peggy &
Alan Bialosky, 24pp. Created by Peggy
& Alan Bialosky.

LG0620 **Big Bird Brings Spring to Sesame Street** 1 - 2
by Lauren Collier Swindler,
illus by Marsha Winborn
©1985 by CTW & Muppets, Inc., 24pp

LG0630 **Big Bird's Day on the Farm**   1 - 2
by Cathi Rosenberg-Turow,
illus by Maggie Swanson
©1985 by CTW & Muppets, Inc., 24pp

LG0640 **Biggest, Most Beautiful Christmas Tree, The** 1 - 3
written & illus by Amye Rosenberg
©1985 by Amye Rosenberg, 24pp

LG0650 **Bugs Bunny Marooned!**   1 - 3
by Justine Korman, illus by Joe Messerli

LG0610

LG0620

©1985 by Warner Bros., Inc., 24pp

LG0660 **Cheltenham's Party** 1 - 3
by Jan Wahl, illus by Lucinda McQueen
©1985 by Jan Wahl (text), Lucinda McQueen
(illus), 24pp (See also: LL1630)

LG0670 **Count All the Way to Sesame Street** 1 - 3
by Dina Anastasio, illus by Richard Brown
©1985 by CTW & Muppets, Inc., 24pp

LG0680 **Day in the Jungle, A** 1 - 2
by Pat Patterson, illus by Olena Kassian
©1985 by Pat Patterson (text),
Olena Kassian (illus), 24pp

LG0690 **Grandma and Grandpa Smith** 1 - 2
by Edith Kunhardt, illus by Terri Super
©1985 by WPC, illus by Terri Super, 24pp

LG0700 **Happy Farm Animals, The** 1 - 2
by Annie North Bedford, illus by Tibor Gergely
©1978/p1985(A), 24pp. Formerly titled:
The Jolly Barnyard (LE0670).

LG0710 **How Does Your Garden Grow?** 1 - 2
by Pat Patterson,
illus by Brenda Clarke & Debi Perna
©1985 by Pat Patterson (text),
Brenda Clarke & Debi Perna (illus), 24pp

LG0720 **Little Brown Bear** 1 - 2
written & illus by Wendy Watson
©1985 by Wendy Watson, 24pp
(See also: LL1632)

LG0730 **Little Golden Book of Holidays, The** 1 - 2
by Jean Lewis, illus by Kathy Wilburn
©1985 by WPC, illus by Kathy Wilburn, 24pp

LG0740 **Little Golden Book of Hymns, The** 1 - 2
by Elsa Jane Werner & E.D. Ebsun,
illus by Frances Score Mitchell
©1985 by WPC, illus by Frances Score
Mitchell, 24pp

LG0750 **My First Book of the Planets** 1 - 2
by Elizabeth Winthrop, illus by John Nez
©1985 by Elizabeth Winthrop Mahony (text),
John Nez (illus), 24pp

LG0760 **Pink Panther & Sons/Fun at the Picnic** 1 - 4
by Sandra Beris, illus by David Gantz

LG0630   LG0640

LG0650   LG0660

LG0670   LG0680

LG0690   LG0700

LG0710   LG0720

LG0730   LG0740

LG0750   LG0760

LG0770 and LG0780

LG0790 and LG0800

LG0810 and LG0820

LG0830 and LG0840

LG0850 and LG0860

| LG0770 | **Poky Little Puppy's Naughty Day, The** | 2 - 4 |

©1985 by United Artists Corp., 24pp

written & illus by Jean Chandler
©1985, 24pp

LG0780 **Rags** 1 - 2
by Patricia Scarry, illus by J.P. Miller
©1970/p1985, 24pp. Cover redesigned.
Previously published as LE5860.

LG0790 **Road Runner/Mid-Mesa Marathon** 2 - 4
by Teddy Slater, illus by John Costanza
©1985 by Warner Bros., Inc., 24pp

LG0800 **Robotman & Friends at School** 1 - 2
by Justine Korman, illus by Joan Costanza
©1985 by United Feature Syndicate, Inc., 24pp

LG0810 **Scarebunny, The** 1 - 2
by Dorothy Kunhardt, illus by Kathy Wilburn
©1985 by Estate of Dorothy M. Kunhardt (text),
Kathy Wilburn (illus), 24pp. Later printings
retitled: *The Friendly Bunny* (LG1010).
(See also: LL1634)

LG0820 **Snoring Monster, The** 1 - 2
by David L. Harrison, illus by Richard Walz
©1985 by David L. Harrison (text),
Richard Walz (illus), 24pp

LG0830 **Tale of Peter Rabbit, The** 1 - 2
by Beatrix Potter, illus by Adriana Mazza Saviozzi
©1970/p1985(A), 24pp. Cover art changed.
Previously published w/cover title *Peter Rabbit*
(LE3130, LE5050).

LG0840 **Ten Items or Less** 1 - 2
by Stephanie Calmenson, illus by Terri Super
©1985 by Stephanie Calmenson (text),
Terri Super (illus), 24pp

LG0850 **Baby Sister** 1 - 2
by Dorothea M. Sachs, illus by Joy Friedman
©1986 by Dorothea M. Sachs (text),
Joy Friedman (illus), 24pp

LG0860 **Bugs Bunny and the Health Hog** 1 - 3
by Teddy Slater, illus by Darrell Baker
©1986 by Warner Bros., Inc., 24pp.

LG0870 **Curious Little Kitten Around the House, The** 1 - 3
by Linda Hayward, illus by Maggie Swanson
©1986 by Linda Hayward (text),
Maggie Swanson (illus), 24pp

LG0880 **Flying Is Fun!** 1 - 2
by Carol North, illus by Terri Super
©1986 by WPC, illus by Terri Super, 24pp.
Reprinted as: *A First Airplane Ride* (LG1250).

LG0890 **How Things Grow** 1 - 2
by Nancy Buss, illus by Kathy Allert
©1986 by Nancy Buss (text),
Kathy Allert (illus), 24pp

LG0900 **Missing Wedding Dress featuring Barbie** 1 - 3
by Karen Krugman, illus by Laura Westlake
©1986 by Mattel, Inc., 24pp

LG0870 and LG0880

LG0910 **Pound Puppies/Pick of the Litter** 1 - 2
by Teddy Slater,
illus by Carol Bouman & Dick Codor
©1986 by Tonka Corp., 24pp

LG0920 **Pound Puppies/Problem Puppies** 1 - 2
by Justine Korman,
illus by Carol Bouman & Dick Codor
©1986 by Tonka Corp., 24pp

LG0930 **Story of Jonah, The** 1 - 2
by Pamela Broughton (adp),
illus by Roberta Collier
©1986 by WPC, illus by Roberta Collier, 24pp

LG0940 **Summer Vacation** 1 - 2
by Edith Kunhardt, illus by Kathy Allert
©1986 by WPC, illus by Kathy Allert, 24pp

LG0950 **The Lord Is My Shepherd** 1 - 2
(Psalms 23), illus by Tom LaPadula
Special contents ©1986 by WPC, illus by
Tom LaPadula, 24pp

LG0960 **Theodore Mouse Up in the Air** 1 - 4
by Michaela Muntean, illus by Lucinda McQueen
©1986 by Michaela Muntean (text),
Lucinda McQueen (illus), 24pp

LG0970 **Bunnie's ABC** 1 - 3
illus by Garth Williams
©1957/p1987(A), 24pp (See also: BB1305)

LG0980 **Christmas Tree That Grew, The** 1 - 3
by Phyllis Krasilovsky, illus by Kathy Wilburn
©1987 by Phyllis Krasilovsky (text),
Kathy Wilburn (illus), 24pp

LG0990 **Daniel in the Lions' Den** 1 - 2
by Pamela Broughton (retold),
illus by Tom LaPadula
©1987 by WPC, illus by Tom LaPadula, 24pp

LG1000 **Fox Jumped Up One Winter Night, A** 1 - 2
written & illus by Nina Barbaresi
©1985/p1987(A) by Nina Barbaresi, 24pp
(See also: LL1631)

LG1010 **Friendly Bunny, The** 1 - 2
by Dorothy Kunhardt, illus by Kathy Wilburn
©1985/p1987 by Estate of Dorothy M.
Kunhardt (text), Kathy Wilburn (illus),

LG0930   LG0940

LG0950   LG0960

LG0970   LG0980

LG0890   LG0900

LG0990   LG1000

LG0910   LG0920

LG1010   LG1020

LG1030   LG1040

LG1050   LG1060

LG1070   LG1080

LG1090   LG1100

LG1110   LG1120

24pp., Formerly titled: *The Scarebunny*.

| LG1020 | **Funny Bunny** | 1 - 3 |

by Rachel Learned,
illus by Alice & Martin Provensen
©1950/p1987(A), 24pp (See also: BB1870)

| LG1030 | **Grover Takes Care of Baby** | 1 - 2 |

by Emily Thompson, illus by Tom Cooke
©1987 by CTW & Muppets, inc., 24pp

| LG1040 | **Lady Lovely Locks...Silkypup Saves the Day** | 1 - 2 |

by Kristin Brown, illus by Pat Paris
©1987 by Those Characters from
Cleveland, Inc., 24pp

| LG1050 | **Let's Fly a Kite, Charlie Brown!** | 1 - 3 |

by Harry Coe Verr, illus by Charles M. Schultz,
backgrounds by Art & Kim Ellis
©1987 by United Feature Syndicate, Inc., 24pp

| LG1060 | **Lily Pig's Book of Colors** | 1 - 2 |

written & illus by Amye Rosenberg
©1987 by Amye Rosenberg, 24pp

| LG1070 | **Lion's Mixed-Up Friends** | 1 - 2 |

by Lucille Hammond,
illus by Christopher Santoro
©1987 by Lucille Hammond (text),
Christopher Santoro (illus), 24pp

| LG1080 | **Little Red Riding Hood** | 1 - 3 |

by Rebecca Heller, illus by Marsha Winborn
©1985/p1987(A) by WPC, illus by Marsha
Winborn, 24pp (See also: LL1633)

| LG1090 | **Littlest Christmas Elf, The** | 1 - 3 |

by Nancy Buss, illus by Terri Super
©1987 by Nancy Buss (text), Terri Super (illus),
24pp

| LG1100 | **Moving Day** | 1 - 3 |

by Leone Castell Anderson,
illus by Eugenie Fernandes
©1984/p1987(D) by Leone Castell Anderson
(text), Eugenie Fernandes (illus), 24pp
Formerly titled: *The Good-by Day* (LG0490)
Cover art changed.

| LG1110 | **My Book of Poems** | 1 - 2 |

by Ben Cruise (sel), illus by Gloria Solly
©1985/p1987(A) by WPC, illus by Gloria Solly,
24pp (See also: LL1634)

| LG1120 | **My Little Golden Word Book** | 1 - 2 |

written & illus by Joe Kaufman
©1968/p1987, 24pp. Formerly titled: *Things
in My House* (LE5700). New cover art.

| LG1130 | **My Own Grandpa** | 1 - 2 |

by Leone Castell Anderson,
illus by Kathy Wilburn
©1987 by Leone Castell Anderson (text),
Kathy Wilburn (illus), 24pp

| LG1140 | **Night Before Christmas, The** | 1 - 3 |

by Clement C. Moore, illus by Kathy Wilburn
©1987 by WPC, illus by Kathy Wilburn, 24pp

| LG1150 | **Old MacDonald Had a Farm** | 1 - 3 |

LG1130   LG1140

(Nursery Song), illus by Carl & Mary Hague
©1975/p1987(A), 24pp

LG1160 **Things I Like** 1 - 2
by Margaret Wise Brown, illus by Garth Williams
©1982/p1987, 24pp. Formerly titled: *The Friendly Book* (LE1990, LE5920)

LG1170 **Tortoise and the Hare, The** 1 - 2
by Margo Lundell, illus by John Nez
©1987 by WPC, illus by John Nez, 24pp

LG1180 **Very Best Home for Me!, The** 1 - 2
©1953/p1987(S), 24pp. Cover art changed.
(See also: LG0220)

LG1190 **What's Up in the Attic?** 1 - 2
by Liza Alexander, illus by Tom Cooke
©1987 by CTW & Muppets, Inc., 24pp

LG1200 **Words** 1 - 2
©1974/p1987(W), 24pp. New cover art.
(See also: LG0120)

LG1210 **Xavier's Birthday Surprise**
(Cabbage Patch Kids) 1 - 2
written & illus by Ari Hill
©1987 by Original Appalachian Artworks,
Inc., 24pp

LG1220 **Beach Day** 1 - 2
by Fran Manushkin, illus by Kathy Wilburn
©1988 by Fran Manushkin (text),
Kathy Wilburn (illus), 24pp

LG1230 **Bear's New Baby, The** 1 - 3
written & illus by Joan Elizabeth Goodman
©1988 by Joan Elizabeth Goodman, 24pp

LG1240 **Day Snuffy Had the Sniffles, The** 1 - 2
by Linda Lee Maifair, illus by Tom Brannon
©1988 by CTW & Muppets, Inc., 24pp

LG1250 **First Airplane Ride, A** 1 - 2
by Carol North, illus by Terri Super
©1986/p1988 by WPC, illus by Terri Super,
24pp. Previous published as: *Flying Is Fun!*
(LG0880)

LG1260 **Garfield and the Space Cat** 1 - 3
by Leslie McGuire
©1988 by United Feature Syndicate,
Inc., 24pp. Created by Jim Davis.

LG1270 **Good Old Days, The** 1 - 2
by Dave Werner, illus by Deborah Borgo
©1988 by WPC, illus by Deborah Borgo, 24pp

LG1280 **Let's Go Shopping!** 1 - 2
by Steven Lindblom, illus by Kathy Allert
©1988 by Steven Lindblom (text),
Kathy Allert (illus), 24pp

LG1290 **My Little Golden Book About Cats** 1 - 2
by Joanne Ryder, illus by Dora Leder
©1988 by Joanne Ryder (text),
Dora Leder (illus), 24pp

LG1300 **Old Mother Goose and Other Nursery
Rhymes** 1 - 3

LG1150   LG1160

LG1170   LG1180

LG1190   LG1200

LG1210   LG1220

LG1230   LG1240

LG1250   LG1260

LG1270 LG1280

LG1290 LG1300

LG1310 LG1320

LG1330 LG1340

LG1370 LG1380

(Nursery Rhymes), illus by Alice &
Martin Provensen
©1988, 24pp (See also: GB1600)

LG1310 Timothy Tiger's Terrible Toothache   1 - 3
by Jan Wahl, illus by Lisa McCue Karsten
©1988 by Jan Wahl (text),
Lisa McCue Karsten (illus), 24pp

LG1320 Tiny Dinosaurs   1 - 3
by Steven Lindblom, illus by Gino D'Achille
©1988 by Steven Lindblom (text),
Gino D'Achille (illus), 24pp

LG1330 Where's Woodstock?   1 - 3
by Margo Lundell, illus by Charles M. Schultz,
backgrounds by Art & Kim Ellis
©1988 by United Feature Syndicate, Inc., 24pp

LG1340 Buster Cat Goes Out   1 - 2
by Joanna Cole, illus by Rose Mary Berlin
©1989 by Joanna Cole (text),
Rose Mary Berlin (illus), 24pp

LG1350 Frosty, The Snowman   1 - 2
by Annie North Bedford, illus by Terri Super
©1989 by Warner/Chappell Music, 24pp.
All new illustrations, changed from LE1420.

LG1360 I Can't Wait Until It's Christmas   1 - 2
by Linda Lee Maifair, illus by Joe Ewers
©1989 by CTW & Muppets, Inc., 24pp

LG1370 I Don't Want to Go   1 - 2
by Justine Korman, illus by Amye Rosenberg
©1989 by Justine Korman (text),
Amye Rosenberg (illus), 24pp

LG1380 Kitty on the Farm   1 - 2
by Phyllis McGinley, illus by Feodor Rojankovsky
©1948/p1989(A), 24pp. Formerly titled:
A Name for a Kitty (LE0550). New cover art.

LG1390 Little Lost Kitten   1 - 2
by Nina, illus by Feodor Rojankovsky
©1951/p1989(A), 24pp. Formerly titled: *The
Kitten's Surprise* (LE1070). New cover art.

LG1400 My Little Golden Book of Manners   1 - 2
by Peggy Parish, illus by Richard Scarry
©1962/p1989(A), 24pp. New cover art.
Previously published as LE4600.

LG1350 LG1360

LG1390 LG1400

LG1410 **New Puppy, The**   1 - 2
by Kathleen N. Daly, illus by Lilian Obligado
©1969/p1989(S), 24pp. New cover art.
Previously published as LE3700.

LG1420 **Oh, Little Rabbit!**   1 - 2
by Joan M. Lexau, illus by Kathy Wilburn
©1989 by Joan M. Lexau (text),
Kathy Wilburn (illus), 24pp

LG1430 **Puppy on the Farm**   1 - 2
by Marilyn Elson, illus by Lisa McCue
©1984/p1989(A) by WPC, illus by Lisa McCue
24pp. First LGB printing. Previously published
as *Duffy on the Farm*.

LG1440 **Silly Sisters, The**   1 - 2
by Dave Werner, illus by Lucinda McQueen
©1989 by WPC, illus by Lucinda McQueen,
24pp

LG1450 **Time for Bed**   1 - 2
written & illus by Joan Elizabeth Goodman
©1989 by Joan Elizabeth Goodman, 24pp

LG1460 **Arthur's Good Manners**   1 - 2
by Stephanie Calmenson,
illus by Lisa McCue Karsten
©1987/p1990 by Stephanie Calmenson (text),
Lisa McCue Karsten (illus), 24pp. Previously
titled: *Spaghetti Manners*.

LG1470 **Big Elephant, The**   1 - 2
by Kathryn & Byron Jackson,
illus by Feodor Rojankovsky
©1949/p1990(A), 24pp (See also: BB1285)

LG1480 **Bugs Bunny and the Pink Flamingos** 1 - 2
by Gina Ingoglia, illus by John Costanza
©1987/p1990(A) by Warner Bros., Inc., 24pp

LG1490 **Bugs Bunny Calling!**   1 - 2
by Cindy West, illus by Joe Messerli
©1988/p1990(A) by Warner Bros., Inc., 24pp

LG1500 **Bugs Bunny, Party Pest**   1 - 2
by William Johnston,
illus by Al Andersen & Tom McKimson
©1976/p1990(A) by Warner Bros., Inc., 24pp

LG1510 **Bunny's New Shoes**   1 - 2
by Stephanie Calmenson,
illus by Lisa McCue Karsten
©1987/p1990(A) by Stephanie Calmenson
(text), Lisa McCue Karsten (illus), 24pp
Previously published as *One Red Shoe (The
Other One's Blue)*.

LG1520 **But, You're a Duck**   1 - 2
by Michael Teitelbaum, illus by Rose Mary Berlin
©1990 by Michael Teitelbaum (text),
Rose Mary Berlin (illus), 24pp

LG1530 **Flying Dinosaurs**   1 - 2
by Steven Lindblom, illus by Christopher Santoro
©1990 by Steven Lindblom (text),
Christopher Santoro (illus), 24pp

LG1410   LG1420

LG1430   LG1440

LG1450   LG1460

LG1470   LG1480

LG1490   LG1500

LG1510   LG1520

154

LG1530   LG1540

LG1550   LG1560

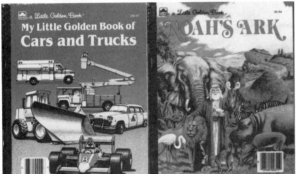

LG1570   LG1580

LG1590   LG1600

LG1601   LG1602

LG1540	**Garfield, The Cat Show** by Norma Simone, illus by Mike Fentz ©1990 by United Feature Syndicate, Inc., 24pp. Created by Jim Davis.	1 - 2
LG1550	**Just Imagine/A Book of Fairyland Rhymes** written & illus by Guy Gilchrist ©1990 by Guy Gilchrist, 24pp	1 - 2
LG1560	**My First Book of Sounds** by Melanie Bellah, illus by Trina Schart ©1963/p1990(A), 24pp. Previously titled: *Bow Wow! Meow! A First Book of Sounds* (See LE5230)	1 - 2
LG1570	**My Little Golden Book of Cars & Trucks** by Chari Sue, illus by Richard & Trish Courtney ©1990 by WPC, illus by Richard & Trish Courtney, 24pp	1 - 2
LG1580	**Noah's Ark** (Based on Genesis 6:5-9:17), by Pamela Broughton (adp), illus by Tom LaPadula ©1985 by WPC, illus by Tom LaPadula	1 - 2
LG1590	**Tickety-Tock, What Time Is It?** written & illus by Julie Durrell ©1990 by Julie Durrell, 24pp	1 - 2
LG1600	**Tiny Toon Adventures/Happy Birthday, Babs!** by Linda Aber, illus by John Costanza ©1990 by Warner Bros., Inc., 24pp	1 - 2
LG1610	**Tiny Toon Adventures/Lost in the Fun House** by Jack Harris, illus by John Costanza ©1990 by Warner Bros., Inc., 24pp	1 - 2
LG1620	**Water Babies** by Gina Ingoglia, illus by Lisa Bonforte ©1990 by Gina Ingoglia (text), Lisa Bonforte (illus), 24pp	1 - 2

Little Golden Books – Activity Books

A special series, augmenting the activity books that were already part of the regular LGB line. This activity series was published from 1955 through 1963. Books are identified as "A Little Golden Activity Book" at the top of the cover, and book numbers start with "A". (One book - A12 - states "A Little Golden Stamp Book", instead of "Activity Book." Also, one book in the regular series, LGB 1-285, *How to Tell Time*, is marked "A Little Golden Activity Book", but was never a part of this separate activity series.)

The same general format was used as for LGBs, with number of pages sometimes reduced to allow for the activity. All stamp books were done in duo-tone, with 3 pages of color stamps to stick on the story pages.

The first value range given always refers to a book in complete condition with unused activity pieces. However, since the books are most often found used, with stamps in place, dolls cut out, etc., values for books in used, but complete condition are also given. Books that retain their story content even with activities missing are generally collected only as "fill-ins" until a complete copy can be found. Values for books with partial activity pieces, etc. should be determined in relation to values given for complete items.

A special color plate depicts many of the activity books from this series and the regular LGB series.

The Tomart code begins with LH1, followed by the 2-digit Activity series number. Last digit is used for variant copies.

Note: No books are known to have been published for numbers A23, A35, A37, A38, A40, A42, A46 and A49.

LH1010 **Words** (A1)   4 - 8
by Selma Lola Chambers, illus by Gertrude Elliott
©1955, 20pp. A wheel book, with 12 words
matched to pictures. Adapted from LE0450,
the book repeats at LH1300 an LH1450.
LH1011 Same as LH1010, without wheel   1 - 3
LH1020 **Circus Time** (A2)   4 - 10
by Marion Conger, illus by Tibor Gergely
©1955, 20pp. A wheel book, with animals
revolving in the center ring. Adapted from
LE0320.
LH1021 Same as LH1020, without wheel   2 - 4
LH1030 **Paper Dolls** (A3)   20 - 35
written & illus by Hilda Miloche & Wilma Kane
©1955, 20pp. A paper doll book adapted
from LE1135. This version has punch-out
dolls in both covers.
LH1031 Same as LH1030, w/all dolls & clothes, cut 15 - 25
LH1032 Same as LH1030, book only   2 - 6
LH1040 **Animal Paint Book** (A4   5 - 15
written & illus by Hans Helweg
©1955, 20pp. A watercolor book with cover
die-cut to show three paints on card inside.
LH1041 Same as LH1040, without paints   2 - 4
LH1050 **Clown Coloring Book** (A5)   15 - 35
illus by Art Seiden
©1955, 20pp. Pictures to color, with a box
of crayons attached to the front cover
LH1051 Same as LE1050, lacking crayons   8 - 12
LH1060 **Trucks** (A6)   20 - 40
by Kathryn Jackson, illus by Ray Quigley
©1955, 24pp. Two punch-out International
Harvester trucks to assemble
LH1061 Same as LH1060, without punch-out trucks   6 - 12
LH1070 **Animal Stamps** (A7)   7 - 14
by Kathleen N. Daly, illus by William J. Dugan,
stamps by James Gordon Irving
©1955, 20pp
LH1071 Same as LH1070, with stamps in place   3 - 6
LH1080 **Bird Stamps** (A8)   7 - 14
by Kathleen N. Daly,
illus by James Gordon Irving
©1955, 20pp
LH1081 Same as LH1080, with stamps in place   3 - 6
LH1090 **Dog Stamps** (A9)   7 - 14
by Ann McGovern, illus by Edwin Megargee
©1955, 20pp
LH1091 Same as LH1090, with stamps in place   3 - 6
LH1100 **Mickey Mouse Club Stamp Book, Walt
Disney's** (A10)   15 - 35
by Kathleen N. Daly,
illus by WDS, adp by Julius Svendsen
©1956 by WDP, 20pp. Listed with MMC
books as "D58". No book published at that
number.
LH1101 Same as LH1100, with stamps in place   6 - 12
LH1110 **Cowboy Stamps** (A11)   7 - 14
by John Lyle Shimek, illus by Richard Scarry
©1957, 20pp
LH1111 Same as LH1110, with stamps in place   3 - 6
LH1120 **Story of Baby Jesus** (A12)   10 - 18
by Jane Werner Watson, illus by Eloise Wilkin
©1957, 20pp. A Stamp Book.
LH1121 Same as LH1120, with stamps in place   4 - 10
LH1130 **Indian Stamps** (A13)   7 - 14
by Edward Huberman, illus by Edwin Schmidt
©1957, 20pp
LH1131 Same as LH1130, with stamps in place   3 - 6
LH1140 **Ginger Paper Doll** (A14)   10 - 35

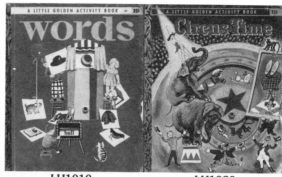

LH1010   LH1020

LH1030   LH1040

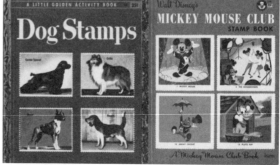

LH1050   LH1060

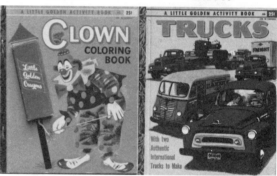

LH1070   LH1080

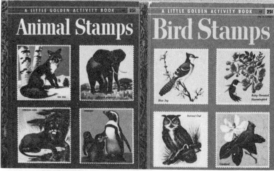

LH1090   LH1100

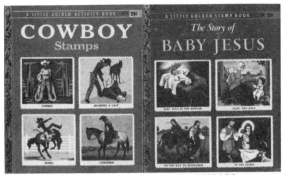

LH1110   LH1120

LH1130   LH1140

LH1150   LH1160

LH1170   LH1180

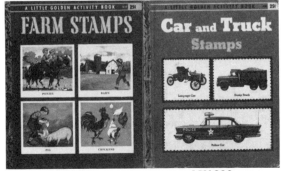

LH1190   LH1200

by Kathleen N. Daly,
illus by Adriana Mazza Saviozzi
©1957 Ginger® by Cosmopolitan
Doll & Toy Corp., 20pp. Doll on
heavy board. Book repeats at LH1320

LH1141 Same as LH1140, doll and clothes, cut   15 - 20
LH1142 Same as LH1140, book only   2 - 6
LH1150 **Trim the Christmas Tree** (A15)   10 - 30
by Elsa Ruth Nast,
illus by Doris & Marion Henderson
©1957, 24pp. A punch-out tree in both
covers, w/10 cut-out Christmas ornaments
to make. (See also: LH1500)
LH1160 **Count to Ten** (A16)   4 - 8
by Lilian Moore, illus by Beth Krush
©1957, 20pp. A wheel book, w/10 object &
number pictures. Book repeats at LH1440.
LH1161 Same as LH1160, without wheel   1 - 3
LH1170 **Stop and Go** (A17)   7 - 14
by Loyta Higgins, illus by Joan Walsh Anglund
©1957, 20pp. A wheel book, w/red & green
traffic lights cued to safety pictures.
LH1171 Same as LH1170, without wheel   2 - 6
LH1180 **ABC Around the House** (A18)   4 - 8
by Kathleen N. Daly, illus by Violet LaMont
©1957, 20pp. A wheel book, w/a word &
picture for each letter of the alphabet. Book
repeats at LH1440
LH1181 Same as LH1180, without wheel   1 - 3
LH1190 **Farm Stamps** (A19)   7 - 14
by Kathryn Jackson,
illus by Adriana Mazza Saviozzi
©1957, 20pp
LH1191 Same as LH1190, with stamps in place   4 - 9
LH1200 **Car and Truck Stamps** (A20)   7 - 14
by Kathleen N. Daly, illus by E. Joseph Dreany
©1957, 20pp
LH1201 Same as LH1200, with stamps in place   4 - 9
LH1210 **Let's Save Money** (A21)   5 - 10
by Loyta Higgins, illus by Violet LaMont
©1958, 20pp. A wheel book, with coin-
saver dial that holds over $1 in change.
LH1211 Same as LH1210, without wheel   2 - 6
LH1220 **Paper Doll Wedding, The** (A22)   10 - 30
written & illus by Hilda Miloche & Wilma Kane
©1954/p1957(B), 24pp. Dolls on heavy
board. Closet on last page. Adapted from
LE1930.
LH1221 Same as LH1220, w/all dolls & clothes, cut 15 - 25
LH1222 Same as LH1220, book only   3 - 8
LH1240 **Reading, Writing and Spelling** (A24)   7 - 14
by Carol Kaufman, illus by Violet LaMont,
stamps by Lilian Obligado
©1959, 20pp
LH1241 Same as LH1240, with stamps in place   2 - 6

LH1210   LH1220

LH1250	**Insect Stamps** (A25)	7 - 14
	by Richard A. Martin, illus by Jean Zallinger	
	©1958, 20pp	
LH1251	Same as LH1250, with stamps in place	2 - 6
LH1260	**Train Stamps** (A26)	8 - 14
	by Kathleen N. Daly, illus by E. Joseph Dreany	
	©1958, 20pp	
LH1261	Same as LH1260, with stamps in place	4 - 8
LH1270	**Firemen and Fire Engine Stamps** (A27)	8 - 14
	by Jane Goldsmith, illus by Richard Scarry, stamps by Ric Estrada	
	©1959, 20pp	
LH1271	Same as LH1270, with stamps in place	4 - 8
LH1280	**Colors** (A28)	5 - 12
	by Kathleen N. Daly, illus by Richard Scarry ©1959, 20pp. A wheel book, w/color pictures matched to objects.	
LH1281	Same as LH1280, without wheel	2 - 4
LH1290	**Animals and Their Babies** (A29)	4 - 10
	by Barbara Shook Hazen, illus by Lilian Obligado ©1959, 20pp. A wheel book, w/names of baby animals matched to pictures of the parent animal.	
LH1291	Same as LH1290, without wheel	2 - 4
LH1300	**Words** (A30)	4 - 8
	by Selma Lola Chambers, illus by Gertrude Elliott ©1955/p1959(B), 20pp. A wheel book, w/12 picture/word combinations, the same as LH1010. Same book repeats at LH1450. Adapted from LE0450.	
LH1301	Same as LH1300, without wheel	1 - 3
LH1310	**Mike and Melissa** (A31)	25 - 40
	by Jane Werner Watson, illus by Adriana Mazza Saviozzi ©1959, 20pp. Two punch-out paper dolls on heavy board, clothes were on outside half of each page, leaving cut book w/tall narrow story pages.	
LH1311	Same as LH1310, w/all dolls & clothes, cut	15 - 25
LH1312	Same as LH1310, book only	3 - 8
LH1320	**Ginger Paper Doll** (A32)	10 - 35
	by Kathleen N. Daly, illus by Adriana Mazza Saviozzi ©1957/p1959(C) Ginger® by Cosmopolitan Doll & Toy Corp., 20pp. Doll on heavy board. (See also: LH1140)	
LH1321	Same as LH1320, w/all dolls & clothes, cut	15 - 20
LH1322	Same as LH1320, book only	2 - 6
LH1330	**Sleeping Beauty** (A33)	25 - 65
	(Fairy Tale), illus by WDS, adp by Julius Svendsen, Frank Armitage, C.W. Satterfield & Thelma Witmer ©1959 by WDP, 20pp. Sleeping Beauty and Prince Phillip paper dolls on heavy board. Adapted from LI0610.	
LH1331	Same as LH1330, w/all dolls & clothes, cut	20 - 50
LH1332	Same as LH1330, book only	5 - 12
LH1340	**Little Red Riding Hood** (A34)	20 - 40
	(Fairy Tale), illus by Sharon Koester ©1959, 24pp. Paper dolls of Little Red Riding Hood and the wolf (with his own granny gown!)	
LH1341	Same as LH1340, w/all dolls & clothes, cut	15 - 30
LH1342	Same as LH1340, book only	9 - 12
LH1360	**Cinderella** (A36)	20 - 40
	(Fairy Tale), illus by Gordon Laite ©1960, 20pp. Paper dolls for Cinderella, Prince Charming ... and the clock.	

LH1240   LH1250

LH1260   LH1270

LH1280   LH1290

LH1300   LH1310

LH1320   LH1330

LH1340   LH1360

LH1390   LH1410

LH1430   LH1440

LH1450   LH1470

LH1480   LH1500

LH1361	Same as LH1360, w/all dolls & clothes, cut	15 - 30
LH1362	Same as LH1360, book only	3 - 9
LH1390	**My Little Golden Calendar for 1961** (A39)	7 - 15

         illus by Richard Scarry
         ©1960, 28pp. A soft cover book which
         opens into a fun calendar.

LH1410	**Hansel and Gretel** (A41)	20 - 40

         by Jacob & Wilhelm Grimm,
         illus by Judy & Barry Martin
         ©1961, 24pp. First printings have punch-out
         paper dolls, "B" printings have cut-out dolls.
         Values are the same for both styles.

LH1411	Same as LH1410, w/all dolls & clothes, cut	15 - 30
LH1412	Same as LH1410, book only	4 - 9
LH1430	**Count to Ten** (A43)	4 - 8

         by Lilian Moore, illus by Beth Krush
         ©1957/p1961(B), 20pp. A wheel book,
         w/10 number/picture combinations. Same
         as LH1160.

LH1431	Same as LH1430, without wheel	1 - 3
LH1440	**ABC Around the House** (A44)	4 - 8

         by Kathleen N. Daly, illus by Violet LaMont
         ©1957/p1961(D), 20pp. A wheel book
         w/26 letter, word & picture combinations,
         same as LH1180.

LH1441	Same as LH1440, without wheel	1 - 3
LH1450	**Words** (A45)	4 - 8

         by Selma Lola Chambers,
         illus by Gertrude Elliott
         ©1955/p1961(C), 20pp. A wheel book
         w/12 picture/word combiantions, same as
         LH1010 & LH1300. Adapted from LE0450.

LH1451	Same as LH1450, without wheel	1 - 3
LH1470	**Paper Dolls** (A47)	10 - 30

         written & illus by Hilda Miloche & Wilma Kane
         ©1951/p1961(B), 20pp. Paper dolls on
         heavy board, adapted from LE2800.

LH1471	Same as LH1470, w/all dolls & clothes, cut	15 - 25
LH1472	Same as LH1470, book only	2 - 6
LH1480	**Gordon's Jet Flight** (A48)	20 - 40

         by Naomi J. Glasson, illus by Mel Crawford
         ©1961, 20pp. A punch-out book with an
         American Airlines Astrojet to assemble.

LH1481	Same as LH1480, without Astrojet	6 - 10
LH1500	**Trim the Christmas Tree** (A50)	4 - 10

         by Elsa Ruth Nast,
         illus by Doris & Marion Henderson
         ©1957/p1962(B), 24pp. A cut-out book
         w/10 Christmas ornaments to make. Does
         not have punch-out Christmas tree in cover
         as w/LH1150. Cut books are considered
         uncollectible.

LH1520	**Tammy** (A52)	15 - 35

         by Kathleen N. Daly, illus by Ada Salvi
         ©1963(C) by Ideal Toy Corporation, 24pp
         Tammy® and Pepper® paper dolls.

LH1520   *Activity Back Cover*

LH1521 Same as LH1520, w/all dolls & clothes, cut 10 - 20
LH1522 Same as LH1520, book only   2 - 6
Back Cover: The first few titles in the Activity series were specially advertised in a box at the top of the book list. This format was used only on Activity books.

Little Golden Ad Backs (See Ad Backs)

Little Golden Books – Billion Golden Memories
In 1987, the billionth Little Golden Book was published ... a copy of *Poky Little Puppy*. In celebration of this publishing milestone, Western sponsored a sweepstakes with prizes including Caribbean cruises, camcorders, video recorders and LG videos, TVs, and Golden Junior Classic books. In addition, folks were invited to share their "favorite Little Golden Book" memory and receive a free book. A gold "Billion Golden Memories" seal identified Golden books that included sweepstakes entry forms.

A "Billion Golden Memories" coin was also distributed by Western during the celebration. A "Billion Golden Memories" program was televised, and the Racine *Journal Times* issue for July 26, 1987 featured a 52-page section that chronicled the history of Western, its books and its people, chock full of congratulatory ads from local businesses and nationwide publishing and licensing affiliates.

Billion Golden Memories Logo

Keepsake Books
A deluxe keepsake set of 3 special volumes, each containing 12 favorite LGB stories was published for a limited time in 1987 as part of the Billion Golden Memories celebration.

LH2000 LGB Keepsake Set   30 - 45
        ©1987, 3 volumes, 96pp each
Individual Books in LH2100
LH2010 **Animal Friends**   6 - 12
LH2020 **Disney Friends**   10 - 18
LH2030 **Trains, Boats and Trucks**   6 - 12

LH2000

Single book commemorative editions of all-time favorite LGB titles were also published as part of the celebration. These keepsake books had the gold seal on the cover, a sweepstakes entry form inside and a special "Commemorative Edition" front end paper. At present, the value of these keepsake editions has not appreciated tremendously, but they are a nice addition to any collection, and will probably grow in value over the years. Value range is for specially marked LGBs only.

LH2100 Billion Golden Memories editions, each   1 - 3

LH2100   ***Commemorative Edition
                       front end paper***

Little Golden Books – Cloth bound
Special cloth bound editions of Little Golden Books with full color covers, both front and back, including the Golden spine, were produced in the late '40s. These colorful covers draw special collector attention as opposed to the regular Goldencraft bindings, which are generally done in limited color, or have only a small color picture on the cover.

The following books are known to have been released in these special bindings. There may have been more.

LH3023 **Shy Little Kitten** (23)   8 - 15
LH3024 **New House in the Forest, The** (24) 8 - 15
LH3025 **Taxi That Hurried, The** (25)   6 - 12
LH3029 **Noises and Mr. Flibberty-Jib** (29) 10 - 18
LH3032 **Fix It, Please** (32)   10 - 18
LH3036 **Saggy Baggy Elephant** (36)   8 - 15
LH3039 **Animal Babies** (39)   7 - 12

LH3032   **LH3024**

Little Golden Books – Ding Dong School Book Series

"Ding Dong School" was an immensely popular TV program for pre-schoolers, aired by NBC in the 1950s. "Miss Frances", school mistress for the program, was one of the country's foremost educators, Dr. Frances Horwich. The program's combination of sound educational principals and nursery-school fun appealed to both parents and children. The books retell popular stories from the TV program.

The series actually began with Rand McNally, which produced at least 22 titles between 1953 and 1954; at least six of which were repeated in the Little Golden Series. The Rand McNally books were the same size as LGBs, with silver spines.

Eight titles were produced for the Little Golden series. The first four books retain the same front cover format as the Rand McNally books, with "Golden Press" noted at the bottom. The text and illustrations remained the same, and a plain gold spine was used, but the back cover and end papers were the standard LGB format used in 1954. The last four books are identified as LGBs at the bottom of the cover, and can be found with both plain gold spines and the regular LG spine. The white border, which was used throughout the Rand McNally series, was also dropped. The series has a unique "Din" number and, although the standard LGB book list ran on the inside back cover, Ding Dong School books were never listed.

LH4010 **Jingle Bell Jack** (Din1)   3 - 10
by Frances R. Horwich, illus by Katherine Evans
©1955/p1959(A) by Frances R. Horwich,
24pp

LH4020 **Mr. Meyer's Cow** (Din2)   3 - 8
by Frances R. Horwich, illus by William Neebe
©1955/p1959(A) by Frances R. Horwich,
24pp

LH4030 **My Daddy Is a Policeman** (Din3)   3 - 10
by Frances R. Horwich, illus by Helen Prickett
©1955/p1959(A) by Frances R. Horwich,
24pp

LH4040 **We Love Grandpa** (Din4)   3 - 8
by Frances R. Horwich, illus by Dorothy Grider
©1955/p1959(A) by Frances R. Horwich,
24pp

LH4010   LH4020

LH4030   LH4040

LH4050 **Here Comes the Band** (Din5)   3 - 8
by Frances R. Horwich, illus by William Timmins
©1955/p1960(A) by Frances R. Horwich,
24pp

LH4060 **Magic Wagon, The** (Din6)   3 - 10
by Frances R. Horwich,
illus by Elizabeth Webbe
©1955/p1960(A) by Frances R. Horwich,
24pp

LH4070 **Lucky Rabbit** (Din7)   5 - 10
by Frances R. Horwich, illus by Ruth Bendel
©1955/p1960(A) by Frances R. Horwich,
24pp

LH4080 **Our Baby** (Din8)   5 - 12
by Frances R. Horwich, illus by Priscilla Pointer
©1955/p1960(A) by Frances R. Horwich,
24pp

LH4050   LH4060

LH4070   LH4080

Little Golden Books – Disney

First published as "Walt Disney's Little Library", the Disney LG series was listed separately from the regular LG line until the numbering system was revised and "D" numbers were replaced with stocking codes. Books have the same format as the regular LGBs of the same period, with the exception of the first 2 books and the Mickey Moue Club series. The first 3 books were issued with dust jackets. (See color plate)

Stories were adapted from WD films as well as created especially for the series. Many were illustated by top Disney animators. While some books have undergone several chagnes during their printing history, others have remained virtually untouched. As major animated films are re-released, their LGB counterparts are often updated. Special attention has been given to noting cover and contents changes throughout the series.

Official Mickey Mouse Club Books were produced in 1955 and 1956. MMC editions have the MMC logo in the upper right corner of the front cover, special end papers, a Mickey Mouse red & silver spine and special back cover, listing other MMC books. They have no LGB identification. However, the series was listed in numerical sequence with the regular books. Some numbers were produced only as MMC editions, some are found in both MMC and regular LGB editions. Cover art was usually the same for both versions. Designs which differ are shown. A few books, usually later printings, are a mixture of LGB and MMC formats. In 1977 a few titles were produced for the new MMC, but no special series was developed and the books are not considered "Official" MMC editions.

The first series of Disney books was numbered D1 thru D140, and with a few exceptions was chronological. Tomart codes adapt the "D" number as explained for the regular LGB series. Mickey Mouse Club listings are all followed by (MMC).

Disney, 1st Series

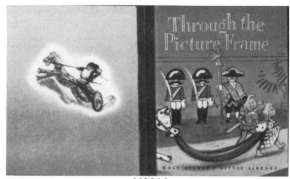
LI0010

LI0010	**Through the Picture Frame** (D1)	10 - 30
	by Robert Edmunds, illus by WDS	
	©1944 by WDP, 24pp. Based on "Ole	
	Lukoie" by Hans Christian Andersen.	
LI0011	Same as LLI0010, in dj of same design	20 - 40
LI0020	**Cold Blooded Penguin, The** (D2)	10 - 30
	by Robert Edmunds, illus by WDS	
	©1944 by WDP, 24pp. From "The	
	Three Caballeros."	
LI0021	Same as LI0020, in dj of same design	20 - 40

LI0020

Books 1 & 2: Full color covers with Disney characters front and back, and special end papers. Books were not numbered, and no title list was printed on the books. Both books were 24-page war editions with dust jackets. Books are marked S&S only and have no LGB identification. Although 10 titles were listed as being part of the "Library", no more books were issued in this format.

End papers for Walt Disney's Little Library had a bookplate and Disney characters. Used only on D1 & D2.

LI0030	**Dumbo** (D3)	10 - 25
	illus by WDS	
	©1947 by WDP, 42pp. Format same as	
	regular LGB series except "WDLL" identifi-	
	cation on cover. Unstated 1st, rare in dust	
	jacket. Adapted from the WD film.	
LI0031	Same as LI0030, in dj of same design	25 - 45
LI0035	Same as LI0030 (MMC)	5 - 10
	©1947/p1955(S) by WDP, 28pp.	
	All new cover design w/yellow background,	
	contents rearranged for 28-page book. This	
	format used for MMC and all later printings.	

LI0030

LI0040	**Snow White and the Seven Dwarfs** (D4)	8 - 15
	by Jacob & Wilhelm Grimm,	
	illus by WDS, adp by Ken O'Brien	
	©1948 by WDP, 24pp. Adapted from the	
	WD film. (See also: LI0660)	
LI0043	Same as LI0040	4 - 8
	©1948/p1951(K) by WDP, 28pp. Cover	
	has plain white background.	
LI0045	Same as LI0043 (MMC)	5 - 10
	©1948/p1955(N) by WDP, 28pp. Cover	
	background changed to light blue for MMC	
	and all later printings.	
LI0050	**Peter and the Wolf** (D5)	6 - 12
	(Fairy Tale), illus by WDS, adp by Dick Kelsey	
	©1947 by WDP, 42pp. From the WD film	
	Make Mine Music adapted from the musical	
	theme by Serge Prokofieff. (See also: LI0560)	
LI0060	**Uncle Remus** (D6)	5 - 10
	by Marion Palmer (adp),	
	illus by WDS, adp by Bob Grant	
	©1947 by WDP, 42pp. Based on Joel	
	Chandler Harris' "Uncle Remus" stories.	
	Adapted from *Song of the South*. Title in	
	red for A & B printings, changed to black	
	for later printings. A proposed title, *Uncle	
	Remus, Brer B'ar and the Honey Orchard*,	
	was never used.	

LI0035   LI0040

LI0045   LI0050

LI0060   LI0065

LI0070   LI0080

LI0090   LI0100

MMC Back Cover   LI0105

LI0110   LI0120

LI0065	Same as LI0060 (MMC) ©1947/p1955(N) by WDP, 24pp. New cover illustration for MMC edition and all later printings. Contents revised for shorter book. (*See also:* LI0850)	5 - 10
LI0070	**Bambi** (D7) illus by WDS, adp by Bob Grant ©1948 by WDP, 42pp. Adapted from the WD film, based on the original story by Felix Salten. (*See also:* LI0900)	5 - 10
LI0075	Same as LI0070 (MMC) by 1948/p1955(O) by WDP, 24pp	5 -8
LI0080	**Pinocchio** (D8) illus by WDS, adp by Campbell Grant ©1948 by WDP, 42pp. Adapted from the WD film, based on the story by Collodi. (*See also:* LI1000)	6 - 12
LI0085	Same as LI0080 (MMC) ©1948/p1955(N) by WDP, 24pp	5 - 8
LI0090	**Bongo** illus by WDS, adp by Campbell Grant ©1948 by WDP, 42pp. Adapted from the film *Fun and Fancy Free*, based on the original story by Sinclair Lewis. (*See also:* LI0620)	5 - 10
LI0100	**Three Little Pigs, The** (D10) (Nursery Tale), illus by WDS, adp by Milt Banta & Al Dempster ©1948 by WDP, 28pp. Adapted from the WD film.	4 - 10
LI0105	Same as LI0100 (MMC) ©1948/p1955(P) by WDP, 24pp. Cover illustration for MMC edition and all later printings. (*See also:* LI0780)	4 - 10

Back Cover design for Official Mickey Mouse Club Books. Additional Mouse Club Books were listed. Books also had a red spine with a Mickey Mouse design. Covers were either totally redone or simply adapted the MMC format. Book contents were not changed.

LI0110	**Johnny Appleseed** (D11) illus by WDS, adp by Ted Parmalee ©1949 by WDP, 42pp. From the WD film *Melody Time*.	6 - 12
LI0120	**Once Upon a Wintertime** (D12) illus by WDS, adp by Tom Oreb ©1950 by WDP, 42pp. From the film *Melody Time*.	6 - 12
LI0130	**Cinderella** (D13) (Fairy Tale), illus by WDS, adp by Campbell Grant ©1950 by WDP, 28pp. Adapted from the WD film. (*See also* LI0590, LI1140)	5 - 12
LI0135	Same as LI0130 (MMC) ©1950/p1955(E) by WDP, 28pp. Cover changed to light green, title type style changed.	4 - 9
LI0140	**Donald Duck's Adventure** (D14) by Annie North Bedford, illus by WDS,	5 - 10

LI0130   LI0140

	adp by Campbell Grant ©1950 by WDP, 28pp	
LI0145	Same as LI0140 (MMC) ©1950/p1955(E) by WDP, 28pp. Color of title type changed to green for MMC & all later editions.	4 - 9
LI0150	**Mickey Mouse's Picnic** (D15) by Jane Werner, illus by WDS, adp by WDS ©1950 by WDP, 28pp	6 - 12
LI0154	Same as LI0150 (MMC) ©1950/p1955(E) by WDP, 24pp	5 - 9
LI0156	Same as LI0150 ©1950/p1968(J), 24pp. Cover background plain blue, title type style changed.	1 - 4
LI0160	**Santa's Toy Shop** (D16) illus by WDS, adp by Al Dempster ©1950 by WDP, 28pp. J & L: Christmas spine.	4 - 9
LI0162	Same as LI0160 (MCC) ©1950/p1955(C) by WDP, 24pp	4 - 9
LI0166	Same as LI0160 ©1950/p1969(N) by WDP, 24pp. Cover background changed to yellow, w/central Santa figure only.	1 - 4
LI0170	**Cinderella's Friends** (D17) by Jane Werner, illus by WDS, adp by Al Dempster ©1950 by WDP, 28pp. Story based on characters from the WD film. Several other books develop original stories, not found in the films, but using the film characters. (See also: LI0580, LI1150)	8 - 12
LI0180	**Donald Duck's Toy Train** (D18) by Jane Werner, illus by WDS, adp by Dick Kelsey & Bill Justice ©1951 by WDP, 28pp. From the WD film, *Out of Scale*.	5 - 10
LI0185	Same as LI0180 (MMC) ©1951/p1955(F) by WDP, 24pp	4 - 8
LI0190	**Alice in Wonderland Meets the White Rabbit** (D19) by Jane Werner, illus by WDS, adp by Al Dempster ©1951 by WDP, 28pp. Adapted from the WD film, based on the story by Lewis Carroll.	4 - 10
LI0200	**Alice in Wonderland Finds the Garden of Live Flowers** (D20) by Jane Werner, illus by WDS, adp by Campbell Grant ©1951 by WDP, 28pp. Adapted from the WD film, based on the story by Lewis Carroll.	6 - 12
LI0210	**Grandpa Bunny** (D21) by Jane Werner, illus by WDS, adp by Dick Kelsey & Bill Justice ©1952 by WDP, 28pp. Adapted from the WD film *Funny Little Bunnies*. Reissued as *The Bunny Book* (LI1110).	6 - 14
LI0220	**Ugly Duckling, The** (D22) by Annie North Bedford, illus by WDS, adp by Don MacLaughlin ©1952 by WDP, 28pp. Adapted from the WD film, based on the Hans Christian Andersen story.	6 - 12
LI0230	**Mad Hatter's Tea Party, The** (D23) by Jane Werner, illus by WDS, adp by Dick Kelsey & Don Griffith ©1952 by WDP, 28pp. Adapted from the WD film, based on the story by Lewis Carroll.	6 - 14
LI0240	**Peter Pan and Wendy** (D24) by Annie North Bedford, illus by WDS,	5 - 10

LI0150

LI0156

LI0160

LI0166

LI0170

LI0180

LI0190

LI0200

LI0210   LI0220

LI0230 LI0240

LI0250 LI0260

LI0270 LI0275

LI0280 LI0290

LI0300 LI0310

adp by Eyvind Earle
©1952 by WDP, 28pp. Adapted from the
WD film, based on the story by James M.
Barrie. (See also: LI0720, LI1100)

| LI0242 | Same as LI0240 (MMC) | 4 - 9 |

©1952/p1955(C) by WDP, 24pp

| LI0250 | **Peter Pan and the Pirates** (D25) | 5 - 10 |

illus by WDS, adp by Bob Moore
©1952 by WDP, 28pp. Adapted from the
WD film, based on the story by James M.
Barrie. (See also: LI0730)

| LI0260 | **Peter Pan and the Indians** (D26) | 6 - 12 |

by Annie North Bedford, illus by WDS,
adp by Brice Mack & Dick Kinney
©1952 by WDP, 28pp. Adapted from the
WD film, based on the story by James M.
Barrie. (See also: LI0740)

| LI0270 | **Donald Duck and Santa Claus** (D27) | 5 - 10 |

by Annie North Bedford, illus by WDS,
adp by Al Dempster
©1952 by WDP, 28pp

| LI0272 | Same as LI0270 (MMC) | 4 - 9 |

©1952/p1955(C) by WDP, 24pp

| LI0275 | Same as LI0270 | 1 - 4 |

©1952/p1965(F) by WDP, 28pp. Cover
w/plain yellow background.

| LI0280 | **Noah's Ark** (D28) | 5 - 12 |

by Annie North Bedford, illus by WDS,
adp by Campbell Grant
©1952 by WDP, 28pp

| LI0290 | **Mickey Mouse and His Space Ship** (D29) | 8 - 14 |

by Jane Werner, illus by WDS,
adp by Milt Banta & John Ushler
©1952 by WDP, 28pp (See also: LI1080)

| LI0300 | **Pluto Pup Goes to Sea** (D30) | 6 - 10 |

by Annie North Bedford, illus by WDS,
adp by Yale Gracey
©1952 by WDP, 28pp. Story line
includes Black Pete.

| LI0310 | **Hiawatha** (D31) | 6 - 12 |

illus by WDS, adp WDS
©1953 by WDP, 28pp. From WD film
Hiawatha.

| LI0320 | **Mickey Mouse and Pluto Pup** (D32) | 5 - 9 |

by Elizabeth Beecher, illus by WDS,
adp by Campbell Grant
©1953 by WDP, 28pp (See also: LI0760)

| LI0322 | Same as LI0320 (MMC) | 5 - 10 |

©1953/p1955(C) by WDP, 24pp. New
cover illustration for MMC edition only.
Contents adapted to 24-page book.

| LI0330 | **Mickey Mouse Goes Christmas Shopping** (D33) | 5 - 10 |

by Annie North Bedford, illus by WDS,
adp by Bob Moore & Xavier Atencio
©1953 by WDP, 28pp

LI0320 LI0322

LI0332   Same as LI0330 (MMC)   ?
         Title noted, but MMC copy unavailable for
         verification.
LI0334   Same as LI0330   2 - 6
         ©1953/p1968 by WDP, 24pp. Cover
         background changed to plain green.
LI0340   **Donald Duck and the Witch** (D34)   8 - 12
         by Annie North Bedford, illus by WDS,
         adp by Dick Kelsey
         ©1953 by WDP, 28pp. Based on the film
         Tricks or Treats.
LI0350   **Seven Dwarfs Find a House, The** (D35) 5 - 10
         by Annie North Bedford, illus by WDS,
         adp by Julius Svendsen
         ©1952 by WDP, 28pp (See also: LI0670)
LI0351   Same as LI0350 (MMC)   5 - 10
         ©1952/p1955(B) by WDP, 28pp
LI0360   **Mother Goose** (D36)   8 - 20
         (Nursery Rhymes), illus by WDS,
         adp by Al Dempster
         ©1952 by WDP, 28pp (See also: LI0510,
         LI0790)
LI0370   **Ben and Me** (D37)   6 - 10
         illus by WDS, adp by Campbell Grant
         ©1954 by WDP, 28pp. Adapted from the
         WD film, based on the book by Robert Lawson.
LI0380   **Chip 'N' Dale at the Zoo** (D38)   6 - 10
         by Annie North Bedford, illus by WDS,
         adp by Bill Bosche
         ©1954 by WDP, 28pp. Adapted from the
         WD film, *Working for Peanuts*.
LI0390   **Donald Duck's Christmas Tree** (D39)   5 - 10
         by Annie North Bedford, illus by WDS,
         adp by Bob Moore
         ©1954 by WDP, 28pp
LI0400   **Donald Duck's Toy Sailboat** (D40)   4 - 10
         by Annie North Bedford, illus by WDS,
         adp by Samuel Armstrong
         ©1954 by WDP, 28pp. Adapted from the
         WD film, *Chips Ahoy*.
LI0410   **Donald Duck's Safety Book** (D41)   6 - 12
         by Annie North Bedford, illus by WDS,
         adp by Manuel Gonzales & George Wheeler
         ©1954 by WDP, 28pp
LI0411   Same as LI0410 (MMC)   5 - 10
         ©1954/p1955(B) by WDP, 28pp
LI0420   **Lady** (D42)   5 - 9
         illus by WDS, adp by Samuel Armstrong
         ©1954 by WDP, 28pp. Adapted from the
         WD film, *Lady and the Tramp*, based on the
         story by Ward Greene.
LI0425   Same as LI0420 (MMC)   ?
         Title noted, but MMC copy unavailable for
         verification.
LI0430   **Disneyland on the Air** (D43)   8 - 12
         by Annie North Bedford, illus by WDS,

LI0330   LI0340

LI0350   LI0360

LI0370   LI0380

LI0390   LI0400

LI0410   LI0420

LI0430   LI0431

LI0432   LI0440

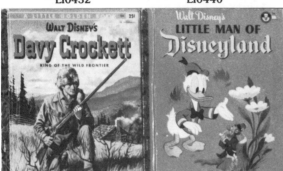

LI0450   LI0460

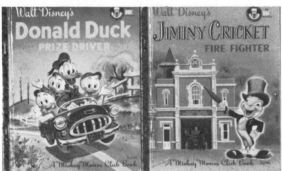

LI0470   LI0480

LI0490   LI0500

LI0510   LI0520

	adp by Samuel Armstrong	
	©1955 by WDP, 28pp	
LI0431	Same as LI0430 (MMC)	8 - 12
	©1955(B) by WDP, 24pp. Picture shows typical cover adaption for MMC edition.	
LI0432	Same as LI0430	4 - 9
	©1955/p1965(C) by WDP, 24pp. Cover background changed to solid red.	
LI0440	**Donald Duck in Disneyland** (D44)	6 - 9
	by Annie North Bedford, illus by WDS, adp by Campbell Grant	
	©1955 by WDP, 28pp (See also: LI0920, LI1090)	
LI0442	Same as LI0440 (MMC)	6 - 9
	©1955/p1956(C) by WDP, 24pp	
LI0450	**Davy Crockett, King of the Wild Frontier** (D45)	6 - 12
	by Irwin Shapiro, illus by WDS, adp by Mel Crawford	
	©1955 by WDP, 28pp. Based on the TV series.	
LI0455	Same as LI0450 (MMC)	?
	Title noted, but MMC copy unavailable for verification.	
LI0460	**Little Man of Disneyland** (D46)(MMC)	6 - 10
	by Annie North Bedford, illus by WDS, adp by Dick Kelsey	
	©1955 by WDP, 28pp	
LI0470	**Davy Crockett's Keelboat Race**(D47)(MMC)	8 - 16
	by Irwin Shapiro, illus by WDS, adp by Mel Crawford	
	©1955 by WDP, 24pp. Adapted from the TV series.	
LI0480	**Robin Hood** (D48)(MMC)	4 - 8
	by Annie North Bedford, illus w/photos	
	©1955 by WDP, 24pp. Adapted from the WD film starring Richard Greene. (See also BD1010)	
LI0490	**Donald Duck Prize Driver** (D49)(MMC)	6 - 12
	by Annie North Bedford, illus by WDS, adp by Neil Boyle	
	©1956 by WDP, 24pp	
LI0491	Same as LI0490	5 - 10
	©1955(B) by WDP. B: not an MMC edition. Same cover design.	
LI0500	**Jiminy Crickett, Fire Fighter** (D50)(MMC)	6 - 14
	by Annie North Bedford, illus by WDS, adp by Samuel Armstrong	
	©1956 by WDP, 24pp	
LI0510	**Mother Goose** (D51)(MMC)	5 - 10
	(Nursery Rhymes), illus by WDS, adp by Al Dempster	
	©1952/p1956(A) by WDP, 24pp. New cover illustration. (See also: LI0360, LI0790)	
LI0520	**Goofy, Movie Star** (D52)(MMC)	7 - 12
	by Annie North Bedford, illus by WDS, adp by Samuel Armstrong	
	©1956 by WDP, 24pp. Based on the Disneyland TV show.	
LI0530	**Mickey Flies the Christmas Mail** (D53)(MMC)	4 - 9
	by Annie North Bedford, illus by WDS, adp by Julius Svendsen & Neil Boyle	
	©1956 by WDP, 24pp	
LI0531	Same as LI0530	5 - 10
	©1956/p1957(B) by WDP, 24pp. Regular LGB format except for MMC logo. Later editions of other books from the MMC series also have mixed formats.	
LI0540	**Perri and Her Friends** (D54)(MMC)	4 - 8

by Annie North Bedford (adp), illus w/photos ©1956(A) by WDP, 24pp. Adapted from the WD film, based on the story by Felix Salten.

LI0541   Same as LI0540   4 - 8
©1956/p1957(B) by WDP, 24pp. Regular LGB edition.

LI0550   **Donald Duck and the Mouseketeers**
(D55)(MMC)   6 - 12
by Annie North Bedford, illus by WDS, adp by Samuel Armstrong
©1956 by WDP, 24pp. Based on the Disneyland TV program "A Day With Donald Duck".

    MMC Book front end paper design. Back end paper also had mouseketeers.

LI0560   **Peter and the Wolf** (D56)(MMC)   6 - 12
(Fairy Tale), illus by WDS, adp by Dick Kelsey
©1947/p1956(A) by WDP, 24pp. From the WD film *Make Mine Music*, adapted from the musical theme by Serge Prokofieff. (See also: LI0050)

LI0565   Same as LI0560   6 - 12
©1947/p1976(B) by WDP, 24pp. Regular LGB edition. Several of the WD books were never redone in full color. This 1976 printing still has pictures in color and duotone.

LI0570   **Mickey Mouse and the Missing Mouseketeers** (D57)(MMC)   3 - 8
by Annie North Bedford, illus by WDS, adp by Julius Svendsen & Bob Totten
©1956 by WDP, 24pp

LI0575   Same as LI0570   1 - 4
©1956/p1976(B) by WDP, 24pp. B: not an "Official MMC" edition. New emblem for 1976 "Walt Disney's MMC". Otherwise regular LGB format.

    Mickey Mouse Club Stamp Book (D58) Not published at this number (See LH1100)

LI0580   **Cinderella's Friends** (D58)(MMC)   5 - 10
by Jane Werner, illus by WDS, adp by Al Dempster
©1950/p1956(A) by WDP, 24pp. Cover change from LI0170.

LI0582   Same as LI0580   4 - 9
©1950/p1959(E) by WDP, 24pp. E: MMC logo only, rest of book is regular LGB format. (See also: LI0170, LI1150)

LI0590   **Cinderella** (D59)(MMC)   3 - 9
(Fairy Tale), illus by WDS, adp by Campbell Grant
©1950/p1956(A) by WDP, 24pp. Adapted from the WD film.

LI0595   Same as LI0590   2 - 7
©1950/p1959(I) by WDP, 24pp. MMC logo only. (See also: LI0130, LI1140)

No Book Published (D60)

LI0610   **Sleeping Beauty** (D61)   6 - 10
by Annie North Bedford, illus by WDS, adp by Julius Svendsen, Frank Armitage & Walt Peregoy
©1957 by WDP, 24pp. Adapted from the WD film. Different illustrations than the Big & Giant GBs. An abridged version of this edition is used with LH1330, a paper doll book.

LI0620   **Bongo** (D62)(MMC)   5 - 9
illus by WDS, adp by Campbell Grant
©1948/p1956(A) by WDP, 24pp. Adapted from the film *Fun and Fancy Free*. Back cover not MMC design. Last book in the "Official MMC" series. (See also: LI0090)

LI0530   LI0531

LI0540   LI0550

MMC End Paper   LI0560

LI0570   LI0575

LI0580   LI0590

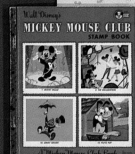

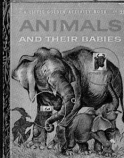

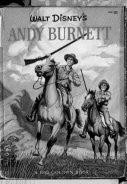

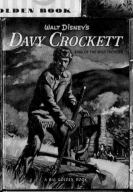

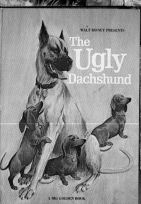

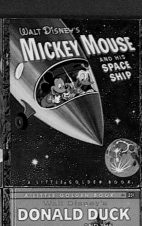
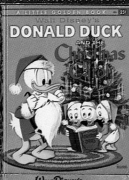

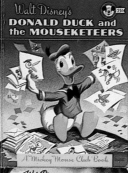

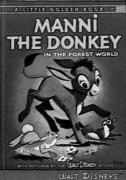

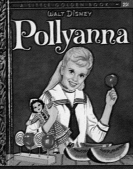
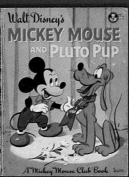

Hanna-Barbera
THE FLINTSTONES
A Big Golden Book

Hanna-Barbera
TOP CAT
A BIG GOLDEN BOOK

HANNA-BARBERA'S
Yogi Bear
A Big Golden Book

Hanna-Barbera
The Jetsons
A LITTLE GOLDEN BOOK

HANNA-BARBERA'S
THE FLINTSTONES
A LITTLE GOLDEN BOOK

Hanna-Barbera
PEBBLES FLINTSTONE
A LITTLE GOLDEN BOOK

Hanna-Barbera
BAMM-BAMM
WITH PEBBLES FLINTSTONE
a Little Golden Book

Hanna-Barbera
CAVE KIDS
a Little Golden Book

Hanna-Barbera
Touché Turtle
A LITTLE GOLDEN BOOK

Hanna-Barbera
Wally Gator
A LITTLE GOLDEN BOOK

Hanna-Barbera
LIPPY the LION
AND HARDY HAR HAR
A LITTLE GOLDEN BOOK

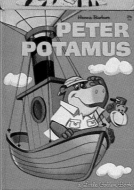
Hanna-Barbera
PETER POTAMUS
a Little Golden Book

Hanna-Barbera
TOP CAT
A LITTLE GOLDEN BOOK

Hanna-Barbera
Yakky Doodle AND Chopper

Hanna-Barbera
Hey there— it's YOGI BEAR!
a Little Golden Book

HANNA-BARBERA'S
Cindy Bear
FEATURING Yogi Bear

HANNA-BARBERA'S
Huckleberry Hound
SAFETY SIGNS
PUBLISHED IN COOPERATION WITH
THE NATIONAL SAFETY COUNCIL
A LITTLE GOLDEN BOOK

HANNA-BARBERA'S
PIXIE and DIXIE
AND MR. JINKS
WITH PAGES FIGURES TO CUT OUT AND ASSEMBLE
A LITTLE GOLDEN BOOK

QuickDraw McGRAW
A LITTLE GOLDEN BOOK

Hanna-Barbera's
SCOOBY-DOO and the Pirate Treasure
a Little Golden Book

Bullwinkle
A LITTLE GOLDEN BOOK

Bob Clampett's
Beany Goes To Sea
a Little Golden Book
LEAKIN' LENA

Winky Dink
A LITTLE GOLDEN BOOK

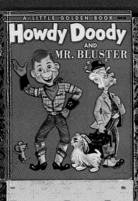

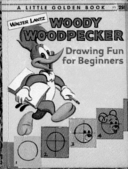

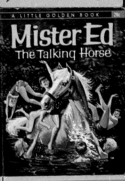

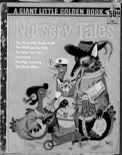

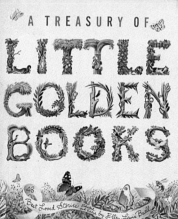
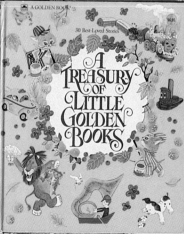

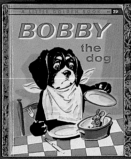

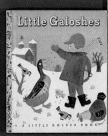

LI0610	LI0620

LI0630	LI0640

LI0650	LI0654

LI0660	LI0670

LI0630 **Scamp, The Adventures of a Little Puppy** (D63)   5 - 10
by Annie North Bedford, illus by WDS, adp by Norm McGary & Joe Rinaldi ©1957 by WDP, 24pp

LI0640 **Paul Revere** (D64)   4 - 9
by Irwin Shapiro, illus by WDS, adp by Paul Luhrs ©1957 by WDP, 24pp

LI0650 **Old Yeller** (D65)   5 - 10
by Irwin Shapiro, illus by WDS, adp by Edwin Schmidt & E. Joseph Dreany ©1957 by WDP, 24pp. Adapted from the WD film, based on the novel by Fred Gipson.

LI0654 Same as LI0650   3 - 6
©1957/p1965(D) by WDP, 24pp. Cover background changed to solid blue.

LI0660 **Snow White and the Seven Dwarfs** (D66)   3 - 6
by Jacob & Wilhelm Grimm, illus by WDS, adp by Ken O'Brien & Al Dempster ©1948/p1958(P) by WDP, 24pp. Adapted from the WD film. Illustrations still printed in color and duotone. P: earliest printing at this number. (See also: LI0040)

LI0670 **Seven Dwarfs Find a House, The** (D67)   5 - 10
by Annie North Bedford, illus by WDS, adp by Julius Svendsen ©1952/p1958(D) by WDP, 24pp. D; earliest printing at this number. (See also: LI0350)

LI0680 **Zorro** (D68)   8 - 14
by Charles Spain Verral, illus by WDS, adp by John Steel ©1958 by WDP, 24pp. Based on the Johnston McCulley character, adapted from the WD TV series.

LI0684 Same as LI0680   5 - 12
©1958/p1965(D) by WDP, 24pp. Cover background changed to yellow.

Pluto Pup Goes to Sea (D69) Not published at this number. (See LI0300)

LI0700 **Scamp's Adventure** (D70)   4 - 8
by Annie North Bedford, illus by WDS, adp by Joe Rinaldi & Neil Boyle ©1958 by WDP, 24pp (See also: LI0880)

LI0710 **Sleeping Beauty & the Good Fairies** (D71)   6 - 10
by Dorothy Strebe & Annie North Bedford, illus by WDS, adp by Julius Svendsen & C.W. Satterfield ©1958 by WDP, 24pp. Characters adapted from the WD film.

Ad Backs noting other Golden series were carried on the back of Disney LGBs in the same manner as the regular LGB series. (See: AB1000)

LI0720 **Peter Pan and Wendy** (D72)   3 - 8
by Annie North Bedford, illus by WDS,

LI0680	LI0684

LI0700	LI0710

adp by Eyvind Earle
©1952/p1958(D) by WDP, 24pp. Adapted
from the WD film, based on the story by
James M. Barrie. D: earliest printing at this
number. (See also: LI0240, LI1100)

LI0730 **Peter Pan and the Pirates** (D73)   3 - 6
illus by WDS, adp by Bob Moore
©1952/p1958(B) by WDP, 24pp. Adapted
from the WD film, based on the story by
James M. Barrie. B: earliest printing at this
number. (See also: LI0250)

LI0740 **Peter Pan and the Indians** (D74)   4 - 8
by Annie North Bedford, illus by WDS,
adp by Brice Mack & Dick Kinney
©1952/p1958(B) by WDP, 24pp. Adapted
from the WD film, based on the story by
James M. Barrie. B: earliest printing at this
number. (See also: LI0260)

LI0750 **Manni the Donkey in the Forest
World** (D75)   6 - 10
by Emily Broun (adp), adp & illus by WDS
©1959 by WDP, 24pp. Based on the
story by Felix Salten.

LI0760 **Mickey Mouse and Pluto Pup** (D76)   3 - 6
by Elizabeth Beecher, illus by WDS,
adp by Campbell Grant
©1953/p1958(E) by WDP, 24pp. E: earliest
printing at this number. (See also: LI0320)

LI0770 **Zorro and the Secret Plan** (D77)   8 - 14
by Charles Spain Verral,
illus by Hamilton Greene
©1958 by WDP, 24pp. Adapted from
the WD TV series. Based on the famous
Johnston McCulley character.

LI0771 Same as LI0770   6 - 10
©1958/p1965(B) by WDP, 24pp. Cover
background changed to red.

LI0780 **Three Little Pigs, The** (D78)   2 - 6
(Nursery Tale), illus by WDS,
adp by Milt Banta & Al Dempster
©1948/p1958(S) by WDP, 24pp.
Illustrations in color & duotone. The
"Y" edition (1965) has all color pictures.
(See also: LO0100)

LI0790 **Mother Goose** (D79)   2 - 6
(Nursery Rhymes), illus by WDS,
adp by Al Dempster
©1952/p1959(E) by WDP, 24pp. E: earliest
printing at this number. (See also: LI0360,
LI0510)

LI0800 **Tonka** (D80)   5 - 10
by Elizabeth Beecher (adp), illus w/photos
©1959 by WDP, 24pp. Photos from the
WD film, *Comanche*. Based on the story
by David Appel.

LI0810 **Darby O'Gill** (D81)   5 - 10

Ad Back   LI0720

LI0730   LI0740

LI0750   LI0760

LI0770   LI0771

LI0780   LI0790

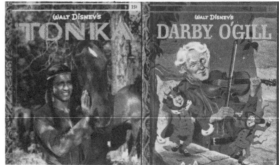

LI0800   LI0810

LI0820   LI0830

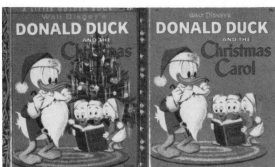

LI0840   LI0841

LI0850   LI0860

LI0870   LI0880

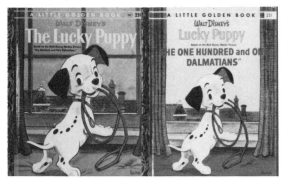

LI0890   LI0891

by Annie North Bedford, illus by WDS,
adp by David Gantz
©1959 by WDP, 24pp. Adapted from the
WD film, *Darby O'Gill and the Little People*.

LI0820	**Shaggy Dog, The** (D82)	5 - 12

by Charles Spain Verral (adp),
illus by WDS, adp by Joseph Cellini
©1959 by WDP, 24pp. Story contains the
full text of *The Hound of Florence* by Felix
Salten, illus adapted from the WD film.

LI0830	**Goliath II** (D83)	6 - 12

written & illus by Bill Peet
©1959 by WDP, 24pp. Adapted from the
WD film

LI0840	**Donald Duck & the Christmas Carol** (D84)	6 - 15

by Annie North Bedford, illus by WDS,
adp by Norm McGary
©1960 by WDP, 24pp. Story line includes
Uncle Scrooge McDuck.

LI0841	Same as LI0840	6 - 15

©1960/p1963(B) by WDP, 24pp.
Title type style changed, cover background
changed to solid green, Christmas spine.

LI0850	**Uncle Remus** (D85)	3 - 7

by Marion Palmer (adp), illus by WDS,
adp by Bob Grant
©1947/p1959(Q) by WDP, 24pp. Based on
Joel Chandler Harris' "Uncle Remus", adapted.
from the film *Song of the South*. Q: earliest
printing at this number. (See also: LI0060)

LI0860	**Donald Duck, Lost and Found** (D86)	5 - 10

by Carl Buettner, illus by Bob Grant &
Bob Totten
©1960 by WDP, 24pp

LI0870	**Toby Tyler** (D87)	5 - 10

by Carl Memling, illus by WDS,
adp by Sam McKim
©1960 by WDP, 24pp. Based on the story
by James Otis Kaler.

LI0880	**Scamp's Adventure** (D88)	3 - 7

by Annie North Bedford, illus by WDS,
adp by Joe Rinaldi & Neil Boyle
©1958/p1960(C) by WDP, 24pp. C: earliest
printing at this number. (See also: LI0700)

LI0890	**Lucky Puppy, The** (D89)	6 - 10

by Jane Werner Watson (adp), illus by WDS,
adp by Allen Hubbard & Don Bestor
©1960 by WDP, 24pp. Based on the book
101 Dalmatians by Dodie Smith. Only the
1st edition shows window panes.

LI0891	Same as LI0890	6 - 10

©1960(B) by WDP, 24pp. Cover variation;
2nd printing, smaller dog, no window panes,
new title type.

LI0894	Same as LI0890	4 - 8

©1960/p1964(F) by WDP, 24pp.New cover

LI0894   LI0895

with green background, film name dropped.

LI0895   Same as LI0894   4 - 8
©1960/p1964(G) by WDP, 24pp. Film name added to cover.

LI0900   **Bambi** (D90)   3 - 9
illus by WDS, adp by Bob Grant
©1948/p1960(T) by WDP, 24pp. T: earliest printing at this number (See also: LI0070). A reprint of *Dumbo* had been planned for D90, but did not materialize.

LI0901   Same as LI0900   1 - 6
©1948/p1965(X) by WDP, 24pp. Cover has plain white background.

LI0910   **Pollyanna** (D91)   8 - 15
by Elizabeth Beecher (adp),
illus by WDS, adp by Karen Hedstrom
©1960 by WDP, 24pp. Adapted from the WD film, based on the novel by Eleanor H. Porter.

LI0920   **Donald Duck in Disneyland** (D92)   4 - 8
by Annie North Bedford,
illus by WDS, adp by Campbell Grant
©1960(D) by WDP, 24pp. New cover design. D: earliest printing at this number.
(See also: LI0440, LI1090)

LI0930   **Bedknobs and Broomsticks** (D93) 2 - 7
illus by WDS
©1971 by WDP, 24pp. Unstated 1st. Adapted from the WD film. (See also: BD1100)

LI0940   **Donald Duck/Private Eye** (D94)   6 - 15
by Carl Buettner, illus by WDS,
adp by Al White & Homer Jonas
©1961 by WDP, 24pp

LI0950   **Swiss Family Robinson** (D95)   5 - 10
by Jean Lewis (adp), illus by Paul Granger
©1961 by WDP, 24pp. Based on the story by Johann Wyss.

LI0960   **Flying Car, The** (D96)   5 - 10
by Charles Spain Verral, illus by Fred Irvin
©1961 by WDP, 24pp. Adapted from rom *The Absent-Minded Professor*.

LI0970   **Babes in Toyland** (D97)   5 - 10
by Barbara Shook Hazen, illus by WDS,
adp by Earl & Carol Marshall
©1961 by WDP, 24pp. Adapted from the WD film.

LI0971   Same as LI0970   4 - 8
©1961(C), 24pp. Cover background changed to green.

LI0980   **Ludwig Von Drake** (D98)   6 - 12
by Gina Ingoglia & George Sherman,
illus by WDS, adp by Hawley Pratt & Herbert Stott
©1961 by WDP, 24pp

LI0990   **Toy Soldiers, The** (D99)   5 - 9
by Barbara Shook Hazen, illus by WDS,
adp by Robert Thompson

LI0900   LI0901

LI0910   LI0920

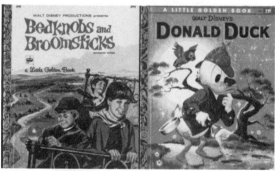

LI0930   LI0940

LI0950   LI0960

LI0970   LI0980

LI0990   LI1000

LI1010   LI1020

LI1030   LI1040

LI1050   LI1060

LI1070   LI1080

LI1090   LI1100

©1961 by WDP, 24pp. Adapted from the
WD film *Babes in Toyland.*

LI1000   **Pinocchio** (D100)   4 - 8
illus by WDS, adp by Campbell Grant
©1948/p1961(V) by WDP, 24pp. Adapted
from the WD film, based on the story by
Collodi. V: earliest printing at this number.
(See also: LI0080)

LI1010   **Pinocchio and the Whale** (D101)   7 - 15
by Gina Ingoglia, illus by WDS, adp by Al White
©1961 by WDP, 24pp. Adapted from the
WD film, based on the story by Collodi.

LI1020   **Big Red** (D102)   4 - 7
by Kathleen N. Daly, illus by WDS,
adp by Mel Crawford
©1962 by WDP, 24pp. Adapted from the
WD film.

LI1030   **Lady** (D103)   3 - 6
illus by WDS, adp by Samuel Armstrong
©1954/p1961(E) by WDP, 24pp. Adapted
from the WD film *Lady and the Tramp,* based
on the story by Ward Greene. E: earliest printing at this number.

LI1050   **Savage Sam** (D104)   3 - 8
by Carl Memling, illus by Hamilton Greene
©1963 by WDP, 24pp. Adapted from the
WD film, based on the novel by Fred Gipson.

LI1050   **Surprise for Mickey Mouse** (D105)   3 - 6
illus by WDS
©1971 by WDP, 24pp. A "Walt Disney World"
book ... story line centered on "The Mickey
Mouse Revue."

LI1060   **Sword in the Stone, The** (D106)   5 - 12
by Carl Memling, illus by WDS,
adp by Norm McGary
©1963 by WDP, 24pp. Adapted from the WD
film, suggested by the story by T.H. White.

LI1070   **Wizard's Duel, The** (D107)   5 - 12
by Carl Memling, illus by WDS,
adp by Al White & Hawley Pratt
©1963 by WDP, 24pp. Adapted from the
WD film, suggested by the story, *The Sword
in the Stone* by T.H. White.

LI1080   **Mickey Mouse and His Space Ship** (D108) 8 - 12
by Jane Werner, illus by WDS, adp by Milt
Banta & John Ushler, cover by Norm McGary
©1963/p1963(C) by WDP, 24pp. New cover
art. Inside text unchanged. (See also: LI0290)

LI1090   **Donald Duck in Disneyland** (D109)   5 - 10
by Annie North Bedford, illus by WDS,
adp by Campbell Grant
©1960/p1963(F) by WDP, 24pp. Cover
background changed to plain orange. F: earliest
printing at this number. (See also: LI0440,
LI0920)

LI1100   **Peter Pan and Wendy** (D110)   2 - 6
by Annie North Bedford, illus by WDS,
adp by Eyvind Earle
©1952/p1964(E) by WDP, 24pp. Adapted
from the WD film, based on the story by Sir
James M. Barrie. E: earliest printing at this
number. Cover design changed to pink
background. (See also: LI0240, LI0720)

LI1110   **Bunny Book** (D111)   5 - 12
by Jane Werner, illus by WDS,
adp by Dick Kelsey & Bill Justice
©1951/p1964(C) by WDP, 24pp. C: earliest
printing at this number. Adapted from the WD
film *Funny Little Bunnies.* Previously pub-

lished as *Grandpa Bunny* (LI0210).
(See also: BD1160)

LI1120 Mary Poppins/A Jolly Holiday (D112) 4 - 10
by Annie North Bedford,
illus by Beverly Edwards & Leon Jason
©1964 by WDP, 24pp. Based on the WD
film, adapted from the stories by P.L. Travers.

LI1130 Mary Poppins (D113) 4 - 9
by Annie North Bedford, illus by Al White
©1964 by WDP, 24pp. Based on the WD
film, adapted from the stories by P.L. Travers.

LI1140 Cinderella (D114) 2 - 6
(Fairy Tale), illus by WDS,
adp by Campbell Grant
©1950/p1964(N) by WDP, 24pp. Adapted
from the WD film. N: earliest printing at this
number. (See also: LI0130, LI0590)

LI1150 Cinderella's Friends (D115) 3 - 7
by Jane Werner, illus by WDS,
adp by Al Dempster
©1950/p1964(F) by WDP, 24pp. F: earliest
printing at this number. Cover background
changed to plain purple. (See also: LI0170,
LI0580)

LI1160 Winnie-the-Pooh/The Honey Tree (D116) 3 - 7
by A.A. Milne, illus by WDS, adp by Bob Totten
©1965 by WDP, 24pp. Text © 1954 by A.A.
Milne

LI1170 Winnie-the-Pooh Meets Gopher (D117) 3 - 7
illus by WDS, adp by George Desantis
©1964 by WDP, 24pp. Based on a story
by A.A. Milne.

LI1180 Ugly Dachshund, The (D118) 7 - 15
by Carl Memling (adp), illus by Mel Crawford
©1966 by WDP, 24pp Adapted from the
WD film. (See also: BD2100)

L1190 Thumper (D119) 4 - 12
illus by WDS
©1942/p1965(A) by WDP, 24pp. 1st LGB
printing. Previously printed by Grosset &
Dunlap in a longer version. Based on the
character created for the WD film *Bambi*.

LI1200 Jungle Book, The (D120) 3 - 7
by Annie North Bedford, illus by WDS,
adp by Mel Crawford
©1967 by WDP, 24pp. Based on the WD
film, adapted from the Mowgli stories by
Rudyard Kipling. NOTE: 29¢ copies are
1sts; 39¢ copies are imprinted with both an
"A" and a "B" on the same page.

LI1210 Winnie-the-Pooh and Tigger (D121) 3 - 7
by A.A. Milne, illus by WDS
©1968 by WDP, 24pp. Text ©1956 by
A.A. Milne

LI1220 Aristocats, The (D122) 4 - 9

LI1110   LI1120

LI1130   LI1140

LI1150   LI1160

LI1170   LI1180

LI1190   LI1200

LI1210   LI1220

LI1230   LI1240

LI1250   LI1260

LI1270   LI1280

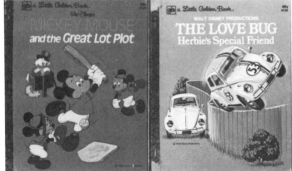

LI1290   LI1300

LI1310   LI1320

illus by WDS
©1970 by WDP, 24pp. Unstated 1st.
Adapted from the WD film.

LI1230 **Disneyland Parade with Donald Duck** (D123) 3 - 9
illus by WDS
©1971 by WDP, 24pp.

LI1240 **Pluto and the Adventure of the
Golden Scepter** (D124)   4 - 8
illus by WDS
©1972 by WDP, 24pp. A "Walt Disney World"
book ... story line centered on Disney World
attractions.

LI1250 **Favorite Nursery Tales** (D125)   3 - 8
(Nursery Tales), illus by WDS
©1973 by WDP, 24pp. Two stories
selected from BD1720.

LI1260 **Robin Hood** (D126)   3 - 9
illus by WDS
©1973 by WDP, 24pp. Unstated 1st.
Adapted from the animated feature.

LI1270 **Donald Duck & the Witch Next Door** (D127) 3 - 7
illus by WDS
©1974 by WDP, 24pp. Unstated 1st.

LI1280 **Robin Hood and the Daring Mouse** (D128) 5 - 10
illus by WDS
©1974 by WDP, 24pp. Unstated 1st.
Adapted from the animated feature.

LI1290 **Mickey Mouse & the Great Lot Plot** (D129) 2 - 6
illus by WDS
©1974 by WDP, 24pp. Unstated 1st.
Story line includes Uncle Scrooge.

LI1300 **Love Bug, The** (D130)   4 - 10
illus by WDS
©1974 by WDP, 24pp. Unstated 1st.
Adapted from the WD film.

LI1310 **Donald Duck in America on Parade** (D131) 3 - 8
illus by WDS
©1975 by WDP, 24pp. Story based on the
Disney Bicentennial parade. Unstated 1st.

LI1320 **Bambi/Friends of the Forest** (D132)   2 - 6
illus by WDS
©1975 by WDP, 24pp. Unstated 1st.

LI1330 **Mickey Mouse/The Kitten Sitters** (D133) 2 - 6
illus by WDS
©1976 by WDP, 24pp. New MMC logo.
Not an "Official" MMC edition. Unstated 1st.

LI1340 **Mickey Mouse & the Best Neighbor
Contest** (D134)   2 - 6
illus by WDS
©1977 by WDP, 24pp. Unstated 1st.

LI1350 **Mickey Mouse and the Mouseketeers/
Ghost Town Adventure** (D135)   2 - 6
illus by WDS
©1977 by WDP, 24pp. New MMC logo.
Not an "Official" MMC edition. Unstated 1st.

LI1330   LI1340

LI1350   LI1360

LI1360   **Rescuers, The** (D136)   3 - 9
illus by WDS
©1977 by WDP, 24pp. Based on the WD
film, adapted from *The Rescuers and Miss
Bianca* by Margery Sharp. Unstated 1st.

LI1370   **Pete's Dragon** (D137)   3 - 7
illus by WDS
©1977 by WDP, 24pp. Unstated 1st.
Adapted from the WD film, based on a story
by Seton I. Miller & S.S. Field.

LI1380   **Mickey Mouse and Goofy/The Big
Bear Scare** (D138)   2 - 6
illus by WDS
©1978 by WDP, 24pp. Unstated 1st.

LI1390   **Donald Duck and the One Bear** (D139)   2 - 6
illus by WDS
©1978 by WDP, 24pp. Unstated 1st.

LI1400   **Donald Duck/Instant Millionaire** (D140)   3 - 8
illus by WDS
©1978 by WDP, 24pp. Story line includes
Uncle Scrooge and the Beagle Boys.
Unstated 1st.

Disney, 2nd series

Books issued since 1979, with stocking codes instead of "D"
numbers. List is chronological with Tomart codes assigned that
are not adapted from the book number. In order to avoid duplication, only new titles or revisions of previously produced titles
are included in the listing.

LI1370   LI1380

LI2010   **Black Hole, The**   1 - 3
©1979 by WDP, 24pp. Adapted from the WD
film. The LGB #501 is a transitional stocking
code number without the appendix.

LI2030   **Winnie-the-Pooh and the Honey Patch**   1 - 3
©1980 by WDP, 24pp.

LI2040   **Winnie-the-Pooh/The Special Morning**   1 - 3
©1980 by WDP, 24pp.

LI2050   **Fox and Hound/Hide & Seek**   2 - 6
©1981 by WDP, 24pp. A: edition noted on
last page. Adapted from the WD film, based
on the story by Dan Mannix.

LI2060   **Toad Flies High**   4 - 10
©1982 by WDP, 24pp. From "Ichabod and
Mr. Toad", adapted from Kenneth Grahame's
The Wind in the Willows. A: noted "available
only in the U.S. until Jan. 1, 1983."

LI2070   **Mickey's Christmas Carol**   1 - 5
©1983 by WDP, 24pp. Adapted from the
animated featurette based on story by Charles
Dickens. (See also: BD1660, MB2770)

LI2080   **Snow White and the Seven Dwarfs**   1 - 3
©1984 by WDP, 24pp. All new edition,
with 50th Anniversary logo.

LI2090   **Sport Goofy and the Racing Robot**   3 - 9

LI1390   LI1400

LI2040   LI2050

LI2010   LI2030

LI2060   LI2070

LI2080   LI2090

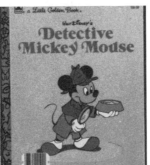

©1984 by WDP, 24pp. "Sport Goofy" was the official mascot of the 1984 French Olympic Team.

LI2100 Black Cauldron/Taran Finds a Friend   2 - 5
©1985 by WDP, 24pp. Adapted from the WD film, based on *The Chronicles of Pridain* by Lloyd Alexander.

LI2110 Detective Mickey Mouse   1 - 2
©1985 by WDCo., 24pp

LI2120 101 Dalmatians   1 - 3
©1985 by WDCo., 24pp. Adapted from the WD film, based on the story by Dodie Smith. (See also: BD1760)

LI2130 Return to Oz/Dorothy Saves the Emerald City   3 - 10
©1985 by WDP, 24pp. Aapted from the WD film, based on the Oz stories by Frank L. Baum.

LI2140 Return to Oz/Escape from Witch's Castle   3 - 10
©1985 by WDP, 24pp. Adapted from the WD film, based on the Oz stories by Frank L. Baum.

LI2150 Bambi   1 - 2
©1984 by WDP, 24pp. All new edition. Adapted from the WD film.

LI2160 Cinderella   1 - 2
©1968 by WDP, 24pp. All new edition. Adapted from the WD film.

LI2170 Donald Duck and the Biggest Dog in Town   2 - 5
©1986 by WDP, 24pp. Reprinted as *Donald Duck and the Big Dog* (LI2190)

LI2180 Sleeping Beauty   1 - 2
©1986 by WDP, 24pp. All new edition. Adapted from the WD film.

LI2190 Donald Duck and the Big Dog   1 - 3
©1986/p1987(C) by WDP. 24pp. Previously titled: *Donald Duck and the Biggest Dog in Town* (LI2170).

LI2200 Donald Duck/Some Ducks Have All the Luck   1 - 3
©1987 by WDCo., 24pp

LI2210 Duck Tales/Hunt for the Giant Pearl   1 - 4
©1987 by WDCo., 24pp

LI2100   LI2110

LI2120   LI2130

LI2140   LI2150

LI2160   LI2170

LI2180   LI2190

LI2200   LI2210

LI2220	**Jungle Book, The**	1 - 2
	©1954/p1987(A) by WDCo., 24pp. Cover change only. Adapted from the WD film, based on the Mowgli stories by Rudyard Kipling.	
LI2230	**Lady and the Tramp**	1 - 2
	©1954/p1987 by WDCo., 24pp. Previous title: *Lady*. New cover only. Adapted from the WD film.	

LI2220   LI2230

LI2240	**Mickey Mouse Heads for the Sky**	1 - 2
	©1987 by WDCo., 24pp	
LI2250	**Pinocchio**	1 - 2
	illus by WDS, adp by Campbell Grant ©1948/p1987(KK) by WDP, 24pp. New cover art only. Adapted from the WD film, based on the story by Collodi.	

LI2240   LI2250

LI2260	**Aristocats, The**	1 - 2
	©1970/p1988(A), 24pp. Cover art changed, contents unchanged. Adapted from the WD film.	
LI2270	**Duck Tales/Secret City Under the Sea**	2 - 4
	by Paul S. Newman, illus by Bill Langley & Annie Guenther ©1988 by WDCo., 24pp	

LI2260   LI2270

LI2280	**Dumbo**	1 - 2
	by Teddy Slater (adp), illus by Ron Dias & Annie Guenther ©1988 by WDCo., 24pp. All new edition.	
LI2290	**Mickey and the Beanstalk**	1 - 2
	by Dina Anastasio (adp), illus by Sharon Ross ©1988 by WDCo., 24pp	

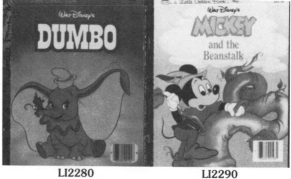

LI2280   LI2290

LI2300	**Mickey Mouse Heads for the Sky**	1 - 2
	©1987/p1988 by WDCo., 24pp. Enhanced cover graphics. See LI2240.	
LI2310	**Mickey Mouse/Those Were the Days**	1 - 2
	by Mary Carey, illus by Mones ©1988 by WDCo., 24pp	
LI2320	**Mickey Mouse's Picnic**	1 - 2
	by Jane Werner, illus by WDS ©1950/p1988(M) by WDP, 24pp. Cover art changed, contents same as LI0150.	
LI2330	**Rescuers, The**	1 - 2
	©1977/p1988(A) by WDP, 24pp. Cover art changed, contents same as LI1360.	
LI2340	**Little Mermaid/Ariel's Underwater Adventure**	1 - 4
	by Michael Teitelbaum (adp), illus by Ron Dias ©1989 by WDCo., 24pp. Adapted from the WD film.	
LI2350	**Peter Pan**	1 - 2
	by Eugene Bradley Coco (adp), illus by Ron Dias ©1989 by WDCo., 24pp. All new edition. Adapted from the WD film.	
LI2360	**Cowboy Mickey**	1 - 2
	by Cindy West, illus by Guelle ©1990 by WDCo., 24pp	

LI2300   LI2310

LI2320   LI2330

LI2340   **LI2350**

LI2360   **LI2370**

LI4000

LJ1800   **LJ1801**

LJ1802   **LJ1803**

LI2370	**Lady and the Tramp**	1 - 2

©1990 by WDCo., 24pp. Adapted from the WD film, based on the story by Ward Greene. Cover art changed, contents unchanged. (See also: LI0420, ILI1030, LI2230)

Little Golden Books – Disney – Mickey's 60th Birthday

A special boxed set of 12 "Mickey" LGBs and a 60th Birthday poster were issued by American Family Publishers in 1988. All the books in the set were also released as regular issue LGBs. However, these books do not have price codes, and all are marked "American Family Publishers" on the inside front cover. Values given for individual books are for these specially marked copies. Order of listing is same as stated on slipcase.

LI4000	**Mickey's 60th Birthday**	20 - 45

©1988 by WDCo. Distributed by American Family Publishers. Set of 12 LGBs in slipcase with poster.

Individual books in LI4000:

LI4010	**Detective Mickey Mouse**	1 - 3
LI4020	**Mickey and the Beanstalk**	1 - 3
LI4030	**Mickey's Christmas Carol**	1 - 3
LI4040	**Mickey Mouse and Goofy/The Big Bear Scare**	1 - 3
LI4050	**Mickey Mouse & the Best Neighbor Contest**	1 - 3
LI4060	**Mickey Mouse and the Great Lot Plot**	1 - 3
LI4070	**Mickey Mouse Heads for the Sky**	1 - 3
LI4080	**Mickey Mouse/The Kitten Sitters**	1 - 3
LI4090	**Mickey Mouse/Those Were the Days**	1 - 3
LI4100	**Mickey Mouse's Picnic**	1 - 3
LI4110	**Surprise for Mickey Mouse**	1 - 3
LI4120	**Mother Goose**	1 - 3

Little Golden Books – Eager Reader

A new beginning reader series that ran in 1974 and 1975. All books had a standard cover format that featured the series name, a back cover design that included a listing of other titles, and specially designed end papers. Spines were plain gold. First printings are unstated, later printings are noted on title page below copyright. (See also: Read-It-Yourself)

LJ1800	**New Home for Snow Ball, A** (800)	1 - 4

by Joan Bowden, illus by Jan Pyk
©1974, 24pp

LJ1801	**Pet in a Jar, The** (801)	1 - 4

by Judy Stang, illus by Jan Pyk
©1974, 24pp

LJ1802	**Hat for a Queen, A** (802)	1 - 4

by Joan Chase Bacon, illus by Olinda Giacomini
©1974, 24pp

LJ1803	**Boo and the Flying Flews** (803)	1 - 4

by Joan Chase Bacon, illus by Donald Leake
©1974, 24pp

LJ1804	**Little Black Puppy, The** (804)	2 - 6

by Charlotte Zolotow, illus by Lilian Obligado
©1974, 24pp

LJ1805	**Who Took the Top Hat Trick?** (805)	1 - 4

by Joan Bowden, illus by Jim Cummins
©1974, 24pp

LJ1806	**Cat Who Stamped His Feet, The** (806)	2 - 6

by Betty Ren Wright, illus by Tom O'Sullivan
©1974, 24pp

LJ1807	**Elephant on Wheels, The** (807)	1 - 4

by Alice McKay Thatcher, illus by Jerry Scott
©1974, 24pp

LJ1808 **Monster! Monster!** (808)   1 - 4
by David Harrison, illus by Rosalind Fry
©1975, 24pp

LJ1809 **Bear's Surprise Party, The** (809)   1 - 4
by Joan Bowden, illus by Jerry Scott
©1975, 24pp

LJ1804   LJ1805

Little Golden Books – Foreign

By 1953, LGBs were advertised as being available to "children of all nations." Foreign language editions from European, Mid-Eastern and South American countries turn up, as well as Australian, Canadian and English versions. Foreign editions generally repeat the American titles, but there are also books that are unique to their country of origin. Big and Giant Golden Books, as well as books from other series, were also produced in foreign editions. Examples can be found with Big Golden Books, Shape Books and Giant LGBs. Books generally have the same value as their American counterparts.

LJ1806   LJ1807

AUSTRALIA (A Little Golden Book)

Over 600 LGBs have been published in Australia, including many titles unique to that country. The LGB format is similar to the American books, with a slightly darker spine and bright yellow end papers. Disney books, activity books, Giant, Deluxe and other Golden Books are also available in Australia.

LK2010 **Aboriginal Tales** (453)   6 - 12
by Victor Barnes, illus by Hal English
©1971, 24pp

LK2020 **Skippy** (379)   6 - 12
by Walter Stackpool
©1969, 24pp

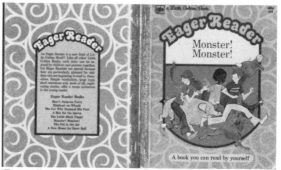

Eager Reader Back Cover   LJ1808

ENGLAND (A Little Golden Book)

Very similar to American editions, except for the "16p" price on the cover, and the Disney and Sesame Street characters very obviously missing from the LGB train on the back cover. This 1973 printing lists 36 other LGBs.

LK2040 **Fuzzy Duckling, The**   2 - 6
by Jane Werner,
illus by Alice & Martin Provensen
©1973, 16pp

LK2010   LK2020

DUTCH (Een Gouden Boekje)

Books numbered in excess of 300 are listed on the back cover, quite a few unique to the Netherlands. Format similar to American books.

LK2060 **Kijk Eens Wat Ik Zie!** (*1–2–3, Juggle w/Me*)   2 - 6
written & illus by Ilse-Margret Vogel
©1970, 24pp

FRANCE (Un Petit Livre D'or)

A variety of formats can be found, incorporating many of the styles used for American LGBs through the years. Contemporary printings use a plain gold spine, a variety of end paper designs and a back cover that features a character from the book and a short list of other titles available.

LK2080 **Doctor Chevefeuille** (*Dr. Goat*)   9 - 15
by Georgianna, illus by Charles Clement
©1965, 20pp. Not published in America
as an LGB, but available as a TopTop Tale
from Whitman.

LK2090 **Le Chien-Matelot** (*Sailor Dog*)   9 - 15
by Margaret Wise Brown,
illus by Garth Williams

LK2040   LK2060

©1964, 20pp
LK2100 **Le Petit Chat Qui Croyait Etre Une Souri**
(*The Kitten Who Thought He Was a Mouse*) 9 - 18
by M. Norton, illus by Garth Williams
©1954, 28pp
LK2110 **Le Petit Chien Fantaisiste** (*The Poky
Little Puppy*)   3 - 9
by Janette Sebring Lowrey,
illus by Gustaf Tenggren
©1962, 16pp

GERMANY (Ein Goldenes Kinderbuch)

Format very similar to American editions of the '50s, with character frame back and Golden end papers. Book listed 20

LK2080   LK2090

LK2100   LK2110

LK2130   LK2150

LK2170   LK2180

other German LGBs available at the time.

LK2130 **Die Lustige Autofahrt** (*Happy Man
and His Dump Truck*)   3 - 9
by Miriam, illus by Tibor Gergely
©1950, 28pp.

HEBREW

Plain gold spine and character frame back, LGB ends. Twenty-six other titles were also available in Hebrew.

LK2150 **(A Day At the Zoo)**   3 - 8
by Marion Conger, illus by Tibor Gergely
24pp. No song at end of book as in regular
LGBs.

MEXICO (Un Pequeno Libro De Oro)

Books shown are from the '50s, with format the same as American LGBs of the same period. Thirty-six other books were available at the time. Soft cover books were also produced.

LK2170 **Caperucita Roja** (*Little Red Riding Hood*) 5 - 14
illus by Elizabeth Orton Jones
©1959, 24pp
LK2180 **El Raton Miguelito Y Su Nave Interplane-
taria** (*Mickey Mouse and His Space Ship*) 8 - 12
by Jane Werner, illus by WDS
© by WDP, 24pp

Little Golden Books – Golden Medallion Series

This series featured all-time best-selling LGBs. Books have a Golden Medallion Series sticker on the front cover, and a special front end paper. The series ran in the early '80s and it is not known how many titles were included. At present, "Medallion" issues have no particular premium value over other reprints of the same time period, but may increase in value in the future.

LK3000   Golden Medallion Books

LK3000

Little Golden Books – Soft Cover

Soft cover versions of LGBs have been popular since the publication of "Little Silver Books" in the '50s. Some books are marked "A Little Golden Book" and some even have a printed Golden spine reproduced on the cover, while others only carry the Golden imprint at the copyright notice. Big Little Golden Books are also published in soft cover. Copies with no price were probably originally included with a cassette tape or in a packet of several copies sold as a unit. Soft cover books are simply cheaper versions of the regular issues and are collected mainly as interesting "go withs." Older copies (1970 and earlier) with Golden spines, especially Disney and other character books, arouse some collector interest and bring $1-4, depending on the subject and condition. Most other copies are valued at $2 and under.

LK4000   Soft cover books

LK4000

Little Golden Books – Special Editions

In 1985, a limited number of new LGBs were published in Special Editions. They were slightly larger than LGBs, 6-7/8" x 8-1/4" (mainly because they were bound in regular book casings), with 28 pages, illustrated end papers and dust jackets. The books retailed for $4.95. All of the books were also issued as part of the regular LGB series.

LL1630   **Cheltenham's Party** (11630)   6 - 10
by Jan Wahl, illus by Lucinda McQueen
©1985 by Jan Wahl (text), Lucinda

LL1630

LL1631   LL1633

LL1634   LL1635

McQueen (illus), 28pp (See also: LG0660)

LL1631   **Fox Jumped Up One Winter's Night**(11631)6 - 10
adp & illus by Nina Barbaresi
©1985 by Nina Barbaresi, 28pp (See also: LG1000)

LL1632   **Little Brown Bear** (11632)   6 - 10
written & illus by Wendy Watson
©1985 by Wendy Watson, 28pp (See also: LG0720)

LL1633   **Little Red Riding Hood** (11633)   6 - 10
by Martha Heller (retold),
illus by Marsha Winborn
©1985 by WPC, illus by Marsha Winborn, 28pp (See also: LG1080)

LL1634   **My Book of Poems** (11634)   6 - 10
by Ben Cruise (sel), illus by Gloria Solly
©1985 by WPC, illus by Gloria Solly, 28pp (See also: LG1110)

LL1635   **Scarebunny, The** (11635)   6 - 10
by Dorothy Kunhardt, illus by Kathy Wilburn
©1985 by the Estate of Dorothy Kunhardt (text), Kathy Wilburn (illus), 28pp (See also: LG0810)

LL2010   LL2020

Little Golden Books – Special Edition, Post "Crispy Critters"

In 1988, Post Cereals packaged special edition LGBs, featuring "Crispy Critters" with their cereal. Three books were produced, two of which were available on the boxes, and a third which could be ordered by mail for 85¢. The books are soft cover, 36 pages and have the standard LGB end papers and a printed spine. They were only available through the cereal promotion and were never issued as part of the regular LGB series.

LL2010   **Crispy in No Place Like Home** (100)   4 - 10
         by Justine Korman, illus by Dean Yeagle,
         painted by Mike Favatta
         ©1987 by General Foods Corp., 36pp

LL2020   **Crispy in the Birthday Band** (200)   4 - 10
         by Justine Korman, illus by Dean Yeagle,
         painted by Mike Favatta
         ©1987 by General Foods Corp., 36pp

LL2030   **Crispy's Bedtime Book** (300)   4 - 10
         by Justine Korman, illus by Dean Yeagle,
         painted by Mike Favatta
         ©1987 by General Foods Corp., 36pp.
         Mail-in premium.

LN1030

LN1010

LN1020

LLGB Package

LITTLE LITTLE GOLDEN BOOKS

Miniature versions of LGBs, right down to the traditional gold spine, 2-3/4" square with 24 pages and end papers the same as regular issue LGBs. Back cover design is the same as the front cover art work for the latest "Treasury of Little Golden Books." (See Treasury Books) The first 12 LLGBs - in their first printings - have spine designs the same size as used on the larger books. Later books and reprints of the first 12 have a "miniaturized" spine design. First used as promotional items (see next listing), the books were issued as a regular Golden line in 1989. Almost all of the books in the series were originally LGBs, and copyright dates given will not agree with actual date of publication. Edition information (but not date of actual publication) is noted on the inside back cover of each book. All books are numbered. The books are sold in packages of two, with other titles in the series listed on the back of the pack.

LN1010   **Poky Little Puppy, The** (1)   1 - 2
         by Janette Sebring Lowrey,
         illus by Gustaf Tenggren
         ©1942/p1989, 24pp (See also: LE0080)

LN1020   **Fire Engines** (2)   1 - 2
         illus by Tibor Gergely
         ©1959/p1989, 24pp (See also: LE3820)

LN1030   **Little Red Hen, The** (3)   1 - 2
         (Folk Tale), illus by J.P. Miller
         ©1954/p1989, 24pp (See also: LE2090)

LN1040   **Saggy Baggy Elephant, The** (4)   1 - 2
         by Kathryn & Byron Jackson,
         illus by Gustaf Tenggren
         ©1947/p1989, 24pp (See also: LE0360)

LN1050   **Scuffy the Tugboat** (5)   1 - 2
         by Gertrude Crampton, illus by Tibor Gergely
         ©1955/p1989, 24pp (See also: LE3630)

LN1060   **Theodore Mouse Goes to Sea** (6)   1 - 2
         by Michaela Muntean, illus by Lucinda McQueen
         ©1983/p1989 by Michaela Muntean (text),
         Lucinda McQueen (illus), 24pp
         (See also: LG0440)

LN1070   **Curious Little Kitten Around the House** (7)   1 - 2
         by Linda Hayward, illus by Maggie Swanson
         ©1986/p1989 by Linda Hayward (text),
         Maggie Swanson (illus), 24pp (See also: LG0870)

LN1080   **Tootle** (8)   1 - 2
         by Gertrude Crampton, illus by Tibor Gergely
         ©1945/p1989, 24pp (See also: LE0210)

LN1090   **Fuzzy Duckling, The** (9)   1 - 2
         by Jane Werner,
         illus by Alice & Martin Provensen
         ©1949/p1989, 24pp (See also: LE0780)

LN1100   **Sleepy Book, The** (10)   1 - 2
         by Margaret Wise Brown, illus by Garth Williams
         ©1949/p1989, 24pp (See also: LG0140)

LN1110   **We Help Mommy** (11)   1 - 2
         by Jean Cushman, illus by Eloise Wilkin
         ©1959/p1989, 24pp (See also: LE3520)

LN1120   **Baby Farm Animals** (12)   1 - 2
         written & illus by Garth Williams
         ©1958/p1989, 24pp (See also: LE3330)

LN1130   **Animals of Farmer Jones, The** (13)   1 - 2
         by Leah Gale, illus by Richard Scarry
         ©1953/p1989, 24pp (See also: LE2110)

LN1140   **We Help Daddy** (14)   1 - 2
         by Mini Stein, illus by Eloise Wilkin
         ©1962, p1989, 24pp (See also: LE4680)

LN1150   **Four Little Kittens** (15)   1 - 2
         by Kathleen N. Daly,
         illus by Adrianna Mazza Saviozzi
         ©1957/p1989, 24pp (See also: LE3220)

191

LN1210   LN1220

LN1270   LN1280

LN1250   LN1260

LN1160	**Three Little Pigs, The** (16) by Elizabeth Ross, illus by R.O. Fry ©1973/p1989, 24pp (See also: LE5440)	1 - 2
LN1170	**Very Best Home For Me, The** (17) by Jane Werner Watson, illus by Garth Williams ©1981, p1989, 24pp (See also: LG0220)	1 - 2
LN1180	**Little Red Riding Hood** (18) by Les Grey, illus by Mabel Watts ©1972, p1989, 24pp (See also: LF2320)	1 - 2
LN1190	**Four Puppies, The** (19) by Anne Heathers, illus by Lilian Obligado ©1960/p1989, 24pp (See also: LE4050)	1 - 2
LN1200	**Tawny Scrawny Lion** (20) by Kathryn & Byron Jackson, illus by Gustaf Tenggren ©1952/p1989, 24pp (See also: LE1380)	1 - 2
LN1210	**Pinocchio, Walt Disney's** (21) illus by WDS, Campbell Grant (adp) ©1948/p1989 by WDP, 24pp. Based on the story by Collodi. (See also: LI0080)	1 - 2
LN1220	**Three Bears, The** (22) (Folk Tale), illus by Feodor Rojankovsky ©1946/p1989, 24pp (See also: LE0470)	1 - 2
LN1230	**Snow White and the Seven Dwarfs, WD** (23) (Fairy Tale), illus by WDS, adp by Ken O'Brien & Al Dempster ©1948/p1989 by WDP, 24pp (See also: LI0040)	1 - 2
LN1240	**Jack and the Beanstalk** (24) by Stella Williams Nathan, illus by Dora Leder ©1973/p1989, 24pp (See also: LE5450)	1 - 2
LN1250	**I Can Dress Myself** (25) by Anna H. Dickson, illus by Carol Nicklaus ©1983/p1990 by CTW & Muppets, Inc., 24pp. Previously published as FLGB.	1 - 2
LN1260	**Big Bird's Busy Day** (26) by Jessie Smith, illus by Ellen Appleby ©1987/p1990 by CTW & Muppets, Inc.	1 - 2
LN1270	**We Like Kindergarten** (27) by Clara Cassidy, illus by Eloise Wilkin ©1965/p1990, 24pp (See also: LE5520)	1 - 2
LN1280	**My First Book of Sounds** (28) by Melanie Bellah, illus by Trina Schart ©1963/p1990, 24pp (See also: LG1560)	1 - 2

LITTLE LITTLE GOLDEN BOOKS — Hardee's Promotions

LLGBs were used as fast-food promotional items before they were released in the series listed above. The books were attached to a Children's Meal™ box, which had games and a punch-out bookmark designed to go with the book. Promotional LLGBs are not numbered, and are all identified "Hardee's" LLGBs. Each series has the list of all four books included in the promotion on the back cover. Back cover design for these books is the same as the back cover used on current production LGBs. All of the spines are in the large pattern.

Story Book Promotion

LN3010	**Little Red Hen, The** (Folk Tale), illus by J.P. Miller ©1954, 24pp (See also: LE2090)	1 - 3
LN3020	**Little Red Riding Hood** by Les Grey, illus by Mabel Watts ©1972 by Les Grey (text), Mabel Watts (illus), 24pp (See also: LE2320)	1 - 3
LN3030	**Poky Little Puppy, The** by Janette Sebring Lowrey, illus by Gustaf Tenggren ©1942, 24pp (See also: LE0080)	1 - 3
LN3040	**Three Little Pigs, The** by Elizabeth Ross, illus by R.O. Fry ©1973, 24pp (See also: LE5440)	1 - 3
LN3045	Book with Children's Meal box	8 - 12

Nursery Tales Promotion

LN3050	**Little Red Caboose** by Marian Potter, illus by Tibor Gergely ©1953, 24pp (See also: LE1620)	1 - 3
LN3060	**Old MacDonald Had a Farm** (Nursery Song), illus by Moritz Kennel ©1960, 24pp (See also: LE4000)	1 - 3
LN3070	**Three Little Kittens** (Nursery Tale), illus by Masha ©1942, 24pp (See also: LE0010)	1 - 3

LN3020 & Children's Meal Box

LN4010   LN4020

LN4030   *Back Cover*

LP2000   LP2050   LP2060

LP2070   LP2080   LP2090

LN3010 & Children's Meal Box

LN3080	**Three Bears, The**	1 - 3
	(Nursery Tale), illus by Feodor Rojankovsky	
	©1948, 24pp (See also: LE0470)	
LN3085	Book with Children's Meal box	8 - 12

Pound Puppy & Pound Purries Promotion

These books have not yet been reprinted as part of the regular issue LLGB series.

LN4010	**Kitten Companions**	2 - 5
	by Justine Korman, illus by John Nez	
	©1987 by Tonka Corp., 24pp	
LN4020	**Pick of the Litter**	2 - 5
	by Teddy Slater,	
	illus by Dick Codor & Carol Bouman	
	©1986 by Tonka Corp., 24pp	
	(See also: LG0910)	
LN4030	**Problem Puppies**	2 - 5
	by Justine Korman,	
	illus by Carol Bouman & Dick Codor	
	©1986 by Tonka Corp., 24pp	
	(See also: LG0920)	
LN4040	**Puppy Nobody Wanted, The**	2 - 5
	by A.C. Chandler, illus by Pat Paris	
	©1986 by Tonka Corp., 24pp	
LN4045	Book with Children's Meal box	10 - 15

LITTLE SILVER BOOKS (soft bound)

Full color, approximately 6" x 8-1/2", these books are counterparts of their LGB editions, issued in soft cover, with 24 pages. They sold for 19¢ and no publication date other than the original copyright notice is available. More titles have yet to be cataloged.

LP2000	**Mother Goose** (1200)	1 - 4
	by Phyllis Fraser, illus by Gertrude Elliott	
	©1942, 24pp (See also: LE0040)	
LP2020	**Come Play with Me**	3 - 9
	by Edith Osswald, illus by Eloise Wilkin	
	©1948, 24pp (See also: LE0040)	
LP2050	**Katie the Kitten** (1205)	1 - 4
	by Kathryn & Byron Jackson,	
	illus by Alice & Martin Provensen	
	©1949, 24pp (See also: LE0750)	
LP2060	**Jerry at School** (1206)	1 - 4
	by Kathryn & Byron Jackson,	
	illus by Corinne Malvern	
	©1950, 24pp (See also: LE0940)	
LP2070	**When I Grow Up** (1207)	1 - 4
	by Kay & Harry Mace, illus by Corinne Malvern	
	©1950, 24pp (See also: LE0960)	
LP2080	**Wild Animal Babies** (1208)	1 - 4
	by Kathleen N. Daly, illus by Feodor Rojankovsky	
	©1958, 24pp (See also: LE3320)	
LP2090	**Kitten Who Thought He Was a Mouse** (1209)	3 - 9
	by Miriam Norton, illus by Garth Williams	
	©1954, 24pp (See also: LE2100)	
LP2100	**My Baby Sister** (1213)	3 - 8
	by Patsy Scarry, illus by Sharon Koester	
	©1958, 24pp (See also: LE3400)	

LOOK AND LEARN LIBRARY (Richard Scarry)

A 4-volume set of Richard Scarry learning books published in 1978 and offered as a mail-order item. The set came in a "Library Building" slipcase, and retailed for just under $25.

LS1010

LT1060

LT1050

- **LR1000**

Books are 9-1/2" x 11", with cover design complimenting the Library slipcase.

LR1000 **Look and Learn Library**, in slipcase 20 - 40
by Richard Scarry
©1978 by Richard Scarry. Complete
set of 4 volumes.

Individual volumes of LR1000:
LR1010 Fun with Words 4 - 10
LR1020 Things to Know 4 - 10
LR1030 Best Stories Ever 4 - 10
LR1040 Going Places 4 - 10

LOOK INSIDE

A "Big Golden" size book. Instead of regular text pages, the book opens to reveal 5 smaller books. Cover is die cut. (See also: Open Door Books)

LS1010 **Mary Poppins** 10 - 25
stories by Alice Chase, illus by WDS
©1964 by WDP. Adapted from the
motion picture, based on the original
stories by P.L. Travers.

LOOK-LOOK BOOKS

Instituted in the mid-1970s, the "Look-Look" Books have come into their own as a major Golden series. All books are 24 pages and identified by the Look-Look design in the upper right corner of the cover. Edition information is carried at the copyright notice. Most of the books carry a listing of additional titles on the back. Originally issued at 95¢, they now sell for $1.95. Although the series is not yet firmly established in the collectible market, we have included a very limited selection of various subjects as an indication of collector awareness. Books by established artists (Richard Scarry, Mercer Mayer, Cyndy Szekeres) which are featured in this series, bear watching as future collectibles, as do Disney and other character titles. While these special books have already begun to appreciate, most of the books in this soft cover series can be found at flea markets and yard sales for under a dollar.

LT1010 **Dinosaurs** 1 - 2
by Kathleen N. Daly,

LT1070 **LT1080**

illus by Tim & Greg Hildebrandt
©1977, 24pp
LT1020 **Just Me and My Little Sister** 1 - 2
written and illus by Mercer Mayer
©1986 by Paperwing Press™, 24pp
LT1030 **Learn to Count** 1 - 2
illus by Richard Scarry
©1976 by WPC, ©1966 by Richard Scarry,
24pp
LT1040 **My House** 1 - 2
illus by Richard Scarry
©1976, 24pp
LT1050 **There"s No Such Thing as a Dragon** 1 - 4
written & illus by Jack Kent
©1975, 24pp
LT1060 **Black Cauldron: Taran and the Fair Folk** 2 - 6
adapted from the WD film
©1985 by WDP, 24pp
LT1070 **Return to Oz: Dorothy Returns to Oz** 3 - 9
©1985 by WDP, 24pp. Based on the WD film.
LT1080 **Who Framed Roger Rabbit: A Different Toon** 1 - 4
based on the film from WD Pictures and
Steven Spielberg
©1985 by WDCo and Amblin Entertainment
Inc., 24pp

MB2420   MB2430

MB2450   MB2740   MB2750

MB2400   MB2410

MB2760   MB2770   MB2780

MELODY BOOKS

Books come with a tiny electronic chip "music box" in the cover which plays when the book is opened. Most books are 5-1/2" x 7", page length varies. "A Golden Melody Book™" in a music staff on the front cover identifies the series, which was launched in 1983 with the biggest advertising campaign ever mounted by the publishers. Although the books are designed for "thousands of playings", it is difficult to find any on the secondary market which still play music.

MB2400 **Silent Night** (12240)   2 - 4
(Hymn) by Joseph Mohr & Franz Gruber,
illus by Ann Schweninger
©1983 by WPC, illus by Ann Schweninger
A fold-out panorama book w/7 scenes.
Song on last page.

MB2410 **We Wish You a Merry Christmas** (12241)   2 - 4
(Christmas Carol), illus by Amy Rosenberg
©1983 by WPC, illus by Amy Rosenberg
A fold-out panorama book w/7 scenes.
Song on last page.

MB2420 **Good Night** (12242)   2 - 6
by Jane Werner Watson, illus by Eloise Wilkin
©1949/p1983, 24pp. Plays "Rock-A-Bye,
Baby" (See also: LE0610)

MB2430 **Twinkle, Twinkle, Little Star** (12243)   2 - 6
(Nursery Song), illus by Sharon Kane
©1960/p1983, 24pp

MB2440 **Old MacDonald Had a Farm** (12244)   2 - 4
(Nursery Song), illus by Carl & Mary Hague
©1975/p1983, 28pp

MB2450 **My ABC Book** (12245)   2 - 4
(ABC), illus by Alys Nugent
©1956/p1983, 28pp. Plays "The Alphabet
Song"

MB2730 **People in Your Neighborhood** (12273)   2 - 6
by editors of "Sesame Street"
©1984 by CTW & Muppets, Inc., 24pp.
Plays "The People in Your Neighborhood"
from "Sesame Street"

MB2740 **It's a Small World, WD** (12274)   2 - 8
illus by WDS
©1981/p1984 by WDP, 24pp

MB2750 **Monchhichi™ Happy Birthday** (12275)   2 - 4
by Sally Trimble, illus by Manny Campana

©1983 by Sekiguchi Co., Ltd., 24pp
Plays "Happy Birthday to You"

MB2760 **Snow White and the Seven Dwarfs,
Walt Disney's** (12276)   2 - 8
©1984 by WDP, 24pp. Plays "Heigh-Ho"

MB2770 **Mickey's Christmas Carol, WD** (12277)   2 - 8
©1983 by WDP, 24pp

MB2780 **Rainbow Brite Saves Spring** (12278)   2 - 4
by Dorothy Eyre, illus by Roy Wilson
©1985 by Hallmark Cards, Inc., 24pp.
Plays "Over the Rainbow"

MB4200 **Rudolph the Red-Nosed Reindeer** (14020)   3 - 10
illus by Richard Scarry
©1988 by Robert L. May; ©1976 by WPC
(illus), 24pp. Adapted from the story by Robert
L. May. A Big Golden Melody Book,
8" x 10-3/4"

MB4210 **Frosty the Snow Man** (14021)   3 - 10
illus by Corinne Malvern
©1988 by Warner/Chappell Music, 24pp.
Adapted from the song of the same name.
A Big Golden Melody Book, 8" x 10-3/4".

MOVIE STORYBOOKS

Full color storybook adaptions of favorite films, illustrated with stills from each movie. The story line generally encompasses the entire story, as opposed to smaller format Golden Books which adapt only a portion of the story. New films as well as classic favorites have been included. All books are 8-3/4" x 11-1/4", page length varies.

ME1020 **Basil of Baker Street** (15840)   3 - 9
©1986 by WDP, 48pp. Official picture-story
adaption of the entire film.

ME1040 **Black Cauldron Storybook, The** (15380)   4 - 10
©1985 by WDP, 44pp. Adapted from the
WD film, based on the *Prydain Chronicles*
by Lloyd Alexander.

ME1060 **Clash of the Titans** (16801)   2 - 6
by Hans Pemsteen, illus by Mike Eagle
©1981 by MGM Film Col, 36pp. Based on
the screenplay by Beverley Cross.

ME1220

ME1200

ME1080 **Dick Tracy: The Movie Storybook** (15951)   3 - 8
by Justin Korman (adp)
©1990 by WDCo., 44pp. Adapted from the
WD film, based on the Chester Gould
character.

ME1200 **Fox and the Hound, The** (16802)   6 - 10
©1981 by WDP, 36pp. Official picture-story
adaption of the entire film.

ME1220 **Gremlins** (15820)   3 - 9
by Marey Carey (adp)
©1984 by Warner Bros., Inc., 48pp.
Adapted from the Steven Spielberg film.

ME1225 **Gremlins 2: The New Batch** (15950)   3 - 9
by Michael Teitelbaum (adp)
©1990 by Warner Bros., Inc., 48pp

ME1350 **Oliver and Company** (11995)   3 - 8
©1988 by WDCo., 48pp. Official picture-
story adaption of the entire film.

ME1400 **Return to Oz Storybook** (15831)   4 - 10
©1985 by WDP, 44pp. Based on the WD
film, adapted from the original stories by
L. Frank Baum.

ME1440 **Secret of Nimh Storybook** (16821)   4 - 10
by Seymour Reit (adp)
©1982 by Mrs. Brisby Ltd, 48pp. Adapted
from Don Bluth Productions *The Secret of
Nimh*, based on the book *Mrs. Brisby and
the Rats of Nimh* by Robert C. O'Brien

ME1520 **Who Framed Roger Rabbit? Movie
Storybook** (15847)   3 - 9
by Justin Korman (adp)

©1988 by WDCo and Amblin Entertainment,
Inc., 44pp. Based on the film from WD and
Steven Spielberg

ME1540 **Wizard of Oz, The (Movie Storybook)**(15848)3 - 9
by Jan Wahl
©1989 by Turner Entertainment Co., 44pp.
Illustrated with stills from the 1939 movie.

MY FIRST LEARNING LIBRARY

This series is not an "ABC" in the usual sense ... in effect, it is a pre-schooler's "encyclopedia." Chief consultant was Dr. Bertha Morris Parker, editor of the famous *Golden Book Encyclopedia*. The series was conceived in response to inquiries for a similar encyclopedia, designed for younger readers. Five years in planning, the text for the series was prepared by Jane Werner Watson and illustrations were done by William Dugan.

Although the numbering appears to have been assigned in sequence with the first series of Little Golden Books, they are not designated as "Little Golden" and form their own distinct Library. The same size as LGBs, the books were 24 pages with a plain gold spine. An individual price of 39¢ is noted on the books and they were originally sold individually as well as in sets. Boxed sets, complete with carrying handle were available.

ML1600 **My First Learning Library**   16 - 48
by Jane Werner Watson,
illus by William Dugan
©1965, 16-volume set
ML1605 Same as ML1600, in carrying case   40 - 60
Individual volumes of ML1600:
ML1615 Book of A, The (615)   1 - 3
ML1616 Book of B, The (616)   1 - 3
ML1617 Book of C, The (617)   1 - 3
ML1618 Book of D & E, The (618)   1 - 3
ML1619 Book of F, The (619)   1 - 3
ML1620 Book of G & H, The (620)   1 - 3
ML1621 Book of I–J–K, The (621)   1 - 3
ML1622 Book of L, The (622)   1 - 3
ML1623 Book of M, The (623)   1 - 3
ML1624 Book of N & O, The (624)   1 - 3
ML1625 Book of P & Q, The (625)   1 - 3
ML1626 Book of R, The (626)   1 - 3
ML1627 First Book of S, The (627)   1 - 3
ML1628 Second Book of S, The (628)   1 - 3
ML1629 Book of T–U–V, The (629)   1 - 3
ML1630 Book of W–X–Y–Z, The (630)   1 - 3

ML1616

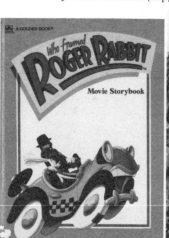

ME1520

ME1540

ML1605

PA1060

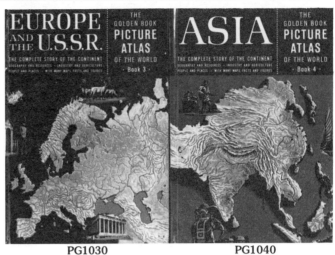

OD1010

PG1030   PG1040

OPEN DOOR BOOK

Large format books with die cut covers, they opened to reveal smaller books, each behind a "door." (See also: Look Inside Books)

OD1010 **Cinderella, WD**   10 - 30
     ©1965 by WDP. A Golden Press Book, created by Capitol. Book opens to reveal 5 little books inside, each with its own "door" cover.
OD1020 **Mother Goose Rhymes**   ?
     Title noted, but copy unavailable for verification.
OD1030 **Say with Me, ABC**   ?
     Title noted, but copy unavailable for verification.

PANORAMA BOOKS

Sturdy board-page fold-up books which open up to a free-standing panorama. Most of the books were drawn from LGB series. These 22-page books were advertised on LGBs in 1963, but the exact period of publication and the extent of the series is not know.

PA1050 **Animal ABC**   ?
     Title noted, but copy unavailable for verification.
PA1060 **Animal Friends**   3 - 10
     by Jane Werner, illus by Garth Williams ©1953, 22pp (See also: LE1670)
PA1080 **Baby's First Christmas**   5 - 18
     by Esther Wilkin, illus by Eloise Wilkin ©1959, 22pp (See also: LE5680)
PA1090 **Baby's Mother Goose**   3 - 8
     (Nursery Rhymes), illus by Aurelius Battaglia ©1948, 22pp (See also: LE3030)
PA1200 **How Big**   3 - 8
     written & illus by Corinne Malvern ©1949, 22pp (See also: LE0830)
PA1260 **Jolly Barnyard**   5 - 10
     by Annie North Bedford, illus by Tibor Gergely ©1950, 22pp (See also: LE0670)
PA1300 **Little Red Hen**   3 - 8
     (Nursery Tale), illus by Rudolf Freund ©1942, 22pp (See also: LE0060)
PA1340 **Mr. Noah and His Family**   3 - 10
     by Jane Werner, illus by Alice & Martin Provensen ©1948, 22pp (See also: LE0490)

PA1360 **My Toy Box**   ?
     Title noted, but copy unavailable for verification.
PA1380 **Night Before Christmas, The**   5 - 20
     by Clement C. Moore, illus by Eloise Wilkin ©1955, 22pp (See also: LE2410)

PICTURE ATLAS OF THE WORLD

A 6-volume set, each book dealing with the complete story of a continent, including geography, history, industry, people and places, etc. Uniform in size with the *Golden Book Encyclopedia* and the *Golden Treasury of Knowledge*.

PG1000 **Golden Book Picture Atlas**   6 - 18
     by Phillip Bacon (ed), illus w/photos & maps ©1960, 96pp each. 6-volume set.
Individual volumes of PG1000:
PG1010   Vol. 1 North America   1 - 3
PG1020   Vol. 2 South America   1 - 3
PG1030   Vol. 3 Europe & the USSR   1 - 3
PG1040   Vol. 4 Asia   1 - 3
PG1050   Vol. 5 Africa   1 - 3
PG1060   Vol. 6 Australia, Oceania and the Polar Lands   1 - 3

PICTURE CLASSICS

Based on classic novels, these books were published both in hard and soft cover. hard cover books were 7-1/2" x 10-1/2"; soft cover books were slightly smaller. All books were 96 pages, with color illustrations on each page. Front paste-down had a brief overview of the story and the back paste-down told something about the author. All stories were especially edited and abridged for the series. Some of the same books selected for this series have been redone for the new Classic Library.

There is no edition/printing information given beyond the copyright. The high acid content of the text paper is already producing brittle pages.

PI1010 **Treasure Island** (1)   3 - 10
     by Robert Louis Stevenson, adp by Anne Terry White, illus by Hamilton Greene

	©1956, 96pp. Hard cover	
PI1011	Same as PI1010, soft cover	1 - 5
PI1020	**Tom Sawyer** (2)	3 - 10
	by Mark Twain, adp by Anne Terry White, illus by Hans H. Helweg	
	©1956, 96pp. Hard cover	
PI1021	Same as PI1020, soft cover	1 - 5
PI1030	**Black Beauty** (3)	3 - 10
	by Anne Sewell, adp by Barbara Nolen, illus by Tom Gill	
	©1956, 96pp. Hard cover	
PI1031	Same as PI1030, soft cover	1 - 5
PI1040	**Little Women** (4)	4 - 12
	by Louisa May Alcott, adp by Emma Gelders Sterne, illus by Julian Paul	
	©1956, 96pp. Hard cover	
PI1041	Same as PI1040, soft cover	1 - 5
PI1050	**Heidi** (5)	4 - 12
	by Johanna Spyri, adp by Deborah Hill, illus by Grace Dalles Clarke	
	©1956, 96pp. Hard cover	
PI1051	Same as PI1050, soft cover	1 - 5
PI1060	**Ben-Hur** (6)	3 - 10
	by Lew Wallace, adp by Willis Lindquist, illus by Mario Cooper	
	©1956, 96pp. Hard cover	
PI1061	Same as PI1060, soft cover	1 - 5
PI1070	**Around the World in 80 Days** (7)	3 - 10
	by Jules Verne, adp by Charles Spain Verral, illus by Tom Gill	
	©1957, 96pp. Hard cover	
PI1071	Same as PI1070, soft cover	1 - 5
PI1080	**Sherlock Holmes** (8)	4 - 12
	by Arthur Conan Doyle, sel by Charles Spain Verral, illus by Tom Gill	
	© 1956, 96pp. Hard cover	
PI1081	Same as PI1080, soft cover	1 - 5
PI1090	**Three Musketeers, The** (9)	3 - 10
	by Alexandre Dumas, adp by Marjorie Mattern, illus by Hamilton Greene	
	©1956, 96pp. Hard cover	
PI1091	Same as PI1090, soft cover	1 - 5
PI1100	**Merry Adventures of Robin Hood, The** (10)	5 - 15
	by Howard Pyle, adp by Willis Lindquist, illus by Don Lynch	
	©1956, 96pp. Hard cover	
PI1101	Same as PI1100, soft cover	1 - 5
PI1110	**Hans Brinker** (11)	3 - 10
	by Mary Mapes Dodge, adp by Anne Terry White, illus by Al Schmidt	
	©1957, 96pp. Hard cover	
PI1111	Same as PI1110, soft cover	1 - 5
PI1120	**Count of Monte Cristo, The** (12)	3 - 10
	by Alexandre Dumas, adp by Edward Robinson, illus by Hamilton Greene	
	©1957, 96pp. Hard cover	
PI1121	Same as PI1120, soft cover	1 - 5

PI1040   PI1050

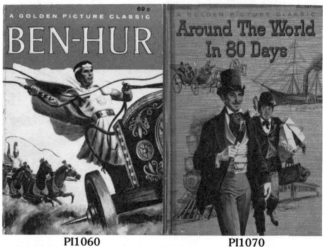

PI1060   PI1070

Play and Learn Books

PLAY AND LEARN BOOKS

Books had a large back with a smaller spiral-bound book attached to the front and were sturdy board construction. They were designed for learning activities such as telling time, tying shoes, and use as a "push toy." Due to their toy/activity nature, not many of these books have survived. Books were originally packaged in boxes that identified the "Play and Learn" series, and a small "Swan" design on each book cover carried the "Play and Learn" designation. The series was advertised on LGB backs in 1964. New titles were added to the series as late as 1981. Collector interest is limited and books of this type are generally available for $3-6.

POP-UP BOOKS

Pop-Up Books were produced in cooperation with Intervisual Communications, Inc., who have produced many of the modern fine pop-up books. Mechanicals include action pictures and 3-dimensional scenes. Several books in other series contain pop-ups and mechanicals as an "added feature" (See color plate), but are not totally designed as Pop-Up Books. (See BB1870, GB1090)

PU1010	**Fox and the Hound, The**	10 - 20
	©1981 by WDP, 22 action pages.	

PU1010

RE1070

RE1090

RE1140   RE1360

PU1040 **Rudolph the Red-Nosed Reindeer**   8 - 14
illus by Darrell Baker
©1983 by Robert L. May. Adapted from the
story by Robert L. May, paper engineering by
Ib Penick. Published by arrangement with
Follett Publishing Co.

QUESTION AND ANSWER– See ADVENTURE BOOKS

READ-IT-YOURSELF & BEGINNING READER BOOKS
Designed for children learning to read "on their own", Read-It-Yourself Books were introduced in 1960. Either especially written for the series or adapted from previously published books, the series went through several different format and numbering changes. Originally published at 30¢, later at 50¢, some titles were also available in "Kivar" (cloth) bindings with dust jacket for $1.
Golden Beginning Readers were an extension of the series. The "sunrise" design on the cover was color-keyed to 3 different reading levels, which were explained on the back of Beginning Readers. Printing information is generally inside the back cover or with the copyright block, although sometimes it's inside the front cover. Also printed in soft cover in a slightly larger size. The modern "Easy Reader" and "Very Easy Reader" books are an equivalent series designed for beginning readers.

RE1050 **Animals Search for Summer, The**   1 - 3
by Nathalie Caputo
©1966, 32pp. From the stories of Pere Castor.
RE1070 **Belling the Cat and Other Stories**   1 - 3
by Leland B. Jacobs, illus by Harold Berson
©1960, 32pp
RE1090 **Bird Nests**   1 - 3
by Nina Shackleford & Gordon E. Burks,
illus by James Gordon Irving
©1962, 28pp
RE1140 **Dog's Life, A**   1 - 3
by Mido, illus by Gerda Muller
©1964, 32pp. From the stories of Pere Castor.
RE1180 **George the Gentle Giant**   1 - 3
by Adelaide Holl, illus by Frank Daniel
©1962, 32pp
RE1190 **Good Friends, The**   1 - 3
by Paul Francois (Faucher), illus by Gerda Muller
©1966, 32pp. Adapted from the story by Fang Yi-K'iun
RE1300 **Jonathan and the Dragon**   1 - 3
by Irwin Shapiro, illus by Tom Vroman
©1962, 32pp

RE1320 **Just for Fun**   2 - 6
by Patricia Scarry, illus by Richard Scarry
©1960, 32pp (See also: LF2640)
RE1360 **King Who Learned to Smile, The**   1 - 3
by Seymour Reit, illus by Gordon Laite
©1960, 28pp
RE1380 **Large and Growly Bear, The**   1 - 3
by Gertrude Crampton, illus by J.P. Miller
©1961, 32pp (See also: LF5100)
RE1400 **Little Black Puppy, The**   1 - 3
by Charlotte Zolotow, illus by Lilian Obligado
©1960, 30pp
RE1420 **Look! Look! A Clown Book**   1 - 3
by Seymour Reit, illus by Joanne Nigro
©1962, 30pp
RE1460 **My Very Own Puppy**   1 - 3
by Albertine Deletaille
©1966, 32pp. From the stories of Pere Castor.
RE1500 **Old Gray and the Little White Hen**   1 - 3
by Paul Francois (Faucher),
illus by Lucile Butel
©1966, 32pp. From the stories of Pere Castor.
RE1520 **Pear-Shaped Hill, The**   1 - 3
by Irving A. Leitner, illus by Bernice Myer
©1960, 32pp
RE1540 **Pickle for a Nickle**   1 - 3
by Lilian Moore, illus by Susan Perl
©1961, 28pp
RE1600 **Round, Round World**   1 - 3
written & illus by Michael Douglas
©1960, 30pp
RE1640 **Sylvester the Mouse with the Musical Ear**   1 - 3
by Adelaide Holl, illus by N.M. Bodecker
©1961, 30pp
RE1680 **Too Many Bozos**   1 - 3
by Lilian Moore, illus by Susan Perl
©1960, 30pp
RE1690 **Turtles**   1 - 3
by Bertie Ann Stewart & Gordon E. Burks,
illus by William Hutchinson
©1962, 30pp
RE1710 **Whale Hunt, The**   1 - 3
by Jane Werner Watson & Kenneth S. Norris,
illus by Claude Humbert
©1960, 32pp
RE1711 Same as RE1710, in dj of same design   4 - 6
RE1730 **Where Do You Live?**   1 - 3
by Eva Knox Evans, illus by Beatrice Darwin
©1962, 32pp
RE1740 **Where's Willie?**   1 - 3
by Seymour Reit, illus by Eric Blegvad
©1961, 32pp
RE1760 **Wolf and the Kids, The**   1 - 3
by Paul Francois (Faucher), illus by Gerda Muller

SA1041   SA1091   SA1021

©1966, 36pp. From the stories of Pere Castor.

RE1780 **Wonderful House, The**   2 - 6
by Margaret Wise Brown, illus by J.P. Miller
©1960, 32pp (See also: LE0760)

SANDPIPER BOOKS

Sandpiper Books are not technically Golden Books, but a supplemental series published by S&S under the Sandpiper Press imprint. Title lists for the series can be found on the backs of some older Big Golden Books, advertised as "a brand new series" designed for young readers who have outgrown their LGBs. In addition, the books repeat some stories that were part of the Golden Story Book series. They also share the same advisory board.

The books are 5-1/4" x 7-1/2", hard bound with plain covers printed in one color ink. However, all the books were issued with full-color dust jackets. Edited for easy reading, the books had color pictures on each of the 78 pages. End paper illustrations were adapted to each story.

SA1010 **Gene Autry and the Red Shirt** (S1)   3 - 8
by Elizabeth Beecher, illus by Jesse March
©1961 by Gene Autry, 78pp
(See also: SS1170)
SA1011 Same as SA1010, in dj   10 - 25
SA1020 **Donald Duck and the Hidden Gold** (S2)   3 - 8
by Jane Werner, illus by WDS,
adp by Al Taliaferro
©1951 by WDS, 78pp (See also: SS1180)
SA1021 Same as SA1020, in dj   10 - 25
SA1030 **Airplane Stories** (S3)   1 - 3
by Marian Conger, illus by Harlow Rockwel
©1951, 78pp
SA1031 Same as SA1030, in dj   5 - 10
SA1040 **Rob Whitlock** (S4)   1 - 3
by Kathryn & Byron Jackson,
illus by Cornelius DeWitt
©1951, 78pp

SA1041 Same as SA1040, in dj   5 - 10
SA1050 **Wishing Stick, The** (S5)   1 - 3
by Jane Werner, illus by Corinne Malvern
©1951, 78pp (See also: SS1020)
SA1051 Same as SA1050, in dj   5 - 10
SA1060 **Pirates Cove and Other Sea Stories** (S6)   3 - 6
©1951, 78pp. Title noted, but copy
unavailable for verification.
SA1070 **Roy Rogers on the Double-R Ranch** (S7)   3 - 10
by Elizabeth Beecher, illus by Ernest Nordli
©1951 by Roy Rogers Enterprises, 78pp
SA1071 Same as SA1070, in dj   10 - 25
SA1080 **Lost Silver Mine, The** (S8)   ?
Title noted, copy unavailable for verification.
SA1090 **Lone Ranger's New Deputy, The** (S9)   3 - 10
by Fran Striker, illus by Ted Shearer
©1951 by The Lone Ranger, Inc., 78pp.
Based on the original story by George Trendle.
SA1091 Same as SA1090, in dj   10 - 20
SA1100 **Alice in Wonderland, WD** (S10)   3 - 10
illus by WDS
©1951 by WDP, 78pp. Adapted from the
WD film, based on the original story by Lewis
Carroll.
SA1101 Same as SA1100, in dj   10 - 22

SCRATCH AND SNIFF BOOKS

Books incorporate "Microfragrance™ Labels", supplied by 3M Company, into the story illustrations. Originally called "Golden Frangrance Books", the series was later designated "Scratch & Sniff." Books are square, measuring 9-1/2" x 9-1/2". Printing information is generally shown inside back cover, when given. Many titles are still in print.

SC5240 **Big Bird Gets Lost** (13524)   3 - 9
by Patricia Thackray, illus by Carol Nicklaus
©1978 by CTW & Muppets, Inc., 32pp
SC5250 **Once-Upon-A-Time Scratch & Sniff
Book, The** (13525)   6 - 12
by Ruthanna Long, illus by Eloise Wilkin
©1978, 28pp
SC5260 **Professor Wormbog's Gloomy Kerploppus**
(13526)   1 - 3
written & illus by Mercer Mayer
©1978 by Mercer Mayer, 32pp
SC5270 **Sweet Smell of Christmas, The** (13527)   2 - 6
by Patricia Scarry, illus by J.P. Miller
©1970, 36pp
SC5280 **Winnie-the-Pooh Scratch & Sniff Book,
The** (13528)   3 - 9
by A.A. Milne, illus by WDS

SC5250   SC5270   SC5280

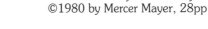

SC5300

SC5350   SC5440

©1954 by A.A. Milne (text), ©1974 by WDP (illus), 28pp. Based on the A.A. Milne story.

written & illus by Mercer Mayer
©1980 by Mercer Mayer, 28pp

SC5300	**Bambi's Fragrant Forest, WD** (13530) ©1975 by WDP, 28pp. Based on the Felix Salten story.	3 - 9
SC5340	**Nose for Trouble, A** (13534) by Barbara Shook Hazen, illus by Greg & Tim Hildebrandt ©1975, 28pp	2 - 6
SC5350	**Detective Arthur on the Scent** (13535) by Mary J. Fulton, illus by Aurelius Battaglia ©1971, 32pp	2 - 6
SC5360	**Little Bunny Follows His Nose** (13536) by Katherine Howard, illus by J.P. Miller ©1971	2 - 6
SC5400	**Max, The Nosy Bear** (13540) by Katherine Howard, illus by J.P. Miller ©1972, 28pp	2 - 6
SC5410	**See No Evil, Hear No Evil, Smell No Evil** (13541) by the editors of Sesame Street ©1978 by CTW & Muppets, Inc., 32pp	3 - 9
SC5420	**Raggedy Ann's Sweet & Dandy, Sugar Candy Scratch & Sniff Book** (13542) by Patricia Thackray, illus by Carol Nicklaus ©1976 by Bobbs-Merrill Co., Inc., 28pp	4 - 8
SC5430	**To Market, To Market** (13543) written & illus by Richard Scarry ©1979, 32pp	3 - 9
SC5440	**Mickey Mouse & the Marvelous Smell Machine, WD** (13544) ©1979 by WDP, 28pp	3 - 9
SC5441	**Mickey Mouse Scratch and Sniff Book** (135441) ©1990 by WDCo., 28pp. Previously published as SC5440. Reissued in 1990 with new cover art and title change.	2 - 5
SC5460	**Little Monster's Scratch & Sniff Mystery** (13546)	4 - 10

SHAPE BOOKS

Soft cover, with die-cut edges to conform to the cover art, these 24-page books first appeared in 1964. Books that repeat stories from the LG series usually have a notation on the title page, "From the World of Little Golden Books." The artwork, however, may not be the same as the original Little Golden Book, and the text is usually edited for a younger child. Most of the books show the title in a circle surrounded by the words "A Golden Shape Book." Shape Books were also published in library bindings (without their "shape") and foreign language editions.

All of the books are numbered, but no listing was carried on the back, and a complete list of all titles is not available. Near the end of the '70s, the numbering system was revised and tied to ISBN numbers, and a numerical listing of titles becomes impossible. Edition information is shown as a letter code at the bottom of the back page or carried with the copyright notice. No strong collectors market has been established, but interest has been shown in associated items, such as Disney and other characters as well as LGB tie-ins. This short listing is intended only as a representation of general values for different categories of Shape Books.

SH1020	**Elephant Book, The** written & illus by Charles Nicholas ©1965, 24pp	1 - 4
SH1040	**Lively Little Rabbit, The** ©1972, 24pp. Adapted from the LGB story.	2 - 6
SH1060	**Kitten Book, The** written & illus by Jan Pfloog ©1986, 24pp	1 - 4
SH1062	**Kitten Book (Los Gatitos)** Same as SH1060, written in Spanish. Shown in full color Goldencraft binding.	3 - 9

SH1020   SH1040

SH1060   SH1062

SH1080   SH1300

SH2020   SH2030

SH2010   SN2030

SN2040

SO6710

SH1080 **Raggedy Ann and Andy Book, The**   2 - 6
        by Jan Sukus, illus by Ruth Ruhman & Gavy
        ©1972 by Bobbs-Merrill Co., Inc., 24pp

SH1200 **Saggy Baggy Elephant, The**   2 - 6
        ©1972, 24pp. Adapted from the LGB.

SH1300 **Mouseketeer's Train Ride, WD**   2 - 6
        ©1977 by WDP, 24pp

SH1310 **Winnie-the-Pooh: Hidden Pictures**   2 - 6
        ©1965 by WDP, 24pp. 1977 printing shown.

Shape Books – Carry-Me

A special series of "Carry-Me" books, which incorporated a
handle in the book design, was issued in the '70s. Story lines
were developed around cases, bags and baskets. At least 6
carry-me books were done.

SH2010 **My Doctor Bag**   2 - 6
        by Kathleen N. Daly, illus by Marc Brown
        ©1977, 24pp

SH2020 **My Picnic Basket Book**   2 - 6
        by Kathleen N. Daly, illus by Jerry Scott
        ©1975, 24pp

SH2030 **My Sports Bag Book**   2 - 6
        by Kathleen N. Daly, illus by Jim Robinson
        ©1977, 24pp

Shape Books: Super Shape

In 1987, the Shape Book series was redesigned as "Super
Shape" books, with glossy laminated covers. The size and format of the original series was retained. The initial offering of 32
titles sold over 3,000,000 copies in 1987.

In addition to a constant supply of new titles, many of the
original Shape Books have been reissued as Super Shapes.
Older titles usually begin a new print series when reissued as
Super Shapes, starting with "A." Their original copyrights are
shown and there is no indication of actual publication date,
although all Super Shape editions would have to be 1987 or
later.

As a relatively new series, a collectors market has not yet
been firmly established, but the interest and values will probably
develop along the same lines as the older Shape series and
Look-Look Books.

SNIFF IT BOOKS

A smaller version of "Scratch and Sniff" books, 7" x 8-1/4",
with 12 pages, probably designed for younger children with
shorter attention spans. Eight fragrance labels were included in
the story.

SN2010 **What! No Spinach?** (13201   4 - 9
        by Edward Knapp, illus by Manny Campana
        ©1981 by King Features Syndicate, 12pp.
        A Popeye book.

SN2020 **Fox & Hound: Lost and Found, WD** (13202) 2 - 6
        ©1981 by WDP, 12pp. Adapted from the
        WD film.

SN2030 **Poky Little Puppy at the Fair, The** (13203) 2 - 6
        by E.K. Davis, illus by Jean Chandler
        ©1981, 12pp

SN2040 **Mouse Family's New House, The** (13204) 1 - 4
        by Edith Kunhardt, illus by Diane Dawson
        ©1981, 12pp

SN2050 **Hedgehog's Christmas Tree, The** (13205) 1 - 4
        by Kathryn Jackson, illus by Amye Rosenberg
        ©1982, 12pp

SN2060 **Curious Little Kitten Sniff Sniff Book, The**
        (13206)   2 - 6
        by Linda Hayward, illus by Maggie Swanson
        ©1983, 12pp

SN2070 **Donald Duck in Where's Grandma?** (13207) 2 - 6
        ©1983 by WDP, 12pp

SN2090 **Mrs. Brisby's Remembering Game** (13209) 2 - 6
        by E.K. Davis (adp), illus by Jean Chandler
        ©1982 by Mrs. Brisby, Ltd., 12pp. Adapted
        from the Don Bleuth production, *The Secret
        of Nimh.*

SP0170   SP0300

SP0400   SP0420

SP0490   SP0550

SP0610   SP0740

SQUARE BOOKS

Square books were approximately 10" square, with pictorial covers and full color illustrations. The book title was shown in a square on the cover. They were first published in the late '60s. How many books were produced in this series is not known.

SO6710 **Three Bears, The** (10671)   8 - 12
by Kathleen N. Daly,
illus by Feodor Rojankovsky
©1967, 24pp. Illustrations are different
from LE0470.

STAMP BOOKS

Soft cover books with 4 pages of full color gummed stamps to be pasted throughout the book. Books were 8-3/8" x 10-7/8", generally 48 pages in length, with black and white illustrations. An edition letter was sometimes noted on the last page, bottom right or on the bottom left corner of the back cover. The series began in the early '50s, and was advertised on LGB backs in 1958 and 1959. Several of the original books were reissued with new cover designs and new titles were added to the series well into the '70s. An assortment of 8 titles was still being offered by the publishers as late as 1980.

Values: These books are most often found with the stamps glued in place and the values have been determined with that condition in mind. Books with unused stamp sheets which are not stuck together command a premium, dependent on overall condition, of up to double the values shown. (See also: LG Activity Books, Giant Golden Books)

Stamp Books "P" Series

SP1001	Animals (1)	1 - 4
SP1002	Automobiles (2)	2 - 6
SP1003	Dolls and Toys (3)	2 - 6
SP1004	Airplanes (4)	2 - 6

SP1005	Flags (5)	1 - 3
SP1006	Picture Stamps for the Very Young (6)	1 - 3
SP1007	Dogs (7)	1 - 6
SP1008	Birds (8)	1 - 5
SP1009	Golden Fun Book (9)	1 - 3
SP1010	Trains (10)	1 - 4
SP1011	Wonders of the World (11)	1 - 3
SP1012	American History (12)	1 - 3
SP1013	Indians (13)	2 - 6
SP1014	Insects (14)	1 - 2
SP1015	Ships and Boats (15)	2 - 6
SP1016	Airplane Stamps (16)	2 - 6
SP1017	Bible Stamps, 1954 (17)	1 - 3
SP1018	Presidents of the U.S. (18)	1 - 3
SP1019	Truck Stamps (19)	2 - 6
SP1020	Rainy Day Play Book (20)	1 - 3
SP1021	Westward Ho! (21)	1 - 4
SP1022	Wonders of Space (22)	1 - 3
SP1023	George Washington, 1954 (23)	1 - 4
SP1024	Abraham Lincoln (24)	1 - 4
SP1025	Animals of the Past (25)	1 - 4
SP1026	Pirates (26)	2 - 6
SP1027	Marco Polo (27)	1 - 3
SP1028	Napoleon (28)	1 - 3
SP1029	Transportation (29)	1 - 3
SP1030	Cowboy Stamps, 1955 (30)	2 - 4
SP1031	Gulliver's Travels (31)	1 - 3
SP1032	Treasure Island (32)	1 - 3
SP1033	Trains (33)	1 - 4
SP1034	Early Man (34)	1 - 3
SP1035	Discoveries and Explorers (35)	1 - 3
SP1036	Musical Instruments (36)	1 - 4
	No title noted for 37	
SP1038	In Days of Old (Middle Ages) (38)	1 - 4
SP1039	Boats and Ships (39)	2 - 6

SP0760   SP0750

SP0890   SP0900

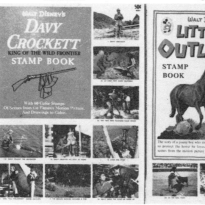

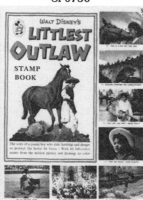

SP3010   SP3020

SP3050   SP3061

SP3030   SP3040

SP1040	Animals of the Sea, 1956 (40)	1 - 3
SP1041	Daniel Boone (41)	1 - 4
SP1042	Robinson Crusoe, 1956 (42)	1 - 4
SP1043	King Arthur (43)	1 - 4
SP1044	Kit Carson (44)	1 - 4
SP1045	Moby Dick (45)	1 - 4
SP1046	Story of Jesus (46)	2 - 6
SP1047	Soldiers (47)	2 - 6
SP1048	Automobiles of Today and Yesterday (48)	2 - 6
SP1049	Sea Shells, 1957 (49)	1 - 3
SP1050	Birds of the World (50)	1 - 4
SP1051	Fish Stamps (51)	1 - 3
SP1052	Rocks and Minerals (52)	1 - 3
SP1053	Science and Inventions (53)	1 - 3
SP1054	Baby Wild Animals (54)	1 - 4
SP1055	Snakes, Turtles & Lizards, 1958 (55)	1 - 4
SP1056	United States (56)	1 - 3
SP1057	Wyatt Earp (57)	2 - 6
SP1058	Wild Life Wonders (58)	1 - 3
SP1059	Mammals of North America (59)	1 - 3
SP1060	Smokey the Bear (60)	3 - 8
SP1061	Cats, 1959 (61)	2 - 6
SP1062	Space Wonders (62)	1 - 4
SP1063	Bible Stories (63)	1 - 3
SP1064	Wonders of the World (64)	1 - 3
SP1065	Dinosaurs (65)	1 - 4
SP1066	Space Travel (66)	1 - 5
SP1067	Horses (67)	1 - 3
SP1068	Natural History (68)	1 - 3
SP1069	Washington, D.C. (69)	1 - 3
SP1070	Trees (70)	1 - 3
SP1071	Story of Jesus (71)	2 - 6
SP1072	Toads, Frogs and Salamanders (72)	1 - 4
SP1073	Zoo Animals (73)	1 - 3
SP1074	Birds, 1953 (74)	1 - 3
SP1075	Pets, 1959 (75)	1 - 3

SP1076	Butterflies and Moths, 1959 (76)	2 - 8
SP1077	Presidents of the U.S. (77)	1 - 3
SP1078	Costumes (78)	2 - 6
SP1079	Scouting (79)	4 - 10
SP1080	Williamsburg (80)	1 - 3
SP1081	Natural Wonders (81)	1 - 3
SP1082	Atomic Energy (82)	1 - 3
SP1083	Dogs (83)	1 - 4
SP1084	Automobiles (84)	2 - 6
SP1085	American History (85)	1 - 3
SP1086	Indians (86)	2 - 6
	No title noted for 87	
SP1088	Insects (88)	1 - 4
SP1089	Huckleberry Hound, 1960, 32pp (89)	6 - 12
SP1090	Wonders of Africa (90)	1 - 3

Sports Series:

SP1201	New York Giants (1)	10 - 20
SP1202	Milwaukee Braves (2)	10 - 20
SP1203	Brooklyn Dodgers (3)	10 - 20

| SP1204 | Cleveland Indians (4) | 7 - 15 |

Disney Series:
SP1301	Davy Crockett, 1955, 32pp (1)	6 - 12
SP1302	Littlest Outlaw, 1955 (2)	1 - 4
SP1303	Robin Hood, 1955 (3)	1 - 4
SP1304	True-Life Adventures, 1955 (4)	1 - 4
SP1305	Davy Crockett & Mike Fink 1955, 32pp (5)	6 - 12
SP1306	Disneyland, 1956 (6)	8 - 15
SP1307	Animals of Africa, 1956 (7)	1 - 4
SP1308	Snow White (8)	8 - 10
SP1309	Secrets of Life (9)	1 - 4
SP1310	Sleeping Beauty, 1958, 32pp (10)	8 - 12
SP1311	White Wilderness (11)	1 - 4

New and Reissued Books:
SP6113	Bible Stamps, ©1968 (6113)	1 - 2
SP6123	Earth and Ecology, 1972 (6123)	1 - 2
SP6131	Animals of the Sea, ©1974 (6131)	1 - 2
SP6132	George Washington, ©1975 (6132)	1 - 2

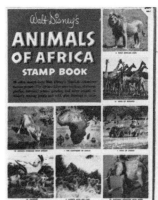

SP3070   SP3100

STAR BOOKS (Golden Star Library, Golden Star Book)

The Golden Star Library is reminiscent of the "Big Little Book" format. Star Books, however, have a glossy full color cover and color illustrations. The back cover, spine, and end papers are decorated with stars. The 12 books in the series sold for 59¢ each. No edition information was found in the books examined.

SR1010 Adventure Tales   5 - 15
by Kathryn & Byron Jackson,
illus by Gustaf Tenggren
©1967, 252pp. Compiled from stories previously published in *Pirates, Ships & Sailors* and *Cowboys & Indians*, both originally published as Giant Golden Books.

SR1020 Adventures of Henry Rabbit   5 - 10
by A.M. Dalmais, illus by Paul Durand
©1967, 252pp

SR1030 Adventures of Little Tiger, The 5 - 10
by Kathleen Daly, illus by J.P. Miller
©1967, 252pp

SR1040 Animal Tales   5 - 10
by Georges Duplaix,
illus by Feodor Rojankovsky
©1944/p1967, 252pp. Stories and poems adapted from the GGB, *Animal Stories*.

SR1050 Animals of the Little Woods   5 - 10
by A.M. Dalmais, illus by Paul Durand
©1967, 252pp

SR1060 Autumn Tales   5 - 10
by Kathryn Jackson, illus by Richard Scarry
©1967, 252pp

SR1070 Peter Pan, WD   5 - 18
by Edith Vincent, illus by WDS
©1967 by WDP, 252 pp. Adapted from the

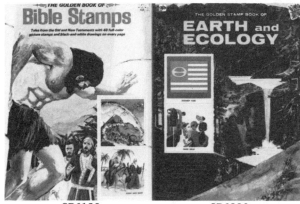

SP6130   SP6230

WD film, based on the story by J.M. Barrie.
SR1080 Pinocchio, WD   5 - 18
by Jay O'Brien (adp), illus by WDS
©1967 by WDP, 252pp. Adapted from the WD film, based on the story by Collodi.

SR1090 Sleeping Beauty & Cinderella, WD 5 - 18
by Marie Ponsot (adp), illus by WDS
©1967 by WDP, 252pp. Adapted from the WD film.

SR1100 Snow White, WD   5 - 18
by Carl Morse (adp), illus by WDS
©1967 by WDP, 252pp. Adapted from the WD film.

SR1110 Springtime Tales   5 - 10
by Kathryn Jackson, illus by Richard Scarry
©1967, 252pp

SR1120 Winter Tales   5 - 10
by Kathryn Jackson, illus by Richard Scarry
©1967, 252pp

STORY BOOKS (A Golden Story Book)

Story Books were 5" x 7", with 128 pages and full color pictures throughout. All books were numbered and additional books were listed on the back cover. Most of the books have a

SR1040   SR1070   SR1080   SR1090   SR1100   SS1160

| SS1010 | SS1020 | SS1030 | SS1040 | SS1050 | SS1060 |

| SS1070 | SS1080 | SS1090 | SS1100 | SS1110 | SS1120 |

"basket weave" gold colored spine, but copies have been found with the regular LGB paper spine. No edition information is given, other than copyright. No retail price is stated on the books, and whether they were available singularly or only in sets is not known. Boxed sets containing 6 books, "The New Golden Story Library", selected by the editors of *Weekly Reader* were available. Several of the titles were repeated as Sandpiper Books.

SS1010 **Herbert's Zoo and Other Lively Stories** (1)   3 - 9
(Anthology), illus by Julian
©1949, 128pp

SS1020 **Magic Wish and Other Johnny and Jane Stories** (2)   3 - 9
by Elsa Ruth Nast, illus by Corinne Malvern
©1949, 128pp

SS1030 **Christopher Bunny and Other Animal Stories** (3)   3 - 9
by Jane Werner, illus by Richard Scarry
©1949, 128pp

SS1040 **Boss of the Barnyard and Other Barnyard Stories** (4)   3 - 9
by Joan Hubbard, illus by Richard Scarry
©1949, 128pp

SS1050 **Stagecoach Robbery** (5)   3 - 9
by Peter Archer, illus by Joe & Beth Krush
©1949, 128pp

SS1060 **Train Stories** (6)   4 - 12
by Robert Garfield & Jessie Knittle,
illus by Tibor Gergely
©1949, 128pp

SS1070 **Mystery in Disneyville, WD** (7)   4 - 12
illus by WDS, adp by Richard Moores &
Manuel Gonzales
©1949 by WDP, 128pp

SS1080 **Circus Stories** (8)   3 - 9
by Kathryn & Byron Jackson,
illus by Charles E. Martin
©1949, 128pp

SS1090 **Penny Puppy and Other Dog Stories** (9)   3 - 9
by Robert Garfield, illus by Aurelius Battaglia
©1949, 128pp

SS1100 **Bugs Bunny's Treasure Hunt** (10)   4 - 12
written & illus by Warner Bros.

Cartoons, Inc., adp by Tom McKimson
©1949 by Warner Bros. Cartoons, Inc., 128pp

SS1110 **Tom & Jerry and Their Friends** (11)   3 - 9
written & illus by MGM Cartoons,
adp by Harvey Eisenberg
©1950 by Loew's Inc., 128pp

SS1120 **So Dear to My Heart, WD** (12)   4 - 12
by Helen Palmer (adp),
illus by WDS, adp by Bill Peet
©1950 by WDP, 128pp. Based on the
story by Sterling North.

SS1130 **Chatterly Squirrel and Other Animal Stories** (13)   3 - 9
by Jane Werner, illus by J.P. Miller
©1950, 128pp

SS1140 **Horse Stories** (14)   3 - 9
by Jack Bechdolt, illus by Cornelius DeWitt
©1950, 128pp. Listed as *Crazy About Horses*.

SS1150 **Merry Piper, The** (15)   3 - 9
(Anthology), illus by Harlow Rockwell
©1950, 128pp

SS1160 **Cat Who Went to Sea and Other Cat Stories** (16)   3 - 9
by Kathryn & Byron Jackson,
illus by Aurelius Battaglia
©1950, 128pp

SS1170 **Gene Autry and the Red Shirt** (17)   4 - 12

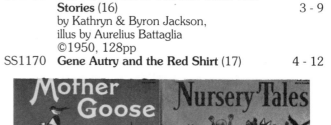

| ST1010 | ST1030 |

by Elizabeth Beecher, illus by Jesse March
©1950, 128pp

SS1180 **Donald Duck & the Hidden Gold, WD** (18) 4 - 12
by Jane Werner, illus by WDS,
adp by Al Taliaferro
©1950 by WDP, 128pp

SS1190 **Magic Pot, The** (19)   ?
Title noted, but copy unavailable for verification.

SS1200 **Christmas Book** (20)   ?
Title noted, but copy unavailable for verification.

STORYTIME BOOKS (Original Series)

This series was produced in both hard and soft cover editions. Hard cover books were 128 pages (7-1/2" x 10-1/2"); soft cover versions were 96 pages (7-1/4" x 10-1/4"). *Nursery Tales* has been found as a Big Golden Book with similar, but more detailed illustrations than the Storytime Book.

ST1010 **Mother Goose** (SC-101)   4 - 10
(Nursery Rhymes)
illus by Adrianna Mazzo Saviozzi
©1957, 128pp

ST1012 Same as ST1010, soft cover, 96pp   3 - 6

ST1020 **Bedtime Stories** (SC-102)   ?
Title noted, but copy unavailable for verification.

ST1030 **Nursery Tales** (SC-103)   5 - 20
by Elsa Jane Werner, illus by Tibor Gergely
©1948/p1957, 128pp (See also: BB2090)

ST1031 Same as ST1030, soft cover, 96pp   6 - 12

ST1040 **Animal Stories** (SC-104)   4 - 10
by Carol Denison (sel), illus by Frank Szasz
©1957, 128pp

ST1041 Same as ST1040, soft cover, 96pp   3 - 6

ST1040

ST2010

ST2020   ST2060

Storytime Books (New Series)

One of the newer Golden Book series, Storytime Books are designed to be read aloud, with lots of "busy" illustrations. Introduced in the fall of 1980, this new series of Golden Storytime Books was designed as a beginning library of high quality books. They are 8-1/4" x 9-1/4", with 22 pages (counting the end papers). All books have a "Bear & Book" design on the cover with the series name. Printing information is carried with the copyright notice.

Listing is chronological and code numbers are not related to book numbers.

ST2010 **Goldilocks and the Three Bears** (11980)   4 - 10
(Fairy Tale), illus by Lilian Obligado
©1980 by WPC, 22pp

ST2020 **Little Wheels, Big Wheels** (11983)   4 - 10
illus by Frank Fitzgerald
©1980 by WPC, illus by Frank Fitzgerald, 22pp

ST2030 **My First Book of Words** (11982)   4 - 10
illus by Jan Palmer
©1980 by WPC, illus by Jan Palmer, 22pp

ST2040 **My First Mother Goose Book** (11981)   4 - 10
(Nursery Rhymes), illus by Jane Chambless-Rigie
©1980 by WPC, illus by Jane Chambless-Rigie,
22pp

ST2110   ST2120

ST2190   ST2210

ST2050 **My First Mother Goose Book** (11987)   1 - 3
(Nursery Rhymes), illus by Aurelius Battaglia
©1980, 22pp

ST2060 **Raggedy Ann and Andy Go Flying** (11986) 6 - 12
by Mary Fulton, illus by Judith Hunt
©1980 by Bobbs-Merrill Co., Inc., 22pp.
Based on the characters by Johnny Gruelle.

ST2070 **That New Baby!** (11989)   4 - 8
by Patricia Relf, illus by DyAnne DiSalvo
©1980 by Patricia Relf (text), DyAnne
DiSalvo (ills), 22pp

ST2080 **Too Many Monkeys!** (11984)   4 - 8
illus by Kelly Oechsli
©1980 by WPC, 22pp

ST2140   ST2160

ST2090 **Who Lives on the Farm?** (11985)   4 - 8
illus by Lisa Bonforte
©1980 by WPC, illus by Lisa Bonforte, 22pp

ST2100 **First Day of School, The** (11957)   4 - 8
by Patricia Relf, illus by DyAnne DiSalvo
©1981 by Patricia Relf (text), DyAnne
DiSalvo (illus), 22pp

ST2110 **Night Before Christmas, The** (11956)   6 - 12
by Clement C. Moore,
illus by Greg & Tim Hildebrandt
©1981 by WPC, illus by Greg & Tim
Hildebrandt, 22pp

ST2120 **Three Little Pigs, The** (11955)   4 - 8
(Nursery Tale), illus by Nina Barbaresi
©1981, 22pp

ST2130 **Who Lives in the Zoo?** (11958)   4 - 8
illus by Lisa Bonforte
©1981 by WPC, Lisa Bonforte (illus), 22pp

ST2140 **Animal Poems for Children**   1 - 3
by DeWitt Conyers (sel), illus by Ann Schweninger
©1982 by WPC, illus by Ann Schweninger, 22pp

ST2150 **Big and Little Stories** (11963)   4 - 8
by Michaela Muntean, illus by Maggie Swanson
©1982 by CTW & Muppets, Inc., 22pp

ST2160 **Curious Little Kitten** (11952)   6 - 10
by Linda Hayward, illus by Maggie Swanson
©1982 by WPC, illus by Maggie Swanson, 22pp

ST2170 **Jack and the Beanstalk** (11951)   4 - 8
retold by Carol North, illus by Brenda Dabaghian
©1982 by WPC, illus by Brenda Dahaghian, 22pp

ST2180 **Monkeys' ABC, The** (11953)   4 - 8
written & illus by Kelly Oechsli
©1982, 22pp

ST2190 **Nativity, The** (11960)   4 - 8
retold by Juliana Bragg, illus by Sheilah Beckett
©1982 by WPC, illus by Sheilah Beckett, 22pp

ST2200 **Once Upon a Time in the Meadow** (11962)   4 - 8
written & illus by Rose Selarose
©1982 by Rose Selarose, 22pp. A "Six
Cousins" story.

ST2210 **Tale of Peter Rabbit, The** (11950)   4 - 8
by Beatrix Potter, illus by Amye Rosenberg
©1982 by WPC, illus by Amye Rosenberg, 22pp

ST2220 **Time for Bed, Sleepyheads** (11964)   4 - 8
by Sandra Chartier, illus by Normand Chartier
©1983 by Sandra & Normand Chartier, 22pp

ST2230 **Kitty's New Doll** (11965)   4 - 8
by Dorothy Kunhardt, illus by Lucinda McQueen
©1984 by the estate of Dorothy Kunhardt (text),
Lucinda McQueen (illus), 22pp

ST2240 **Little Red Hen, The** (11990)   4 - 10
(Nursery Tale), illus by Amye Rosenberg

©1984 by WPC, illus by Amye Rosenberg, 22pp

ST2250 **Pudge Pig's Counting Book** (11991)   3 - 6
written & illus by Amye Rosenberg
©1985 by Amye Rosenberg, 22pp

ST2260 **Bunny's Get-Well Soup** (11967)   4 - 8
written & illus by Joan Elizabeth Goodman
©1987 by Joan Elizabeth Goodman, 22pp

ST2270 **My Bible Alphabet** (11968)   3 - 6
by Maida Silverman, illus by Kathy Mitchell
©1987 by Maida Silverman (text), Kathy
Mitchell (illus), 22pp

ST2280 **Puss in Boots** (11969)   3 - 6
by Charles Perrault, illus by Lucinda McQueen
©1987 by WPC, illus by Lucinda McQueen, 22pp

ST2290 **Show Must Go On, The** (11970)   3 - 6
written & illus by Emily Arnold McCully
©1987 by Emily Arnold McCully, 22pp

ST2300 **Travels of Freddie & Frannie Frog** (11966) 3 - 6
by Betsy Macsiro, illus by Guillo Macsiro
©1987 by Betsy & Guillo Macsiro, 22pp

ST2310 **Ugly Duckling, The** (11971)   3 - 6
by Hans Christian Andersen, illus by Lisa McCue
©1987 by WPC, illus by Lisa McCue, 22pp

ST2320 **Little Dragon's Grandmother** (10969)   3 - 6
by Jan Wahl, illus by Lucinda McQueen
©1988 by Jan Wahl (text), Lucinda McQueen
(illus), 22pp

ST2330 **You Lucky Duck** (10970)   3 - 6
written & illus by Emily Arnold McCully
©1988 by Emily Arnold McCully, 22pp

STURDY BOOKS

These picture books are designed for very young learners, and are constructed to withstand rugged treatment. They typically have heavy board pages, with large illustrations and very little text. Several sturdy series have been released. Additional books can be found under: Giant Sturdy Books, Happy Books, and Sturdy Shape Books.

The current Golden Sturdy Book® series was introduced in the mid-70s, and includes several titles from the *Happy Book* series. Books are 5-1/2" x 9-7/8", with 22 pages, cased in regular book bindings. Printing is usually noted on the inside back cover.

SU1200 **Cyndy Szekeres' ABC** (12120)   2 - 4
written & illus by Cyndy Szekeres
©1983, 22pp

SU1220 **Animal Sounds** (12122)   1 - 3
illus by Aurelius Battaglia
©1981, 22pp

SU1230 **I Can Do It All By Myself** (12123)   1 - 3
illus by June Goldsborough

SU1330   SU1340   SU1390

| | SU1300 | SU2520 | SU2531 | SU2680 | SU2580 |

©1981, 22pp

SU1240 **Who Am I?** (12124)   1 - 3
illus by Normand Chartier
©1978 by CTW & Muppets, Inc., 22pp

SU1250 **I Am A Bunny** (12125)   1 - 3
by Ole Risom, illus by Richard Scarry
©1963, 22pp

SU1260 **I Am A Mouse** (12126)   2 - 4
by Ole Risom, illus by J.P. Miller
©1963, 22pp

SU1290 **Words** (12129)   1 - 3
written & illus by Joe Kaufman
©1963, 22pp

SU1300 **What Animals Do** (12130)   1 - 4
written & illus by Richard Scarry
©1963, 22pp. Originally published as
The Rooster Struts.

SU1320 **Counting** (12132)   1 - 3
illus by Helen Frederico
©1963, 22pp

SU1330 **I Am a Kitten** (12133)   1 - 3
by Ole Risom, illus by Jan Pfloog
©1970, 22pp

SU1340 **I Am a Puppy** (12134)   1 - 3
by Ole Risom, illus by Jan Pfloog
©1970, 22pp

SU1390 **I Am a Monster** (12139)   1 - 4
by H. Monster, illus by Joe Mathieu
©1976 by CTW & Muppets, Inc., 22p

SU1410 **Cyndy Szekere's Counting Book** (12140)   2 - 4
written & illus by Cyndy Szekeres
©1984, 22pp

SU1420 **Inside Sesame Street** (12142)   1 - 3
by the editors of Sesame Street,
illus by Marsha Winburn
©1986 by CTW & Muppets, Inc., 22pp

Sturdy Shape Books

Sturdy Shape Books, introduced in 1980, are 6" x 9-1/2" "shaped" to their cover design with 14 pages, printed on heavy coated boards in a self-cover binding. With limited text, they are advertised as combining "the attraction of a toy with the educational value of a good book." This popular series, featuring licensed characters and illustrations by well-known artists was still active in 1990 with new titles added regularly. Printing code is noted inside the back cover or with the copyright statement.

SU2500 **Baby Animals** (12250)   1 - 4
illus by Lisa Bonforte
©1980, 14pp

SU2510 **This Is My House** (12251)   1 - 4
illus by John E. Johnson

©1981, 14pp

SU2520 **Poky Little Puppy's Counting Book** (12252)   2 - 6
illus by Jean Chandler
©1980, 14pp. Illustrations from this book were
adapted for gift wrap. See Collectibles section.

SU2530 **Mother Goose Rhymes** (12253)   2 - 6
(Nursery Rhymes), illus by Lilian Obligado
©1980, 14pp

SU2531 **Nursery Rhymes** (12253-0)   2 - 4
(Nursery Rhymes), illus by Lilian Obligado
©1980/p 1985, 14pp. Originally titled
Mother Goose Rhymes. New cover design.

SU2540 **Big Bird's Color Game** (12254)   2 - 6
by the editors of Sesame Street,
illus by Tom Cooke
©1980 by CTW & Muppets, Inc. 14pp

SU2550 **Truck Book, The** (12255)   2 - 6
illus by William Dugan
©1980, 14pp

SU2560 **Here Comes a Train** (12256)   2 - 4
illus by Leonard Shortall
©1980, 14pp

SU2580 **My Goodnight Book** (12256)   4 - 10
illus by Eloise Wilkin
©1981, 14pp

SU2600 **Winnie-the-Pooh All Year Long** (12260)   2 - 6
illus by WDS
©1981 by WDP, 14pp

SU2610 **Fox Finds a Friend** (12261)   2 - 6
illus by WDS
©1981 by WDP, 14pp

SU2640 **Hound Finds a Friend** (12264)   2 - 6
illus by WDS
©1981 by WDP, 14pp

SU2660 **Saggy Baggy Elephant, The** (12266)   1 - 4
by Cassandra Conyers, illus by Darrell Baker
©1982, 14pp

SU2670 **Here Comes Santa Claus** (12267)   2 - 6
by M. Hover, illus by Christopher Santoro
©1982, 14pp

SU2680 **Honey Rabbit** (12268)   2 - 4
by Margo Hopkins, illus by Cyndy Szekeres

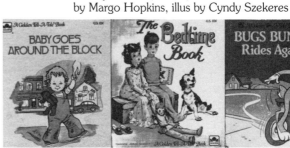

Tell-A-Tale Books

	©1982 by Cyndy Szekeres (illus), 14pp	
SU2690	**Play With Me** (12269)	2 - 6
	written & illus by Mercer Mayer	
	©1982, 14pp	
SU2700	**Mrs. Brisby's Children** (12270)	3 - 8
	By Margo Hopkins, illus by A.O. Williams	
	©1982 by Mrs. Brisby's, Ltd., 14pp	
SU2710	**My Good Morning Book** (12271)	4 - 10
	illus by Eloise Wilkin	
	©1983, 14pp	

TELL-A-TALE BOOKS

Golden Tell-a-Tell Books are a combination of reissued old favorites from the original Tell-a-Tale line (published under the Whitman imprint) and newly issued books, published since the series was changed to "Golden Tell-a-Tales" in 1986. Western Publishing Co. acquired the assets of Whitman in 1916, and many books that were originally published as Whitman titles have been reissued under the Golden imprint over the years. Paperback versions of many of these Tell-a-Tale Books have also appeared under the "Merrigold" imprint. Golden Tell-a-Tales are too new to generate much interest as collectibles, and copies can be picked up at flea markets and yard sales for 25¢ or less. As usual, licensed characters and popular artists will attract collector attention and grow in value more rapidly than general titles.

TB1070	TB1050	TB1010

TINY BOOKS

Hard cover Golden Tiny Books were 4" x 5-1/4", 24 pages with an overall plaid design on the back cover and plain spines in different colors. End papers have pastel drawings showing children reading books. The first 12 books are the same as the Golden Hours Library (GH1000), including the clock in the lower left corner of the front cover. Whether more books were produced in this hard cover format has not been determined. The books were marketed in the late '60s and sold for 19¢. No edition information is given in the books.

Mini-Golden Tales and Golden Tiny Tales were soft cover spin-offs, with the same size and general design.

Tiny Books

TB1010	**How to Tell Time** (1)	1 - 4
	by Jane Werner Watson, illus by Eleanor Dart	
	©1957, 24pp (See also: LE2850)	
TB1020	**Hop, Little Kangaroo** (2)	1 - 4
	by Patricia Scarr,m illus by Feodor Rojankovsky	
	©1965, 24pp (See also: LE5580)	
TB1030	**Heidi** (3)	1 - 4
	by Johanna Spyri, illus by Corinne Malvern	
	c. 1954, 24pp (See also: LE1920)	
TB1040	**Four Puppies** (4)	1 - 4
	by Anne Heathers, illus by Lilian Obligado	
	©1960, 24pp (See also: LE4050)	
TB1050	**Big Little Book** (5)	1 - 4
	by Dorothy Hall Smith, illus by Moritz Kennel	
	©1962, 24pp (See also: LE4820)	

TB1060	**Littlest Racoon, The** (6)	1 - 4
	by Peggy Parish, illus by Claude Humbert	
	©1961, 24pp (See aso: LE4570)	
TB1070	**Old MacDonald Had a Farm** (7)	1 - 4
	(Nursery Song), illus by Moritz Kennel	
	©1960, 24pp (See also: LE4000)	
TB1080	**Tommy's Camping Adventure** (8)	1 - 4
	by Gladys Saxon, illus by Mel Crawford	
	©1962, 24pp (See also: LE4710)	
TB1090	**Four Little Kittens** (9)	1 - 4
	by Kathleen N. Daly,	
	illus by Adriana Mazza Saviozzi	
	©1957, 24pp (See also: LE5300)	
TB1100	**Colors Are Nice** (10)	1 - 4
	by Adelaide Holl, illus by Leonard Shortall	
	©1962, 24pp (See also: LE4960)	
TB1110	**Rumpelstiltskin and the Princess and the Pea** (11)	1 - 4
	by Hans Christian Andersen,	
	illus by William J. Dugan	
	©1962, 24pp (See also: LE4980)	
TB1120	**Little Cottontail** (12)	1 - 4
	by Carl Memling, illus by Lilian Obligado	
	©1960, 24pp (See also: LE4140)	

TG1000	TG2000

TINY GOLDEN BOOKS

Tiny Golden Books made their appearance in 1948, with *Tiny Animal Stories*, followed in 1949 by *Tiny Nonsense Stories* and Disney's *Tiny Movie Stories* in 1950.

Each set was housed in its own "book shelf box", protected by a slipcase, with a cellophane window to show the name of each book. Full page color ads appeared in *Life* magazine for both *Tiny Animal* and *Tiny Nonsense Stories*. Boxed sets of each series, and combinations of the different series, were produced.

Each Tiny Book, 2-1/4" x 3-1/4", has 24 pages, with heavy board covers and color illustrations throughout. Covers and end paper designs are different for each series. All books are identified as "A Tiny Golden Book."

TG1000	**Tiny Animal Stories**	20 - 45
	by Dorothy Kunhardt, illus by Garth Williams	
	©1948, 24pp. 12 books in a Jungle House box.	
TG1005	Same as TG1000, in slipcase	30 - 50

Individual books of TG1000:

TG1010	Baby Camel and His Naughty Father, The	1 - 3
TG1020	Baby Hippopotamus's Adventure, The	1 - 3
TG1030	Brave Father Gorilla, The	1 - 3
TG1040	Hop, Hop Little Kangaroo	1 - 3
TG1050	Little Leopard and His Fat Stomach, The	1 - 3
TG1060	Look Out, Baby Bears, Here He Comes!	1 - 3
TG1070	"Meow" said the Fierce Baby Lion	1 - 3
TG1080	Shame on You, Little Whale!	1 - 3
TG1090	This Little Giraffe Wants to Play	1 - 3
TG1100	Tiger Kitten's Poor, Poor Tail	1 - 3
TG1110	Two Stuck-in-the-Mud Rhinoceroses	1 - 3
TG1120	Why the Little Elephant Got Spanked	1 - 3
TG2000	**Tiny Movie Stories, Walt Disney**	25 - 60
	by WDS	

Tiny Golden Books as numbered for TG5000, boxed set. With the exception of the numbers and the titles on the "Tiny Animal" series placed in ovals, the covers are the same as when issued in single sets.

©1960 by WDP, 24pp. 12 books in a Movie Theatre Box.

TG2005	Same as TG2000, in slipcase	35 - 70

Individual books of TG2000:

TG2010	Bambi Plays Follow the Leader	2 - 5
TG2020	Bongo Stars Again	2 - 5
TG2030	Bootle Beetle's Adventures	2 - 5
TG2040	Brer Rabbit Plays a Trick	2 - 5
TG2050	Cinderella's Ball Gown	2 - 5
TG2060	Donald Duck's Wild Goose Chase	2 - 5
TG2070	Dopey and the Wicked Witch (Seven Dwarfs)	2 - 5
TG2080	Dumbo's Magic Feather	2 - 5
TG2090	Mickey's New Car	2 - 5
TG2100	Pablo the Penguin Takes a Trip	2 - 5
TG2110	Pinocchio's Surprise	2 - 5
TG2120	Three Little Pigs Fool a Wolf	2 - 5
TG3000	**Tiny Nonsense Stories**	20 - 45

by Dorothy Kunhardt, illus by Garth Williams ©1949, 24pp. 12 books in a Nonsense

	Town City Block box.	
TG3005	Same as TG3000, in slipcase	30 - 55

Individual books of TG3000: 1 - 3

TG3010	April Fool!	1 - 3
TG3020	Cowboy Kitten, The	1 - 3
TG3030	Easter Bunny, The	1 - 3
TG3040	Happy Valentine	1 - 3
TG3050	Little Squirrel's Santa Claus	1 - 3
TG3060	Mrs. Sheep's Little Lamb	1 - 3
TG3070	Naughty Little Guest, The	1 - 3
TG3080	Poor Frightened Mr. Pig	1 - 3
TG3090	Roger Mouse's Wish	1 - 3
TG3100	Two Snowbulls, The	1 - 3
TG3110	Uncle Quack	1 - 3
TG3120	Wonderful Silly Picnic, The	1 - 3
TG4000	**Tiny Theater, Walt Disney**	15 - 35

©1981 by WDP. 12 books in a Theater Box w/small pop-up stage.

Individual books of TG4000:

TG4010	Fox and Hound Become Friends (1)	1 - 2
TG4020	Rescuers Save Penny, The (2)	1 - 2
TG4030	Mickey's New Car (3)	1 - 2
TG4040	Donald Duck's Wild Goose Chase (4)	1 - 2
TG4050	Dumbo's Magic Feather (5)	1 - 2
TG4060	Pablo the Penguin Takes a Trip (6)	1 - 2
TG4070	Three Little Pigs Fool a Wolf (7)	1 - 2
TG4080	Pinocchio's Surprise (8)	1 - 2
TG4090	Cinderella's Ball Gown (9)	1 - 2
TG4100	Dopey and the Wicked Witch (10)	1 - 2
TG4110	Bambi Plays Follow the Leader (11)	1 - 2
TG4120	Brer Rabbit Plays a Trick (12)	1 - 2

(*Bootle Beetle* and *Bongo Stars Again* were dropped from this new series.)

Tiny Golden Library Sets

TG5000	**Tiny Golden Library (Animal, Nonsense and Movie Stories)**	40 - 80

by Dorothy Kunhardt, illus by Garth Williams, Disney books by WDS

TG6000

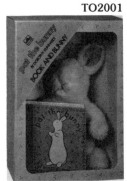

TO2001

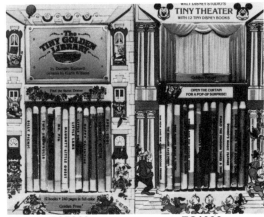

TG7000   TG4000

©1964, 36 books in a wood-pattern box.
Contains books from TG1000, TG2000
and TG3000.

TG6000 **Tiny Golden Library (Animal &**
Nonsense Stories)   30 - 55
by Dorothy Kunhardt, illus by Garth Williams
©1968, 24pp. 24 books in a Nonsense
Town City Block box. Contains books from
TG1000 and TG3000.

TG6005 Same as TG6000, in slipcase   40 - 65

TG7000 **Tiny Golden Library (Nonsense Stories)**   15 - 30
by Dorothy Kunhardt, illus by Garth Williams
©1949/p1981, 24pp. Reprints of TG3000.
All books numbered. 12 books in Apartment
House box w/secret drawer.

TG7005 Individual books of TG7000, each   1 - 2

TO2000   TO2010

TOUCH AND FEEL BOOKS

The initial success of two Richard Scarry books, *Is This the House of Mistress Mouse?* and *The Egg in the Hole*, along with Dorothy Kunhardt's *Pat the Bunny*, gave rise to a whole series of books for very young children that have things to touch, move, or smell, as well as hidden surprises. As a distinct series, "Touch and Feel" books are a rather recent grouping. The series incorporates both new books and titles previously published in other Golden series.

TO2000 **Pat the Bunny** (12000)   2 - 5
written & illus by Dorothy Kunhardt
©1940 by Dorothy Kunhardt. Originally
created for the author's daughter, this book has
sold over 4 million copies, and has been one
of the best-loved children's books in the 50
years since its debut. Value given is for "Touch
& Feel" printings. Earlier printings from the
'40s would appreciate sharply.

TO2001 Same as TO2000, boxed w/plush rabbit   8 - 20
First packaged thus in 1987.

TO2010 **Pat the Cat** (12001)   2 - 6
by Edith Kunhardt
©1984 by Edith Kunhardt, 20pp

TO2290 **Is This the House of Mistress Mouse?**
(12029)   5 - 16
written & illus by Richard Scarry
©1964 by GP, 20pp, 8" x 8". A hole book.

TO2290   TO2300

Spiral bound, heavy board construction.

TO2300 **Egg in the Hole Book, Richard Scarry's**
(12030)   5 - 16
written & illus by Richard Scarry
©1967 by GP, 20pp, 8" x 8". A hole book.
Spiral bound, heavy board construction.

TO2440 **Telephone Book, The** (12144)   2 - 6
by Dorothy Kunhardt
©1961, 20pp

TO2460 **Touch Me Book, The**   1 - 4
by Pat & Eve Witte, illus by Harlow Rockwell
©1961, 18pp

TO2480 **Santa's Beard Is Soft and Warm** (12148)   2 - 6
by Bob Ottum & Jo Anne Ward,
illus by Rod Ruth
©1974, 18pp

TO2510 **Whose Baby?** (12151)   1 - 4
by Mary DeBall Kwitz
©1978, 18pp

TO2520 **Winnie-the-Pooh: Hungry for Honey, WD**
(12152)   2 - 5
illus by WDS
©1979 by WDS, 18pp

TO2530 **What's Inside?** (12153)   1 - 4
by editors of Sesame Street
©1980 by CTW & Muppets, Inc., 18pp

TO2540 **Good Morning Book, The** (12154)   1 - 4
illus by Eugenie Fernandez
©1983, 20pp. Paper engineering by Ib Penick.

TO2550 **Good Night Book, The** (12155)   1 - 4
illus by Eugenie Fernandez
©1983, 20pp. Paper engineering by Ib Penick.

TO2560 **Just a Snowy Day** (12156)   1 - 4
written & illus by Mercer Mayer
©1983 by Mercer Mayer, 20pp. A Little
Critter™ Book. Paper engineering by Ib Penick.

TO2570 **Who's Hiding?** (12157)   1 - 4
by editors of Sesame Street, illus by Tom Cooke
©1986 by CTW & Muppets, Inc., 14pp

TO2590 **Good Night, Sweet Mouse** (12159)   1 - 4
written & illus by Cyndy Szekeres
©1988 by Cyndy Szekeres, 14pp

TO2591 Same as TO2590, boxed w/toy mouse   2 - 6

TO2620 **Poky Little Puppy's Day at the Fair** (12162)   1 - 4
by Rita Walsh, illus by Jean Chandler
©1990, 20pp

TO2460   TO2620

TOY BOOKS

These "toy book" titles were advertised both as a group by themselves and as part of the Big Golden Book series. Other toy-type books, with puppets and paper dolls, can be found under LGB-Activity Books, Big Golden Books, Funtime Books and Golden Books.

TP1010 **Cinderella Puppet Show, WD**   15 - 50
illus by Retta Worcester
©1949 by WDP. 5 scenes & 10 puppets.

TR1005

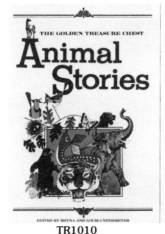

TR1010

TR1020

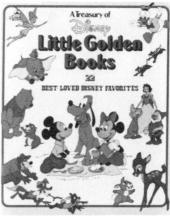

TS1150

TP1010

TS1100

TS1210

TP1020	**Golden Christmas Manger, The**	10 - 30
	written & illus by Helen Sewell ©1949 Folding manger w/32 cut-out figures.	
TP1030	**Judy & Jim, A Paper Doll Story**	40 - 60
	written & illus by Hilda Miloche & Wilma Kane ©1947. A story book w/scenes in which to insert the dolls and their toys. Published under S&S imprint, w/no Golden identification.	
TP1031	Same as TP1030, new cover design ©1949	40 - 60
TP1040	**Let's Go Fishing**	8 - 20
	by Kathryn & Byron Jackson, illus by Richard Scarry ©1949. W/fishing rod & cut-out fish in 6 pocket pages.	
TP1050	**Mother Goose Land with Judy and Jim**	40 - 60
	written & illus by Hilda Miloche & Wilma Kane ©1949, 52pp. Scenes & costumes all related to Nursery Rhymes, w/a trunk at the back of the book to hold the clothes. Published under S&S imprint, w/no Golden identification.	

TREASURE CHEST, THE GOLDEN

A 4-volume story set, issued in a green "Treasure Chest" slip-case. Illustrated in color and black & white. Classic legends and tales. Many stories were previously published in other Golden series supplemented by some new story material not previously published by Golden. Each volume is identified as "Golden Treasure Chest", followed by volume title.

TR1000	**Golden Treasure Chest, The**	16 - 40
	by Bryna and Louis Untermeyer (ed) ©1968, 4-volume set, 256pp per volume.	
TR1005	Same as TR1000, in slipcase	25 - 50
Books in TR1000:		
TR1010	**Animal Stories** (15601)	4 - 10
TR1020	**Tales and Legends** (15602)	4 - 10
TR1030	**Adventure Stories** (15603)	4 - 10
TR1040	**Favorite Classics** (15604)	4 - 10

TREASURY BOOKS

Treasury Books have been grouped together in view of their "best-loved story" content, and not necessarily because they are a distinct series. They are compiled from stories printed elsewhere in the Golden series. Many of the stories included in these anthologies are out-of-print and difficult to find in their original editions.

TS1100	**Story Land: An All Colour Bedtime Book for Children**	10 - 25
	by Ellen Lewis Buell ©1960, 156pp. A British "Treasury of Little Golden Books", same as TS1210, w/title change and new cover by Angier Scott. Released by Golden Pleasure Books.	
TS1150	**Treasury of Disney Little Golden Books**	3 - 10
	©1978 by WDP, 94pp. 22 best-loved Disney favorites.	
TS1210	**Treasury of Little Golden Books**	10 - 30
	by Ellen Lewis Buell	

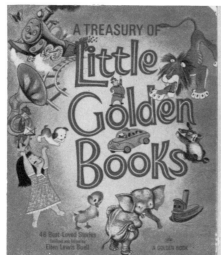

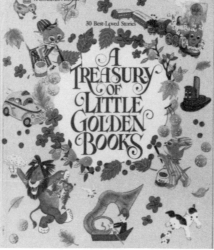

TS1220

TS1240

TS1280

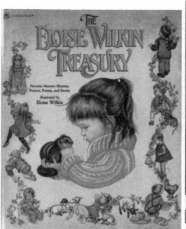

TS1250

TS1270

TS2040

TS2200

©1960, 156pp. 48 best-loved LGBs, original text and art rearranged for larger format. Cover and end papers by Feodor Rojankovsky.

TS1220	Same as TS1210	10 - 25

©1972, 156pp. Contents same as TS1210, new cover design.

TS1230	**Treasury of Little Golden Books**	5 - 10

by Ellen Lewis Buell
©1976, 94pp. Soft cover edition, w/26 stories selected from TS1210. Cover art similar to, but varied slightly from TS1220.

TS1240	**Treasury of Little Golden Books**	8 - 15

by Ellen Lewis Buell
©1982, 92pp. 30 stories selected from TS1210. A special release for Golden's 40th anniversary. New cover art and end papers by Kathy Allert.

TS1250	**Donald Duck Treasury, The**	3 - 9

©1984 by WDP, 62pp. A combination of LGBs and Tell-a-Tale books.

TS1270	**Eloise Wilkin Treasury**	6 - 12

by Linda C. Falken (ed), illus by Eloise Wilkin
©1985, 70pp. Adaptations from various books.

TS1280	**Treasury of Little Golden Books**	2 - 8

by Ellen Lewis Buell
©1989(A), 116pp. "Newly expanded", w/36 stories selected from TS1210; new cover design.

A new "Golden Treasury" series of 8-1/2" x 11" books was introduced in 1989. Some of the material is derived from LGBs (usually 3 LGBs are combined to form 1 book). Several of the books have totally new content. No collector value has yet been established.

TREASURY OF CHILDREN'S LITERATURE

From classic stories to Tall Tales, *The Golden Treasury of Children's Literature* was a veritable gold mine of juvenile stories. The 10 volumes which comprise the *Treasury* were compiled over a 4-year period, carefully edited and selected by Bryna and Louis Untermeyer. Some of the material was culled from previously published Golden Books, but much was designed and selected especially for the series.

TS2000	**Treasury of Children's Literature**	40 - 100

by Bryna & Louis Untremeyer (ed)
©1962, 10 volume set

Volumes in TS2000:

TS2010	**Big and Little Creatures** (V1)	4 - 10
	1962, 176pp	
TS2020	**Beloved Tales** (V2)	4 - 10
	1962, 152pp	
TS2030	**Fun and Fancy** (V3)	4 - 10
	1962, 164pp	
TS2040	**Old Friends and Lasting Favorites** (V4)	4 - 10
	©1962, 152pp	
TS2050	**Wonder Lands** (V5)	4 - 10
	©1962, 152pp	

TS2060	**Unfamiliar Marvels** (V6)	4 - 10
	©1962, 152pp	
TS2070	**Creatures Wild and Tame** (V7)	4 - 10
	©1963, 152pp	
TS2080	**Adventurers All** (V8)	4 - 10
	©1963, 152pp	
TS2090	**Legendary Animals** (V9)	4 - 10
	©1963, 152pp	
TS2100	**Tall Tales** (V10)	4 - 10
	©1963, 152pp	
TS2200	**Treasury of Children's Literature**	8 - 15
	©1966, 544pp. Selections from 10-volume set made into one volume.	

TS3005

TREASURY OF KNOWLEDGE

A 16-volume set, uniform in size with *The Golden Book Encyclopedia* and *The Golden Book Picture Atlas*. The three sets are designed as complimentary reference sources. Articles are not alphabetically arranged as with the *Encyclopedia*, but each volume includes a time chart placing the subjects discussed historically, as well as relating them to the content of other volumes. A good portion of the last volume is given over to an index for the entire series. Each 94-page book is hard bound, with pictorial covers and color illustrations throughout.

TS3000	**Golden Treasury of Knowledge**	16 - 32
	by Margaret Bevans (ed)	
	©1961, 94pp each. Index in Vol. 16.	
	Cover illustrations differ w/each volume.	
	16-volume set.	
TS3005	Individual volumes of TS3000, each	1 - 2

WALT DISNEY'S LIBRARY

Disney books were issued within the Giant and Big Golden series that were sometimes identified as "Walt Disney Library" books, other times as Big or Giant Golden Books. A specific WDL listing was not issued, but there was no unique format to the books that set them apart from regular issue Golden Books. They were produced under the S&S imprint and books as late as 1956 can carry WDL identification. For the purposes of this guide, we have listed WDL titles in their respective Big and Golden categories. No particular difference in value is noted for "WDL editions" over regular issue of the same books.

WALT DISNEY'S LITTLE LIBRARY

A short-lived classification for Disney books produced in LGB size. Although as many as 10 Disney books are listed as being part of "Walt Disney's Little Library" on LGB lists, only the first 3 books ever carried the identification. Of those 3, only the first 2 were totally given to a unique "WDLL" format. (See Little Golden Books-Disney for listings.)

WALT DISNEY PARADE

A Disney showcase. Four volumes in a slipcase, a great collection of Disney's best. Compiled from various Disney books in the Golden series and some new material. Also issued in a condensed 1-volume version.

WP1000	**Walt Disney Parade** (23015)	32 - 48
	by WDS	
	©1970 by WDP, 4-volume set, 256pp each volume	
WP1005	Same as WP1000, in slipcase	40 - 60
Individual volumes of WP1000:		
WP1010	**Fun Favorites** (V1)	8 - 12

WP2005   WW1100

WP1020   WP1030   WP2010

WP1020	**Adventures in Fact** (V2)	8 - 12
WP1030	**Fantasy on Parade** (V3)	8 - 12
WP1040	**Great Moments in Fiction** (V4)	8 - 12
WP2000	Same as WP1000, revised edition ©1977 by WDP. 4-volume set, 256pp each. New cover art.	20 - 40
WP2005	Same as WP2000, in slipcase	25 - 50
WP2010	Individual volumes of WP2000	5 - 10
WP2100	**Walt Disney's Parade of Fun, Fact, Fantasy and Fiction** by WDS ©1970 by WDP, 459pp. Single volume edition. Contents selected from WP1000. Actual date of publication not stated.	15 - 30

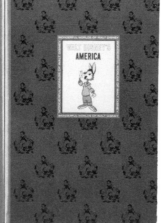

WW1005   WW1030

WONDERFUL WORLDS OF WALT DISNEY

Compiled from Little, Big and Giant Golden Books and other Disney material, the books were 7-3/4" x 10-1/2", 256 pages, with green bindings and a different color spine for each book. The set of 4 volumes came in a slipcase. Originally published in 1965 and reissued in 1978. Books were available by mail order only, and many LGBs have ads for the set bound in at the back of the book.

WW1000	**Wonderful Worlds of Walt Disney** WDS, illustrated w/photos & dwgs. ©1965 by WDP. 4-volume set, 256pp each.	24 - 48
WW1005	Same as WW1000, in slipcase	35 - 60

Individual volumes of WW1000:

WW1010	**Fantasyland** (15590)	6 - 12
WW1020	**Worlds of Nature** (15591)	6 - 12
WW1030	**America** (15592)	6 - 12
WW1040	**Stories from Other Lands** (15593)	6 - 12
WW1100	Same as W1000, in Goldencraft bindings, individual volumes, each	6 - 12
WW2000	Same as WW1000, revised edition	20 - 40

	©1956/p1978 by WDP. 4 volumes, 256pp each	
WW2005	Same as WW2000, in slipcase	25 - 50
WW2010	Individual volumes of WW2000, each	5 - 10

AUDIO–VISUAL PRODUCTS

RECORDS

One of the early spin-offs from Golden Books was the production of records, which began in 1948 with the release of 12 Little Golden Records. It was a natural step from Little to Big Golden Records ... in short order EPs, LPs, Record Chests, and Book and Record Sets were being produced, and Golden was well on its way to becoming the leading producer of children's records. As with Golden Books, the best musical, vocal and artistic talent was employed to produce the records. Original director of Music was Mitch Miller, and narrations and vocals were done by many "name" artists, including Bing Crosby, Jimmy Durante, Irene Wicker (The Singing Lady), Roy Rogers ... and even Phil Rizzuto. Disney songs, character-based records, learning and game recordings supplied children with endless hours of listening fun. (There were even "Little Golden Needles ... the perfect needles for children's phonographs.")

Little Golden Records (1948)

This initial record offering of 12 titles was based on 8 LGBs, 1 BGB and 3 other stories. They came in a heavy paper jacket, the same size as a Little Golden Book, utilizing the LG back cover design for the back of the record jacket. With full color pictures inside and out, and a bright yellow unbreakable record, the 20¢ records were an immediate success, with one retailer selling out their entire 10,000 record stock in 3 days.

AV1001	Scuffy the Tugboat (1)	3 - 9
AV1002	Lively Little Rabbit, The (2)	3 - 9
AV1003	Shy Little Kitten, The (3)	3 - 9
AV1004	Tootle (4)	3 - 9
AV1005	Poky Little Puppy (5)	3 - 9
AV1006	Circus Time (6)	3 - 9
AV1007	Funny Little Mouse, The (7)	2 - 6
AV1008	Wynken, Blynken & Nod (8)	2 - 6
AV1009	Little Peewee (9)	3 - 9
AV1010	Golden Egg, The (10)	3 - 9
AV1011	Big Brown Bear, The (11)	3 - 9
AV1012	Out of the Window (12)	2 - 6

Little Golden Records – Singles

While trading on the popularity of the "Little Golden" image, these records are not necessarily tied to books in the way that the "See and Hear" records are. Records that are derived from book titles are complimentary to the story, rather than an actual reading of the book. These records - both yellow and orange - were 78 rpm and originally came in full color paper sleeves, 7-3/4" x 6-3/4", often with a headline similar to that used on LGBs in the '50s. "Little Golden Record" and "Golden Record"

AV1003   AV1001   AV1010   AV1011   AV1805

AV1178   AV1309   AV1310   AV1490   AV1522

AV1160   AV1176

AV1840   AV1195

AV1450   AV1590

were used interchangeably in the series, and both names are often found on the same record. Many of the records were reissued in a 6-1/2" x 7-3/4" sleeve, in both 45 and 78 rpm, and new records were added to the series in this format. Records redone in 45 rpm were standard black records. Extended Play records, which combined 3 Little Golden Records in 1, were also offered. A representative listing of records in each of these categories is included, but the lists are by no means complete.

While most of the general records - nursery rhymes, sing alongs, etc. - generate very little collector interest, specialized subjects within the series do. Therefore, rather than list the records in strict numerical or alphabetical sequence, they are grouped by subject (much as they were on the back of the original jackets), then listed alphabetically. Records without their jackets are considered uncollectible.

Singles (45 & 78 rpm)
Characters & Personalities – TV, Movies, Cartoons
AV1100	Annie Oakley (184)	3 - 8
AV1110	Bill Barker (Terry Toons) (218)	1 - 5
AV1120	Bugs Bunny (180)	1 - 5
AV1125	Bugs Bunny and Tweetie Pie (159)	1 - 5
AV1130	Daffy Duck (186)	1 - 3
AV1135	Elmer Fudd (189)	1 - 5
AV1140	Howdy Doody: Cowabonga! (221)	2 - 10
AV1142	Howdy Doody: Laughing Song (220)	2 - 10
AV1144	Howdy Doody: Little One, Lean One (212)	2 - 10
AV1146	Howdy Doody: Look! Look! (219)	2 - 10
AV1150	Oz: Over the Rainbow (49)	2 - 6
AV1155	Oz: We're Off to See the Wizard (50)	2 - 6
AV1160	Popeye the Sailor Man (60)	5 - 15
AV1165	Porky Pig (206)	1 - 3
AV1170	Rootie Kazootie (98)	3 - 8
AV1172	Rootie Kazootie and Galapoochie Pup (149)	3 - 8
AV1174	Rootie Kazootie and Mr. Deetle Dootle (131)	3 - 8
AV1176	Rootie Kazootie: Polka Dottie's Garden (109)	3 - 8
AV1178	Songs of Bozo (735)	3 - 8
AV1180	Sylvester the Cat (203)	1 - 3
AV1190	Tarzan (67)	2 - 7
AV1195	Tom Corbett Space Cade Song (89)	10 - 30
AV1200	Tweetie: I Taut I Saw a Puddy Tat (159)	1 - 3
AV1220	Woody Woodpecker's Song (WL) (58)	1 - 5

Christmas Records
AV1270	Boy at a Window, Bing Crosby (356)	1 - 5
AV1300	Frosty the Snowman (69)	1 - 3
AV1302	I Saw Mommy Kissing Santa Claus (110)	1 - 3
AV1304	I Want a Hippopotamus for Christmas (155)	1 - 3
AV1306	Jingle Bells (35)	1 - 3
AV1308	Little Fir Tree (166)	1 - 3
AV1309	Merry Merry Christmas (772)	1 - 3
AV1310	Night Before Christmas (33 - Eloise Wilkin cover)	4 - 10
AV1312	O Little Town of Bethlehem (37)	1 - 2
AV1314	Rudolph the Red-Nosed Reindeer (68)	1 - 3
AV1316	Santa Claus is Coming to Town (47)	1 - 3
AV1318	Silent Night (34)	1 - 2
AV1320	Sleigh Ride, Captain Kangaroo (125)	1 - 3
AV1322	White Christmas (103)	1 - 3

Folk Songs
AV1340	Blue-Tail Fly, The (31)	1 - 2
AV1342	De Camptown Races (21)	1 - 5
AV1344	Dixie (19)	1 - 2
AV1346	Oh, Susanna (17)	1 - 2

Little Golden Books
AV1360	Animals of Farmer Jones (13)	1 - 5
AV1365	Big Brown Bear, The (11)	1 - 5
AV1370	Brave Cowboy Bill (46)	1 - 5
AV1380	Circus Time (6)	1 - 5
AV1390	Doctor Dan, The Bandage Man (51)	3 - 8
AV1400	Five Little Firemen (14)	1 - 5
AV1410	Gaston and Josephine (152)	3 - 8
AV1415	Golden Egg, The (10)	1 - 5
AV1425	Happy Man and His Dump Truck (54)	1 - 5
AV1440	Little Fat Policeman (45)	1 - 5
AV1450	Little Golden Sleepy Record (40)	1 - 5
AV1460	Little Lulu (59)	5 - 12

	AV1306	AV1300
	AV1525	
	AV1720	
	AV2590	

AV1470	Little Peewee (9)	1 - 5
AV1480	Lively Little Rabbit, The (2)	1 - 5
AV1490	Me and My Teddy Bear (572)	4 - 12
AV1500	Poky Little Puppy (86)	2 - 6
AV1510	Poor Mr. Flibberty Jib (53)	3 - 8
AV1520	Saggy Baggy Elephant, The (42)	2 - 6
AV1522	Saggy Baggy Elephant (707)	1 - 3
AV1525	School Days: Jerry at School (279)	1 - 3
AV1530	Scuffy the Tugboat (55)	2 - 6
AV1540	Seven Sneezes, The (43)	3 - 8
AV1550	Shy Little Kitten (3)	2 - 6
AV1570	Timmy is a Big Boy Now (52)	3 - 8
AV1580	Tootle (4)	2 - 6
AV1585	Tootle (56)	2 - 6
AV1590	White Bunny and His Magic Nose, The (41)	1 - 5

Nursery Songs

AV1650	Frog He Would a-Wooing Go (29)	1 - 2
AV1660	Humpty Dumpty (23)	1 - 2
AV1670	Muffin Man, The (20)	1 - 2
AV1680	Old King Cole (24)	1 - 2
AV1690	Three Little Kittens (16)	1 - 2

Roy Rogers & Dale Evans

AV1700	Daniel the Cocker Spaniel (187)	2 - 6
AV1705	Goodnight Prayer (205)	2 - 6
AV1710	Happy Trails to You (176)	3 - 10
AV1715	Little Shoemaker, The (196)	2 - 6
AV1720	Lord's Prayer, The (240)	2 - 6
AV1725	Open Up Your Heart (179)	2 - 6
AV1730	Roy Rogers Had a Farm (199)	3 - 10
AV1735	Swedish Rhapsody (185)	2 - 6

Song Hits and General Titles

AV1800	Alexander's Ragtime Band (72)	1 - 2
AV1805	Cinderella (628)	1 - 3
AV1810	Daddy's Report Card (134)	1 - 2
AV1820	Easter Parade (75)	1 - 2
AV1830	Good Ship Lollipop (101)	1 - 2
AV1840	Happy Birthday (374)	1 - 3
AV1850	How Much is that Doggie in the Window?(145)	1 - 2
AV1860	I'm Gonna Get Well Today (102)	1 - 2
AV1870	MacNamara's Band (118)	1 - 2
AV1875	Magic Golden Record (44)	1 - 5
AV1880	Mairzy Doats (147)	1 - 2
AV1885	Never Be Afraid, Bing Crosby (355)	1 - 5
AV1890	Oklahoma! (239)	1 - 4

AV1900	Peter Cottontail (57)	1 - 2
AV1905	Pig Polka (135)	1 - 2
AV1910	Pirates & Sailors Songs (48)	1 - 2
AV1930	Romper Room Sing Along Songs (1032)	1 - 3
AV1950	Star-Spangled Banner (79)	1 - 2
AV1960	Syncopated Clock (126)	1 - 2
AV1980	Three Little Fishes (133)	1 - 2

Disney Singles (45 & 78 rpm)
General

AV2500	At the Country Fair	2 - 6
AV2510	Bang! Goes Old Betsy! (213)	1 - 7
AV2530	Goofy the Toreador (151)	2 - 6
AV2540	Happy Birthday (WD)(12)	1 - 5
AV2550	Hi Diddle Dee Dee (43)	1 - 5
AV2570	Mr. Chip 'n Mr. Dale (46)	1 - 5
AV2590	Saga of Andy Burnett (449)	1 - 5
AV2595	Santa's Toy Shop (14)	2 - 6
AV2600	Toot and a Whistle a Plunk and a Boom (162)	1 - 5
AV2610	Trick or Treat (WD)(39)	1 - 5

AV2600	AV2720

Donald Duck

AV2700	Donald Duck and Pluto Pup	2 - 7
AV2710	Donald Duck Around the World (605)	2 - 7
AV2720	Donald Duck's Singing Lesson (6)	2 - 7
AV2730	Donald Duck, Baby Sitter (8)	2 - 7
AV2740	Donald Duck, Cowboy (13)	2 - 7

Mickey Mouse

AV2800	Mickey Mouse & His Friends (5)	2 - 6
AV2820	Mickey Mouse's New Car (7)	2 - 6
AV2830	Mickey Mouse's Birthday Party (60)	2 - 6
AV2840	Mickey Mouse's Christmas Party (62)	2 - 6

AV2710	AV3010	AV3040	AV3300	AV3306

AV2830   AV2840

Mickey Mouse Club
AV2910	Mickey Mouse Picture House Song (225)	1 - 5
AV2920	Official MMC Pledge (223)	1 - 5
AV2930	Official MMC Song and March (222)	1 - 5
AV2950	You, the Human Animal (224)	1 - 5

Disneyland
AV3000	Adventureland (303)	1 - 5
AV3010	Disneyland (TV theme song)	1 - 5
AV3020	Fantasyland	1 - 5
AV3040	Tomorrowland (302)	1 - 5

Films: Animated Features
Alice in Wonderland
AV3200	A Very Merry UnBirthday (24)	1 - 5
AV3202	Alice in Wonderland (18)	1 - 5
AV3204	All in a Golden Afternoon (22)	1 - 5
AV3206	I Give Myself Very Good Advice (20)	1 - 5
AV3208	I'm Late (19)	1 - 5
AV3210	Painting the Roses Red (25)	1 - 5
AV3212	Twas Brillig (23)	1 - 5
AV3214	Walrus and the Carpenter (21)	1 - 5

Bambi
| AV3220 | Bambi (164) | 2 - 6 |

Cinderella
AV3240	Bibbidi-Bobbidi-Boo (9)	2 - 6
AV3242	Cinderella Work Song (10)	2 - 6
AV3244	Dream is a Wish Your Heart Makes (11)	2 - 6

Davy Crockett
| AV3250 | Ballad of Davy Crockett (197) | 6 - 15 |

Dumbo
| AV3260 | Dumbo (169) | 1 - 5 |

Lady and the Tramp
| AV3270 | Siamese Cat Song (214) | 1 - 5 |
| AV3272 | Songs from Lady and the Tramp (190) | 2 - 6 |

101 Dalmatians
| AV3276 | 101 Dalmatians | 2 - 6 |

Peter Pan
AV3280	Peter Pan Theme Song (35)	1 - 5
AV3282	Pirate's Life, A (38)	1 - 5
AV3284	Second Star to the Right (36)	1 - 5
AV3286	What Made the Red Man Red (37)	1 - 5

Pinocchio
AV3290	Give a Little Whistle (3)	1 - 5
AV3292	I've Got No Strings (4)	1 - 5
AV3294	When You Wish Upon a Star (42)	1 - 5

Sleeping Beauty

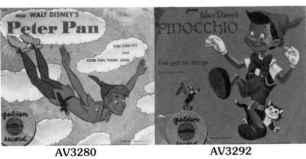

AV3280   AV3292

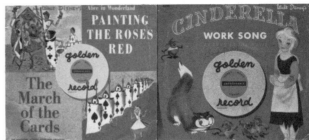

AV3200   AV3242

AV3300	Hail Princess Aurora (480)	2 - 7
AV3302	I Wonder	2 - 7
AV3304	Once Upon a Dream (481)	2 - 7
AV3306	Sing a Smiling Song (482)	2 - 7
AV3308	Skumps	2 - 7
AV3310	Sleeping Beauty Song (486)	2 - 7

Snow White
AV3400	Bluddle Uddle Um Dum (30)	2 - 6
AV3402	Hi-Ho, Hi-Ho (1)	2 - 6
AV3404	Snow White Yodel Song (29)	2 - 6
AV3406	Whistle While You Work (2)	2 - 6

Song of the South
| AV3420 | Zip-A-Dee-Doo-Dah (27) | 1 - 5 |

AV3402   AV3404

Films: Short Subjects
AV3480	Babes in Toyland (661)	1 - 5
AV3500	Bongo the Circus Bear (26)	1 - 5
AV3510	Ferdinand (16)	1 - 5
AV3520	Funny Little Bunnies (17)	1 - 5
AV3540	Johnny Appleseed (168)	1 - 5
AV3550	Little Toot (28)	1 - 5
AV3560	Melody (Adventures in Music) (44)	1 - 5
AV3565	Perri (347)	1 - 5
AV3570	Peter and the Wolf (65)	2 - 6
AV3580	Snoopy the Seal (174)	1 - 5
AV3590	Toby Tyler	1 - 3
AV3600	Tonka	1 - 5
AV3610	Who's Afraid of the Big Bad Wolf? (15)	1 - 5

Record - Extended Play (3-in-1)
Songs from 3 favorite singles combined in one 45 rpm.

Characters & Personalities – TV & Movie
| AV3650 | Dale Evans' Songs of Faith (325) | 2 - 6 |
| AV3655 | Howdy Doody and Buffalo Bob Songs (327) | 3 - 10 |

AV3540   AV3550

AV3762

AV3720

AV3801

AV4150

AV4031

AV4103

AV4106

AV4108

AV3660	Looney Tunes (323)	2 - 6
AV3665	Roy Rogers' Cowboy Songs (324)	3 - 10
AV3670	TV Wild West Favorites (321)	2 - 6

Christmas

| AV3675 | Golden Christmas Favorites (322) | 1 - 5 |

Nursery Songs

| AV3680 | Golden Mother Goose (317) | 1 - 5 |
| AV3690 | Golden Nursery Songs (328) | 1 - 3 |

Song Hits

AV3700	Golden Songs About America (326)	1 - 3
AV3710	Golden Toy Parade (320)	1 - 3
AV3720	School Days (711)	1 - 3
AV3730	Songs About Animals (319)	1 - 3
AV3740	Train Songs (318)	1 - 5

Little Golden Record Albums

| AV3761 | My Little Golden Christmas album (LGR1) 4 records | 3 - 8 |
| AV3762 | Rudolph the Red-Nosed Reindeer (LGR2) 2 records | 2 - 6 |

Record Chests

Golden Record Chests were colorful boxed sets of 8 records. The "chests" had carrying handles and individual holders for the records. They were marketed in the mid-50s for $3.95 and came in both 78 and 45 rpms. (Set 1 was also produced in 33-1/3 rpm.)

AV3800	**Child's Introduction to the Orchestra, A** (GRC1) 17 songs w/orchestral variations & a mini-symphony	9 - 20
AV3801	**Walt Disney's Song Parade** (GRC2) 29 Disney movie song hits	10 - 30
AV3802	**Golden Treasury of Hymns** (GRC3) 32 favorite hymns	9 - 20
AV3803	**Child's Introduction to the Great Composers** (GRC4) 32 instrumental selections	9 - 20

Book and Record Sets
Little Golden Books (That Read Themselves)

Marketed in the late '50s, these sets consisted of a cardboard envelope/jacket, with a regular issue LGB, and an extended play record that included the entire text of the book. The record had a picture of the book cover on the label. Advertised as a step to help the child learn to read, it also had the advantage of letting "the phonograph take over the job of reading 'just one more'."

AV4029	**Night Before Christmas, The** (C329)	9 - 15
AV4030	**Hansel and Gretel** (C330)	9 - 15
AV4031	**Heidi** (C331)	6 - 12
AV4032	**Saggy Baggy Elephant, The** (C332)	6 - 12
AV4033	**Roy Rogers and Cowboy Toby** (C333)	7 - 18
AV4034	**Little Man of Disneyland, The** (WD)(C334)	7 - 15

Little Golden Book & Record (Read-Along Books & Disneyland Records)

Soft cover, 24-page books, 7-1/4" x 7-1/4", with a Disneyland 33-1/3 rpm record in a holder in the back cover, distributed by Buena Vista Distributing Co. Inc. in the '60s and '70s. Record labels include a sketch of the main character from the book. A list of additional LGB titles was carried inside the back cover. Many of the Disney LGBs were redone in the Read-Along series, but the cover art was changed and they are not identified as a LGB & Record. A boxed set of 12 Little Golden Record Books was produced in 1978. Records are listed alphabetically.

Read-Along Books and Records (Disneyland)

AV4101	Chicken Little (209)	1 - 3
AV4102	Circus Time (221)	1 - 3
AV4103	Color Kittens, The (212)	1 - 3
AV4104	David and Goliath (218)	1 - 3
AV4105	Frosty the Snowman (253)	1 - 3
AV4106	Happy Man and His Dump Truck (213)	1 - 3
AV4107	Jingle Bells (255)	1 - 3
AV4108	Large and Growly Bear, The (210)	1 - 3
AV4109	Little Boy with a Big Horn, The (207)	1 - 3
AV4110	Little Engine that could, The (216)	1 - 3
AV4111	Little Fat Policeman (224)	1 - 3
AV4112	Lively Little Rabbit, The (220)	1 - 3
AV4113	Noah's Ark (219)	1 - 3
AV4114	Poky Little Puppy (203)	1 - 3

AV4121   AV4122

AV4214   AV4227

AV4115	Puss 'n Boots (208)	1 - 3
AV4116	Pussycat Tiger, The (217)	1 - 3
AV4117	Rudolph the Red-Nosed Reindeer (252)	1 - 3
AV4118	Rumpelstiltskin (204)	1 - 3
AV4119	Saggy Baggy Elephant (201)	1 - 3
AV4120	Scuffy the Tugboat (205)	1 - 3
AV4121	Seven Little Postmen (222)	1 - 3
AV4122	Smokey the Bear (215)	1 - 3
AV4123	Tawny Scrawny Lion (202)	1 - 3
AV4124	Taxi that Hurried, The (214)	1 - 3
AV4125	There's No Such Thing as a Dragon (223)	1 - 3
AV4126	Thumbelina (206)	1 - 3
AV4127	Tootle (211)	1 - 3
AV4128	Twelve Days of Christmas, The (254)	1 - 3
AV4150	Read-Along Collection (boxed set)	20 - 40

Little Golden Book & Record (Read and Hear)

These sets combined a 45 rpm record with a LGB. The full 24-page story was bound in soft cover, with a holder for the record inside the front cover. Cover art from the original LGB was used in the cover design, and some of the records also have the book cover on the label. "Read and Hear" records were also produced for other children's book series, but this list is comprised of LGB combinations only. The original Read and Hear number follows the record title. Books without the records are considered uncollectible. Records are listed here alphabetically.

AV4201	ABC Rhymes (233)	1 - 3
AV4202	Ali Baba (245)	1 - 3
AV4203	Animals of Farmer Jones (218)	1 - 3
AV4204	Baby's Mother Goose (158)	1 - 3
AV4205	Big Brown Bear, The (220)	1 - 3
AV4206	Boy with the Drum, The (254)	1 - 5
AV4207	Bozo Finds a Friend (169)	1 - 5
AV4208	Bozo the Clown (212)	1 - 5
AV4209	Bravest of All, The (260)	1 - 3
AV4210	Chicken Little (162)	1 - 3
AV4211	Child's Garden of Verses, A (236)	1 - 5
AV4212	Chitty Chitty Bang Bang (238)	1 - 5
AV4213	Cinderella (172)	10 - 25
	(A paper doll book & record set)	
AV4214	Circus Time (239)	1 - 3
AV4215	Corky's Hiccups (262)	1 - 3
AV4216	Counting Rhymes (237)	1 - 3
AV4217	Country Mouse and the City Mouse (174)	1 - 3
AV4218	Day on the Farm, A (235)	1 - 3
AV4219	Five Little Firemen (241)	1 - 5
AV4220	Frosty the Snowman (179)	1 - 3
AV4221	Fuzzy Duckling (256)	1 - 3
AV4222	Gingerbread Man, The (164)	1 - 3
AV4223	Hansel and Gretel (151)	1 - 3
AV4224	Happy Birthday Party (Cut-outs) (171)	5 - 12
AV4225	Happy Days (252)	1 - 3
AV4226	Happy Man and His Dump Truck (219)	1 - 5
AV4227	Heidi (152)	1 - 3

AV4228	How to Tell Time (160)	2 - 8
AV4229	Jack and the Beanstalk (163)	1 - 3
AV4230	Little Boy with a Big Horn (183)	1 - 3
AV4231	Little Engine that Could, The (216)	1 - 3
AV4232	Little Fat Policeman (246)	1 - 3
AV4233	Little Indian (255)	1 - 3
AV4234	Little Red Caboose (159)	1 - 3
AV4235	Little Red Hen (166)	1 - 3
AV4236	Little Red Riding Hood (156)	1 - 3
AV4237	Lively Little Rabbit, The (243)	1 - 3
AV4238	Mister Dog (250)	5 - 10
AV4239	Musicians of Bremen, The (177)	1 - 3
AV4240	Naughty Bunny (251)	2 - 6
AV4241	Night Before Christmas, The (168)	1 - 3
AV4242	Numbers (167)	1 - 3
AV4243	Nursery Songs (161)	1 - 3
AV4244	Old MacDonald Had a Farm (182)	1 - 3
AV4245	Peter Rabbit (173)	1 - 3
AV4246	Poky Little Puppy (154)	1 - 5
AV4247	Puss 'n Boots (175)	1 - 3
AV4248	Pussycat Tiger, The (259)	1 - 3
AV4249	Riddles, Riddles, From A to Z (234)	1 - 5
AV4250	Rudolph the Red-Nosed Reindeer (178)	1 - 3
AV4251	Rumpelstiltskin/Princess and the Pea (165)	1 - 3
AV4252	Saggy Baggy Elephant (153)	1 - 5
AV4253	Scuffy the Tugboat (181)	1 - 5
AV4254	Seven Little Postmen (214)	1 - 3
AV4255	Shy Little Kitten, The (242)	1 - 3
AV4256	Smokey the Bear (170)	1 - 3
AV4257	Snow White & Rose Red (176)	1 - 3
AV4258	Susan in the Driver's Seat (264)	1 - 3
AV4259	Tawny Scrawny Lion, The (247)	1 - 5
AV4260	Taxi that Hurried, The (240)	1 - 5
AV4261	Three Bears, The (155)	1 - 3
AV4262	Three Bedtime Stories (157)	1 - 3
AV4263	Three Billy Goats Gruff, The (221)	1 - 3
AV4264	Three Little Kittens (213)	1 - 5
AV4265	Three Little Pigs, WD (209)	1 - 5
AV4266	Thumbelina (184)	1 - 3
AV4267	Tiger's Adventure (253)	1 - 3
AV4268	Tootle (208)	1 - 5
AV4269	Twelve Days of Christmas	1 - 3

AV4246   AV4249

AV4250   AV4259

AV4270	Ugly Duckling (WD) (211)	1 - 5
AV4271	Ukelele and Her New Doll (249)	1 - 3
AV4272	Visit to the Children's Zoo, A (232)	1 - 3
AV4273	Wacky Witch (261)	1 - 3
AV4274	When I Grow Up (244)	1 - 3
AV4275	White Bunny and His Magic Nose, The (217)	1 - 3
AV4276	Who Comes to Your House (263)	1 - 3
AV4277	Wonderful School, The (248)	1 - 3

Book and Record Sets (LP)

A Hi-Fi LP in a folding jacket, packaged with a 32-page Golden Book with full color illustrations made up the Golden Book and Record Sets. Six sets are known to have been produced, there may have been more.

AV4310	Golden Treasury of Bedtime Stores (1) Record and book	8 - 20
AV4311	Same as AV4310, record only, in jacket	3 - 9
AV4320	Golden Treasury of Mother Goose Stories (2) Record and book	8 - 20
AV4321	Same as AV4320, record only, in jacket	3 - 9
AV4330	Yogi Bear's Songs and Stories (3) Record and book	10 - 30
AV4331	Same as AV4330, record only, in jacket	5 - 10
AV4340	Golden Treasury of Christmas Songs and Stories (4) Record and book	10 - 20
AV4341	Same as AV4340, record only, in jacket	5 - 10
AV4350	Golden Bible: Songs and Stories of the Old Testament (5) Record and book	5 - 15
AV4351	Same as AV4350, record only, in jacket	2 - 7
AV4360	An Introduction to the Instruments of the Orchestra (6) Record and book	6 - 12
AV4361	Same as AV4360, record only, in jacket	3 - 10

Storytime Records (LP)

Storytime Records are LPs boxed with soft cover LGBs. Most of the Storytime sets contained 6 LGBs, with the book covers shown on the record jacket, all narrated in the same "read

AV6000

AV5223

Book and Record Sets

along" style as the single story sets. Other Storytime Records included books and party kits and other activities. At least 11 records were included in the series. Insufficient examples in collectible condition have been observed to establish either an accurate listing or determine value.

TAPES: Books and Audio Cassettes

Book and tape combinations were introduced in the '70s, with "A Little Golden Book & Cassette" in the Read-Along series produced by Disneyland Records.

Little Golden Book and Cassette (Read-Along Books and Cassettes)

Format is the same as the Read-Along Records, with a "B" added to the book number. Listing values are for books with tapes.

AV5201	Saggy Baggy Elephant (201B)	1 - 3
AV5202	Tawny Scrawny Lion (202B)	1 - 3
AV5203	Poky Little Puppy (203B)	1 - 3
AV5204	Rumpelstiltskin (204B)	1 - 3
AV5205	Scuffy the Tugboat (205B)	1 - 3
AV5206	Thumbelina (206B)	1 - 3
AV5213	Happy Man and His Dump Truck (213B)	1 - 3
AV5214	Taxi that Hurried, The (214B)	1 - 3
AV5216	Little Engine that Could (216B)	1 - 3
AV5222	Seven Little Postmen (222B)	1 - 3
AV5223	There's No Such Thing As a Dragon (223B)	1 - 3
AV5224	Little Fat Policeman, The (224B)	1 - 3

BOOK 'n TAPE™: Youth Electronics

Golden Youth Electronics℠ includes both audio and video tapes, marketed in a wide variety of forms, from the familiar "read-along" activities to sing-alongs, learning tapes, exercise activites and more.

Golden Book 'n Tape sets now being marketed come in a variety of forms, all including soft cover versions of LGB favorites, Look-Look Books and specially prepared books-for-tapes. Sets are available in single and twin-packs and special 3-book gift packs, as well as "Tape Totes", designed to hold 10 books and audio tapes. (The Tote comes with a special book/audio edition of The Poky Little Puppy, to start the young collector off right.) Most tapes and books are quickly separated, accounting for a lot of the soft cover books that turn up at yard

AV7822

AV7837

CC1010

CC1140

CC1110

sales and flea markets. With the exception of the original Read-Along sets, the field is too new to have attracted much collector attention.

| AV6000 | Book 'n' Tape, unopened packages, depending upon whether they are single or multiple books | 4 - 12 |

VIDEOS

Video tapes of Golden Books, bringing the Poky Little Puppy and his friends "to life" via the living room VCR, were brought out in 1985. The 8 tapes released sold nearly 3 million tapes in the first year of distribution.

Golden Book Videos® include Music and Step Ahead videos as well as "Storybooks Brought to Life" with a host of licensed characters. Videos are done in "Picturemation"™, a blend of camera moves, animation and special effects. Collectors interest is centered on titles that include favorite Golden stories, most of which are found in the Golden Book Video Classics series.

Golden Book Video Classics

Released in 1989, "Golden Book Video Classics" feature the familiar Golden Book spine on their packages and include stories from Big and Little Golden Books as well as several other Golden series. Series sources are noted where known. Available primarily on the retail market at this time, most Golden Book videos retail for under $10.

AV7821	Scuffy the Tugboat and Friends (13821-6) Originally released as *3 Favorite Golden Stories*, includes *Scuffy the Tugboat* & *Theodore Mouse Goes to Sea* from the LGB series.	3 - 8
AV7822	Poky Little Puppy's Favorite Stories (13822-4) Originally released as *3 Best Loved Golden Stories*, includes *Sailor Dog* from the LGB series and *Poky Little Puppy and the Patchwork Blanket*, a BGB.	3 - 8
AV7837	Tawny Scrawny Lion's Jungle Tales (13837-2)	3 - 8

Originally released as *3 Jungle Animal Tales*, includes *Saggy Baggy Elephant*, *Tawny Scrawny Lion* and *Rupert the Rhinoceros* from the LGB series.

AV7838	Fairy Tale Classics (13838-0) includes *Little Red Riding Hood* from the 3rd LGB series.	2 - 6
AV7840	Three Tales from Care Bears (13840-2) w/stories from the Look-Look series.	2 - 5
AV7841	Old MacDonald's Farm and Other Animal Tales (13841-0)	2 - 5
AV7844	Merry Mother Goose and Other Tales (13844-5) includes *There's No Such Thing as a Dragon* from the book and cassette series.	2 - 5
AV7845	Ugly Duckling and Other Treasured Tales, The (13845-3) includes *The Ugly Duckling* from the Storytime series.	2 - 5
AV7849	Favorite Fairy Tales (13849) 3 stories, including *Cinderella*	2 - 5
AV7860	Three Sesame Street Stories (13860-7)	2 - 5
AV7863	Five Sesame Street Stories (13863-1) *Big Bird Brings Spring to Sesame Street* from LGB series.	2 - 5
AV7870	Peter Rabbit and Other Tales (13870-4) Originally released as *3 Golden Amye Rosenberg Stories*, includes *Peter Rabbit* and *Little Red Hen* from the Storytime series and *Polly's Pet* from the LGB series.	3 - 8
AV7871	Gingerbread Man and Other Nursery Tales, The (13871-7) Originally released as *3 Richard Scarry Animal Nursery Tales*, includes *The Gingerbread Man* from the LGB series.	3 - 8
AV7898	Our Dwelling Place: The Birth of Jesus (13898-4)	2 - 4
AV7899	Our Dwelling Place: The Trials of Jesus (13899-2)	2 - 4
AV8408	Little Golden Book Land: The Great Harbor Rescue (14080) Golden's first full animation video.	3 - 10

COLLECTIBLES

"Go withs" are the added attractions to any collecting interest. A variety of merchandise using Golden characters and books has been produced over the years. In addition to the items shown here, there are probably many more waiting to be discovered.

CC1230-CC1270

CC1300   CC1310

CC1210 & CC1220

CC1290   CC1280

CANDY TINS

Illustrations from the very first LGB *Three Little Kittens* (LE0010) adorn an English candy tin. Similar tins with characters from other children's books of the same period have been noted, but it is not known if any more tins with LGB illustrations were produced.

CC1010   Three Little Kittens tin   30 - 65

CERAMICS

Ceramic shop items, produced from molds, both licensed and unmarked items have been seen. How many molds were produced is not known.

CC1110	Saggy Baggy Elephant planter, unmarked	8 - 14
CC1120	Saggy Baggy Elephant seated figure, unmarked	8 - 12
CC1140	Scuffy the Tugboat figure, marked WPC	4 - 8

LITTLE GOLDEN BOOK LAND (Enesco)

"Baby and juvenile gifts" were introduced in 1990 by Enesco as part of Western's Little Golden Book Land promotion. The collection includes porcelain and ceramic figures, paper goods, dinnerware and other items, all featuring Golden's star characters.

Figurines, Porcelain
CC1210	Poky Little Puppy	2 - 5
CC1220	Shy Little Kitten	2 - 5

Trains, Porcelain
CC1230	Tootle, musical	9 - 17
CC1240	Poky Little Puppy	3 - 6
CC1250	Tawny Scrawny Lion	3 - 6
CC1260	Baby Brown Bear	3 - 6
CC1270	Katy Caboose	4 - 8

Night Lights, Porcelain
CC1280	Saggy Baggy Elephant	10 - 15
CC1290	Scuffy the Tugboat	10 - 15
CC1300	Tootle bank, ceramic	5 - 9
CC1310	Scuffy the Tugboat, musical	9 - 17

Gift Items (as pictured, clockwise from top right)
CC1340	Tootle/Katy Caboose bookends	10 - 18
CC1350	Child's dinner set, 7 pieces, Bib, tray, bowl, cup, spoon, fork & book	10 - 18
CC1360	Sipper cup, melamine	1 - 3
CC1370	Child's cup, melamine (w/toothbrush)	2 - 4

CC1340-CC1380

CC2050   CC2040

224

CC2400

CC2201 & CC2202

CC2200

CC2450 & CC2455

| CC1380 | Tin box w/handles & coloring book | 3 - 7 |
| CC1380 | Paper gift bags, assorted sizes | 1 - 2 |

party paper. Included were hot and cold cups, paper plates and a tablecloth. All pieces depicted "Tootle" and a "Golden Book" sign post.

LITTLE GOLDEN JEWELRY

Stevano-Silbro Exclusives manufactured Little Golden Jewelry in the early '50s. Wholesaled at 75¢ a dozen, the plastic pins were carded and came in assorted colors.

CC2010	Lively Little Rabbit	8 - 16
CC2020	Poky Little Puppy	10 - 20
CC2030	Saggy Baggy Elephant	8 - 16
CC2040	Scuffy the Tugboat	8 - 16
CC2050	Shy Little Kitten	8 - 16
CC2060	Tootle	8 - 16

LITTLE GOLDEN WRITING PAPER

Boxed sets of stationery, decorated in color with LGB characters were manufactured in the early '50s. The set included postcards, single and double sheets of paper and envelopes.

CC2200	Stationery, boxed set	20 - 75
CC2201	Stationery sheets, each	3 - 6
CC2202	Postcards, each	3 - 8

PARTY GOODS
Happy Birthday Party Paper

Beach Products of Kalamazoo, MI licensed "Happy Birthday"

CC3100

CC3108

CC3102

CC4105 - *boxed*

CC4402

| CC2400 | Happy Birthday Party Paper, Beach Products, sealed packages, ea | 2 - 6 |

Gift Wrap

Contempo Gift Wrap, produced in 1987, featuring "Tootle" and "The Poky Little Puppy", was offered in rolled and folded packages. Gift tags were also available.

| CC2450 | Gift wrap paper, Contempo | 3 - 12 |
| CC2455 | Gift tags, Contempo | 1 - 3 |

PICTURE PORTFOLIOS

As early as 1945, picture portfolios with large size full-color pictures of Golden Book illustrations were available. In addition to *Mother Goose* pictures by Feodor Rojankovsky, portfolios were also done by Garth Williams and Eloise Wilkin, but complete information on the number of portfolios issued and the participating artists has yet to be determined.

| CC3100 | Pictures from *Mother Goose* by Feodor Rojankovsky Complete portfolio w/8 pictures. | 80 - 110 |

Individual pictures from CC3100:

CC3101	Jack and Jill	10 - 15
CC3102	Mary Had a Little Lamb	10 - 15
CC3103	Little Boy Blue	10 - 15
CC3104	Old Woman in the Shoe	10 - 15
CC3105	Little Tommy Tittlemouse	10 - 15
CC3106	Rain, Rain, Go Away	10 - 15
CC3107	Little Miss Muffet	10 - 15
CC3108	Pussy Cat, Pussy Cat	10 - 15

PUZZLES

In addition to being the world's largest producer of children's books, Western's Consumer Products Division is also the largest jigsaw puzzle manufacturer in the world, producing nearly a third of the world's supply. While puzzles of all descriptions have been manufactured, for the purpose of this guide we are including only puzzles that are related to Golden Books and characters used in Golden Books. A list of LGB Puzzle Books is

CC4104   CC4010

included in the category listing in the Appendix. (See also: puzzle color plate)

Little Lifters™ Knobbed Puzzles

A series of beginner puzzles issued by Western in 1985, "Little Lifter" puzzle pieces are knobbed and come in a fitted plastic tray. Each piece is lifted to reveal a surprise picture. At least 4 different sets were released, but only one set used Golden Book characters.

| CC4010 | Little Golden Book Friends | 3 - 9 |

Little Golden Picture Puzzles

Issued in the late '40s and early '50s, Little Golden Picture Puzzles were individually boxed puzzles, reproducing cover art from LGBs, on a slightly smaller scale (6-1/2" x 7-3/4"), mounted on heavy cardboard. The box and puzzle were framed with the same Golden design used on the back cover of the books, with a picture of the cover on the lid and additional titles in the series listed on the bottom. Some were in frames, others

CC5051 CC5052

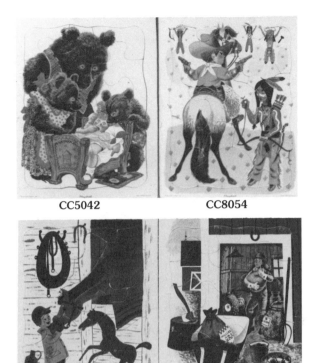

CC5042 CC8054

CC5024 CC5053

CC5072 CC5074

were loose. Four series of 6 puzzles were produced. Values given are for puzzles only. With original box, value increases 50-75%.

First Series

CC4101	Five Little Firemen	6 - 12
CC4102	Jolly Barnyard	6 - 12
CC4103	Lively Little Rabbit	6 - 12
CC4104	Poky Little Puppy	8 - 15
CC4105	Shy Little Kitten	6 - 12
CC4106	Tootle	6 - 12

Second Series

CC4201	Alphabet from A to Z	5 - 10
CC4202	Dr. Dan, The Bandage Man	8 - 15
CC4203	Johnny's Machines	5 - 10
CC4204	Marvelous Merry Go Round	5 - 10
CC4205	A Year on the Farm	5 - 10
CC4206	Wonderful House	5 - 10

Third Series

CC4301	Busy Timmy	8 - 15
CC4302	A Busy Day at the Playground	8 - 15
CC4303	Happy Man and His Dump Truck	6 - 12
CC4304	Little Black Sambo	10 - 30
CC4305	Little Yip-Yip and His Bark	6 - 10
CC4306	When You Were a Baby	5 - 10

Fourth Series

CC4401	Brave Cowboy Bill	5 - 10
CC4402	Day at the Beach	5 - 10
CC4403	How Big	5 - 10
CC4404	Katy the Kitten	6 - 12
CC4405	Little Golden ABC	5 - 10
CC4406	Train to Timbuctoo	5 - 10

Little Golden Puzzles™, Woodboard

"From the creators of Little Golden Books", these durable woodboard puzzles, framed in a box which uses the familiar LGB spine design, were introduced in 1987. All of the subjects produced deal with modern LGB subjects, including "Pound Puppies", "Disney's Duck Tales" and pictures by Richard

Scarry. They are still available on the retail market, $2-6.

Playskool Frame Tray Puzzles (8" x 10")

Were released in the late '50s and came in boxed sets of 4. They were grouped by subject, with illustrations from various LGBs. All of the puzzles are marked with their set number in the lower right corner. Twelve sets were included in the series.

CC5010	**Animal Babies** (80-1), boxed set	20 - 38
CC5020	**Ways to Travel** (80-2), boxed set	20 - 38
	Based on illustrations from LE1800	
	Puzzles shown from CC5020:	
CC5024	Airplanes (80-2D)	4 - 8
CC5030	**Horses and Colts** (80-3), boxed set	20 - 38
CC5040	**Fairy Stories** (80-4), boxed set	20 - 38
	Based on illustrations from LE0420	
	Puzzles shown from CC5040:	
CC5042	Three Bears	4 - 8
CC5050	**Life of a Cowboy** (80-5), boxed set	20 - 38
	Based on illustrations from LE0930, LE0960	
	Puzzles shown from CC5050:	
CC5051	Cowboy & Bronco (80-5A)	4 - 8
CC5052	Cowboy & Lasso (80-5B)	4 - 8
CC5053	Brave Cowboy & Guitar (80-5C)	4 - 8
CC5054	Brave Cowboy & Indian (80-5D)	4 - 8
CC5060	**Indian Pals** (80-6), boxed set	20 - 38
CC5070	**Farms and Farming** (80-7), boxed set	25 - 45
	Based on illustrations from LE0680, LE2110	
	Puzzles shown from CC5070:	
CC5072	Little Galoshes (80-7B)	6 - 10
CC5074	Farmer Jones (80-7D)	4 - 8
CC5080	**Children and Religion** (80-8), boxed set	20 - 38
	Based on illustrations from LE3400	
	Puzzles shown from CC5080:	
CC5081	Baby Sister (80-8A)	4 - 8
CC5090	**Funny Animals** (80-9), boxed set	20 - 38
CC5100	**Workers We Know** (80-10), boxed set	22 - 40
	Based on illustrations from LE0600, LE0910	
	Puzzles shown from CC5100:	

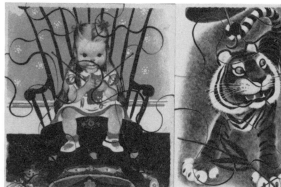
CC5220

CC5240

CC5260

CC5280

CC5081

CC5101

CC5102

CC5112

CC5114

CC5103

CC5111

CC5101	Milkman (80-10A)	6 - 10
CC5102	Mailman (80-10B)	6 - 10
CC5103	Policeman (80-10C)	4 - 8
CC5110	**Dogs and Puppies** (80-11), boxed set	25 - 45
	Based on illustrations from LE0560, LE0730, LE1310	
Puzzles shown from CC5110:		
CC5111	Dogs (80-11A)	6 - 10
CC5112	Our Puppy (80-11B)	6 - 10
CC5114	Little Yip-Yip (80-11D)	6 - 10
CC5120	**Children in Action** (80-12), boxed set	20 - 38

Playskool Masonite Puzzles

Probably boxed, but whether they came in sets or individually has not been determined. All of the puzzles found are 8-1/2" x 9-1/4" and reproduce illustrations from LGBs. Puzzles are not dated or numbered, and have been found marked both "S&S" and "Golden Press". Name at the bottom of the puzzle refers to subject matter, not the LGB from which the illustration was taken.

CC5220	Knitting Time (LGB 1-61)	9 - 20
CC5240	Little Black Sambo (LGB 1-57)	15 - 35
CC5260	Make Believe Wedding (LGB 1-44)	10 - 25
CC5280	Three Little Kittens (LGB 1-1)	9 - 20

Playskool Puzzles, Picture Block

Golden Book Picture Block Puzzles had 9 interchangeable dimensional blocks making up 6 different pictures. The set shown was produced in 1961. How many picture block puzzles were produced has not been determined.

CC5410	Trucks & Machines (86G)	8 - 20

Playskool Puzzles, Woodboard

Boxed in a similar fashion to LGB puzzles, complete with LGB spine design, the series features characters and adventures from the LGBL promotion.

CC5452

CC5410

| CC5452 | Scuffy the Tugboat | 2 - 4 |
| CC5454 | Poky Little Puppy | 2 - 4 |

CC6000

Capitol Adventure Kits

TOYS & GAMES

| CC6000 | Black Hole Game (Walt Disney Productions) | 5 - 10 |

©1979 by WDP
Game set included the LI2010, a Golden Poster Storybook and a *Golden Book of Things to Do* w/stickers & cut-outs along with other activity items.

Capitol Adventure Kits

A spin-off from Junior Golden Guides and other nature/science books, Golden Capitol Adventure kits were boxed sets containing all the equipment and information for a beginning hobby in natural science. Birds, seashells, rocks and a weather analysis kit were among the kits offered. Specimens, basic hobby equipment and a 94-page book on the subject were included in each kit. They were advertised on LGBs in 1960. Most of the kits self-destructed with use, and no known examples have appeared on the secondary market.

Fisher-Price Classics

This 1987 toy assortment was a combination of best-loved LGB stories and familiar Fisher-Price pull toys. The effect was not to duplicate the book character, but rather to provide a companion piece for a "play and read" activity. The sets came in special Classic display packages, and the books were all specially marked on the covers with a Fisher-Price symbol identifying them as part of the set.

CC7500	Fire Engine (2250), toy in box w/LE3820	5 - 15
CC7501	Same as CC7500, book and toy, no box	3 - 6
CC7502	Same as CC7500, specially marked book only	1 - 4
CC7510	Little Snoopy (2251), toy in box w/LE0080, *The Poky Little Puppy*.	5 - 15
CC7511	Same as CC7510, book and toy, no box	3 - 6
CC7512	Same as CC7510, specially marked book only	1 - 2
CC7520	Tag-Along Turtle (2252), toy in box w/LG1170	5 - 15

CC7520

CC7500

CC7510

CC7530

CC7903 CC7902 CC7901 CC7904

CC7603

CC7602

CC7521	Same as CC7520, book and toy, no box	3 - 6
CC7522	Same as CC7520, specially marked book only	1 - 4
CC7530	Toot-Toot Engine (2253), toy in box w/LE0210	5 - 15
CC7531	Same as CC7530, book and toy, no box	3 - 6
CC7532	Same as CC7530, specially marked book only	1 - 4

Little Golden Games

For children ages 5-9, were manufactured in the late '70s by Western. They featured LGB characters, and the box lid had the same illustration as the cover of the corresponding LGB.

CC7601	Jack and the Beanstalk based on LF5450	6 - 12
CC7602	Old MacDonald Had a Farm based on LE5000	6 - 12
CC7603	Three Bears, The based on LF2040	6 - 12
CC7604	Three Little Pigs, The based on LF5440	6 - 12

Mechanical Toys (Ideal)

Ideal produced a series of mechanical toys in the late '50s which featured LGB characters. Toys were hand-painted and came in colorful litho boxes, with cover designs similar to the LGB. The extent of the series has not yet been determined.

| CC7800 | Poky Little Puppy, w/crank-wind talking device | 50 - 90 |

Plush Toys, Little Golden Book Land

Manufactured by Playskool/Hasbro, 4 "cute, cuddly friends" helped Little Golden Book Land come alive for young readers in 1989. The washable polyester toys came boxed with a small paper story/activity book. Toys were approximately 12" tall and each one wore a bow made of special ribbon done in the same design as the LGB spine.

CC7901	Poky Little Puppy	10 - 20
CC7902	Saggy Baggy Elephant	15 - 25
CC7903	Shy Little Kitten	10 - 20
CC7904	Tawny Scrawny Lion	20 - 35

Smokey the Bear Book and Toy Sets (Tonka Toys)

Boxed sets containing movable figures, Tonka mini-vehicles and LGBs provided entertainment and instructions for Jr. Forest Rangers.

| CC8520 | Camping the Smokey Bear Way (5020) 15-piece set w/mini-Tonka camper & accessory pieces, including LE4230. | 15 - 30 |

CC8520

CC8535

| CC8530 | Smokey Bear and the Forest Rangers (5030) 16-piece set w/mini-Tonka wagon, ranger station and accessories, including LF3450. | 15 - 30 |
| CC8535 | Smokey Bear and His Forest Friends (5035) 22-piece set w/mini-Tonka stake truck, mini-Tonka pickup with pumper, mini-Tonka jeep and accessory pieces, including LE3870. | 20 - 35 |

AUTHOR AND ILLUSTRATORS

A keynote of Golden publications has always been the quality of the editorial staff, the authors and the artists. The Artists and Writers Guide, based in New York, had access to much top talent and was also in a good position to spot fresh talent. In addition, the licensing of Disney characters by Western gave the Guild access to many established artists. A list of Golden Book authors and illustrators reads like a *Who's Who* in the field of children's lit during the past 50 years. Special notes and awards for many of the authors and artists are noted with the listings. In keeping with the "Golden Dozen" policy of the publishers, we have selected 12 "most asked about" authors and artists for review.

Brown, Margaret Wise (author, 1910-1952)

In her short 15-year writing career, Margaret Wise Brown authored more than 90 picture books, and received many awards. She divided her time between a home in Manhattan and another on a Maine island, turning out 7 or more books a year for her various publishers and establishing herself as a premiere writer of picture books. *Mister Dog* (LE1280) is written about her own Kerry Blue Terrier, Crispin. It was one of her last titles to appear before her early death in 1952.

Gergely, Tibor (illustrator, 1900-1978)

A Caldecott Honor artist (1955), Gergely was born in Budapest, Hungary and came to America in 1939. He was a self-taught artist and much of his work draws on the peasant lifestyle he was familiar with in Austria, Hungary and Czechoslovakia. He did magazine and newspaper illustrations, murals and stage designs, in addition to his work with children's books. *Tibor Gergely's Great Big Book of Bedtime Stories* (GG3860), is a fascinating collection of many of his best works.

Malvern, Corinne (illustrator, 1905-1956)

An award-winning artist, Malvern spent her growing up years as an aspiring actress, but decided in her early twenties to pursue a career as an artist instead. She and her sister, Gladys – who wrote juvenile novels, shared a New York apartment overlooking the Hudson River and often collaborated on books. The "I've seen it before" feeling that collectors associate with her style is largely due to a "captive audience" syndrome: she also illustrated grade-school readers and workbooks in the '40s and '50s.

Provensen, Alice (1918-) **and Martin** (1916-1987) (authors/illustrators)

The Provensens began their illustrating careers working with film animation in California ... Martin for Disney, Alice for Lantz. Following their marriage in 1944, they moved to New York City and began to illustrate children's books together. Beginning with *Animal Fair*, they also wrote many of the books they illustrated. The Provensens, awarded the Caldecott Medal in 1984, have received many awards for their books, including several titles done for Golden. Their favorite book was *The Iliad and the Odyssey* (GB2150), produced for Golden in 1954.

Reed, Mary Maud (editor, 1880-1960)

Assistant Professor of Education for the Teacher's College of Columbia University, Reed held a doctorate in Education. She supervised the content LGBs from 1942 until her death in 1960. She also did editorial advisory work on many books throughout the Golden series and edited *My First Golden Dictionary* (BB3090).

Rojankovsky, Feodor Stepanovich (illustrator, 1891-1970)

Born in Russia in 1891, Rojankovsky began illustrating children's books in the Ukraine during the Russian Revolution. His work received considerable attention when he later worked with the French publisher Pere Castor. In 1941, he came to America, mainly through the intervention of Georges Duplaix, and became one of the country's most popular children's illustrators, as well as Golden's top animal illustrator. A 1956 Caldecott Medalist, he illustrated well over 100 children's books. *The Alphabet of Many Things* (BB3450) was his last children's book.

Scarry, Richard McClure (author/illustrator, 1919-)

Born in Boston, Richard Scarry came to New York "to become some sort of artist" following a stint in the U.S. Army in WWII. After illustrating several books by other authors, he had an idea for a book of his own and the result was *Richard Scarry's Best Word Book Ever* (GB1150), published by Golden in 1963. By 1987, the book had sold over 2 million copies and Scarry, who has at least 35 publishers and well over 55 million copies of his book in circulation, had written and illustrated over 200 books and has been published in 28 languages. He considers Golden his number one publisher. He and his wife Patricia (who also authored many LGBs) live in Gstaad, Switzerland, where they moved in 1968.

Tenggren, Gustaf Adolph (illustrator, 1896-1970)

Born in Sweden, Tenggren came to America in 1920. He spent three years with the Disney studio (1936-39) where he worked on *Snow White*, *The Old Mill* and *Pinocchio*, among other projects. He was also well-known for his many "deco" style magazine and poster illustrations. He made his home in Southport, Maine and became a full time illustrator of children's books in the early '40s. The Annual "50 Books" Exhibition sponsored by the American Institute of Graphics chose his work *The Lively Little Rabbit* (LE0150) for exhibition in 1943 and *Tenggren's Story Book* (GB2600) for exhibition in 1944.

Watson, Jane Werner (author/editor, 1915-)

Perhaps the most prolific Golden Book author, with over 200 books to her credit, Watson was an editorial assistant for Whitman prior to the formation of the Golden Book line. She served as editor and staff writer for the Artists and Writers Guild from 1942 to 1954. An amateur archeologist and seasoned traveler, her social study and history books, such as *The Golden Geography* (GB2010) and *The Golden History of the World* (GB2030) were such first-hand research experiences. See pseudonym list below for the many pen names used by Watson.

Wilkin, Eloise Burns (illustrator, 1904-1987)

For over 60 years, Eloise Wilkin produced award-winning illustrations, for "at least 100 books", according to her daughter, Deborah Springett. Golden Press published 73 books with Wilkin's illustrations, and her last, the book she considered her masterpiece, *Eloise Wilkin's Books of Poems* (BB1720) was published shortly after her death at age 83 in 1987. Her pictures are beloved by collectors for their sensitive portrayal of the wide-eyed wonder and innocence of youth. A native of Rochester, New York, her illustrations often sprang from scenes in and around her home and included her grandchildren as well as the family dog. The most collectible of all Golden Book illustrators at the present time, a color plate features some of her books and "Baby Dear", who has her own LGB (LE4660). A list of all her books included in this guide can be found at the end of the category index.

Williams, Garth Montgomery (illustrator, 1912 -)

Born in America, Williams moved with his family to England as a child. He graduated from the Royal Academy of Art and returned to America in 1941. A "New Yorker" artist, as well as a sculptor (he received the Prix de Rome sculpture award in the

'30s), Williams rose to prominence as a children's illustrator with his pictures for E.B. White's *Stuart Little*, and firmly established himself with his sensitive drawings for the new edition of Wilder's *Little House* books, published in 1953. He recounts how Dorothy Kunhardt begged S&S to have him illustrate her *Tiny Animal* series ... which proved to be the beginning of a long involvement with Golden Books. He now spends much of his time in the Desert Southwest and Mexico.

Zim, Herbert Spencer (author/editor, 1909-)

From his 10-acre tropical headquarters in the Florida Keys, Zim has authored or edited over 100 nature and science guides and received many awards for his work. Over 200 million copies of his books are in print. He was responsible for the initiation and original supervision of the Golden Guides, as well as many other Golden Books, including the *Encyclopedia of Natural Science*. Avidly interested in natural science since his early years, he spent his spare time as a student with his nose in guidebooks or hanging around the high school science lab. He was already teaching science while attending Columbia University and continued teaching while working on his doctorate. He was working primarily with junior and senior high school students when first approached to write a book on science for 7-9 year olds. Since that time, his continued success in this specialized book field has enabled him to realize a personal goal of helping many young people become interested in the natural sciences.

Pseudonymns
Author/illustrator pseudonymns found in book listings include:

Pseudonymn	Proper Name
Alexander, Beatrice	Raymond, Louise
Archer, Peter	Jackson, Kathryn & Byron
Ariane	Georges Duplaix
Bedford, Annie North	Watson, Jane Werner
Broun, Emily	Sterne, Emma Gelders
Carlisle, Clark	Holding, James
George	George Wolfson
Godfrey, Jane	Bowden, Joan Chase
Graham, Kennon	Harrison, David Lee
Hill, Monica	Watson, Jane Werner
Lee, Sing	Mullan, Carol
Masha	Stern, Marie Simchow
Miryam	Yardumian, Myriam
Nast, Elsa Ruth	Watson, Jane Werner
Nicole	Georges Duplaix
Palmer, Helen Marion	Geisel, Helen
Piper, Watty	Bragg, Mabel Caroline
Salten, Felix	Salzman, Siegmund
Simkovitch, Natasha	Stern, Marie Simchow
Werner, Elsa Jane	Watson, Jane Werner
Werner, Jane	Watson, Jane Werner
Williams, Hilda K.	McElroy, Margaret J.

BIBLIOGRAPHY/REFERENCES

Arbuthnot, May Hill and Sutherland, Zena. *Children and Books*. Chicago: Scott, Foresman and Company, 1972 (4th edition).

Bader, Barbara. *American Picture Books from Noah's Ark to the Beast Within*. New York: MacMillan, 1976.

Commire, Anne, et al. *Something About the Author, Vols. 1-61*. Detroit: Gale Research, Inc., 1989.

De Montreville, Doris and Hill, Donna. *Third Book of Junior Authors*. New York: H.W. Wilson Company, 1972.

Doyle, Brian. *Who's Who of Children's Literature*. New York: Schocken Books Inc., 1968.

Eakin, Mary K. *Good Books for Children*. Chicago: University of Chicago Press, 1959.

Fuller, Muriel. *More Junior Authors*. New York: H.W. Wilson Co., 1963.

Kingman, Foster and Lontoft. *Illustrators of Children's Books, 1957-1966*. Boston: Horn Book, Inc., 1968.

Kingman, Hogarth and Quimby. *Illustrators of Children's Books, 1967-1976*. Boston: Horn Book, Inc., 1978.

Lanes, Selma G. *Down the Rabbit Hole*. New York: Atheneum, 1971.

Jones, Delores B. *Bibliography of the Little Golden Books*. Westport: Greenwood Press, 1987.

Jones, Delores B. *Children's Literature Awards & Winners*. Detroit: Neal-Schuman Pub. Inc./Gale Research, Inc., 1988.

Kunitz, Stanley J. and Haycraft, Howard. *Junior Book of Authors*. New York: H.W. Wilson Co., 1951.

Schwed, Peter. *Turning the Pages: An Insider's Story of Simon & Schuster, 1924-1984*. New York: Macmillan Publishing, Co., 1984.

Tebbel, John. *Between the Covers*. New York: Oxford University Press, 1987.

Viguers, Dalphin and Miller. *Illustrators of Children's Books, 1946-1956*. Boston: Horn Book, Inc., 1958.

BOOK INDEX

This index is an alphabetical listing of major book titles only. It does not include soft cover books or individual titles within most multi-volume sets.

The Table of Contents on page 4 provides a page number index to all major categories in this book. Many cross references are included.

In order to simplify location of titles, books are referenced by Tomart code rather than page number. The book categories are listed in alphabetical sequence, defined by a two-letter code, followed by numbers up to 9999. Once the letter code is found, simply locate the number and you will find the exact item indexed, not just the page on which it is located. Variant printings will usually follow at the same location, or will be referenced with the comments.

Our Baby-LH4080
Our Fifty States-FR1120
Our Flag-LE3880
Our Friend the Atom-DL1390
Our Puppy-LE0560, LE2920
Our Sun-FR1090
Our World-LE2420
Out of My Window-LE2450
Owl and the Pussycat, The-LG0280
Pal and Peter-LE2650
Pano the Train-LF1170
Pantaloon-LE1140
Paper Doll Wedding, The-LE1930, LH1220
Paper Dolls-LH1030, LH1470 (see: LG Paper Dolls)
Party in Shariland-LE3600
Party Pig, The-LE1910
Pat the Bunny-TO2000
Pat the Cat-TO2010
Pat-A-Cake/Baby's Mother Goose-LE0540
Paul Revere-LI0640
Pear Shaped Hill, The-RE1520
Pebbles-BB3270
Pebbles Flintstone-LE5310
Penny of Paintrock Books-JF3010
Penny Puppy-SS1090
People and Places-DL1410
People in Your Neighborhood-MB2730
Pepper Plays Nurse-LE5550
Perri-BD1780
Perri and Her Friends-LI0540
Pet in a Jar, The-LJ1801
Pete's Dragon-LI1370
Peter and the Wolf-LI0050, LI0560
Peter Pan-BD1800, BD1820, LI2350, SR1070 (see: Storybook of...)
Peter Pan and the Indians-LI0260, LI0740
Peter Pan and the Pirates-LI0250, LI0730
Peter Pan and the Troll-DR3302
Peter Pan and Wendy-LI0240, LI0720, LI1100
Peter Potamus-LE5560
Peter Rabbit-LE3130, LE5050 (see: Tale of Peter Rabbit)
Petey and I-LF1860
Pets for Peter-LE0820
Pickle for a Nickel, A-RE1540
Pick-up Sticks-LE4610
Picture Dictionary (see: LG Picture Dictionary)
Pierre Bear-LE2120
Piggy Wigglet and the Great Adventure-BB3280
Pink Elephant with Golden Spots, The-BB3290
Pink Panther & Sons/Fun at the Picnic-LG0760
Pink Panther in the Haunted House, The-LF1400
Pinocchio-BD1840, BD1860, GG3320, LI0080, LI1000, LI2250, SR1080
Pinocchio and the Whale-LI1010
Pippi Longstocking (see: The Remarkably Strong...)
Pirates Cove and Other Sea Stories-SA1060
Pirates, Ships and Sailors-BB3300, GB2360
Pixie and Dixie and Mr. Jinks-LE4540
Planets-LB8180 (see: My First Book of Planets)
Plants and Animals-GD5170
Play Ball!-LE3250
Play Street-LE4840
Play with Me-LE5670, SU2690
Pluto & The Adventure of the Golden Scepter-LI1240

Pluto Pup Goes to Sea-LI0300
Poems-FR1060, GG3340 (see: Golden Treasury of Poetry; My Book of Poems)
Poems for the Very Young (see: Golden Book of...)
Poetry (see: LGB of Poetry)
Poky Little Puppy, The-BB3330, LE0080, LE2710, LE5060
Poky Little Puppy and the Lost Bone-LC3030
Poky Little Puppy and the Patchwork Blanket-BB3310
Poky Little Puppy at the Fair-SN2030
Poky Little Puppy Follows His Nose Home, The-LF1300
Poky Little Puppy's Counting Book, The-SU2520
Poky Little Puppy's Day at the Fair-TO2620
Poky Little Puppy's First Christmas, The-BB3320
Poky Little Puppy's Naughty Day, The-LG0770
Poky Little Puppy's Special Day-LD3710
Polar Regions-LB8260
Polly's Pet-LG0550
Pollyanna-LI0910
Pony for Tony, A-LE2200
Porky Pig and Bugs Bunny/Just Like Magic-LF1460
Pound Puppies/Pick of the Litter-LG0910
Pound Puppies/Problem Puppies-LG0920
Prayer Book for Children-BB3350
Prayers for Children-BB3360, LE0050, LE2050
Prehistoric Animals-LB7080, LB8080
Presidents of the United States-FN4920
Professor Wormbog's Gloomy Kerploppus-SC5260
Pudge Pig's Counting Book-ST2250
Puff the Blue Kitten-LE4430
Puppy Love-LG0410
Puppy on the Farm-LG1430
Puss in Boots-LE1370, LE3590, ST2280
Pussy Willow-BB3380, LE3140
Pussycat Tiger, The-LF3620
Questions and Answers-FR1070
Quick Draw McGraw-LE3980
Quiz Fun-GD5240
Rabbit and His Friends-LE1690
Rabbit Is Next, The-LF1730
Rabbit's Adventure, The-LF1640
Raggedy Andy: The I Can Do It, You Can Do It Book-BB3400
Raggey Ann: A Thank You Please and I Love You Book-BB3410
Raggedy Ann and Andy: Five Birthday Parties-LG0090
Raggedy Ann and Andy Go Flying-ST2060
Raggedy Ann and Andy Help Santa Claus-LF1560
Raggedy Ann and Andy/Rainy Day Circus-LF4010
Raggedy Ann and Andy/The Little Gray Kitten-LF1390
Raggedy Ann and Fido-LE5850
Raggedy Ann and the Cookie Snatcher-LF2620
Raggedy Ann's Sweet and Dandy, Sugar Candy...Book-SC5420
Rags-LE5860, LG0780
Rainbow Brite and the Brook Meadow Deer-LG0560
Rainbow Brite Saves Spring-MB2780
Rainy Day Play Book-LE1330, LG0210
Read-It-Yourself Storybook, The-GG3400

Reading, Writing and Spelling-LH1240
Rebecca of Sunnybrook Farm-IC2120
Red Badge of Courage, The-IC2260
Red Little Golden Book of Fairy Tales, The-LE3060
Remarkably Strong Pippi Longstocking, The-LF1230
Reptiles and Their Way of Life-LB8200
Rescuers, The-LI1360, LI2330
Return to Oz/Dorothy Saves the Emerald City-LI2130
Return to Oz/Escape from Witch's Castle-LI2140
Return to Oz Storybook-ME1400
Riddles, Riddles/From A to Z-LE4900
Right's Animal Farm-LG0420
Rin Tin Tin and Rusty-LE2460
Rin Tin Tin and the Hidden Treasure-BB3430
Rin Tin Tin and the Lost Indian-LE2760
Rin-Tin-Tin and the Outlaw-LE3040
Road Runner/A Very Scary Lesson-BB3440, LF1220
Road Runner/Mid-Mesa Marathon-LG0790
Road to Oz, The-LE1440
Rob Whitlock-SA1040
Robert and His New Friends-LE1240
Robin Hood-LI0480 (see: Adventures of...)
Robin Hood (animated)-LI1260
Robin Hood and the Daring Mouse-LI1280
Robinson Crusoe-GB2400
Robotman and Friends at School-LG0800
Rocks and How They Were Formed-LB8210
Rocky and His Friends-LE4080
Roger Rabbit (see: Who Framed Roger Rabbit?)
Rojankovsky's ABC: Alphabet of Many Things-BB3450
Rojankovsky's Wonderful Picture Book-GG3420
Romper Room Do Bees/A Book of Manners-LE2730
Romper Room Exercise Book-LE5270
Ronald McDonald and the Talking Plant-LG0570
Rooster Struts, The-HB1140
Rootie Kazootie Baseball Star-LE1900
Rootie Kazootie Detective-LE1500
Rootie Kazootie Joins the Circus-LE2260
Round, Round World-RE1600
Roy Rogers and Cowboy Toby-LE1950
Roy Rogers and the Indian Sign-LE2590
Roy Rogers and the Mountain Lion-LE2310
Roy Rogers and the New Cowboy-LE1770
Roy Rogers, King of the Cowboys-BB3470
Roy Rogers on the Double-R Ranch-SA1070
Rudolph the Red-Nosed Reindeer-BB3480, LE3310, MB4200
Rudolph the Red-Nosed Reindeer Shines Again-LG0290
Ruff and Reddy-LE3780, LE4770
Rumpelstiltskin and the Princess and the Pea-LE4980
Runaway Squash, The-LF1430
Rupert the Rhinoceros-LE4190
Russian Fairy Tales-GG3460
Rusty Goes to School-LE4790
Saggy Baggy Elephant, The-LE0360, LE3850, SU2660
Saggy Baggy Elephant and the New Dance-LC3020

Saggy Baggy Elephant/No Place for Me-LD3730
Saggy Baggy Elephant's Great Big Counting Book-BB3490
Sailor Dog, The-BB3510, LE1560
Sails, Rails and Wings-GG3480
Sam the Firehouse Cat-LE5800
Santa Claus Book, The-BB3530
Santa's Beard Is Soft and Warm-TO2480
Santa's Surprise Book-LF1210
Santa's Toy Shop-LI0160
Savage Sam-BD1900, LI1040
Scamp-LI0630
Scamp's Adventure-LI0700, LI0880
Scarebunny, The-LG0810, LL1634
School Days-FR1030
Science-FR1080
Scooby-Doo and the Pirate Treasure-LF1260
Scuffy the Tugboat-BB3540, LE0300, LE2440, LE3630
Scuffy's Underground Adventure-LD3750
Sea, The-LB7070, LB8070
Sea and Shore, The-FR1110
Sea Around Us, The-DL1450
Seashore (see: About the Seashore)
Secret of Nimh Storybook-ME1440
See No Evil, Hear No Evil, Smell No Evil-SC5410
Sesame Street (see: Category Index)
Sesame Street Story Land-GG3500
Sesame Street Word Book-GG3520
Seven Dwarfs Find a House, The-LI0350, LI0670
Seven Little Postmen-LE1340, LE5040
Seven Sneezes, The-LE0510
Shaggy Dog, The-LI0820
Shazam! A Circus Adventure-LF1550
Sherlock Holmes-IC2150, PI1080
Shoelace Box, The-LG0580
Show Must Go On, The-ST2290
Shy Little Kitten, The-LE0230, LE2480, LE4940
Shy Little Kitten's Secret Place-LD3720
Silent Night-MB2400
Silly Sisters, The-LG1440
Singing Games-LE0400
Sky (see: My LGB About the Sky)
Sleeping Beauty-BD1920, BD1940, GB2460, GG3560, LH1330, LI0610, LI2180
Sleeping Beauty and Cinderella-SR1090
Sleeping Beauty and the Good Fairies-LI0710
Sleep Book (see: Golden Sleepy Book)
Sleepy Book, The-LG0140
Sly Little Bear-LE4110
Smokey and His Animal Friends-LE3870
Smokey Bear and the Campers-LE4230
Smokey Bear Finds a Helper-LF3450
Smokey the Bear-LE2240, LE4810 (see: True Story of...)
Snoring Monster, The-LG0820
Snow Queen, The-GB2480, GG3620
Snow White-SR1100
Snow White and Rose Red-LE2280
Snow White and the Seven Dwarfs-BD1960, BD1980, LI0040, LI0660, LI2080, MB2760
Snowy the Little White Horse-BB3560
So Big-LE5740
So Dear to My Heart-SS1120
Some Busy Hospital!-GG3630
Songs We Sing From Rogers and Hammerstein-GG3670
Space Flight-LB7100, LB8100
Sport Goofy and the Racing Robot-LI2090
Spotty Finds a Playmate-BB3580

Top Cat-BB3740, LE4530
Touché Turtle-LE4740
Wally Gator-LE5020
Yakky Doodle and Chopper-LE4490

OZ
Emerald City of Oz, The-LE1510
Return to Oz: Dorothy Saves the
Emerald City-LI2130
Return to Oz: Escape from Witch's
Castle-LI2140
Return to Oz Storybook-ME1400
Road to Oz-LE1440
Tin Woodman of Oz, The-LE1590
Wizard of Oz, The-BB3440, LF1190,
ME1540

PAPER DOLLS
Charmin' Chatty-FT3040
Cinderella-LH1360
Ginger-LH1140, LH1320
Hansel and Gretel-LH1410
Judy and Jim-TP1030
Little Golden Paper Dolls, The-LE1130,
LE2800
Little Red Riding Hood-LH1340
Mary Poppins-FT3080
Mike and Melissa-LH1310
Mother Goose Land with Judy and Jim-
TP1050
Paper Doll Wedding, The-LE1930,
LH1220
Paper Dolls-LH1030, LH1470
Pollyanna, WD-FT3130
Sleeping Beauty, WD-LH1330
Tammy-LH1520
Tammy Doll-FT3170

PUZZLE BOOKS-LGB
Baby's House-LE0805
Brave Cowboy Bill-LE0930
Color Kittens, The-LE0865
Happy Man and His Dump Truck, The-
LE0772
Jerry at School-LE0940
Jolly Barnyard, The-LE0672
Katie the Kitten-LE0755
Little Golden ABC, The-LE1010
Little Red Riding Hood-LE0425
Pets for Peter-LE0820
Ukelele and Her New Doll-LE1020
When I Grow Up-LE0960

SCOUTING
Brownie Scouts-LE4090
Cub Scouts-GD5220
Golden Anniversary Book of Scouting-
DL1060
Scouting Stamps-SP1079

SESAME STREET
Amazing Mumford Forgets the Magic
Words!, The-LG0010
Bert's Hall of Great Inventions-LF3210
Big and Little Stories-ST2150
Big Bird Brings Spring to Sesame Street-
LG0620
Big Bird Gets Lost-SC5240
Big Bird's Color Game-SU2540
Big Bird's Day on the Farm-LG0630
Big Bird's Red Book-LF1570
Cookie Monster and the Cookie Tree-
BB1520, LF1590
Count All the Way to Sesame Street-
LG0670
Day Snuffy Had the Sniffles, The-
LG1240
Ernie's Work of Art-LG0030

Four Seasons, The-LG0050
Grover Takes Care of Baby-LG1030
Grover's Own Alphabet-LG0150
I Am a Monster-SU1390
I Can't Wait Until it's Christmas-LG1360
I Think That it is Wonderful-LG0520
I'm My Mommy/I'm My Daddy-BB2760
Inside Sesame Street-SU1420
Many Faces of Ernie, The-LG0080
Monster at the end of this book, the-
BB2960, LF3160
Oscar's Book-LF1200
People in Your Neighborhood-MB2730
Puppy Love-LG0410
See No Evil, Hear No Evil, Smell No Evil-
SC5410
Sesame Street Story Land-GG3500
Sesame Street Word Book-GG3520
Together Book, The-LF3150
What's Inside?-TO2530
What's Up in the Attic?-LG1190
Who Am I?-SU1240
Who's Hiding?-TO2570

SMOKEY THE BEAR
Smokey and His Animal Friends-LE3870
Smokey Bear and the Campers-LE4230
Smokey Bear Finds a Helper-LF3450
Smokey the Bear-LE2240, LE4810
Smokey the Bear Stamps-SP0600
True Story of Smokey the Bear, The-
BB3760

STAMP BOOKS (see: Stamp Book
series)
Animal Stamps-LH1070
Bird Stamps-LH1080
Car and Truck Stamps-LH1200
Cowboy Stamps-LH1110
Dog Stamps-LH1090
Farm Stamps-LH1190
Firemen and Fire Engine Stamps-
LH1270
Giant Golden Stamp Book-GB1640
Indian Stamps-LH1130
Insect Stamps-LH1250
Mickey Mouse Club Stamp Book-
LH1100
Reading Writing and Spelling Stamps-
LH1240
Story of Baby Jesus Stamps-LH1120
Train Stamps-LH1260

TV SHOWS
Captain Kangaroo
Captain Kangaroo-GD5210, LE2610
Captain Kangaroo and the Beaver-
LE4270
Captain Kangaroo and the Panda-
LE2780, LE4210
Captain Kangaroo's Surprise Party-
LE3410
Howdy Doody
Howdy Doody and Clarabell-LE1210
Howdy Doody and His Magic Hat-
LE1840
Howdy Doody and Mr. Bluster-LE2040
Howdy Doody and Santa Claus-LE2370
Howdy Doody and the Princess-LE1350
Howdy Doody in Funland-LE1720
Howdy Doody in the Wild West-BB2690
Howdy Doody's Animal Friends-LE2520
Howdy Doody's Circus-LG0990
Howdy Doody's Lucky Trip-LE1710
It's Howdy Doody Time-LE2230
Lassie
Adventures of Lassie-GD5120
Lassie-FT1160

Lassie and Her Day in the Sun-LE3070,
L35180
Lassie and the Big Clean-up Day-
LF5720
Lassie and the Daring Rescue-LE2770
Lassie and the Lost Explorer-LE3430
Lassie and the Secret Friend-BB2820
Lassie Finds a Way-BB2835
Lassie Shows the Way-LE2550, LE4150
TV Shows-Miscellaneous
Circus Boy-LE2900
Cleo-LE2870
Donny and Marie/The Top Secret
Project-LF1600
Dr. Kildare-FT4240
J. Fred Muggs-LE2340
Land of the Lost/The Surprise Guests-
LF1360
Leave It to Beaver-LE3470
Mister Ed/The Talking Horse-LE4830
Mister Roger's Neighborhood-LF1330
National Velvet-LE4310
Party in Shariland-LE3600
Runaway Squash, The-LF1430
Waltons and the Birthday Present, The-
LF1340
Wild Kingdom, Marlin Perkin's-LF1510

WESTERNS
Andy Burnett-BD1045
Annie Oakley and the Rustlers-LE2210
Annie Oakley: Sharpshooter LE2750
Brave Eagle-LE2940
Broken Arrow-LE2990
Buffalo Bill, Jr.-LE2540
Cheyenne-LE3180
Dale Evans (Prayer Book for Children)-
BB3350
Dale Evans and the Coyote-LE2530
Dale Evans and the Lost Gold Mine-
LE2130
Davy Crockett-BD1300, LI0450,
SP3010
Davy Crockett and Mike Fink-BD1310,
SP3050
Davy Crockett's Keelboat Race-LI0470
Fury-LE2860
Fury Takes the Jump-LE3360
Gene Autry-LE2300
Gene Autry and Champion-LE2670
Gene Autry and the Red Shirt-SA1010,
SS1170
Gunsmoke-LE3200
Hopalong Cassidy and the Bar-20
Cowboy-LE1470
Lone Ranger, The-LE2630
Lone Ranger and the Talking Pony, The-
LE3100
Lone Ranger and Tonto, The-LE2970
Lone Ranger's New Deputy, The-
SA1090
Maverick-LE3540
Rin Tin Tin and Rusty-LE2460
Rin Tin Tin and the Hidden Treasure-
BB3430
Rin Tin Tin and the Lost Indian-LE2760
Rin Tin Tin and the Outlaw-LE3040
Roy Rogers and Cowboy Toby-LE1950
Roy Rogers and the Indian Sign-LE2590
Roy Rogers and the Mountain Lion-
LE2310
Roy Rogers and the New Cowboy-
LE1770
Roy Rogers: King of the Cowboys-
BB3470
Roy Rogers on the Double-R Ranch-
SA1070
Wagon Train-LE3260

Wells Fargo (Tales of...)-LE3280
Wyatt Earp (Life and Legend of...)-
LE3150
Zorro-BD2260, FT4490, LI0680
Zorro and the Secret Plan-LI0770

WILKIN, ELOISE: Book List
Baby Dear-LE4660
Baby Is Born, A-GG1300
Baby Listens-LE3830
Baby Looks-LE4040
Baby's Birthday-LF3650
Baby's First Christmas-LE3680, PA1080
Baby's Mother Goose-BB1160
Birds-BB1365, GD5110, LF1840
Boy With a Drum, The-LE5880
Busy Timmy-LE0500, LE4520
Child's Garden of Verses, A-LE2890,
LE4930
Christmas ABC, The-LE4780
Christmas Story, The-LE1580, LG0240
Come Play House-LE0440
Day at the Playground, A-LE1190
Eloise Wilkin Treasury-TS2190
Eloise Wilkin's Book of Poems-BB1720
First Bible Stories-LE1980
Fix It, Please!-LE0320
Georgie Finds a Grandpa-LE1960
Golden Treasury of Prayers for Boys and
Girls-GG2560
Good Little, Bad Little Girl-LE5620
Good Morning, Good Night-LE0610
Good Night-MB2420
Guess Who Lives Here-LE0600
Hansel and Gretel-LE2170, LE4910
Hi Ho! Three in a Row-LE1880
Jamie Looks-LE5220
Linda and Her Little Sister-LE2140
Little Book, The-LE5830
Little Golden Holiday Book, The-
LE1090
Mother Goose, Eloise Wilkin's-LE5890
My Baby Brother-LE2790
My Big Book of the Outdoors-BB3010
My Big Book of the Seasons-BB3020
My Dolly and Me-LE4180
My Good Morning Book-SU2710
My Goodnight Book-SU2580
My Kitten-LE1630, LE3000, LE5280
My Little Golden Book About God-
LE2680
My Pets-GD5270
My Puppy-LE2330, LE4690
My Snuggly Bunny-LE2500
My Teddy Bear-LE1680, LE4480
My Toy Box-PA1360
New Baby, The-BB3140, LE0410,
LE2910, LE5410
New House in the Forest, The-LE0240
Night Before Christmas, The-FN4960,
LE2410, PA1380
Noises and Mr. Flibberty-Jib-LE0290
Once-Upon-A-Time Scratch & Sniff
Book, The-SC5250
Play With Me-LE5670
Prayers for Children-BB3360, LE2050
So Big-LE5740
Story of Baby Jesus-LH1120
Thank You Book, The-GG3800
This World of Ours-GD5260
Twins, The-LE2270
We Help Daddy-LE4680
We Help Mommy-LE3520
We Like Kindergarten-LE5520
Where Did the Baby Go?-LF1160
Wiggles-LE1660
Wonders of Nature-BB4060, LE2930
Wonders of the Seasons, The-BB4070